D1547985

Suspect Race

SUSPECT RACE

*Causes and Consequences
of Racial Profiling*

Jack Glaser

OXFORD
UNIVERSITY PRESS

Kishwaukee College Library
21193 Malta Rd.
Malta, IL 60150-9699

OXFORD
UNIVERSITY PRESS

Oxford University Press is a department of the University of
Oxford. It furthers the University's objective of excellence in research,
scholarship, and education by publishing worldwide.

Oxford   New York
Auckland   Cape Town   Dar es Salaam   Hong Kong   Karachi
Kuala Lumpur   Madrid   Melbourne   Mexico City   Nairobi
New Delhi   Shanghai   Taipei   Toronto

With offices in
Argentina   Austria   Brazil   Chile   Czech Republic   France   Greece
Guatemala   Hungary   Italy   Japan   Poland   Portugal   Singapore
South Korea   Switzerland   Thailand   Turkey   Ukraine   Vietnam

Oxford is a registered trademark of Oxford University Press
in the UK and certain other countries.

Published in the United States of America by
Oxford University Press
198 Madison Avenue, New York, NY 10016

© Oxford University Press 2015

All rights reserved. No part of this publication may be reproduced, stored in
a retrieval system, or transmitted, in any form or by any means, without the prior
permission in writing of Oxford University Press, or as expressly permitted by law,
by license, or under terms agreed with the appropriate reproduction rights organization.
Inquiries concerning reproduction outside the scope of the above should be sent to the
Rights Department, Oxford University Press, at the address above.

You must not circulate this work in any other form
and you must impose this same condition on any acquirer.

Library of Congress Cataloging-in-Publication Data
Glaser, Jack.
Suspect race : causes and consequences of racial profiling / Jack Glaser.
  pages cm
Includes bibliographical references and index.
ISBN 978–0–19–537040–9
1. Racial profiling in law enforcement—United States.   2. Stereotypes (Social psychology)—
United States.   3. Race discrimination—United States.   I. Title.
HV7936.R3G53 2015
363.2308900973—dc23
2014018847

9 8 7 6 5 4 3 2 1
Printed in the United States of America
on acid-free paper

CONTENTS

ACKNOWLEDGMENTS

This book is the product of many years of research and writing but also of countless conversations with students, colleagues, police officers, and friends. I am forever indebted to those who provided such capable research assistance, Amanda Charbonneau, Chrissie Grover-Roybal, and Rik Jeffery. Incisive and helpful comments on earlier drafts were given by Paul Figueroa, Phil Goff, Dacher Keltner, Kandaswami Paramasivan, and Jody Stiger. For their collaboration, support, and inspiration, I thank Mahzarin Banaji, Henry Brady, David Epel, Amy Hackney, David Harris, Delores Jones-Brown, Erik Kahn, Tracie Keesee, Rob MacCoun, Karin Martin, Steve Raphael, and Meredith Gamson Smiedt. Special thanks and appreciation go to my wife, Elissa Epel, and son, Danny Glaser, for their consistent encouragement, patience, and insights. I dedicate this book to the loving memory of my parents, Agathe and Joe Glaser.

PREFACE

As I sat working on Chapter 2 of this book in a coffee shop in my neighborhood on a winter day, I overheard a gray-haired, heavyset, Middle Eastern man sitting near me recount to his friends several instances of being stopped and questioned by local police without cause: "He was asking me questions like I was lying..." I was struck that this testimony fell into my lap while I was writing the book. I know that, even though I am a scientist, I am not immune to the psychologically distorting influence of coincidences, so I am not going to jump to any conclusions about the representativeness of my neighbor's experience. Nevertheless, it reminded me that what I have been studying and writing about is not merely an abstract concept but something very real, fairly commonplace, and troubling.

Years later, I am sitting in a different cafe in a different San Francisco neighborhood editing the manuscript, overhearing the discussion of four police officers sitting at the next table on a coffee break (no doughnut in evidence, I hasten to note). They are speaking in the relaxed, humorous banter of coworkers in any field: some business, some personal. But their discussion is sprinkled with very heavy topics, like active homicide investigations. They are casually using the term *CSI* and not referring to a TV show. It is a poignant reminder to me that the primary objects of my research on racial profiling—police officers—are very real, normal, vulnerable people.

Much has happened in American law enforcement, policy, and politics since I began writing this book in 2008. Of particular significance, the country elected an African American president. As I reflect on this period, I am struck by how little has happened on the racial profiling front. Federal legislation continues to be stymied. Few new state laws have been enacted, and none have had meaningful enforcement mechanisms. In fact, laws have been enacted in Arizona and Alabama that make racial profiling (in immigration law enforcement) *more* likely. New studies indicate continued evidence of racially biased decisions to stop and search. The one area where significant progress appears to be occurring is at the agency level, with an increasing number of police departments partnering with social scientists to develop methods to monitor for and mitigate racial profiling. Spoiler alert: This is where the chapters of this book will ultimately take us—to an understanding of the normal human psychological functions that give rise to racial profiling, and how they can be addressed at the agency and individual officer level to mitigate the problem. At this point this is occurring mostly by agency-level initiative, in some cases with the active intervention of the U.S. Department of Justice and the courts, but there is no reason it could not be complemented and facilitated by legislative action and possibly a shift in jurisprudential disposition.

As a public policy professor trained in social psychology, I divide my time between training professional policy analysts and conducting basic and applied research at the intersection of public policy and psychology. As a social psychologist interested in stereotyping, prejudice, and discrimination, and a policy researcher interested in improving the function of government, I find racial profiling is a near-perfect nexus for my interests and expertise. Racial profiling is, after all, stereotype-based policing. Social psychologists like me have been studying stereotyping scientifically for nearly a century. We know a tremendous amount about the content, function, structure, and process of stereotypes and stereotyping. We know that stereotyping is a normal cognitive process, but that it leads to undesirable, discriminatory effects. The primary purpose of this book, therefore, is to bring to bear the social psychological understanding of stereotyping on the policy problem of racial profiling. One key insight is that stereotyping often occurs outside of our conscious awareness and control, and that even those of us with strong intentions to be fair and equitable can make stereotype-contaminated judgments.

Police are normal people with normal human cognition, and so it is very likely that their judgments of the suspiciousness of others will be biased by racial stereotypes, particularly stereotypes connecting racial and ethnic minorities with crime and aggression. Recognizing this will be helpful for officers, their supervisors, and the people in positions to set or change relevant policies.

My ideal audience for the information in this book would be police officers themselves, and I have tried to write it in such a way that it will be of interest and use to them. Racial profiling is a topic of great concern to a great many people, and so I believe that members of the general public will find it interesting and useful. However, at this stage, much of the material is covered with an expectation of some degree of social scientific expertise. Academics in criminology, law, sociology, political science, ethnic studies, public policy, and related fields should find the social psychological perspective herein of value. And psychologists who wish to embed their understanding of stereotyping in a very real policy problem, one where stereotypes have immediate and life-altering effects, will find help with that in these pages.

This book is focused almost exclusively on profiling in the United States. Racial profiling, no doubt, is a problem that exists wherever there is law enforcement and racial or ethnic stereotypes about groups regarding crime and related traits. However, laws and law enforcement practices vary by country, as do interethnic relations and attitudes. The concepts considered here will certainly apply in the United Kingdom, Canada, Oceania, and many European countries. They may well apply to other countries, but I cannot guarantee that.

One area of racial profiling that has been the source of increasing concern and controversy in recent years is in immigration law enforcement. The passage of state laws requiring local and state police to enforce immigration law is an incitement to ethnic profiling. In Arizona, the flashpoint of immigration law enforcement, the enactment of SB1070 in 2010, necessitated that more people of Hispanic descent would be subjected to searches by police, who the law requires to verify immigration status for anyone they stop for whom there is basis for suspicion of immigration law violation. This means that a much larger proportion of Latino Americans are going to be asked for immigration documentation. Many will, in reaction, begin carrying documents that can verify status, something the rest of us do not have to do. Others will fail to comply, or will affirmatively and civilly disobey the rule, and many of them will end up spending time in jail because they cannot immediately document their status. This has a troubling potential to create a two-tiered hierarchy of classes of citizens and legal residents in the United States (or, for now, in Arizona)—those who "seem American" and those who "seem foreign." Right now, because they are the largest group, Whites are the default "American" ethnicity. These immigration issues are the topic of hot debate and will be for some time. Nevertheless, I am not covering immigration profiling in this book because there is not much in the way of a systematic analytic literature, but also because it is dramatically different from other forms of profiling. This is the case primarily because of the very close link between ethnic identity and the crime that is being profiled, particularly in regions bordering Mexico. One thing, however, is very clear: The negative effects of profiling seen in drug law and counterterrorism profiling apply to immigration profiling too. Namely, profiling necessitates that a greater proportion of the targeted minority group will be subjected to intrusion, and this is true for the innocent population as well.

Social psychology has a lot to offer law enforcement, especially those interested in racial profiling. As I mentioned earlier, racial profiling is essentially stereotype-based policing. Social psychologists know far more about it than scholars in any other discipline. And yet, while psychologists have published thousands of scientific journal articles, chapters, and books about stereotypes and stereotyping, they have published only a handful about racial profiling. This book reflects an effort to build a bridge between these two important topics.

For nonscientists, some of the material in this book will seem technical. The social psychological research described (concentrated in Chapters 3 and 4) has been published in high-quality scientific journals. These are journals with rigorous peer review systems that publish only a small proportion of the articles submitted to them. In order to be published, studies in these journals need to compellingly rule out alternative explanations to those the authors posit, usually through extensive investigation and statistical analysis. This can make the reports dense and seemingly obscure, and therefore comprehensible, let alone exciting, only to those of us steeped in the discipline. In bringing the social psychological scientific research to bear on the issue of racial profiling, I have tried to describe the research in plain language, avoiding jargon as much as possible.

Furthermore, scientists are careful to not make overzealous claims based on just a few demonstrations. Accordingly, readers may notice that I use seemingly awkward and tentative language like "demonstrates compellingly" where more affirmative words like "proves" would feel more satisfying. This reflects the scientific norm inherent in hypothesis testing: Scientists generally do not "prove" things. Rather, we construct our experiments to reject "null hypotheses." When we have empirically falsified all the plausible alternatives to a given theory, we regard the theory as "accepted" but not proven, recognizing that there may be some as-yet-unimagined alternative explanation for the phenomena predicted by the theory. Even gravity is regarded as a theory, although it is universally accepted.

OVERVIEW

Chapter 1 begins the discussion by, in good policy analytic form, defining the core problem, which is racially discriminatory law enforcement, and examining its societal implications. This is accomplished primarily by looking at Bureau of Justice Statistics and U.S. Census data, and I readily acknowledge that the dramatic racial disparities evidenced in American criminal justice are caused by many things, not just biased policing. Chapter 2 addresses the latter, covering research on racial profiling that has been carried out with a wide array of methodologies (e.g., anecdotal, surveys, correlational analysis, and econometric modeling). The primary conclusion is that it is overwhelmingly evident that racial bias is operative in policing in many locales, but there are also places and times where it is not evident.

Chapters 3 and 4 infuse psychological theory and research into the discussion, moving beyond just *whether*, and *when and where*, profiling is happening to *how and why* it happens. The many decades of social psychological science on stereotyping, prejudice, and discrimination are considered and yield a fundamental understanding: Stereotyping—generalizing traits and behavioral tendencies to members of racial, ethnic, gender, and other groups—is normal human cognition that causes us to make inferences about individuals that are often erroneous. These inferences cause us to behave differentially and can give rise to discrimination. Stereotypes, like most human mental processes, can and do operate outside of conscious awareness, and so they can influence us whether we want them to or not. As a consequence, much of what we call racial profiling is likely spontaneous and unintended.

Some commentators have argued that racial profiling is worth the sacrifice to civil liberties because it enhances public safety. Accordingly, Chapter 5 takes a closer look at the assumption that racial profiling is efficient, examining its likely effects on criminal incapacitation and deterrence. This is a challenging task to accomplish with real data because it is difficult to determine when racial profiling has occurred, let alone to establish how it has reduced crime. My mathematical simulations of many scenarios of criminal offending and profiling indicate that, in general, gains in terms of criminal captures (incapacitation) would be surprisingly modest and can be counterproductive. The simulations also illustrate what some commentators have suspected, which is that profiling exacerbates racial disparities in incarceration rates and will create them where offending rate differences do not exist. With regard to the deterrent effect of profiling, the one known experimental test of racial profiling provides evidence for what we are calling *reverse deterrence*—increased offending by members of the groups that are not profiled. The effect of this could, ironically, be a net *increase* in crime.

Chapter 6 turns the discussion from profiling primarily in the drug war context to the more newly salient case of counterterrorism. Similarities and differences between drug and terrorism profiling are considered. The fundamental and troubling similarity is that profiling will *cause* disadvantaged outcomes for members of the targeted groups. A related consequence is that law enforcement may lose the cooperation of members of those groups, help that is crucial to successful prevention and prosecution.

Chapter 7 attempts to provide a broad review of the policy landscape for racial profiling in the United States. Generally, the chapter is descriptive, but I admittedly detour into prescription (and proscription) in places where it was prudent to point out the promise (or futility) of a particular policy.

Chapter 8 is more prescriptive in the sense that I make affirmative recommendations for policies to mitigate racial profiling. However, the chapter does not attempt to cover the breadth—local, state, federal; administrative, legislative, judicial—reflected in Chapter 7. Rather, it connects the discussion back to the social and cognitive psychological principles explained in Chapters 3 and 4, leveraging our science-based understanding of human thought and behavior to identify methods for reducing the effects of stereotypes about groups on police decisions about individuals.

In my career, I often feel like an emissary between social psychology and public policy. I am in very good and humbling company in this capacity, with Daniel Kahneman, Robert MacCoun, and others, but we are a small club with a range of topics of expertise. I am the "stereotyping and prejudice guy" (in the sense that I study them, but as Chapters 3 and 4 will make clear, I am guilty as well). This book is written in that emissarial spirit. It is my hope that it will help people from different disciplines appreciate each other's approaches and talk to each other about this issue in a more holistic and constructive way. It is my deeper hope that in connecting social psychology with public policy I have succeeded in making both more accessible to a broader audience, because they are both fascinating and, more important, crucial to a better understanding and promotion of a fairer, stronger society.

Suspect Race

CHAPTER 1

What Is Racial Profiling?

Consider that you, as a police officer tasked with apprehending drug couriers, patrolling a stretch of highway known to be a heavy drug transport corridor, see an SUV with tinted windows and two young Black men in the front driving at 1 mile per hour under the speed limit. The vehicle has a broken taillight. Do you pull it over?

The first officer to arrive at the scene of a reported assault, you see two people, a man and a woman, sprinting from the area. You shout at both to stop, but they keep running, in different directions, away from you. Which one do you pursue, and why?

Imagine the same scenario, but this time both people are men, one is White and the other is Black. Which one do you pursue, and why?

In the first assault scenario, you may have opted to go after the man, either because men are more likely than women to commit assaults, or because you may reasonably expect to catch more flak for chasing a woman. But the second scenario probably posed a more difficult dilemma. Maybe part of you felt the Black guy was more likely to be the assailant. Maybe another part of you did not want to operate on that basis. But it is worth noting that the two scenarios are basically equivalent, the only difference being the strength and social acceptability of the stereotypes about gender and crime versus race and crime.

Here is another scenario. You have been briefed that there are very reliable statistics indicating that members of Chinese ethnic gangs are responsible for the lion's share of armed robberies in your jurisdiction. Walking the beat, you see three young Asian men enter a food mart. Do you follow them in or continue on your previous course? Would it affect your decision if you knew that such robberies were very frequent? Or very rare? How big a proportion of young Asian men being involved in such robberies would there need to be for you to feel justified in following these three?

You're a Transit Safety Administration (TSA) screener at an airport. Homeland Security has placed the terrorism threat level at its highest. Three Middle Eastern men approach the screening area. Do you give them special attention? Why or why not? What if the TSA had announced that there was specific information that al-Qaeda was planning to perpetrate an attack in the United States in the next 2 days?[1]

There are no easy answers to most of these questions. But the variations on them surely change the likelihood that a given individual (yourself, perhaps) would choose to detain or search someone. And those decisions are based not on the suspect's specific behavior but on the fact that he fits a "profile" of a criminal who is perhaps more prone to commit a particular type of crime. Clearly, some profiles are more justifiable than others, and some conditions are more acceptable for profiling. For example, in the classic "ticking time bomb" scenario, when there is specific information that a terrorist act is imminent, the use of national origin may be much more palatable than under normal conditions. Similarly, using gender seems more acceptable to more people than using race or ethnicity, perhaps because statistics unambiguously indicate that men commit more crime, or perhaps because men are otherwise generally not a stigmatized or underprivileged group.

In fact, recent history is rife with real-world examples of the application of profiling. On the outrageous side of the spectrum is the case of forensic psychologist Walter Quijano, who testified repeatedly in death penalty cases that specific Latino defendants were more dangerous *because they were Latino*. In upstate New York in 1992, Oneonta police questioned virtually every young Black man in town in one investigation. In 1998, customs officials at Chicago's O'Hare Airport were found to have been searching Black women at a grossly disproportionate rate—Black women were, in fact, particularly *un*likely to be carrying contraband. And in 2009, after the shooting by police of an unarmed, elderly Black man in Homer, Louisiana, the town's police chief declared, "If I see three or four young black men walking down the street, I have to stop them and check their names. I want them to be afraid every time they see the police that they might get arrested" (Witt, 2009). More common examples of racial profiling have to do with traffic stops, which will be discussed extensively in Chapter 2. The point here, however, is that the use of race, ethnicity, gender, and other demographics as a basis for criminal suspicion can occur in many domains of law enforcement, and in all these domains it raises questions about fairness and effectiveness.

Most dramatically overrepresented in criminal justice, and the most common targets of racial profiling, are African Americans. Their race, as the book's title signifies, represents something that is used in suspect descriptions but is also itself often the basis of suspicion. They will, accordingly, be the focus of much of the discussion in this book.

---

1. Credit goes to Stanford law professor R. Richard Banks for this type of scenario. I was first exposed to it at a conference on racial bias in policing, where Professor Banks used it most effectively in his presentation.

WHAT IS RACIAL PROFILING?

I have been using the term *racial profiling* with the assumption that there is reasonably good understanding and consensus about what that is. But it is time to clarify the discussion with a formal definition. I will return to this definition, and compare it with that of other analysts, and distinguish it from similar concepts, like *criminal profiling* and the use of race in suspect descriptions, as well. But for now, I offer the following definition, to be elaborated on later:

> *Racial profiling is the use of race or ethnicity, or proxies thereof, by law enforcement officials as a basis for judgment of criminal suspicion.*

Reasonable people can and do disagree over whether racial profiling is legal, fair, ethical, and effective. And surely it is more or less of all of these depending on the conditions. Nevertheless, public condemnation of racial profiling has been unambiguous. Furthermore, since revelations in the 1990s about its occurrence, law enforcement officials and policymakers have been quick and forceful in disavowing the practice. This condemnation has, in fact, come from the very highest levels of government, with President Bill Clinton stating in June 1999 that racial profiling is "morally indefensible" and "deeply corrosive," and asserting, "It is wrong, it is destructive, and it must stop." His immediate successor, President George W. Bush, declared in February 2001 that racial profiling is "wrong and we will end it in America." Even after the attacks of September 11, 2001, President Bush publicly condemned racial profiling, instructing the Department of Justice to ban the practice in federal law enforcement, although the administration carved out a notable exception for national security (see Chapters 6 and 7 for further discussion).

Indeed, there is legitimate reason for concern about racial profiling, to the extent that it increases the likelihood that disproportionate numbers of minorities will enter the criminal justice system. In other words, *if police pay more attention to (are more likely to stop and/or search) members of some racial or ethnic groups, then regardless of actual criminality or offending rates, those groups will bear a disproportionate share of sanctions.* In a time where millions of Americans are incarcerated, such disproportions can have profound negative effects on minority communities. Additionally, racial profiling will cause disproportionate numbers of *innocent* civilians from those groups to be subjected to stops, searches, and wrongful arrests.

THE HIGH AND HIGHER RATES OF INCARCERATION

There are significant constitutional questions surrounding issues of due process and equal protection that we will consider later. For now we will focus on the current criminal justice climate and on the high rate of incarcerations, especially of African Americans, that gives many analysts, policymakers, and citizens cause for concern about racial profiling.

The U.S. rate of incarceration has grown dramatically over the last three decades. According to data from the Department of Justice's Bureau of Justice Statistics (BJS), the number of persons in prison or jail has gone from 503,586 (about 0.22% of the U.S. population) in 1980 (Bureau of Justice Statistics, 1995) to 2,266,832 (about 0.73% of the U.S. population) in 2010. An additional 1,338,535 people were on probation or parole in 1980; this number had grown to 4,896,190 in 2010 (Bureau of Justice Statistics, 2008b, 2011a). The statistics are more dramatic when we consider just men: In 1980, 0.28% of men in the United States were incarcerated (Bureau of Justice Statistics, 1995). In 2010, this figure was 1.35% (Bureau of Justice Statistics, 2011a).

The biggest influence on this change has been drug arrests stemming from the "War on Drugs" initiated in the early 1970s with the formation of the U.S. Drug Enforcement Agency (DEA). According to Harris (2002b), "The DEA trained tens of thousands of state and local police officers in the tactics of profiling through Operation Pipeline; these officers then went back to their own departments to train others and to set up specialized drug interdiction units" (p. 38).

Western (2006), in his analysis of punishment in the United States, estimated that the rate of drug-related incarcerations in the United States rose by a factor of about 10 from 1980 to 2001, while the rate for violent and property crimes less than tripled (Western, 2006, p. 22). Noting that there were nearly 1.6 million adult and juvenile drug arrests in the United States in 2001, Western (2006) estimated that about 12% of them led to incarceration, with an average sentence of more than 2 years. The BJS reported that in 2009, 17.8% of state prisoners were sentenced for a drug offense. That same year, a drug offense was the most serious offense for 51% of federal prisoners (Bureau of Justice Statistics, 2011b). In 2010, "drug abuse violations" was the largest single category of arrest in the United States, with 1,638,846 arrests (Federal Bureau of Investigation, 2011). The increase in drug-related arrests has been overwhelmingly driven by a precipitous climb in arrests for possession, as opposed to arrests for sales or manufacture, which have been relatively static over the last two and a half decades (Federal Bureau of Investigation, 2011). As a result, possession arrests are by far the largest share of drug arrests (about 81.9% in 2010). In sum, *the proportion of Americans in some form of custody has grown dramatically over the past three decades, and a large portion of that growth has been due to increased arrests for drug violations.*

A disproportionate number of arrests and incarcerations are from the African American and, to a lesser extent, Latino[2] populations. While Blacks represent

2. It is difficult to estimate rates of Latino arrests and incarcerations because Latinos are typically counted as Whites in FBI/BJS statistics (hence the references to "non-Hispanic Whites").

approximately 12.5% of the U.S. population, they accounted for 28.2% of those arrested in 2007, and 35.1% of those arrested for drug abuse violations. These disproportions increased during the decades corresponding to the War on Drugs. The BJS reports that the percentage of White and Black adults under correctional supervision (jail, prison, parole, or probation) went from 1.4% of Whites and 5.7% of Blacks in 1986 to 2% of Whites and 9% of Blacks in 1997 (Bureau of Justice Statistics, 1998). This pattern is reflected in the trends over time for incarceration in state and federal prisons presented in Figure 1.1. The figure illustrates two trends: first that, overall, incarcerations were climbing at a steady rate through the 1980s and 1990s, a trend that began in the 1970s with the advent of the War on Drugs; and second that this increase was dramatically disproportionately borne by the Black population. The rates leveled off after 2000 but remained high and disparate. One might be tempted to conclude that the leveling off of these trends indicates an end to bias, but this would be a mistake. In order for the incarceration rates to remain disparate over time, they must be sustained by continuing disparate prison admissions.

There is considerable variation across regions and states in terms of incarceration rates and racial disparities, but the overall pattern is quite clear: A nontrivial proportion of Americans, especially young men, are under correctional

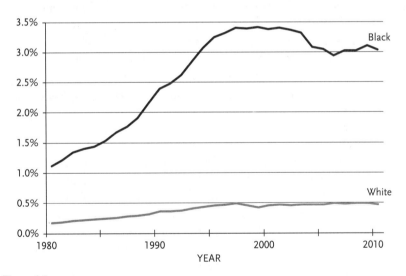

Figure 1.1
Percentage of Black and White American men (aged 18 to 64) serving sentences of 1 year or more in state or federal prison, 1980 to 2010.
Sources: Bureau of Justice Statistics (1996, 2000a, 2000b, 2011a, 2011b, n.d.); U.S. Census data retrieved from IPUMS (King et al., 2010).
Note: For all years but 1998, the BJS provided statistics only for those serving sentences of 1 year or more. For 1998, I interpolated incarceration numbers between 1997 and 1999. Prior to 1999, the BJS included Hispanics in the White category. Accordingly, the percentage of Whites reported in this graph was calculated using all Whites as the denominator prior to 1999 and, from 1999 on, White/non-Hispanic for the prison (numerator) and general population (denominator) counts.

supervision, and that proportion is dramatically higher among minorities, particularly Blacks. The impact is dire; in 2003, the BJS projected that, assuming existing incarceration rates persisted, 5.9% of White men born that year would be incarcerated at some point in their lifetime. For Latinos it would be 17.2%, and for African Americans, 32.2% (Bureau of Justice Statistics, 2003).

WHAT CAUSES THESE DISPARITIES?

An obvious candidate for what could explain these disparities would be higher rates of crime among African Americans. Indeed, the National Crime Victimization Survey (NCVS) indicates that Blacks are identified as perpetrators of crime at relatively high rates. For example, single-offender victimizations in 2006 involved Black offenders 22.4% of the time (Bureau of Justice Statistics, 2008c, Table 40). However, these disparities in offenders reported by victims are insufficient to explain the differences in arrest, conviction, and incarceration rates described earlier, which are considerably larger. Furthermore, it is not clear that these offending rates are relevant to racial profiling.

Racial profiling is most commonly associated with drug law enforcement, and with regard to drug arrests it is harder to find baseline statistics of offending rates against which to compare arrest, prosecution, conviction, and incarceration rates. The NCVS is based on a large annual survey of Americans with regard to crime victimization. Because drug crimes are typically victim*less*, they do not show up in the NCVS. However, survey research on illicit drug use as one indicator of rates of drug law violations indicates that Blacks are not much more likely than others to break drug laws. Specifically, the U.S. Department of Health and Human Services' (2008) National Survey on Drug Use and Health for 2007 found that Blacks were only slightly more likely than Whites to report having used illicit drugs in the preceding month (9.5% and 8.2%, respectively). Johnston, O'Malley, and Bachman (2001), in their report for the National Institute on Drug Abuse, found that, from 1975 to 2000, Black 8th, 10th, and 12th graders consistently reported lower rates of illicit drug use, including crack and methamphetamines, than White and Hispanic youth. This would lead one to expect that Black youth would be arrested for drug abuse violations at a relatively low rate, and yet, according to BJS statistics, Black youth are arrested for drug abuse violations at a significantly higher rate than are White youth (Bureau of Justice Statistics, 2008a, Table 43).

Perhaps the overrepresentation of Blacks (including Black youth) among those arrested has more to do with drug dealing and related offenses like weapons possession, which could be higher among Blacks. Here survey statistics also indicate that Blacks are arrested at rates that are much higher than would be expected based on their behavior. A Centers for Disease Control and Prevention survey of students, the Youth Risk Behavior Survey, found that Black students were less likely (17.2%) to indicate that they had carried a weapon at some point in the preceding 30 days than were White students (18.2%) or Hispanic students (18.5%) (Youth Risk Behavior Survey, 2007). And yet, Black youth are arrested for weapons violations at a per capita rate almost three times the rate of White youth (Bureau of Justice Statistics, 2008a, Table 43).

So, while offense rates appear to be higher among Blacks for some crimes, and lower for others, even when they are higher, these discrepancies are not enough to explain the much more dramatic overrepresentation of Blacks in the criminal justice system. Other causes must contribute to the high rate of criminal justice involvement for Black Americans. One cause is no doubt disparities in sentencing for different types of offenses. For example, penalties for crack cocaine–related offenses are typically far more severe than for powder cocaine, and crack is more commonly associated with Black than with White drug users and dealers. Indeed, according to the U.S. government's Office of Applied Studies, Substance Abuse and Mental Health Services Administration's National Survey on Drug Use and Health, Whites report a higher rate of powder cocaine use, and Blacks report a higher rate of crack cocaine use. As a result, as the U.S. Sentencing Commission concluded in 1995, "The 100-to-1 crack cocaine to powder cocaine quantity ratio is a primary cause of the growing disparity between sentences for Black and White federal defendants" (p. 154). In 2010, the U.S. Congress passed the Fair Sentencing Act, reducing, but not eliminating, the discrepancy in sentencing for crack and powder cocaine.

Another explanation has to do with the locations of drug use and dealing. Some accounts hold that Blacks are more likely to use and sell drugs in public places and are therefore more likely to get caught. This is supported by empirical findings that communities with high proportions of minorities have more visible drug problems, although no greater rate of drug use (Saxe et al., 2001).

We must consider, however, the possibility that some of the racial disparities in those who are caught and punished result from racial bias in law enforcement. In fact, considerable research has addressed this specifically, and a number of studies have found that suspect and defendant race and ethnicity have been direct causes of disparities. For example, a review by Mustard (2001) of sentencing of more than 77,000 federal offenders found that Blacks tended to be given significantly longer sentences, especially for drug trafficking, even after statistically controlling for other variables that could explain the difference, such as demographics and criminal history. Pope and Feyerherm (1995), in their extensive analysis of a representative sample of empirical studies of minority representation in the juvenile justice system, reported that most studies found evidence for overrepresentation of Black youth, even when statistically controlling for other likely causes.

So, statistical analyses clearly indicate that, at least in many places, times, and instances, racial bias exists in criminal justice. Nevertheless, much of this research is "correlational," meaning that racial disparities cannot be proved to be *caused* by racial bias. Studies showing that disparities persist even after statistically controlling for other factors, such as socioeconomic differences, crime severity, and criminal history, allow us to make a fairly strong inference of bias. But another method of research affords stronger inferences of a causal effect of racial bias. Specifically, the *experimental* method, commonly employed by psychological scientists to study human thoughts, feelings, and behaviors, is a powerful tool in this regard.

Just as with natural or medical science, experiments allow us to hold constant all other factors and thereby isolate as causes only those factors that we experimentally manipulate. For example, in medical research, to isolate the effect of a drug on a disease, people are randomly assigned to be given the drug or some medicinally neutral placebo (so that everyone has the same subjective experience of taking something and not knowing if it is the drug or the placebo). Any difference in health outcomes, like a higher cure rate in the drug (or "treatment") group, means that the drug *caused* the desired effect. Nothing else could explain the difference. Similarly, in psychological research, we randomly assign people to one treatment or another and measure some behavior of interest to see what effect the treatment had.

For those of us interested in criminal justice–related behavior, this might mean having people read a description of a crime, varying the race of the defendant, and asking whether our research participants think the defendant should be convicted or acquitted, and if convicted how harsh his or her sentence should be. Psychologists typically try to be subtle in how we manipulate variables like defendant race. First of all, in the typical experiment, only half the sample would get the minority defendant; the other half would get a White defendant. Consequently, it is unlikely that study participants will infer that the experiment is about the defendant's race—they have nothing to compare to. Many experiments, including those I have conducted, manipulate defendant race subtly, merely by using names, like Tyrone or Antoine as opposed to Tyler or Antony, that are stereotypically associated with Blacks and Whites. Other experiments have shown photos or videos of suspects or, more bluntly, have provided demographic information, including suspect race.

Research of this sort has demonstrated that ostensibly Black defendants are more likely to be convicted and receive harsher sentences. Because, in the experiments, all else is held equal, we can isolate the effect of defendant race and conclude that it (or, more precisely, the reaction it evokes) *causes* the disparate outcome. Sommers and Ellsworth (2001) have conducted several such studies and also have carefully reviewed others' work. In so doing, they have noted that, as in other domains, overt racial prejudice is unusual in our post–civil rights era, but, drawing on psychological research that shows that Whites are more likely to display anti-Black prejudice under relatively ambiguous circumstances (see Crosby, Bromley, & Saxe, 1980; Gaertner & Dovidio, 1986), they found that White mock jurors were significantly more likely to convict (and give a harsher sentence to) a Black defendant than a White defendant when race was only subtly evident. More psychological research on racial and ethnic bias will be discussed at greater length and depth in later chapters. For now it should be noted that experimental research indicates that, all else being equal, Whites tend to be more punitive toward minorities. Police, being human beings with normal psychology, are likely subject to similar biases.

The research and statistics described so far implicate the existence of racial and ethnic bias in criminal justice decision-making. Whole books have been written on the subject (see, e.g., Cole, 1999; Kennedy, 1997; Tonry, 1995), so further establishing it is not my primary purpose here. In fact, it is not my intention to argue that racial discrimination is unusually pervasive in criminal justice. The purpose of this book does not depend on an assumption that racial bias is especially ubiquitous in policing, but merely that it is commonplace, as in other domains. Furthermore, it is important that racial bias (meaning, stereotypes and attitudes) is a significant cause, although not necessarily the sole cause, of racial disparities in criminal justice. In this sense, we will discuss racial profiling as stemming from both formal, official descriptions (profiles) of high-probability perpetrators and informal personal beliefs of individual officials. Because we know from psychological research (to be discussed at length in Chapters 3 and 4) that stereotypes are widely shared and that they often influence judgments and behaviors, our primary concern will be with better understanding how that happens and how it can be minimized in law enforcement practice.

PROFILING AND THE WAR ON DRUGS

No doubt, race has influenced law enforcement decisions for as long as there have been stereotypes about race and crime. Formal racial profiling as we know it today, however, stems largely from the War on Drugs. Early drug courier profiles were developed in the mid-1970s by the Federal Bureau of Investigation (FBI) and the newly formed DEA (see Withrow, 2006, for a thorough history of drug courier profiling). The increased emphasis on drug crime interdiction resulting from the War on Drugs caused much of the increase in incarcerations described earlier. Noted legal scholar John Donohue (2005) described the effect cogently: "Between 1933 and 1973, incarceration in the United States varied within a narrow band of roughly 100 to 120 prisoners per 100,000 population. Since then, this rate has been increasing by an average of five percent annually" (p. 48).

Early drug courier profiles, many of which were widely employed, included explicit references to race (usually African American) and ethnicity (typically Latino) as bases for suspicion when combined with other factors, such as age, gender, and type of clothing and car. Several legal scholars have provided comprehensive histories of racial profiling and the War on Drugs (e.g., Harris, 2002a; Withrow, 2006). David Harris (2002a) has noted that many drug courier profiles contained highly ambiguous information that afforded officers considerable discretion. David Cole (1999) provided a list of factors culled from different agencies' profiles that included many conflicting attributes (e.g., "traveled alone" and "traveled with companion" or "acted too nervous" and "acted too calm"), illustrating that the profile may be in the eye of the beholder.

The rationale behind drug courier profiling, including race and ethnicity as factors, holds that members of some social groups have a higher probability of being engaged in particular types of crime. The rationale is logical and intuitively appealing (but there are logical pitfalls, to be discussed in Chapter 5), but the constitutional issues of fairness that are clearly implicated drive general public disapproval. When revelations about profiling emerged across a number of U.S. states in the mid-1990s, public condemnation was wide, and official disavowal was swift and certain. Nevertheless, investigations of profiling since then, to be discussed in Chapter 2, have indicated that racial bias in police stops and searches persists.

THE PROBLEM WITH DRUG CRIME DATA

Perceptions of racial and ethnic drug crime trends, specifically that minorities are more likely to use, transport, and sell illicit drugs, are often based on flawed inferences. Because drug crimes do not appear in the NCVS, statistics about drug crime offenders are derived either from criminal justice statistics (who gets caught) or from surveys asking people their offending rates (who admits to it). In the latter case, it is reasonable to be skeptical about the accuracy of self-reports of crime. Nevertheless, Blacks and Latinos surveyed do not report higher rates of drug crimes (U.S. Department of Health and Human Services, 2008). In the former case, looking for racial or ethnic differences in arrest rates is an inherently problematic way to investigate racial bias in law enforcement, to the point of being perversely circular.

The problem is that if racial bias is causing officers to stop and search Blacks, for example, at a higher rate than Whites, then that alone will *cause* there to be a disproportionate number of Blacks arrested and convicted. In this manner, the profiling itself will *bias* the data. Drug law enforcement is not a scientific survey where research participants are randomly sampled and everyone has an equal probability of being selected. Rather, quite reasonably, police "select" (surveil, stop, question, search) those they believe have the greatest chance of being engaged in crime. But this necessarily has the effect of causing those kinds of people to get arrested more often, regardless of their actual rate of criminal behavior. In other words, *racial profiling can give rise to a self-fulfilling prophecy.*

When these beliefs about criminality are based on factors that are directly and instrumentally related to crime, such as wearing out-of-season clothing that might help conceal contraband, or driving a car with darkly tinted windows on a known drug transport corridor, they generally do not pose a civil liberties problem. When they involve race and ethnicity, they can cause disproportionate numbers of minorities to be sanctioned and disenfranchised, *and* they can also skew our future perception and understanding of who really is responsible for what share of crime. If subsequent law enforcement is based on these skewed perceptions, this can actually undermine the efficiency and effectiveness of policing. This idea will be explored in much greater depth in Chapter 5. For now, suffice it to say that criminal justice statistics are not reliable indicators of actual racial and ethnic trends in drug crimes.

Why is it important to know what the real drug crime rates of different racial or ethnic groups are? Because so-called formal or actuarial profiles that have historically been developed by law enforcement agencies like the FBI and DEA are only as good as the information on which they are based. If the statistics are unreliable, the profiles will be, too. But racial profiling can, and no doubt does, also take a more informal form. That is, police, like everyone else, have stereotypes about different groups, and these stereotypes influence their judgments of members of those groups. In Chapters 3 and 4, I will discuss the psychological research that explains how this happens, often despite our best intentions. This kind of stereotype-based judgment and decision-making is, although generally and rightly disdained, totally normal human cognition. Nevertheless, it leads to discrimination. This is the primary concern of this book.

Racial profiling is at the nexus of social psychology and law enforcement policy. Social psychology is the study of how human thoughts, feelings, and motivations affect interpersonal and intergroup relations, and vice versa. Racial profiling is the application of beliefs (stereotypes) about race and criminality to law enforcement decisions with regard to members of specific groups. Psychologists have conducted thousands of carefully designed studies about stereotyping and, consequently, the field has a lot to offer. Accordingly, the purpose of this book is to bring to bear the vast knowledge from psychology on stereotypes, and how they guide behavior, to understanding racial profiling.

PUBLIC SAFETY AND CIVIL LIBERTIES

Racial profiling resides at another important intersection—the perennial balance (or perhaps *tension*) between civil liberties and public safety. It is said that freedom has a price, and examples such as loss of privacy in exchange for protection are emblematic of this. In this vein, prominent policy scholars have argued for the necessity of racial profiling, particularly in the context of counterterrorism, but sometimes generalizing more broadly. For example, renowned criminologist James Q. Wilson editorialized as follows: "Black men are six to eight times more likely to commit violent crimes than are white men. When the police patrol the streets trying to prevent crime, should they stop white and black men at the same rate?" (Wilson & Higgins, 2002). Even if we accept Wilson's estimate, it is problematic to apply arrest rates for violent crimes, which are responded to based primarily on specific reports, to crimes, like drug possession, that are typically identified through officer-initiated stops. This problem is compounded by the results of previously described survey research indicating that White and Black rates of illicit drug use are approximately equal (U.S. Department of Health and Human Services, 2008). But the quotation illustrates the connection people make between racial profiling and enhanced public safety.

Even those who oppose racial profiling on constitutional grounds and express concerns about its effects on minority communities sometimes indicate beliefs that it represents a rational approach to enhance public safety (e.g., Kennedy, 1999). Some of the research and analysis discussed in this book will challenge the standard assumptions about increased public safety. This is important because, in order to have a meaningful discussion about racial profiling, we need to understand both sides of the trade-off between public safety and civil liberties. To this end, we should consider the extent to which racial profiling really does enhance public safety, and that means considering the extent to which it is based on real and significant differences in criminality, as opposed to flawed generalizations (stereotypes).

We also need to take into account the civil rights side—the extent to which the targeted communities are treated fairly and justly. Here we must consider that incarcerations of Black Americans are higher than they are for other groups, and that they are higher than would be expected based on actual criminal offending rates. We must also look at the totality of the effect on the targeted communities. In this regard, the statistics are troubling. As noted previously, the Bureau of Justice Statistics projected in 2003 that, if existing trends continued, 32.2% of Black males born that year will be incarcerated during their lifetime. The economic effects of a large proportion of any community being incarcerated and then hobbled by a criminal record when seeking future employment are troubling.

Another effect of disproportionate policing of minorities is that many states in the United States revoke the voting rights of convicted felons. As a result, if Blacks are being stopped, arrested, and convicted at rates that are disproportionate to their relative criminality rates, they will be politically disenfranchised in a manner that runs afoul of the Constitution and basic principles of democracy. Additionally, such political disenfranchisement, coupled with the economic hardships of high rates of incarceration, and the disturbances to family and community structure, are no doubt demoralizing.

In conclusion, African Americans are arrested and incarcerated for drug crimes at an alarming rate that is dramatically greater than that for other racial groups. Of considerable concern is evidence from survey research that Blacks are not more likely to engage in drug crimes. No doubt, racial disproportions in criminal sanctions can result from biases throughout the criminal justice process—including decisions to charge, aggressively prosecute, convict, sentence, parole, and so forth. Nevertheless, officers' judgments represent the most common point of entry to the criminal justice system. Whether formal or informal, racial profiling is bound to be influential. The costs of violating minorities' civil liberties through disproportionate criminal suspicion and sanction must be weighed against any presumed gain in public safety. Beyond this practical cost-benefits reckoning is a more fundamental moral one, expressed well by constitutional law professor Jonathan Turley (2002, p. 4): "While the Constitution protects the security and survival of the state, it also guards against the arbitrary and abusive use of power in the name of the public interest."

DEFINING RACIAL PROFILING

Racial profiling is a term that is bandied about quite a bit. Despite its technical origins, it is now a politically volatile term that tends to elicit indignation and defensiveness. In 2008, an offhanded comment that appeared to endorse racial profiling cost Palo Alto, California, police chief Lynn Johnson her job, despite her speedy and emphatic apology and repudiation of profiling. But some of the heat that the term generates may be due to the looseness with which it is defined and used. Some people, in fact, appear to use it to describe any racial stereotyping or discrimination at all. The politicization of the term is interesting and could be the topic of its own lengthy discourse. Its relevance here, however, will be limited to the concern that the insinuation of racism and willful discrimination makes it difficult for law enforcers to acknowledge the possibility that any form of profiling is occurring within their ranks.

In order to have a meaningful and effective consideration of the topic, we need a precise, politically neutral definition. I provided a preliminary definition previously, but in order to move forward with a clear conceptual foundation, it would be helpful to consider carefully the meaning of what we are calling *racial profiling*, taking into account how it has been used and defined by other experts across several fields, including criminology, law, economics, and policy studies.

The closest thing to a federal policy on racial profiling, the End Racial Profiling Act (ERPA), is an as yet unpassed bill to be discussed further in Chapter 7. ERPA is straightforward and specific, defining racial profiling as

> the practice of a law enforcement agent or agency relying, to any degree, on race, ethnicity, national origin, or religion in selecting which individual to subject to routine or spontaneous investigatory activities or in deciding upon the scope and substance

of law enforcement activity following the initial investigatory procedure, except when there is trustworthy information, relevant to the locality and timeframe, that links a person of a particular race, ethnicity, national origin, or religion to an identified criminal incident or scheme. (Section 2.6)

Law professor David Harris is one of the earliest and most authoritative experts on racial profiling. He has written extensively on the subject and raised public consciousness considerably. He defines racial profiling as "the use by law enforcement of racial or ethnic appearance as one factor, among others, in deciding who to stop, question, search, etc." (e-mail communication, January 5, 2009). Importantly, Harris (2002a) differentiates between formal (departmental policy–driven) and informal (discretionary, personal stereotype–driven) profiling, and he notes that profiling need not be conscious or deliberate. These distinctions will prove crucial for the purposes of this book because emphasis will be placed on informal profiling that arises from personal, sometimes nonconscious stereotypes.

Richard Banks (2001), a law professor, says, "Racial profiling constitutes the intentional consideration of race in a manner that disparately impacts certain racial minority groups, contributing to the disproportionate investigation, detention, and mistreatment of innocent members of those groups" (p. 1077). While this definition effectively describes some, perhaps the more "formal," racial profiling, I would argue, and David Harris clearly agrees, that racial profiling need not be intentional and, in fact, most often is not. This does not make Banks's definition *wrong* but only more narrow.

Criminologists Ramirez, McDevitt, and Farrell (2000) define racial profiling as "any police-initiated action that relies on the race, ethnicity, or national origin rather than the behavior of an individual or information that leads the police to a particular individual who has been identified as being, or having been, engaged in criminal activity" (p. 3). In doing so, Ramirez and colleagues explicitly contrast profiling with policing based on individual-level information, as does the ERPA definition. Similarly, Risse and Zeckhauser (2004), in a philosophical discussion of the utility of racial profiling, define it as "any police-initiated action that relies on the race, ethnicity, or national origin and not merely on the behavior of an individual" (p. 136), although they are careful to not imply that profiling and individual behavior–based judgments are mutually exclusive.

Law professor Bernard Harcourt, who has carefully analyzed racial profiling as one form of "actuarial" practices in criminal justice (Harcourt, 2007), defines it as "the practice of stopping and searching minority motorists at a rate in excess of their representation on the road based on the assumption that they are more likely to be transporting drug contraband" (Harcourt, 2004, p. 1276, n. 2). While this definition is narrowly tied to drug courier profiling, Harcourt has examined racial profiling much more broadly. An advantage of this definition is that it provides a concrete criterion—stops disproportional to presence—rather than relying merely on the presumption of a way of thinking on the part of law officers.

Lorie Fridell, a criminology professor and the director of research for the Police Executive Research Forum (PERF), reasonably demurs from defining racial profiling at all, arguing as follows:

> We believe "racial profiling" has frequently been defined so restrictively that it does not fully capture the concerns of both police practitioners and citizens. For instance, racial profiling is frequently defined as law enforcement activities (e.g., detentions, arrests, searches) that are initiated solely on the basis of race. Central to the debate on the most frequently used definitions is the word "solely." In the realm of potential discriminatory actions, this definition likely references only a very small portion.
>
> Fridell, Lunney, Diamond, & Kubu, 2001, p. 3

This is a valid and crucial point. Fridell and colleagues opted to use a different, broader term, "racially biased policing," which she defines as being "when the police inappropriately consider race/ethnicity in deciding with whom and/or how to intervene when acting to enforce the law" (personal communication, May 29, 2012).

Indeed, some commentators (e.g., MacDonald, 2001; Macdonald, 2002; Parker, 2001) have defined racial profiling, or at least one form of it, as involving the use of race as the *sole* factor in a decision to stop or search. This is not a useful definitional approach because, while it may serve the ideological purpose of dismissing the existence of profiling, it is not realistic. The inclusion of *multiple* facets is inherent in the use of the term *profile*. Furthermore, a system wherein people were stopped solely on the basis of race would reasonably be defined not as racial *profiling* so much as full-blown racial *oppression*. So it is a distraction from a serious and productive discussion of racial profiling to assert that it involves stops based solely on race (or ethnicity, etc.).

Criminal justice scholar Brian Withrow (2006), in providing extensive coverage of others' definitions, points out that different researchers and practitioners use different terms, such as "race based policing" and "race biased policing" (pp. 42–43), like Fridell and colleagues' "racially biased policing." In addition to avoiding the "sole factor" distraction, these terms more strongly, if not directly, indicate bias, whereas "racial profiling" allows for the possibility of what Harcourt (2006) would call "actuarial" policing—the use of statistical base rates, however imperfect, for assessments of probabilities of criminality.

For the purposes of keeping the connection to the large and growing literature on racial profiling, I will continue to use that term but will attempt to define it precisely enough to avoid confusion. Using the term *racial profiling* will also serve to more definitively connect the psychological literature on stereotyping to a known police practice, profiling—a central goal of this book.

Serious definitions of racial profiling are not wildly disparate. They typically expand the topic beyond race to ethnicity, national origin, and sometimes religion, and they hold that racial profiling involves the use of these factors as a basis for criminal suspicion and/or police behavior.

Generally consistent with other prominent definitions, I offer the following:

Racial profiling is the use of race or ethnicity, or proxies thereof, by law enforcers as the basis of judgments of criminal suspicion.

The term *ethnicity* is included as a fairly broad category including national origin, religion, and other social memberships that can be (however imperfectly) inferred from appearance, name, and possibly location.

The inclusion of "proxies thereof" is important because it recognizes that law enforcers are typically only making *inferences* about race or ethnicity. For example, officers making traffic stops do not have access to drivers' birth certificates or demographic survey responses. They infer race and ethnicity based on physical characteristics, and they may be wrong. For example, in the case of air transit security screening, Sikhs are often mistaken for Muslims. The point is essentially moot, however, because the effect is the same—individuals are subjected to stops and searches because of a physical appearance that has no direct relation to crime, and not because of their behavior.

The definition is relatively broad in that it applies to any *judgments* of criminal suspicion, not just actual behaviors (e.g., stops and searches). The rationale for this construction of the definition is that racial profiling is largely cognitive—it reflects the thoughts and judgments law enforcers make. These judgments necessarily affect the *probability* that the target of judgment (the suspect) will be stopped. One could argue that if an officer uses race or ethnicity in his or her judgments but never exhibits bias in behavior, this is not racial profiling. If, however, officers' judgments do not reliably relate to their actions, we may have a bigger problem than racial profiling.

I deliberately constrain the definition to law enforcers. It is certainly true that people make judgments about others based on race and ethnicity in many other domains, but we already have a term for this—*stereotyping*. Racial profiling has historically been a term used exclusively for law enforcement. I prefer to respect that precedent because fairness, due process, and nondiscrimination are perhaps more crucial in law enforcement than in any other domain for the maintenance of a free and open society. Accordingly, the topic deserves clear and potent labels for its related phenomena. Restricting the term *racial profiling*, with all the rhetorical and political force it carries, to law enforcement keeps an appropriate level of light and heat focused on the issue.

For my purposes, profiling can be formal or informal, deliberate or unintentional. In fact, it is important for the purposes of this book to consider both kinds because their causes are very different, and, accordingly, so should policies designed to address them.

Needless to say, police are generally not at liberty to stop and investigate anyone they want, and so racial profiling is rarely blatant. Rather, it typically relies on "pretexts"—ostensible violations or suspicious behaviors. For example, police engaged in racial profiling might stop a Black driver based on the *pretext* that he was driving over the speed limit or had a broken taillight, or even for the highly subjective reason of "reckless driving." A pedestrian stop may be based on something as potentially innocuous as loitering or "furtive glances." In 1996, the U.S. Supreme Court issued a unanimous ruling that upheld drug arrests that resulted from stops based solely on traffic violation pretexts and not probable cause related to the drug offense (*Whren v. United States*, 517 U.S. 806 (1996)). Similarly, the Court has ruled that pedestrians can be stopped and lightly frisked without probable cause (*Terry v. Ohio*, 392 U.S. 1 (1968)). Furthermore, the Court has repeatedly acknowledged that criminal profiles are inherently informal, yet permissible (e.g., *Reid v. Georgia*, 448 U.S. 438 (1980)), and that some degree of profiling is permissible in immigration enforcement at U.S. border checkpoints (*United States v. Martinez-Fuerte et al.*, 428 U.S. 543 (1976)).

As a result, the courts have been tolerant of racial profiling, generally rejecting it as a basis for excluding evidence in criminal cases. One prominent exception is New Jersey v. Pedro Soto et al. (1996), wherein, based on statistical analyses demonstrating a *pattern* of racial discrimination in highway stops, the New Jersey Superior Court rejected evidence against a class of defendants. The impact of the statistical evidence was perhaps buttressed by a rising uproar in New Jersey over racial profiling and additional evidence that state troopers were being encouraged to profile. This high evidentiary bar is difficult (and expensive) for most defendants to reach, however. See Alschuler (2002), Banks (2001, 2003), Gould and Mastrofski (2004), Harcourt (2007), Harris (2002a), and Withrow (2006) for more thorough and nuanced legal analyses, and Chapter 7 of this book for further discussion.

Racial Profiling ≠ Criminal Profiling

In understanding what racial profiling is, it is important to distinguish it from what it is not. One term that is sometimes conflated with racial profiling is *criminal profiling*. Criminal profiling involves the use of specific evidence about a particular, known case (the crime has already occurred). Criminal profilers can use statistical base rates about criminals who have committed similar crimes in the past to prepare a demographic and perhaps psychological profile of the perpetrator. This is then used to narrow the pool of potential suspects. This manner of criminal profiling is a relatively formal procedure (although, no doubt, detectives engage in informal, tacit criminal profiling regularly), and still publicly accepted, although less well-known than racial profiling.

Despite the analytic nature of criminal profiling, it has a dubious record (Silke, 2001; Winerman, 2004). Silke (2001) laments that there is a paucity of research on the effectiveness of criminal profiling (aka, "offender profiling") and notes that the few studies that have systematically analyzed the rates at which criminal profiles contribute to criminal captures have found it to be effective in only a small percentage of cases and typically contain many incorrect descriptors. A recent example of the pitfalls of criminal profiling is the case of the DC Sniper, who killed 10 people in 2002. Profilers predicted that the sniper was a White male, in his mid-20s, acting alone (Gettleman, 2002). In fact, he was a 41-year-old Black man, John Allen Muhammad, working with a teenage accomplice, Lee Boyd Malvo, also Black. Misguided profiles are not just a waste of time; they have the potential to steer investigators away from actual perpetrators.

The DC Sniper case also illustrates that race or ethnicity can be part of a criminal profile, so the distinction between *racial* and *criminal* profiling might seem subtle. However, the primary difference between racial and criminal profiling is profound. In the former case, no crime is known to have been committed, but agents suspect individuals of an as yet unidentified crime (e.g., drug possession) based on a profile (e.g., young, Black, male, and driving slowly). In the latter case, a crime or multiple crimes have been committed, and law enforcers are constructing a profile of traits the perpetrator is likely to possess. That race may be a descriptor in a criminal profile of a perpetrator does not render it a "racial profile."

It is also important to distinguish racial profiling from *the use of race in suspect descriptions*. Yale Law professor Peter Schuck (2002), in making a case for racial profiling based on its putative effectiveness, stated:

> No one would think it unjust for [an airport security] officer to screen for Osama bin Laden, who is a very tall man with a beard and turban, by stopping all men meeting that general description. This is so not only because the stakes in apprehending him are immense but also because in making instantaneous decisions about whom to stop, the official can use gender, size, physiognomy, and dress as valuable clues. (p. 61)

However, this conflates racial profiling with using race in suspect descriptions. Using a description of Osama bin Laden to catch Osama bin Laden, even if that description included an ethnic descriptor, would not deprive a class of individuals (except for those who look a lot like bin Laden) of constitutional protections. One can make a compelling argument that racial profiling and the use of race in suspect descriptions represent two points on a continuum, and prominent scholars have done so (Alschuler, 2002; Banks, 2001, 2004b). As suspect descriptions get simpler (e.g., "young, Black male"), they start to resemble profiles. However, the important distinction remains that suspect descriptions involve specific, known crimes and therefore cannot be used in the indeterminate fashion that, for example, drug courier profiles can be and are used. The race in the suspect description is due to a witness or some other race-identifying direct evidence.

Finally, it is important to bear in mind that there are indicators of suspicion that may be correlated with race or ethnicity but that still bear an *instrumental* connection to the crime of interest. For example, SUVs with tinted windows are probably more likely to be drug transport vehicles than are open-bed pickup trucks, and they may be more commonly driven by young Black men. If police stop these vehicles at a relatively high rate because of their practical connection to drug transportation, and young Black men are disproportionately stopped as a result, that is not racial profiling. To illustrate the point with perhaps an absurdly extreme example: If police were looking for elephant smugglers, there would be no point in stopping small cars. But as a result of the police focus on large trucks, truck drivers would necessarily be stopped disproportionately in searches for elephants. This need not reflect any "bias." An attribute (e.g., vehicle type) that is instrumentally related to the type of crime (e.g., transporting contraband) being policed may have a disparate effect on a group of people who happen to tend to share that attribute. This is not necessarily profiling, although it may still have a disparate impact. This distinction will be particularly relevant to the discussion of counterterrorism profiling in Chapter 6. The real group conflict between radical Muslims and Western societies could be seen as justification for profiling Muslims—it is not just a correlation; there is a causal connection. However, as we will discuss, the history of terrorism in the United States, perpetrated primarily by White, Christian militants, strains the utility of this argument.

This book is intended to be both descriptive and prescriptive. It seeks to describe the nature of racial profiling, primarily in terms of human psychology. A deeper understanding of human cognition, especially the process of stereotyping, will allow for policy prescriptions that have a realistic chance of effectively changing human behavior.

A number of excellent books and articles on racial profiling have already been published. This book seeks not to replicate them but rather to complement them with a thorough analysis of the relevant psychological factors, something that has not been more than cursorily considered to date. The central argument of this book is that racial profiling is stereotype-based policing. Because hundreds of social psychologists have devoted decades of research to understanding stereotyping, we know a tremendous amount about how stereotypes operate. This book applies that knowledge to racial profiling. Other writings have not.

Brian Withrow's (2006) *Racial Profiling: From Rhetoric to Reason* is a thorough and highly accessible description of police practices, legal context, empirical techniques for studying profiling, and policy prescriptions, with no reference to psychological processes. Richard Schauer's (2003) philosophically oriented book *Profiles, Probabilities, and Stereotypes* argues thoughtfully in favor of statistically based profiles. However, despite the title, it includes little discussion of the psychology of stereotyping. Bernard Harcourt's *Against Prediction: Profiling, Policing, and Punishing in an Actuarial Age* (2007) is in many ways a counterpoint—and a compelling one—to Schauer's arguments for the rationality of profiling. Harcourt's analysis is highly empirical, while also offering a thorough and thoughtful legal analysis. It too lacks discussion of stereotyping. Fredrickson and Siljander's *Racial Profiling: Eliminating the Confusion Between Racial and Criminal Profiling and Clarifying What Constitutes Unfair Discrimination and Persecution* (2002) argues that there is no such thing as racial profiling, rendering it difficult to apply a psychological understanding of stereotyping to it. David Harris's groundbreaking book (2002a) provides an excellent historical and legal analysis while also putting a human face on the targets of racial profiling. Harris, more than any of the other profiling experts, acknowledges and respects the role of stereotyping in profiling but provides only fleeting coverage of the topic. Similarly, Albert Alschuler's (2002) extensive constitutional analysis of racial profiling offers a thorough and thoughtful discussion of relevant law as well as insights regarding the identification and impact of profiling, but it does not discuss cognitive causes.

All of these predecessors offer considerable depth and sophistication, focusing on history, law, and empirical approaches. This book is primarily psychological, focusing on the cognitive bases of racial profiling and drawing on a vast, rich, fascinating, and rigorously scientific literature. Building on that, as well as some assessment of the utility of racial profiling, we then turn to policy analysis, reviewing the extant laws and regulations and considering new alternatives.

Racial profiling is a topic worthy of analysis only if it is real, of course. Accordingly, in the next chapter I will describe evidence that indicates that racial profiling has occurred in various locations throughout the United States in recent years. However, the important question is not so much exactly when and where racial profiling happens. No doubt, it occurs in some places but not others, and among some officers but not others. The crucial questions are, under what circumstances does it occur, what causes it, and how can it be addressed? Nevertheless, a better understanding of racial profiling requires a historical and empirical analysis, and we will give appropriate attention to that in the next chapter.

CHAPTER 2
Racial Profiling Is Real

In 1999, a drug sting operation in Tulia, Texas, netted 43 defendants, 40 of whom were African American. This was rather striking in a small town not known to have a big drug problem, and where less than 10% of the population was Black. Almost one-third of the Black male Tulia population was arrested. Not surprisingly, this raised concerns about racial profiling. It turned out that the undercover investigator responsible for the arrests had a shady past and was operating alone and with minimal supervision, keeping sloppy or no records of his investigation. Much of the investigator's testimony proved unreliable and many of the charges bogus (Blakeslee, 2005; Yardley, 2000).

Also in 1999, under investigation by major news media organizations and the U.S. Department of Justice, the New Jersey State Police acknowledged after years of denial that there was a consistent pattern of racial profiling by their officers on the New Jersey Turnpike. Records showed that, in addition to there being dramatic statistical disproportions in stops of Black and Latino drivers, officers had in fact been instructed to consider race and ethnicity in making traffic stops. According to the *The New York Times*, "One training plan written by a unit supervisor offered this tip off for recognizing drug courier drivers: 'Hispanics mainly involved'" (Barstow & Kocieniewski, 2000). The revelations from New Jersey resulted in a significant mea culpa from the state police brass and a court-mediated consent decree requiring measures to monitor for racial profiling.

These cases are only two of a larger number of historical examples where fairly extreme manifestations and compelling evidence of racial profiling have occurred. They also represent very different scenarios: one in which a lone, radical actor is primarily responsible, and the other in which the problem is systemic. They occur in very different parts of the country, in small, local versus large, statewide agencies. Probably neither is very representative of the more common forms of racial profiling, but they illustrate that it is very real and probably not isolated.

To provide a better sense of the seriousness and breadth of the problem, this chapter will cover a wide array of evidence. There is considerable variability in the style and persuasiveness of this evidence, with anecdotal and survey accounts being concrete and colorful but rarely airtight, and the more quantitative studies being more convincing, though more abstract and coldly analytical, sometimes inscrutable for nonexperts. The totality and diversity of the evidence, however, are compelling.

Although there is substantial evidence of racial profiling across a wide array of places and types of agencies, the purpose of this review is not to establish that racial profiling is universal or even pervasive, but merely that it is real and relatively common. Like other manifestations of human thought and behavior, racial profiling is not a predictable certainty; rather, it varies in its frequency and intensity across people, times, and situations.

We know from psychological research that everyone holds stereotypes to varying degrees, and that stereotypes often guide behavior. (Exactly how and why this is the case will be covered in depth in Chapters 3 and 4.) Furthermore, we make the reasonable assumption that law enforcement agents have normal human cognition. We also know, and will discuss in greater detail in later chapters, that in carefully controlled experiments, people are more likely to perceive racial and ethnic minorities (in contemporary America, that is primarily Blacks and Latinos) as criminally oriented and to vote to convict them and give them harsher sentences, all else being equal (e.g., Sommers & Ellsworth, 2001; Sweeney & Haney, 1992).

Nevertheless, it is reasonable to believe that law enforcement procedures and training, and the strong cultural taboo associated with racial discrimination would preclude racial profiling. It is therefore worth considering specific evidence of racial profiling and the various methodologies associated with it.

THE BENCHMARK PROBLEM

The main empirical challenge to assessing the effect of suspect race on police decisions to stop and search is what is known as the *benchmark* issue. Simple racial or ethnic disparities (i.e., higher rates of stops and/or searches for one group or another) are not sufficient evidence of biased policing. For example, if Blacks and Latinos have been stopped at rates higher than one would expect based on their presence in the population, that alone would only *suggest* but not *prove* racial profiling. Members of minority groups may be getting stopped and searched at higher rates in some locations simply because they are offending (e.g., speeding) at higher rates or engaged in more behaviors that are direct indicators of criminal suspicion (e.g., visiting a known drug sale point), or even possibly because they are simply present (e.g., driving) more in particular areas.

Benchmarks are measures of representation, offending, and suspicious behavior rates that account for suspect race and ethnicity as well as other demographic variables like gender and age. These *base rates* (the baseline rates at which members of various groups are present and engaged in various behaviors) serve as the denominator in the equation

$$stop\ rate = \frac{stopped}{benchmark}$$

that helps determine whether members of those groups are being policed *disproportionately* when we compare the stop rates for different groups. The more careful and precise the benchmarking, the greater confidence we can have in inferences regarding racial profiling—its presence or its absence.

Identifying and accurately quantifying appropriate benchmarks is such an important and difficult aspect of assessing discriminatory policing that both the U.S. General Accounting Office, now called the Government Accountability Office (GAO; 2000a) and California's similarly analytically rigorous Legislative Analyst's Office (LAO; 2002) concluded that most of the available studies of racial profiling were of ambiguous value because they lacked appropriate benchmarking. The LAO report, illustrating how different agencies vary significantly in their operational definitions of racial profiling, also noted that internal police department analyses sometimes go to lengths to explain away racial disparities in stops. The use of appropriate benchmarks, or alternative approaches (e.g., outcome tests, to be described further below), ideally based on some degree of consensus among analysts, would promote better understanding and more judicious and effective interventions.

Different analysts have attempted to address the benchmark issue in different ways with varying degrees of success (see Withrow, 2006, for an excellent discussion of benchmarks). Some early racial profiling analyses failed to include benchmarks at all. Others have simply used census data to estimate the proportion of drivers or pedestrians from different racial groups that would be expected to be in a given location, failing to account for different pedestrian or driving rates or habits. In contrast, some researchers have gone to great lengths to generate accurate benchmarks based on direct observations, and many of the more recent analyses have very sophisticated mathematical and econometric models to account for base rates. Simplicity has the benefit of straightforwardness but the detriment of imprecision. Complex, sophisticated approaches, in contrast, are more precise but can require esoteric theoretical assumptions that increase uncertainty and cloud interpretations.

As is generally the case with scientific inquiry, greater confidence in our understanding of a phenomenon, and a reasonable assessment of the actual state of affairs, can be achieved by reviewing *multiple studies employing multiple methods*. If there is a reasonably consistent trend across studies, research paradigms, times, and locations, we can be confident that a demonstrated phenomenon is real. Accordingly, we will next review a number of studies and other sources of evidence of racial profiling across a wide array of styles of inquiry. However, we must recognize a few important caveats.

First, we do not expect that, even if racial profiling is a real phenomenon, it is universal—that it will be going on everywhere all the time. Some departments have characteristics that are likely to promote fair and equal treatment (e.g., diverse staff, rigorous training, high accountability), and some jurisdictions lack significant numbers of minorities, and therefore lack the opportunity for racial or ethnic bias to occur or be detectable. Consequently, we do not expect every study to reveal racial disparities, let alone racial profiling. The failure to do so would not mean that racial profiling is not real.

Second, the inverse is also true: Even if we find evidence of racial profiling in all the locations studied, we cannot infer that it happens everywhere.

Third, racial profiling is a politically volatile subject with very serious implications, and so there is the potential for bias to affect the analyses. Some advocacy groups may selectively highlight statistics that indicate profiling, and some police departments may do the opposite when reporting their own internal analyses. They might also interpret similar statistics very differently. Both may be well-intentioned, but their conclusions could be biased by the demonstrated tendency people have to embrace information that confirms our prior conceptions. (Social psychologists have shown that people tend to look for and accept information that supports their prior attitudes and beliefs and ignore or dismiss information that contradicts them; e.g., Lord, Ross, & Lepper, 1979).

Finally, it is good science to recognize that the better the methods, the more reliable the results. For example, when scientists "meta-analyze" phenomena (when they mathematically combine and compare the results of multiple studies of the same topic), they often score each study for its methodological quality and give greater weight to more careful studies when calculating average effects. Similarly, we should give greater credence to higher-quality studies in our investigation of racial profiling.

A number of scholars have provided helpful and thoughtful coverage of empirical studies of racial profiling (e.g., Harcourt, 2006; Harris, 2002a; Withrow, 2006). Without duplicating their efforts completely, I will offer a sampling of analyses here, presented according to categories in order of empirical rigor. Bear in mind that, although the historical/anecdotal evidence comes first because it ranks lower in scientific rigor, this should not be taken to mean that such evidence is inherently inferior. It is of a different sort, and its limitations need to be acknowledged—primarily that it is influenced by the subjective experience of those giving the accounts—but it is valid and informative nonetheless.

HISTORICAL/ANECDOTAL EVIDENCE

Authors like Harris (2002a), Harcourt (2006), Schauer (2003), and Withrow (2006) have provided clear and illuminating historical accounts of how formal racial profiling practices evolved from criminal profiling procedures developed by psychologists, psychiatrists, and FBI and DEA analysts dating back to the early 20th century. Serial killers, for example, were profiled to narrow the pool of suspects for investigation. Investigators were looking for the proverbial needle (the killer) in a haystack (the general population), and they needed to make the haystack much smaller because they could never examine every "piece of hay." Past history of captured serial killers in the United States indicated that they tended to be adult, White, and male, among other characteristics. The history of this sort of criminal profiling is *mixed* at best, with some striking successes and some startling failures, such as the DC Sniper case, referenced in Chapter 1.

For our purposes, the point of interest is the evolution of criminal profiling into formal racial profiling. The crucial shift with regard to present-day racial profiling may have been the application of criminal profiling to airplane hijackers, and then to drug couriers, because the approach became *predictive*. In other words, instead of merely trying to narrow the pool of suspects (make the haystack smaller) for a given crime or set of crimes like serial murders, law enforcement officials were looking for perpetrators of *as yet unknown* or even *unperpetrated* crimes (looking for a larger number of needles that might or might not exist).

In many ways, the logic was the same. As Harcourt (2007) describes, law enforcers (like insurance underwriters trying to assess risk) have used actuarial methods to identify those most likely to engage in particular kinds of behavior, specifically crimes like drug possession and transport. Based on common characteristics of known perpetrators, profiles of predicted perpetrators are constructed. If one of these characteristics is race or ethnicity, it might be no less predictive than gender or age. We will discuss further in Chapter 5 some of the logical limitations of this approach, primarily in that profiles are limited to *known* (i.e., previously apprehended) perpetrators and can therefore miss whole classes of perpetrators and can become self-fulfilling.

The historical record is clear that formal racial profiling is an established technique for capturing and/or deterring perpetrators of as yet unknown or unrealized crimes, developed by the DEA and FBI from previously accepted criminal profiling methods (Harris, 2002a; Withrow, 2006). Harris (2002b) notes that, although the DEA has claimed that its training procedures did not encourage officers to use race in drug courier profiles, "training materials sometimes showed otherwise. For example, one training video shows officers making several mock stops; in each one, the driver stopped has a Hispanic surname. The DEA and other federal agencies were also disseminating intelligence in the 1980s and 1990s that blamed trafficking in particular drugs on identified ethnic groups" (pp. 38–39).

In addition to the history of the evolution of racial profiling, well documented by others, the historical record with regard to modern-day occurrences of racial profiling is also evident in published accounts of revelations about racial profiling, as in the New Jersey State Police and Tulia, Texas, cases described previously. For example, in 2002 it was revealed that police in Delaware were compiling a list of people they projected were likely to break the law in the future. According to news reports, the database included "names, addresses and photographs of the potential suspects—many of whom have clean slates…most of the 200 people included in the file have been minorities from poor, high-crime neighborhoods" (Chronicle News Service, 2002, A7).

In addition to the historical accounts of revealed departmental policies and procedures, there are ample anecdotal examples of Black individuals, often upstanding citizens like off-duty police officers, police chiefs, and high-ranking public officials (including former secretary of state Colin Powell), who report having been stopped and searched by the police without any identifiable basis for suspicion other than their race or ethnicity. Harris (1999, 2002a) has provided a number of compelling stories in this vein. And Russell (1998, p. 36) tendered a long list of prominent Black men who have stories of being racially profiled. These accounts are helpful because of the narrative detail they offer, giving us specific, concrete examples of likely cases of racial profiling and a clear sense of the contours of the experience from the target's perspective. This experience may involve psychological consequences for self-esteem, alienation, and the triggering of destructive emotions like "fear, anger, and humiliation" (Harris, 1999). Given the inherently subjective nature of the accounts, they do not yield incontrovertible evidence. However, they should not be discounted either. In particular, those involving prominent citizens like judges, elected officials, and off-duty or plainclothes police officers (as the suspects) provide legitimate and compelling evidence that race and ethnicity influence at least some officers' judgments and behaviors inappropriately.

It is important to reiterate here the distinction between formal and informal racial profiling. In the New Jersey case, there is evidence of relatively formal profiling—explicit (albeit not readily acknowledged) instructions for the use of race or ethnicity in judgments of criminal suspicion. Because they are from the suspects' perspective, the anecdotes rarely if ever speak to the cause of the profiling, and so it may be that many of those incidents resulted from informal profiling—individual officers, deliberately or not, including suspect race or ethnicity as factors affecting their judgments of suspicion. It is unusual to have direct evidence of formal profiling (e.g., departmental memos, whistle-blowing), probably because formal racial profiling is itself unusual. Nevertheless, we will not be able to make conclusive distinctions about the type of profiling underlying the remaining evidence to be discussed. However, given the tendency for law enforcement leaders to condemn racial profiling—many agencies have officially and publicly banned the practice—most of it is probably informal.

SURVEY EVIDENCE

The Gallup poll has repeatedly included questions in its large, national surveys asking respondents if and how often they felt they had been stopped by the police "just because of [their] race or ethnic background." In 1999, Gallup reported that 42% of Blacks (compared with 6% of Whites) and 72% of Black men aged 18 to 34 (compared with 10.9% of White men of those ages) believed they had been stopped by police on the basis of race or ethnicity (Newport, 1999; Weitzer & Tuch, 2002). Sixty-nine percent of all Blacks who reported having been stopped on the basis of race or ethnicity indicated that it had happened to them 3 times or more (6 times or more for 30%, and 11 times or more for 15%).

Importantly, further analyses revealed that Blacks who were relatively high in education and income were no less likely to report having been profiled, indicating that race was not just an artifact of socioeconomic variables that predict criminality. This also reduces the likelihood that racial differences in stop rates could be explained by police patrolling lower-income, higher-crime neighborhoods more. Furthermore, because the Gallup poll was conducted by telephone, incarcerated people (those most likely to have been stopped by the police, and for whom such stops are most likely to have been justified) were excluded from the sample.

The U.S. Bureau of Justice Statistics found somewhat different results in a study released in 2007 (Durose, Smith, & Langan, 2007). Using U.S. Census interview data from 2002 and 2005 regarding reports of contacts with the police, the BJS study found that Black, Latino, and White drivers reported nearly identical rates of being stopped by the police. These statistics are different from those of the Gallup study because the census respondents were not asked how often the stops were *based on* their race or ethnicity, simply whether or not and how often they had been stopped. It is possible that White and minority drivers could be stopped at similar rates overall while the reasons for their stops would be different. In fact, the 2005 survey asked respondents the reasons for the police stops, and Black drivers were less likely (76.8%) to believe the stops were legitimate than were White (87.6%) and Latino (85.1%) drivers.

It is also possible that some Black drivers in the Gallup poll were incorrectly attributing the stops to their race. However, we must also consider the possibility that minority drivers, being concerned about being stopped for what is sometimes called "driving while black or brown" (i.e., racial profiling), tend to drive more cautiously or even less frequently. If this were the case, equal rates of being stopped (relative to presence in the general population) could reflect disproportionate attention from the police. All of these considerations render these survey results somewhat ambiguous.

But there is more potent evidence of racial profiling in the BJS study. Among those who reported having been stopped by the police, Blacks and Latinos were much more likely than Whites to report having been searched (10.2%, 11.4%, and 3.5%, respectively, in 2002; 9.5%, 8.8%, and 3.6% in 2005). Indeed, these higher search rates help to explain why minority drivers would take measures to avoid being stopped in the first place. Police have considerable discretion regarding whom they search (e.g., Gould & Mastrofski, 2004), particularly in the case of consent searches, which represented 57.6% of searches according to respondents in the 2005 census. In fact, this 57.6% estimate is almost certainly low, given that most civilians do not know they can decline a consent search request; they are therefore unlikely to recognize and report them for what they are. Researchers have estimated the share of searches that are of the consent type to be upwards of 90% (Simmons, 2005, p. 773).

The stop and search statistics indicate that decisions to stop may be based more on objective behavior and suspiciousness, while search decisions may be influenced more by race and ethnicity. Alternatively, the racial and ethnic disproportions in search decisions may also reflect different rates of legitimate suspiciousness. However, some evidence exists in these data that police are searching minority drivers in a manner disproportionate to suspiciousness. Specifically, while the search rate is almost three times as high for minority drivers as for White drivers, the arrest rate is only about twice as high (4.5% of Black, 3.1% of Latino, and 2.1% of White drivers who reported having been stopped). If the racial and ethnic disproportions in search rates are due to higher rates of criminality, a similar disproportion should be evident in the arrest rates.

In sum, the survey data from Gallup and the Census Bureau and Justice Department provide evidence of racial profiling, or at the very least the perception of it by minorities. In the case of the DOJ-analyzed census data, we can make a fairly strong inference about racial bias from the higher rates of searches in the absence of commensurate rates of arrests for minorities. Even though self-reports of these sorts (i.e., based solely on the memories of survey respondents) are bound to be imperfect, because the census questions were not framed with regard to race or ethnicity, it is less likely that the results can be explained by illusory perceptions of bias.

STATISTICAL EVIDENCE EMERGING FROM CRIMINAL TRIALS AND LAWSUITS

Allegations of racial profiling have rarely been effective as a defense in criminal cases, largely because of the considerable deference courts have given to police discretion in decisions to stop and search (see, e.g., the *Terry* and *Whren* U.S. Supreme Court decisions, discussed in Chapters 1 and 7). However, some persuasive statistical evidence of racial profiling has come as a result of criminal defense efforts and civil litigation on behalf of allegedly targeted communities. Among the most notable are the analyses conducted by statistician John Lamberth on behalf of defendants in New Jersey and plaintiffs suing the State of Maryland. In

New Jersey, for example, Lamberth (now a professional statistical consultant to individuals and law enforcement agencies, specializing in racial profiling analyses) worked on behalf of 26 Black defendants to determine whether seemingly high rates of highway stops of Blacks from 1988 to 1991 were, indeed, disproportionate to their share of the population in the region, drivers on the New Jersey Turnpike corridor in question, and traffic law violators in that corridor (Lamberth, 1994). Lamberth conducted labor-intensive data collection, involving direct observation of turnpike traffic, to identify reasonable benchmarks, and compared them with police data on stops, citations, and arrests. He found that cars with Black occupants were stopped at a rate significantly disproportionate to their representation in the particular span of turnpike under investigation. He argued that this discrepancy could not be accounted for by driving habit differences because a systematic audit revealed that Black and White drivers exceeded the speed limit at essentially identical rates. The court drew upon Lamberth's conclusions in ruling in favor of the defendants. Furthermore, this ruling, in addition to revelations from released internal documents that the New Jersey State Police were engaged in racial profiling, spurred a forceful condemnation of the practice and mitigation efforts by the state.

Lamberth's New Jersey study has been criticized because his claim of no racial difference in moving violations was based simply on whether cars were exceeding 60 miles per hour (in a 55 zone) or not, and nearly all cars were. A study released by the state in 2001 found that among observed drivers, Blacks were nearly twice as likely to speed 15 or more miles per hour above the speed limit than were Whites. This is from a different time period, approximately a decade later, and the observed disparity probably cannot alone explain why Blacks were stopped at a rate of 2.6 times their representation on the roads. Furthermore, the New Jersey state attorney general, upon release of the latter report, emphatically indicated that it did not refute the state's own admission that it had been engaged in racial profiling (Peterson, 2002). At the very least, however, the new data illustrate that even relatively rigorous research methods like Lamberth's are not without limitations, nor above criticism.

Another compelling example of statistical experts working effectively with police data comes from Oakland, California. Researchers from the RAND Corporation, a highly regarded, nonpartisan, policy research institute, used court-mandated Oakland Police Department data on vehicle stops to determine whether racial bias was influencing decisions to stop and search (RAND, 2004; see also Grogger & Ridgeway, 2006). Working around the benchmark problem, they compared stop rates for daylight hours with those after dark, when officers should be less likely to detect driver race, finding no significant difference in stop rates. The researchers also found that, among stops, Blacks had slightly lower citation rates, which from an "outcome test" (see further discussion below) perspective suggests bias, and that Black drivers, all else being equal, tended to be subjected to longer stops.

RAND researcher Greg Ridgeway and colleagues have been ahead of the pro-verbial curve in addressing benchmark problems. They have worked with police data to develop "doubly robust internal benchmarks" for estimating the likeli-hood that individual officers are making stop decisions in a racially biased man-ner relative to their department or unit (Ridgeway & MacDonald, 2009). The method is intended to avoid false positive identifications of biased officers. This offers a potentially powerful and statistically rigorous method. However, it relies on an assumption that the typical officer in a given department is not biased, but rather the problem is driven by a few "bad apples," which could lead to underiden-tification of biased policing in departments with systemic problems. It also may work only for very large departments and/or when data from a very long period of time can be analyzed. Nevertheless, researchers like Ridgeway are hot on the trail of a reliable method.

STATISTICAL EVIDENCE EMERGING FROM SCIENTIFIC STUDIES

In 1992, the ABC News show *20/20* conducted and broadcast an experiment investigating racial profiling in Los Angeles. As described in Cole (1999), *20/20* deployed Black and White test drivers who were otherwise highly similar (in terms of appearance, demographics, cars, and driving behavior). Black driv-ers were stopped and questioned repeatedly, but White drivers were passed up consistently.

Of course, this study, designed for mass media consumption, does not likely meet all standards of scientific rigor, such as random selection and assignment. No statistical tests were performed, nor was it submitted to critical "peer review," the vetting system necessary for publication of research in scientific journals. Nevertheless, the basic approach is valid, and the results are straightforward and therefore instructive. Perhaps we should regard this information as more "anecdotal" than scientific, meaning that it represents something that may not be broadly representative, but that actually happened and is illustrative of a real phenomenon, providing us with a narrative (and, in this case, some video) of the nature of profiling. In this sense, the *20/20* evidence is strongly suggestive and is particularly valuable in being a rare experimental test for the presence of racial profiling.

The beauty of experiments, when they are designed, conducted, and analyzed carefully, is that they allow us to control for the influence of all extraneous vari-ables, isolating the cause of what we are interested in. So, if we were somehow able to construct an experiment in which randomly selected police officers were assigned to patrol areas with sets of Black and White drivers or pedestrians who were in every other respect identical (in this sense, the race of the driver would be the experimental variable) and were unaware that their race might affect the behavior of the police, we could draw strong inferences about whether and the extent to which police tend to engage in racial profiling (i.e., stop and/or search people at differential rates *because of* their race).

In isolating a single variable, like race, in this way, experiments allow us to do something very powerful: *infer causality.* This means that experiments enable us to determine whether change in one variable that we *manipulate* (the "predictor" or "independent" variable) *causes* a change in another variable that we *measure* (the "outcome" or "dependent" variable). For example, many experiments have shown that when people are given summaries of criminal trials, and the race or ethnicity of the defendant is manipulated (research subjects are randomly assigned to read a summary with either a White or a minority defendant), the subjects are more likely to indicate that they would convict and give harsh sentences to minority defendants (e.g., see Sommers & Ellsworth, 2001). We can be confident that the defendant being depicted as minority has *caused* the greater punitiveness because nothing else could have; everything else was equivalent.

Without the resources, temerity, and freedom from institutional constraints that a network news organization has, experimental tests of racial profiling with real police are virtually impossible to conduct. And, as discussed, in the case of the *20/20* test, the procedure was not scientifically rigorous and therefore of only limited evidentiary value. Consequently, almost all of the empirical studies of racial profiling have employed a different approach.

The primary scientific alternative to experimental research is *correlational* (or observational) design. In their simplest form, correlational studies involve *measuring* both the predictor and the outcome variables and calculating the extent to which they correspond (or correlate, literally *co-relate*). Correlations index how much one variable goes up or down as a function of the other variable going up or down. More complex correlational designs involve multiple predictor variables and statistically control for their respective influences on the outcome variable using *multiple regression* techniques.

In the case of *dichotomous* variables, where there are only two possible values (e.g., male or female; White or minority; stopped or not stopped), the correlation reflects the probability that the outcome will occur given that the predictor has one value or another (how likely a person is to get stopped given that he is a minority). There are no guarantees that all else is equal—in fact that is almost never the case. So inferences of causality are weaker because any correspondence between variables (e.g., between suspect race and rate of stopping) may be due to some other variable or variables (e.g., racial differences in behavior). The other reason correlational studies preclude causal inference is that, even if we could rule out the influence of all other factors, without manipulating one of the variables, we cannot know which is causing which. So, for example, education may be correlated with wealth, but it could be that higher education promotes higher income, or greater wealth buys more education, or both. However, in the case of studies of racial bias, it cannot be that criminal justice outcomes are causing race. Consequently, "reverse causality" is not one of our concerns.

The rest of the evidence that we will consider is most accurately described as correlational. Researchers, including academics, police department statisticians, government oversight analysts, and journalists, have obtained and analyzed data on civilian demographics, the most important being the race and ethnicity of those who are stopped and searched by police in various locales to see if stop and search rates differ as a function of (are correlated with) driver/pedestrian race or ethnicity.

Aside from the Gallup and census surveys, which are limited in that they represent only subjective self-reports of police contact experiences, no known racial profiling study has *directly* calculated the probability of being stopped conditional upon being from one racial/ethnic group or another. This would be the most straightforward test. However, it would involve costly monitoring of many individuals, waiting for and recording relatively infrequent events. Instead, researchers have generally estimated the probabilities of being stopped and/or searched for different groups, based on police records (including race and ethnicity) of who *was* stopped (and searched and arrested), where and when those data are available. These data do not account for those who were not stopped, and without that information, we can draw only limited conclusions. Accordingly, analysts rely heavily on the benchmarks (estimates of the baseline proportions we would expect to see stopped in the absence of racial bias) discussed previously. Furthermore, a relatively new approach based on an "outcomes test" paradigm has been employed by econometricians to circumvent the benchmark problem.

Increasingly, since revelations about racial profiling in the 1990s and the ensuing public condemnation, police departments require officers to record the race/ethnicity of people they stop, and the departments retain these data. In 2004, the RAND Corporation reported that more than 400 agencies were compiling such data, and that number is likely higher today (although some agencies have allowed their data collection policies to "sunset"). There are reasons to be concerned that these data can be incomplete and unreliable (LAO, 2002). Some agencies (e.g., Atlanta; Washington, DC; San Diego) employ mandatory reporting procedures, such as computer-aided dispatch (CAD), that are triggered as soon as a stop is called in. The reliability of even these has been called into question (Atlanta City Auditor's Office, 2008; McEwen, 2002; Rankin, 2010; Rashbaum, 2010). Officers have some discretion regarding whether or not to call in stops, and racial and ethnic designations can be subjective and unverifiable. On the other hand, Ridgeway, Schell, Riley, Turner, and Dixon (2006) found stop report completion rates in excess of 96% in their audit of Cincinnati officers. Reliability of these data no doubt varies from agency to agency, and from officer to officer. Additionally, the data and their utility will only be as good as the practices used to collect them.

The interpretation of police stop data is further complicated by the fact that, for better or worse, simply measuring a behavior changes it. This *Hawthorne effect* referred originally to factory workers at Hawthorne Electric, who were more productive merely for having been observed, but it is a more general phenomenon. This poses the dilemma that, barring completely unobtrusive observation, it would be difficult to ever get an accurate assessment of the extent of racial profiling. Nevertheless, if observation affects police behavior, it seems most likely that that would militate against evidence of racial profiling because officers under observation, or being required to report, would be more careful to avoid racial disparities. Accordingly, evidence indicating racial profiling (disproportionate rates of stops and searches for minorities) would not be compromised, except perhaps to be underestimated.

Despite the potential for the act of observation to affect the behavior of interest, British researchers (Norris, Fielding, Kemp, & Fielding, 1992), directly observing London police, found that Black citizens were two and a half times more likely to be subjected to police-initiated stops than were Whites. Norris and colleagues broke the stops down by type, differentiating between those that were warranted by "obvious enforcement" (i.e., tangible reasons like broken headlights) and those based on more discretionary "general suspicion." The majority (58%) of stops of Whites were for obvious enforcement; in contrast, the majority (56%) of stops of Blacks were for the more subjective general suspicion. This finding, based on direct, careful observation, provides compelling evidence that *discretionary* police stops are most likely to be influenced by suspect race. It is consistent with psychological theory, to be discussed in subsequent chapters, indicating that stereotype-biased judgments are more likely to occur in ambiguous situations.

"STOP AND FRISK"

One of the early, but nevertheless one of the more rigorous and compelling, analyses was conducted by the Office of the Attorney General of the State of New York (OAGSNY) (1999) in its investigation of New York City's "Stop and Frisk" program, an aggressive crime reduction initiative undertaken by the NYPD's Street Crime Unit. The program involved a high rate of pedestrian stops and pat-downs.

Studying the period over the 15 months beginning January 1, 1998, the Attorney General's Office found, first, that Blacks and Latinos were stopped by the police in much greater proportions than were Whites, relative to their representation in the population. For example, Blacks, who represented 25.6% of New York City's population, were 50.6% of those stopped. The disparities were most likely not attributable to higher rates of patrolling in higher-crime, minority neighborhoods—stop rates of Blacks and Hispanics were disproportionately high in overwhelmingly White neighborhoods as well.

As discussed previously, disproportions in stop rates alone are not evidence of racial profiling. The disparities could be explained by real, race-neutral differences in behavior. However, the Attorney General's Office also found that a smaller proportion of Blacks who were stopped were arrested (1 in 9.5) relative to Whites (1 in 7.9) and Latinos (1 in 8.8). One interpretation of these results would be that Blacks (and Latinos) in New York City were less likely to be engaged in crime (e.g., drugs or weapons possession), but these data cannot speak to such a conclusion. This interpretation would hold only if police were stopping people completely randomly, an assumption undermined by the unequal stop rates for Whites and minorities, not to mention the realities of law enforcement.

A valid conclusion from the lower arrest rates of Blacks and Latinos who were stopped is that a part of the basis for suspicion that at least some officers were using was suspect race/ethnicity. If race and ethnicity were not influencing police decisions to stop *above and beyond other indicators of suspicion*, the arrest rates would have been equivalent.

Another way to think about this is that, given their lower arrest rates (among those stopped), Blacks and Latinos were probably held by police to a lower threshold of suspiciousness. Whites, in contrast, must have had to have been behaving relatively suspiciously to get stopped; consequently, those Whites who were stopped were more likely to have been doing something wrong—hence their higher arrest rate. The sample of Street Crimes Unit actions, approximately 175,000 stops over that period, is more than large enough to allow for a high degree of confidence that disproportions of these magnitudes are not random fluctuations but rather are reliable indicators of racial/ethnic bias.

The OAGSNY's findings of racial bias in policing by the NYPD's Street Crime Unit were corroborated by a subsequent investigation by the U.S. Department of Justice, and an inquiry by the U.S. Commission on Civil Rights (2000) that was precipitated by the wrongful, fatal shooting of an unarmed, innocent Black man, Amidou Diallo. Despite the investigations, these patterns of disparate application of the stop and frisk tactic have persisted. At the same time, rates of stop and frisk have grown dramatically. Jones-Brown, Gill, and Trone (2010) analyzed NYPD stop data from 2003 to 2009 and found a steadily, sharply increasing number of stops (160,851 in 2003 to 575,996 in 2009). Officers are required to indicate the reasons they had for each stop. Looking most deeply at the 2008 data, Jones-Brown et al. found that by far the most commonly recorded rationale for a stop was the highly subjective "furtive movements." More than half of the stops led to frisks, but this rate was higher for Blacks (57%) and Hispanics (56%) than for Whites (42%). Among those stopped, the hit rates were low, with 1.7% yielding contraband, 1.09% yielding non-gun weapons like knives, and 0.15% yielding guns. As Figure 2.1 illustrates, minorities were far more likely be stopped and frisked, and to have force used against them. And yet, among those frisked, knife and contraband hits were considerably lower for minorities (knives: 1.87%; contraband: 3.10%) than for Whites (3.49% and 4.71%). Gun find rates were higher for minorities, but the overall yield rates for guns was low (0.29% of minorities stopped and 0.17% of Whites stopped). The considerably higher contraband and

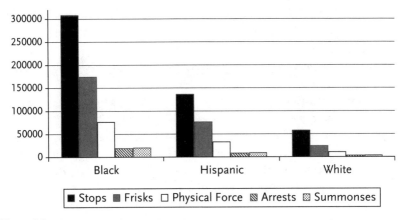

Figure 2.1
Number of Black, Hispanic, and White people subjected to stops, frisks, and so forth by New York Police Department officers in 2008. Adapted with permission from D. Jones-Brown, J. Gill, and J. Torne, *Stop, Question and Frisk Policing Practices in New York City: A Primer* (New York: Center on Race, Crime and Justice, John Jay College of Criminal Justice, 2010).

non-gun weapon hit rates for Whites who were stopped and frisked strongly indicate that minorities are searched based on a lower threshold of suspicion—and this is a potent indicator of biased policing. The NYPD's aggressive Stop and Frisk program appears to have resurged since the turn of the century, but its yields are persistently low, and its effects are racially disproportionate.

CONSENT SEARCHES

"You kiss a lot of frogs before you find a prince." That was an explanation for a large volume of unproductive traffic stops, offered by a California Highway Patrol (CHP) supervisor in a legal deposition (Zamora, 2001, p. A1). A lawsuit had forced the CHP to release data on traffic stops that revealed large racial and ethnic disproportions in who was stopped in its Operation Pipeline drug interdiction program. CHP data revealed that Latinos and Blacks were approximately three and two times as likely as Whites to be stopped, respectively. Instructions for officers to stop drivers who looked out of place probably allowed the kind of discretion that gave rise to the racial/ethnic disparities.

Perhaps most telling were disproportions in consent searches, wherein police can ask to search a car even in the absence of probable cause. That minorities were being subjected to higher rates of consent searches strongly suggests that race and ethnicity were directly influencing CHP officers' judgments of suspicion. If police are requesting consent searches of minority drivers' cars more, in the absence of direct bases for suspicion (e.g., visible contraband), it likely reflects that they are using race/ethnicity as an indicator of suspicion.

Alternatively, they may be using other indirect bases of suspicion (e.g., car type) that are correlated with race/ethnicity. Either way, the discriminatory impact is the same.

Disparities in consent searches do not represent incontrovertible evidence of profiling. Some officers may request consent even in the presence of probable cause, just to ensure the admissibility of evidence resulting from the search. This could explain some of the disparities but is unlikely to explain all.

Similar to the findings from the CHP data are results coming out of an internal audit by the Illinois Department of Transportation, conducted by researchers at the University of Illinois at Chicago (Weiss & Rosenbaum, 2008). According to this study, in 2008 (and results were comparable for all years prior), minorities, and particularly Blacks, were more likely to be stopped. Among those stopped, African Americans and Hispanics were more than three and two times as likely, respectively, as Whites to be submitted to consent searches. It is, however, the *outcome of those consent searches* that offers the most compelling evidence of racial profiling. Among consent searches of White drivers, 24.37% yielded contraband; for Black and Hispanic drivers submitted to consent searches, the hit rates were 17.02% and 11.89%, respectively. These disproportions strongly indicate that in order for Whites in Illinois to be consent searched, they needed to meet a higher threshold of suspicion.

In response to studies showing racial disparities in consent search rates, departments such as the CHP and the New Jersey State Troopers have banned or dramatically cut back the practice (Peterson, 2002; Zamora, 2001).

CUSTOMS SEARCHES

Racially biased searches have been documented in a very different type of law enforcement environment—customs searches. In March 2000, the GAO (2000b) released a study of airline passengers submitted to personal searches (about 102,000) in 1997 and 1998. Most strikingly, the study found that, among other disparities, Black women who were U.S. citizens were nine times more likely to be X-ray searched, but half as likely to be found carrying contraband, than were White women who were U.S. citizens. Ahmed and Rezmovic (2001) also found with regard to racial disparities in U.S. Customs searches that those most often targeted are not necessarily most likely to be found carrying contraband.

INTERNAL AGENCY ANALYSES

Since problems with racial profiling became part of the public consciousness in the mid-1990s, many law enforcement agencies have conducted internal audits of their own pedestrian and vehicle stop data. Some of these analyses, and the data collection efforts that have enabled them, have been voluntary, and others have been in response to court orders (e.g., New Jersey State Police; Oakland, California, Police Department). As indicated earlier, the GAO and California's LAO have rightly identified the limitations typical of these studies, particularly with regard to benchmarks, or the lack thereof. But it is worth noting that a number of major agencies have undertaken analyses. The following are some examples:

- The Texas Department of Public Safety ([TPDS] 2001) found that in 2001 Blacks and Latinos were stopped and searched at rates that are comparable to their representation in the population. This is a crude benchmark: overall state population, not accounting for differential car ownership rates or rates of travel in enforced areas, not to mention rates of legitimately suspicious behavior or traffic violations. Perhaps more important, the TDPS failed to note that, according to their own data, the rate of drug charges from searches of Latinos was less than half that for Blacks and Whites, suggesting bias in decisions to search Latinos (see the section "Outcome Tests" later in this chapter). Furthermore, an independent study conducted for advocacy groups found disproportionately high rates of stops and searches for Blacks and Latinos in Texas (Steward, 2004).
- A report from the Missouri attorney general in 2001 found that Black and Latino motorists were stopped and searched at rates that were dramatically higher than for White motorists. Again, the benchmarks were crude, but the attorney general, Jay Nixon, publicly accepted the results as suggestive of racial profiling (AP, 2001).
- A study of stop and search rates in San Diego found that Black and Hispanic drivers were stopped at rates that were considerably higher than predicted by their representation in the driving-age resident population (Cordner, Williams, & Zuniga, 2000). As with the Missouri study, the benchmark, not taking into account actual rates of driving or offending, was imprecise. Among those stopped, search rates, including consent search rates, were also substantially higher for Blacks and Latinos than for Whites, although arrest rates per search were not reported.
- In 2002, the Nebraska State Patrol released statistics indicating that in the period studied, Black and Hispanic motorists who were stopped were seven and six times more likely, respectively, to be searched than were White motorists who were stopped (AP, 2002).
- A study of rates of tickets and warnings for drivers stopped in Massachusetts in April and May 2001 (the period for which these data were reliably recorded statewide) conducted for the *Boston Globe* did not attempt to identify the appropriate benchmark for estimating stop rates. It did, however, find that among those stopped, Whites received substantially fewer tickets (and more warnings, instead) than did minorities (Dedman, 2003). This pattern was

subtle in the statistics for the state police, who exhibited less leniency (issued tickets at a higher rate) overall. It was, however, pronounced in local agencies, including Boston, where 42.1% of White and 54.7% of minority traffic violators got tickets. The pattern held across types of violations, types of minorities (but was most pronounced for Hispanics), and driver gender, and for hometown as well as out-of-area drivers.

- A state-commissioned study of traffic stop data in Nevada (McCorkle, 2003) found that Blacks and Hispanics were more likely than Whites to be stopped by police in the state. This was based on the crude population baseline. However, the study also found that search rates, and particularly consent search rates, were dramatically higher for Black and Hispanic motorists who were stopped, while seizures from searches were slightly lower for Blacks and Hispanics.

OUTCOME TESTS

As noted previously, quantifying racial bias in policing is fraught with challenges, most prominently the "benchmark" problem, wherein we often lack the right denominator in the equation that allows us to determine the proportion of minorities who are stopped relative to the proportion of Whites. What is the appropriate denominator? The general population? The population passing through the enforcement corridor of interest (assessed by a labor-intensive audit)? The population in observable violation of the law, or exhibiting objectively legitimate evidence of suspicion (assessed by even more, perhaps infeasible, labor-intensive audit)? Benchmarks vary in their precision, and so the statistical inferences based on them vary in their strength.

One analytic approach, the "outcome test," attempts to circumvent the benchmark problem by looking at the outcomes of stops only. The logic behind outcome tests is that, if different groups have different outcomes resulting from some common experience (e.g., being stopped and searched by police), then they are being selected for that experience on an unequal basis (Ayres, 2001, 2002). If, for example, minority mortgage holders are less likely to default (the outcome), it is likely because they had to meet a higher threshold to get a loan (discrimination) in the first place. We do not need information about borrowers' loan qualifications to make this inference.

To be even more concrete (and at the risk of being overly simplistic), if a quality assurance tester in a clothing factory were scanning red and blue shirts for flaws, and was biased toward inspecting more red shirts but was more likely to look for actual indicators of flaws (e.g., loose threads) on blue shirts, among the shirts the tester inspected, fewer red than blue shirts would end up being flawed. Accordingly, a supervisor could detect that the tester had a bias to inspect red shirts based on a finding that fewer flaws were found on inspected red shirts than inspected blue shirts, even without knowing how many red and blue shirts there were. The alternative conclusion would be that the tester is inspecting shirts at random and the red shirts really do have a lesser tendency to have flaws. Outcome tests thus allow for inferences about discrimination without baselines or benchmarks, assuming that officers are not stopping suspects on a purely random basis. If officers were stopping people on a random basis, findings of lower hit rates for minorities would indicate lower offending rates for minorities.

In the context of police stops, we have already seen several examples of outcome tests, particularly with regard to results of searches. If minority civilians who are stopped by the police are less likely to be arrested, it very likely reflects that they had to meet a lower standard of suspicion to get stopped in the first place. The exact mechanics of outcome tests and how well they work is the source of considerable debate among economists constructing "equilibrium models" (e.g., Berkovec, Canner, Gabriel, & Hannan, 1994; Dharmapala & Ross, 2004; Knowles, Persico, & Todd, 2001; Ross, 1997; Sanga, 2009; see legal scholar Harcourt's excellent 2004 and 2007 reviews and critiques), but the fundamental insight is the theoretical basis of a very powerful approach to studying racial profiling.

One important caveat about outcome tests is that they assume that *arrest* decisions are not prone to racial bias. Indeed, it is difficult and risky for an officer to arrest someone falsely, but officers do have some discretion in terms of choosing to *not* arrest someone, just as they have discretion in terms of who to issue a warning versus a citation for a traffic violation. Because police officers are in the business of catching criminals, and are rewarded for doing that, there is not much concern about underarresting biasing outcome test results. Nevertheless, it is a possibility that cannot be ruled out. The result is that outcome tests are probably relatively conservative tests of profiling because minority arrest rates may also be inflated due to bias.

Outcome tests of racial profiling have tended to find evidence of bias against minorities, specifically as evidenced by lower hit (arrest) rates for minority than White drivers, among those stopped. Knowles and colleagues (2001), examining Maryland State Police data for a period following a racial discrimination lawsuit involving stops on Interstate 95, found no evidence of racial bias against Blacks. Data were available only for stops that resulted in searches, but this is not necessarily a problem for the outcome test approach. Knowles and colleagues found that, although Blacks were searched at a rate far in excess of their estimated representation on the highways, Blacks who were searched were slightly *more* likely to be arrested than were Whites who were searched. Hispanics' hit rates were substantially lower than Whites', although Knowles et al. regarded this as only "suggestive" because the data set contained relatively few searches of Hispanics. A number of scholars critiqued these findings, arguing that they were dependent on particular assumptions about economic equilibria (Antonovics & Knight, 2004) and that they failed to account for levels of offense severity (Dharmapala & Ross, 2004).

Sanga (2009) found that when all Maryland data (not just those from the corridor involved in the lawsuit, and from a longer period of time) were examined, anti–Black motorist bias was clearly evident. That an analysis of the data extending farther from the time and place of the lawsuit yields different results is telling. It is probable that officers policing a zone that has recently been the subject of a high-profile and unfavorable lawsuit implicating racial bias would be especially mindful of avoiding such biased behavior. Sanga's finding that lower hit rates for Blacks (and therefore evidence of racial bias) emerge as we move farther from the time and place of the lawsuit supports this explanation and indicates that the default (i.e., when and where the lawsuit is less salient) arrangement involves biased searching of Black motorists.

One of the primary methodological critiques of outcome tests in general has to do with what is called the *infra-marginality* problem (Ayres, 2002). Specifically, discrimination (in mortgage lending, traffic stops, or other domains) is presumed to happen primarily "at the margin," in cases where evidence is not obvious or clear-cut. Bankers will generally grant a loan to someone who has the clear capacity to repay it plus interest, and will deny a loan to someone who clearly does not have the capacity to repay it, regardless of race or ethnicity. Similarly, police officers will generally stop, search, and arrest someone who is in obvious violation of the law and leave alone someone who is obviously unsuspicious (although this last assumption is more tenuous, given the very high rates of stops and frisks and typically low hit rates in locations such as New York). It is in the marginal cases, when the judgment is ambiguous and discretion is high, that you expect to see the most discrimination. However, behavior toward those who are outside the margin (i.e., are infra-marginal) may be overwhelmingly explained by other factors.

In the case of police stops, Whites and minorities may present as obviously suspicious or unsuspicious for very different reasons and at very different probabilities, but outcome test statistics (rates of arrest among those stopped) will conflate the marginal cases with the infra-marginal cases and could bias the results. This may be why studies that have differentiated between stops and searches that involve more or less discretion have found more evidence of discrimination in high-discretion (more likely marginal) cases. For example, Hernández-Murillo and Knowles (2004) found evidence of bias in Missouri when more discretionary searches (i.e., those not "incident to arrest" due to an existing warrant) were examined separately. This harkens back to the findings of Norris and colleagues (1992), who, in their direct observations of London police, found a pronounced tendency to stop Blacks more when operating under "general suspicion" rather than "obvious enforcement."

Consent search (and other high-discretion stop and search) outcomes provide at least a partial solution to the infra-marginality problem because consent searches are more likely to be at the margin—officers need to request consent in the absence of *obvious* evidence (consent searches can still occur in the obvious absence of suspiciousness, however). As we have seen from several of the pieces of evidence discussed previously, consent search data have tended to indicate that minorities who are searched are less likely to possess contraband.

The evidence reviewed in this chapter is not, nor is it intended to be, an exhaustive audit of tests of racial disparities in police stops, searches, and arrests in the United States. It is, however, a clear demonstration, drawing on multiple methodologies by many analysts, that racial profiling has been prevalent in American law enforcement. To social psychologists, this is utterly unsurprising because of what we know about the ubiquity of stereotyping and the difficulty people have in making stereotype-neutral judgments.

The evidence of profiling begs several important questions: What causes it? What effects does it have? How would one prevent it? These are the questions that we will attempt to answer in the coming chapters.

CHAPTER 3
Causes of Racial Profiling

A fourth-grade girl named Hannah works conscientiously to answer the examiner's questions on the aptitude test. She performs reasonably well by any standard, right around grade level. How would you rate her performance if you knew that she came from a lower-class background as opposed to an upper-class background?

This is not merely a thought experiment but a real experiment that was conducted by social psychologists John Darley and Paget Gross (1983). Darley and Gross split their sample randomly, as in any good experiment, and although everyone watched the same exact video of Hannah taking the test, half were given the impression that she came from an upper socioeconomic status (SES) background, and the other half, that she came from a lower SES background. The observers rated Hannah's performance not realizing that they had been given different information. The two groups yielded significantly different ratings: Those in the upper SES experimental condition tended to rate her performance above grade level; those in the lower SES group tended to rate her below grade level. Why? Her performance was identical for both groups.

The observers' judgments were probably well-intentioned, maybe even carefully reasoned. But many of them were affected by something other than Hannah's actual performance. Their preconceptions about how low- and high-income children tend to perform colored their interpretations of her test responses. Ambiguous aspects of her performance were "disambiguated" by the preconception. The result was both inaccurate and discriminatory. The consequences for a real child in this situation could be severe, affecting her placement in school, her teachers' expectations of her performance, her future opportunities, and her self-esteem.

What does this have to do with law enforcement? The raters' biased assessments of Hannah's abilities stemmed from their preconceptions about her, which were based on their beliefs about the intellectual abilities of lower- and upper-class individuals. Beliefs about characteristics of members of social categories defined by class, race, gender, ethnicity, age, religion, and so forth are *stereotypes*. As Darley and Gross (and many other researchers have) demonstrated, stereotypes influence judgments.

Racial profiling is stereotype-based policing—decisions about criminal suspicion based on prior conceptions about groups and their prevailing characteristics.

Studies similar to Darley and Gross's have demonstrated that stereotypes linking Blacks with aggression cause people to judge Blacks' ambiguous behavior as more aggressive than identical behavior by Whites (Duncan, 1976; Sagar & Schofield, 1980). Other experiments have shown that actual police officers also hold stereotypes linking Blacks with violence (Eberhardt, Goff, Purdie, & Davies, 2004, to be discussed in greater detail later in this chapter). This evidence, taken in combination with the overwhelming evidence of disparate treatment of minority suspects, described in the previous chapter, provides ample reason to believe that stereotypes cause police to treat minorities with greater suspicion.

Stereotypes are very well understood by social psychologists, who have studied them systematically for nearly a century, conducting thousands of experiments, surveys, and field studies. In the context of discussing the various causes of racial profiling, I will in this chapter focus primarily on stereotypes because, *whether they arise from careful, actuarial analysis or mindless cognitive errors, stereotypes are the primary cause of racial profiling.* Accordingly, I will provide a complete picture of the nature of stereotypes, including the *functions* they serve, their mental *structure*, how they are *formed* and changed, the *process* by which they affect judgments and behavior, and their specific *contents*. This will provide an understanding of how and why stereotypes can so readily affect our judgments, even when we do not want them to.

STEREOTYPING IS NORMAL

Before launching into a description of the psychological science on stereotyping, it is prudent to recognize that many people associate *psychology* with *psychopathology*. This is common but wrong. Psychology is the scientific study of mental processes and behavior. It is therefore focused for the most part on *normal* phenomena like emotions, memory, and interpersonal relations. The study of stereotyping is no exception. Indeed, stereotyping is a natural and efficient process that probably evolved because it was generally adaptive. However, *"normal" is not always "desirable."* Stereotype-based judgments, particularly when made by people in positions of power, have discriminatory effects, undermining the process of judging an individual on his or her own merits.

It is important to emphasize that stereotyping is normal, because if people perceive it as something deviant or malicious, they either will have difficulty seeing it in themselves (most people, quite reasonably, see themselves as normal and benevolent) or will be actively defensive about it and resist taking steps to avoid making biased judgments. So, while stereotyping can have some very disturbing, even deadly effects, it should not be confused with psychopathology or bigotry. This is not to say that flagrant bigots do not engage in stereotyping; they are just more likely to willfully endorse, even embrace, the use of stereotypes, particularly negative stereotypes of minorities. Stereotyping is generally a more passive, unintentional, and to most people invisible process, which can make it all the more invidious.

MANY ORIGINS, ONE PROCESS

At the core of racial profiling is the belief on some level that members of a particular group are more inclined than others to engage in a particular kind of criminal behavior. This belief may be arrived at through formal empirical analysis (e.g., DEA actuaries developing drug courier profiles, or national security analysts creating terrorist profiles) or informal, spontaneous learning (e.g., people watching news or fictional characters on TV). The belief may be heartily endorsed, grudgingly acknowledged, or strenuously resisted. Whatever the cause or the disposition, stereotypes tend to influence our judgments.

However, different origins most likely demand different interventions, so understanding the spectrum of causes should be helpful in crafting the most effective policy response. If the cause is formal and intentional, then explicit, enforceable prohibitions may be warranted (assuming the objective is to mitigate profiling). If the cause is informal and perhaps even unintentional, then more complicated interventions, including training, monitoring, and incentives, will likely be implicated. Fortunately, these two types of approaches are not mutually exclusive.

Formal Causes of Profiling

As other scholars (Harcourt, 2007; Harris, 2002a; Schauer, 2003; Silke, 2001) have already well documented, racial profiling in law enforcement has its roots in criminal profiling.[1] Nevertheless, criminal profiling is profoundly different from racial profiling. Historically, *criminal profiling has been an investigatory tool*, where, in an effort *to solve a specific, known crime case*, analysts develop a profile of a likely perpetrator based on characteristics of perpetrators of similar

1. Harcourt (2007, Chapter 3) and Harris (2002a, Chapters 2 and 3) provide thorough and excellent histories of formal criminal and racial profiling. See also Becton (1987) and Cole (1999) for enlightening descriptions of the evolution and the varied and often internally inconsistent content of drug courier profiles.

crimes in the past. In contrast, *racial profiling is a projective* enforcement strategy utilizing a more generic profile intended *to identify perpetrators of as yet unknown crimes* (e.g., drug possession, for sale or use; terrorism).

In many cases, criminal profiles have been developed systematically by trained actuaries. Harcourt (2007), in his thorough and cogent critique of actuarial applications, explains and documents how they have become commonplace in modern criminal justice and contributed to the advent of racial profiling. Insurance actuaries use demographic, epidemiological, and personal (driving, medical) records to estimate the likelihood that a given applicant will have a car accident or get terminally ill, and make coverage decisions based on this. Likewise, agencies in most U.S. states utilize similar "risk assessment" techniques, actuarially estimating the likelihood that a given convict will recidivate based on how many characteristics he shares with people who have recidivated in the past. Because of the coldly actuarial, "data-driven" nature of the process, many of these characteristics (e.g., the number of siblings a convict has) bear no direct relation to the criminal behavior at issue, let alone one that could reasonably be deemed a fair and just basis for punishment. Nevertheless, sentencing and parole determinations are often based in part on these actuarial predictions (Harcourt, 2007).

To be sure, it could be said that *informal* criminal profiling is as old as law enforcement, with investigators using prior knowledge of perpetrators to identify and vet suspects in new criminal cases. Not long after the proliferation of actuarial methods in sentencing and parole decision-making in the 1970s, *formal* criminal profiling became a common practice in American law enforcement (Harcourt, 2007, p. 103). Around the same time, *racial profiles* also became prevalent. Agents in the Federal Aviation Administration (FAA) sought to preempt airplane hijackings and bombings, and so, although their undisclosed terrorist profiles were putatively based solely on passenger behavior, there is little doubt that they included religion, ethnicity, and national origin to reflect the recent history of incidents perpetrated by Cubans and Middle Eastern Muslims. The newly formed Drug Enforcement Agency (DEA) worked to develop strategies for breaking up the illicit drug trade by apprehending couriers based on knowledge of past trends in courier characteristics and behavior.

The desire to preempt not yet perpetrated hijackings and bombings (by as yet unknown perpetrators), and to disrupt the conveyance of drugs in a widespread and diffuse market, led to the application of profiling to counterterrorism and the war on drugs. In this manner, criminal profiling evolved from an investigatory tool to a projective interdiction practice—investigators were now using profiles to find perpetrators even in the absence of knowledge of a crime. Furthermore, the perceived correlations, between religion or national origin and terrorism, and between race/ethnicity and drug transporting, caused hijacker and drug courier profiles to include racial and ethnic factors—formal racial profiling was born.

Although agency heads have tended to deny this, formal profiles have often contained explicit or at least tacit racial or ethnic components. As Harris (2002a) and Cole (1999) documented, a number of drug courier profiles have explicitly identified African Americans and Latinos. National security agencies keep their terrorist profiles classified, but there is a near certainty that they include religion (i.e., Muslim) and national origin (i.e., Middle Eastern, South Asian, North African). The disproportionate focus of the U.S. Department of Justice (DOJ) on registration of noncitizen residents of South Asian origins in the period just after the September 11, 2001, attacks betokens the use of national origin in federal counterterrorism. In fact, the DOJ acknowledged that it engages in racial profiling for national security purposes when, in 2003, it carved out an exception for national security in its otherwise blanket ban on racial profiling in federal law enforcement.

A Challenge for Criminal Profiling:
Who Are the "Known" Perpetrators?

Although formal drug courier and terrorist profiles are presumed to be based on systematic, actuarial analysis of valid data, it is difficult to confirm this, given the controversial nature of the practice and reticence of relevant agencies. Stipulating that they are, indeed, systematic and empirical, formal profiles, even those including race or ethnicity, would be developed through the analysis of the characteristics of known perpetrators of the relevant crimes. One fundamental problem with this approach is that *known* perpetrators are those who have been reported or caught. In the case of reported crimes, analysts can rely on police data (to the extent that departments reliably retain records on suspect descriptions in unresolved reported crimes) or the National Crime Victimization Survey (NCVS), a very large survey of a random sample of Americans. As discussed in Chapter 1, because the NCVS seeks victims' reports of crimes, it is not helpful in estimating criminal prevalence in "victimless" crimes like drug possession, transport, or sale or extremely rare crimes like hijackings and terrorism. As a consequence, data on known perpetrators for the most commonly profiled crimes (drug crimes) are based almost entirely on those already caught. If suspect race has already been a factor in agents' assessments of suspicion (and, as demonstrated in Chapter 2, there is every reason to believe it has been), then these known drug crime perpetrators are not representative of the larger population of drug crime perpetrators. In scientific terms, there is a *selection bias* in the sample of known perpetrators— they have been selected from a nonrepresentative population in part because of their race. As a consequence, the minorities who are targeted will be overrepresented among known perpetrators, and actuarial estimates of racial differences in offending rates will be skewed and invalid.

In order to calculate a truly accurate estimate of the rate of criminality of a particular group (to develop an effective profile), one would ideally have a random sample drawn from the population and a valid manner of determining who, among that sample, are criminally inclined. Theoretically, this could be done, but practicably it could not. The institutional review boards that oversee scientific research on human subjects would prohibit social scientists from subjecting people to the intrusive searches that would be required, even if they could somehow do so lawfully. Law enforcement agencies would most likely face intense political reprisals for submitting citizens to random searches. Security screeners at airports do, in fact, submit a random sample of air travelers—in addition to those who trigger searches based on suspicion—to searches, but the hit rate (with regard to terrorist perpetrators) is effectively zero, so would not be informative in developing a profile. Airport random searches serve a primarily deterrent purpose. In the absence of random sampling in drug law enforcement, we are left with a nonrepresentative sample—those who have been caught.

Drawing inferences about racial differences in criminality rate from those who have been caught involves an error akin to what logicians call *affirming the consequent*. Affirming the consequent is the following error: If A then B; B therefore A. A more concrete, illustrative example is: "If pregnant then female; female therefore pregnant." One can imagine the unpleasant social consequences of operating under *that* assumption. Another, more probabilistic example is: "Whenever there is a flood, it has been raining; it has been raining, therefore there will be a flood." It is more likely that there will be a flood after rain, but it is still very unlikely. Inferring that Blacks are likely to be drug criminals because (known) drug criminals are likely to be Black is a similar error (Glaser, 2001), except far worse because, while men cannot be pregnant and floods almost never happen without rain, Whites can be (and many are) drug criminals.

In terms of statistics and probability theory, this issue of the lack of appropriate benchmarks/base rates is a *Bayesian* one, named for the Reverend Thomas Bayes, who, in the 18th century, developed a mathematical formula for calculating conditional probabilities. A conditional probability is the likelihood of one state of affairs given another. For example, the likelihood of a flood is conditional upon rain; a flood is more likely when it rains than it is on the average day. *Bayesian errors* involve a failure to account for unconditional base rates (e.g., how often it rains when estimating the likelihood of a flood; or how many Blacks there are in total when estimating the rate of criminality). It has been demonstrated that people have a tendency to commit Bayesian errors because they overlook base rates (i.e., general prevalences) in favor of ideas that are representative of their intuitions (Kahneman & Tversky, 1973).

Inferring racial and ethnic patterns in criminality from criminal justice data in order to develop profiles is especially problematic, and ironic, when one considers that profiling itself skews these statistics. This subject will be discussed further in Chapter 5. The crux of the problem is that if minorities are already being profiled (and there is ample evidence that they are), they will be arrested and convicted at rates that are disproportionate to their offending rates. They will therefore be overrepresented in the criminal justice system. This leads to a self-fulfilling prophecy, or feedback loop—minorities are more likely to be stopped because they are overrepresented in crime statistics, and they are over-represented in crime statistics because they are more likely to be stopped.

The absence of an appropriate estimate of the probability of being criminal given that one is Black or Latino (as opposed to the probability of being Black or Latino, given that one is a convicted criminal) is a profound challenge for actuarially based profiling. This is a benchmark problem, like the one discussed in Chapter 2, but relating to the construction of the profile rather than to the estimate of the rate of profiling. In both cases, the outcome tests described in Chapter 2 may be the best quantitative solution.

Informal Causes of Profiling

While formal causes of profiling—actuarial derivation of criminal profiles—are widespread and influential, social psychological theory and research point to a less formal cause that may well be more influential and widespread: *stereotypes*. Because of the ubiquity of stereotypes and the subtle and manifold ways they influence our judgments, their at least occasional effect on police behavior is vir-tually inevitable despite the strong social norms against bias operating in con-temporary law enforcement. This will be the subject of the remaining discussion in this and the following chapter.

In addition to drug crimes, the other most commonly profiled crime is ter-rorism, and yet in important ways, these two types of crime are mirror images of each other: Drug crimes occur with very high frequency, but individually they have a relatively small impact on society; terrorist acts, in contrast, occur with extremely low frequency (at least outside the Middle East), but individually they have a very large impact on society. In both cases there are strong prevailing ste-reotypes about the typical perpetrators, yet in both cases there are very compel-ling reasons to question these stereotypes. Specifically, survey research indicates that rates of illicit drug use among White Americans are comparable to those for Black Americans. With regard to terrorism, the prevailing stereotypic perpetrator is Middle Eastern, but the United States has a long history of violent terrorist acts being committed by White Christians like Eric Rudolph (the Atlanta Olympics bomber), Timothy McVeigh (the Oklahoma City bomber), Bruce Ivins (the alleged anthrax perpetrator), and members of the Weather Underground, not to mention Unabomber Ted Kaczynski and Andrew Stack, the man who destroyed an Internal Revenue Service building by intentionally crashing his airplane into it.

These two very different kinds of offenses, with very different motivations and consequences, are in a sense bound together by a common interdiction strategy, profiling. Why is that? Do they share some characteristic that other crimes do not? They seem to have more differences than similarities. In addition to their dramatic differences in frequency and impact, their motivations contrast—terrorism is ideologically motivated, and drug crimes are, for the most part, economically motivated (sale) or hedonistically motivated (possession for use). Terrorism is a collective act, an effort to achieve something for a larger group and cause; drug crime is highly individualistic. And, because of their disparate objectives, terrorism is extremely violent and destructive, while drug crimes are generally not, except for related activities like intergang conflicts and resistance to arrest.

One thing terrorism and drug crime do have in common is that there are strong prevailing stereotypes of perpetrators. We will postpone discussion of the "accuracy" of these stereotypes. For now, we will acknowledge that, contrary to early 20th-century definitions of stereotypes, contemporary definitions do not require that a belief about a group be inaccurate in order to be called a "stereotype."

The reasons for the strength of these stereotypes are very different. In the case of terrorism, there are what psychologists call "availability" and "representativeness" heuristics (cognitive shortcuts) operating (Tversky & Kahneman, 1973). The recency and magnitude of the 9/11 attacks, as well as follow-on attempts on U.S. airliners and attacks in London, Madrid, Bali, and other sites, including recent attempts in the United States, make Muslim extremist terrorists especially *available* and therefore overrepresented in our memories. This skews our perceptions of the "typical" terrorist. In the case of drug crimes, the stereotypes may be driven more by media representations of drug dealers and by past profiling that has caused minorities to be overrepresented among incarcerated drug criminals (see Chapter 5 for a full discussion of how profiling *creates* the overrepresentation).

In the absence of these stereotypes, whatever their origins, profiling would not occur. In other words, if Blacks and Latinos were not perceived as being more likely to commit crimes, they would not attract more law enforcement attention. A clear understanding of stereotypes and stereotyping is, therefore, critical to an understanding of racial profiling. Fortunately, hundreds, of social psychologists have dedicated much of their careers to understanding stereotyping and related phenomena.

Social Psychology and the Understanding of Group-Based Biases

Social psychology is the study of the mental processes (e.g., thoughts, feelings, motivations) that give rise to social behavior (e.g., friendliness, communality, hostility, discrimination) and, likewise, the situations and environments that can give rise to those mental states. In particular, social psychology places emphasis on *situational* determinants of behavior, understanding that a lot of what we do is determined by the situations we are in, what we have experienced in the past, and what social norms dictate about how we should behave.

Being perhaps the most popular topic of study in social psychology, intergroup biases (stereotyping, prejudice, and discrimination) have been the object of intense scrutiny and the subject of many books, edited volumes, and scientific journal articles, including thorough reviews (e.g., Allport, 1954; Brown, 1995; Fiske, 1998; Nelson, 2009; Plous, 2003)[2] that would make excellent sources for in-depth reading. In the sections that follow, I will offer background on the general concepts that are helpful in our understanding of the psychological causes of racial profiling.

Experimental Social Psychological Methods: A Primer

Before discussing the social psychological research that has promoted considerable understanding of stereotyping, prejudice, and discrimination, it would be helpful to review the basic tenets, strengths, and limitations of the methods. As noted in Chapter 2, most of the empirical research on racial profiling to date has been *correlational*—assessing the strength of association between variables (e.g., driver race and stop rate) based on *observation*. This has the advantage of telling us what is happening in the real world (aka "the field") but the disadvantage of allowing limited *causal inference*. In other words, although we may see a relationship between two variables like driver race and stop rate, it is difficult to be confident that driver race itself is causing police to stop people, as opposed to some other intermediary variable or variables, like rate of offense, type of car, geographical distribution, and so forth. I have briefly discussed this challenge in Chapter 1 and the research that has allowed for inferences of varying degrees of strength.

It is crucial for psychological scientists to be able to make strong causal inferences about mental processes. Psychology is a cumulative venture—rarely does any single study stand alone as documentation of a phenomenon. Humans are highly variable beings with extremely complex cognition, and our behaviors are determined by many factors, internal and external. Accordingly, in order for psychologists to build an understanding of how the mind works, we conduct many narrowly constructed *experiments*, isolating how one variable causes another to change. For example, the Darley and Gross (1983) experiment described earlier was designed to isolate the effect of a single variable (perceived SES) on another (assessment of aptitude). Because research subjects were *randomly assigned* to the experimental conditions, meaning that each subject had an equal probability of being in either group, we can make a strong inference that perceptions of SES

---

2. The books by Brown and Plous are especially accessible to nonscientist audiences, as is Plous's comprehensive companion website, www.understandingprejudice.org. Allport's classic book *The Nature of Prejudice* (1954) proved prescient of and an inspiration for many of the theories and findings that would come in the next half century.

caused people to rate the girl lower or higher in aptitude. The groups were otherwise, but for random differences, the same, so *nothing else was likely to have caused the difference.*

In addition to being randomly *assigned* to experimental conditions, research subjects should be randomly *selected* from the population to which the experiment aims to generalize. If we want to generalize to officers in a particular police department, all officers in that department would have to have an equal probability of being selected into the sample.

In addition to random selection and assignment, it is crucial that research subjects not know they are in a particular experimental condition. They can, and almost always do, know they are in an experiment, but if they know what variable is being manipulated and which condition they are in, they may, intentionally or not, attempt to conform to or defy the hypothesis they surmise. This is why medical experiments include *placebo* control conditions, so that, from the subjects' perspective, everyone is getting a treatment (e.g., a drug). Social psychologists construct control conditions that provide experiences that are as equivalent as possible. Ideally, those administering an experiment and recording the data will also not know who is in what condition, lest they treat and/or rate them differently based on their own expectations.

Through careful, rigorous experimental procedures, social psychologists have provided compelling demonstrations of many interpersonal and intergroup phenomena, some of which will be described shortly. Although the studies are careful and the conclusions valid, they are often limited to laboratory settings and narrow populations (e.g., college students). Most of the research, however, is focused on the nature of mental and social *processes* that should operate similarly across populations and settings.

The more important caveat about experimental research (and this applies to conclusions drawn from correlational studies as well) is that the effects (e.g., differences between sample groups) are only *general tendencies*, most typically averages. If the average performance rating given by the people in Darley and Gross's high-SES condition is statistically significantly higher than the average for those in the low-SES condition, that does not mean that every one of them scored higher than every one (or even the average) of the people in the other group. This is not to say that the findings are in any way invalid, but rather that we should interpret them realistically, bearing in mind that group differences are usually only tendencies, and that many factors influence human thoughts, feelings, and behaviors.

Our Three-Dimensional Mental Life

Philosophers and psychologists have long described a "trilogy of mind," indicating that mental processes can be broken down into three types: affect (emotion, mood, evaluation); cognition (attention, perception, memory, belief); and behavior (motivation, action)[3] (Breckler, 1984; Hilgard, 1980; McGuire, 1985, 1989). This idea should be fairly obvious to anyone who has ever felt their gut feelings to be in conflict with their rational thoughts, perhaps vying for control of some ultimate course of action. However, our thoughts, feelings, and actions tend to fall into line with each other (Heider, 1946, 1958; Ostrom, 1969). In fact, when they are in conflict, we feel anxious and work hard to reduce this "cognitive dissonance" (Festinger & Carlsmith, 1959).

Theorists have aptly applied this trichotomy to intergroup relations (Allport, 1954; Harding, Kutner, Proshansky, & Chein, 1954). If our minds respond to things in terms of feelings, thoughts, and actions, this would be true of how we respond to racial, ethnic, national, gender, and other social groups. In the realm of intergroup bias, the terms *affect, cognition,* and *behavior* map on to familiar terms: *prejudice, stereotyping,* and *discrimination,* respectively. This is useful for understanding that prejudice, stereotyping, and discrimination, like their more generic counterparts, are separate but interrelated; that they influence each other in every direction, but they are not redundant. Accordingly, to the extent that we hold predominantly negative stereotypes of a group, this will cause us to have relatively negative feelings (prejudice) toward that group. At the same time, if we have negative feelings toward a group, we will be more likely to accept uncritically information indicating that they have negative traits. These negative thoughts and feelings will cause us to be disparaging toward members of that group. Likewise, disparaging behavior (e.g., avoidance, hostility) toward members of the group may cause us to generate negative beliefs and feelings to justify the behavior.

Categorization

The long and rich tradition of social psychological research on stereotyping, prejudice, and discrimination is a story of discoveries building on each other. Perhaps the most fundamental concept with regard to intergroup biases is *social categorization,* which was built on general theories of cognition. Cognitive psychologists (e.g., Bruner, 1957; Neely, 1977; Rosch, 1975, 1978) demonstrated how humans rapidly, effortlessly, and spontaneously classify objects and concepts into categories (e.g., shapes, foods) in order to make sense of our complex world and predict future events. Humans would not be able to survive without this ability.

---

3. While definitions of affect and cognition are straightforward, the third pillar has been more ambiguous, with motivation and behavior getting lumped together even though the former is an internal state and the latter is usually more outwardly focused.

Henri Tajfel (1981; Tajfel, Billig, Bundy, & Flament, 1971) and colleagues demonstrated that we classify people into "social categories" in a similar fashion, and it has subsequently been shown that this also happens rapidly and effortlessly (Dovidio, Evans, & Tyler, 1986; Gaertner & McLaughlin, 1983). In categorizing people, we include ourselves, and groups to which we perceive ourselves as belonging are referred to in the psychological parlance as *in-groups*. Accordingly, groups we perceive ourselves as not belonging to are called *out-groups*.

The tendency to perceive social groups along gender, racial, and ethnic lines, and thus to put ourselves and others into social categories, is a natural process that arises fairly early in childhood (Aboud, 1988). I have seen this demonstrated firsthand. When my son was little, my wife and I were careful to not describe people in terms of racial or ethnic categories. One day in a toy store, when he was 3 years old, my son started playing with a little Asian boy. When it was time to leave, he patted the boy's hand and said, "Betty." Why? One of the staff at his day-care center was a Chinese woman named Betty. We had never talked with my son about the Asian category, let alone given it a label. He recognized the category himself and gave it his own label, based on an available exemplar, Betty. Now, I think my son is a clever little fellow and all, but I have to acknowledge that this was just normal behavior—people are hardwired to see categories, and that includes categories of people.

Prejudice

Seeking a bias-free control group for his experiments, Tajfel (1978) developed procedures for creating groups based on transparently arbitrary criteria. For example, he had research subjects estimate the number of dots on a page and then told them they were assigned to a group of people who were underestimators or overestimators. In fact, following standard experimental procedures, the group assignments were random. Furthermore, the participants never met each other or had any expectation that they would. Tajfel's expectation was that these people, who clearly shared no real common identity or fate with their in-group (the group they were assigned to), would not show the in-group favoritism that one would expect to see in groups that share real, substantive identities. To his surprise, Tajfel found that even these trivial, arbitrary distinctions led people to show favoritism toward (allocate more monetary rewards to) ostensible members of their own new groups, despite there being no prospect of personal gain. This finding has been replicated with even more transparently arbitrary assignments, like a simple coin toss (e.g., Sachdev & Bourhis, 1985). Tajfel even concocted clever procedures to test if people were just promoting their own group's interests and, by extension, their self-interest. He found, somewhat discouragingly, that on average people would seek to give out money in such a manner that ensured their group got more than the other group, *even if that meant that everybody got less*. These findings, that people will exhibit favoritism toward members of groups for which their membership is based on very little, have come to be known as the *minimal groups* effect. The mere act of social categorization itself gives rise to discriminatory treatment.

As Tajfel's minimal groups work established, people tend to be very ready to categorize themselves and others into groups along multiple, even trivial, dimensions. But more than that, people just as readily show preferences for their own group, even when that group is so new or abstractly defined that they do not have a clear sense of what it is like. Compounding this *mere categorization* effect on group preferences is the *mere exposure* effect; Kunst-Wilson and Zajonc (1980) found that people indicated greater liking for geometric shapes to which they had been previously exposed subliminally. They had no conscious recollection of having seen the shapes; they just liked them better than ones they had not been exposed to. Even in the absence of knowledge about or experience with groups, people prefer their own, and this is a fundamental basis of prejudice.

Prejudice is the *affective* component of intergroup bias, meaning that it is the more emotional, gut-level *preference* for or dislike toward a particular group. The general and common trend is for people to prefer their own group, but it is clear that low-status groups are more ambivalent (Jost & Major, 2001). In a study that was influential in the U.S. Supreme Court's *Brown v. Board of Education* ruling that struck down racial segregation in public schools, Clark and Clark (1950) asked children to choose between two dolls, one with "White" skin, the other brown. White children overwhelmingly chose the White dolls. Black children were more evenly split, most likely because they were influenced by a culture that generally valued things associated with Whites.

To date, hundreds of studies have indicated that people tend to exhibit more positive dispositions toward their own in-groups, especially if the in-group is high in status. This has been shown with explicit questionnaire measures (Henry & Sears, 2002; Schuman, Steeh, Bobo, & Krysan, 1997), indirect, "unobtrusive" measures (Crosby, Bromley, & Saxe, 1980), and computerized reaction time–based measures of nonconscious biases (Greenwald, Poehlman, Uhlman, & Banaji, 2009).

Social psychologists have recently begun pointing a spotlight on the emotional nature of prejudice, identifying specific emotions, such as anger, fear, and disgust, that differentiate dispositions toward groups (e.g., Cottrell & Neuberg, 2005; Tapias, Glaser, Vasquez, Keltner, & Wickens, 2007; Mackie & Smith, 2002). Tapias and colleagues found, for example, that attitudes toward Blacks and gays (relative to Whites and heterosexuals) were both characterized by anger more than other emotions, and attitudes toward gays were also associated with disgust. This takes our understanding of prejudice beyond just the unidimensional good-bad orientation.

No doubt, some racial disparities in criminal justice, including police stops, are due to basic prejudice, with law enforcers acting retributively on their gut-level dislike. It is my assessment, however, that most racial or ethnic bias in policing is attributable to more cognitive factors, specifically stereotyping, to be discussed in the following sections. This assessment is based on two things. First, where profiling tends to occur, in drug interdiction and counterterrorism, there are powerful stereotypes linking the targeted groups to the targeted behaviors. This has been demonstrated empirically with regard to Blacks and crime generally (Dixon & Maddox, 2005; Walsh, Banaji, & Greenwald, 1995; Park & Banaji, 2000), as well as with drug crime in particular (Gordon, Michels, & Nelson, 1996). With regard to stereotypes associating Muslims and Arabs with terrorism, empirical demonstrations (e.g., Meer & Modood, 2009) are few, but the premise is self-evident because of the extensive media coverage of terrorist acts committed by Muslim extremists.

Second, research on one type of law enforcement behavior has revealed that racial prejudice does not predict racial discrimination, whereas stereotypes do. Specifically, in the work of Correll and colleagues (Correll, Park, Judd, & Wittenbrink, 2002), the strength of a stereotype associating Blacks with danger predicted the strength of their measure of *shooter bias*, which is the tendency, in a video simulation, to "shoot" armed Black men faster than armed White men, and to decide to not shoot unarmed White men faster than unarmed Black men. Shooter bias is also found in the tendency to erroneously shoot unarmed Black men more than unarmed White men (see Chapter 4 for a more thorough discussion of shooter bias). Correll and colleagues (2002) found that research subjects who indicated that there was a general cultural stereotype linking Blacks with danger (whether or not they endorsed that stereotype themselves) showed stronger shooter bias. However, measures of prejudice did not correlate with shooter bias. Similarly, Knowles and I (Glaser & Knowles, 2008) found that an implicit (computerized reaction time; see Chapter 4 for more explanation) measure of the stereotypic association between Blacks and weapons predicted shooter bias, but an implicit measure of racial prejudice did not.

In sum, prejudice is still very commonplace in various manifestations, and should be a concern whenever it is present in law enforcement, but it likely represents a relatively small influence on racial profiling. The rest of the chapter will, accordingly, focus on the more influential mental process, stereotyping.

Stereotypes

A stereotype is a belief about a trait being disproportionately possessed by members of a particular social group. For example, people tend to believe that women are more nurturing but less competent than men, and that Blacks are more athletic but less law-abiding than other racial groups. Modern social psychology has built upon research on human thought and memory from another branch of the field, cognitive psychology, to understand stereotypes as, like other beliefs, mental associations between groups and traits. When we possess a stereotype (e.g., that women are nurturing), our mental association between that trait and that group is stronger than it is for other groups. Like many physical objects, stereotypes or "constructs," specifically *mental constructs*, that must be formed, have structure and content, serve functions, and can change, to a point. Social psychologists have studied all these properties of stereotypes, as well as the processes by which they influence judgments and behaviors. To promote a better understanding of how stereotypes give rise to racial profiling, I will review these findings.

Stereotype Function

It makes sense to start by asking why we stereotype in the first place—what functions do stereotypes serve? The primary stereotype functions that have been postulated are (1) to rationalize inequities; (2) to boost in-group esteem and, by extension, self-esteem; and (3) as cognitive shortcuts. Regarding the first function, researchers have shown that people will generate beliefs about groups that help to explain their status or the lack thereof (Eagly & Steffen, 1984; Jost & Banaji, 1994). This can happen in spite of receiving information to the contrary (Hoffman & Hurst, 1990). It is difficult for people to accept that some people just get less and suffer more, or are relegated to subordinate status through no fault of their own, and so they generate and/or accept beliefs about those groups, such as that they tend to have less ability or worthiness, to explain the inequities. This can have a recursive, self-fulfilling effect, where members of those groups are treated differently because of the beliefs and even come to conform to them, as has been shown in research on "stereotype threat" (Steele, 1997). This behavior, in turn, confirms the stereotype.

The second type of function relates to promoting one's self-esteem by association with one's group esteem. This is one of the tenets of social identity theory (Turner, 1975, 1987). In seeking to enhance self-esteem, we associate ourselves with highly esteemed groups. Sometimes, in order to promote group esteem, we must denigrate other groups so that our in-group's esteem is boosted by comparison. This can promote negative stereotyping of (and overall evaluation/prejudice toward) out-groups.

The primary, or at least most extensively researched, function stereotypes serve is a *heuristic* one. As cognitive social psychologists have noted (Fiske & Taylor, 1991), people are continuously bombarded with massive amounts of information through our various senses. In order to manage all of this information with our finite mental resources, we behave as "cognitive misers," processing information efficiently and conserving our capacity for crucial decisions. Some of this efficiency is obtained through automatization (extensive rehearsal that allows some processes to eventually operate very rapidly, with virtually no mental effort), which will be discussed at length in Chapter 4. Cognitive efficiency is also achieved through heuristics, or shortcuts that allow us to make quick inferences without considering all the information one would need to make a 100% certain determination. We see a shiny, red, speckled, roundish object about the size of a fist, with a stem, and we know it is an apple. No need to bite into it to taste it and be sure. Similarly, we see a person of moderate height with delicate features and long hair—we "know" it is a woman. But heuristics are also applied to less clear-cut cases and inferences about less reliably predictable outcomes. Even seemingly clear-cut judgments sometimes trip us up. Is that a real apple or a plastic apple? Is that apple ripe? Is that a woman or a boy with long hair?

When a cognitive shortcut of this sort is applied to predicting attributes or behavior of people who fall into different social categories (e.g., women, Hispanics, seniors), it is a stereotype. As heuristics, stereotypes enable people to process information about other people efficiently, if not always effectively. This has been demonstrated empirically by showing that when people's cognitive resources are limited or depleted (e.g., when they are tired), they are more likely to judge others in a manner consistent with the stereotypes of their group. Likewise, when people are given the opportunity to use stereotypes, their cognitive resources are subsequently less depleted. Specifically, Bodenhausen (1990), in an ingenious application of human physiology to social psychology, found that people's circadian rhythms predicted their rate of stereotyping—morning people (people who are more alert in the morning) made more stereotyped judgments in the afternoon/evening; afternoon/evening people stereotyped more in the morning. Conversely, Macrae, Milne, and Bodenhausen (1994) showed that people who were given the opportunity to use stereotypes in making judgments performed better on a subsequent cognitive task—they had conserved their resources by using the heuristic (taking the shortcut).

In sum, stereotypes enable us to make judgments of and decisions about others under conditions of uncertainty or ambiguity. In fact, when uncertainty becomes less tolerable (when people have a high "need for cognitive closure,") they are more likely to stereotype (Kruglanski & Webster, 1996). The more specific information we have about someone, and the more time we have, the less we have to rely on stereotypes to make inferences about that person. But when making quick judgments and first impressions with incomplete information, as when deciding who to stop and/or search, stereotyping is common.

Stereotype Formation

Stereotypes, like all other mental associations and beliefs, can be formed indirectly (e.g., by reading or hearing about something) or directly (through direct experience with members of the group and perception of their behaviors). Indirect sources of stereotypes are often influenced by historical factors. For example, prevailing stereotypes of African Americans have roots in the circumstances of the slavery era. The specific content of these stereotypes will be discussed later. Humans do not need direct experience, let alone classical conditioning, to learn things. Family, friends, and the media are our primary, indirect sources of stereotypes (Mackie, Hamilton, Susskind, & Rosselli, 1996).

Decades of psychological research have shown that there are a number of mechanisms by which distorted perceptions of groups can be formed. Mackie et al. (1996), for example, made the important observation that people's tendency to attribute others' behavior to stable dispositions or traits instead of external, situational causes (this is called the *fundamental attribution error*) sets us up to perceive patterns in these traits. Without this default tendency to attribute most behavior to internal dispositions, stereotypes would not have as much sway in our judgments. Pettigrew (1979) extended the fundamental attribution error idea further to an *ultimate attribution error*, demonstrating that there is an even stronger tendency to attribute behaviors by out-group members to their dispositions, further promoting out-group stereotyping.

Compounding the tendency to make inferences about stereotypic traits of out-groups is what is called the *out-group homogeneity effect*—the tendency to perceive groups we do not belong to as less differentiated than groups we do belong to (Jones, Wood, & Quattrone, 1981; Park & Rothbart, 1982). In other words, there is a cognitive basis to and empirical support for the old "they all look alike to me" phenomenon. Because we tend to see members of out-groups as relatively similar to each other, stereotypes are more easily generalized across them. Perceptions of one out-group member are applied to many.

It has also been shown that stereotypes can form entirely spuriously through *illusory correlation* (Hamilton & Sherman, 1989). Illusory correlations result from the tendency people have to overestimate the relation between rare events that occur together (Chapman, 1967). Hamilton and Gifford (1976) experimentally demonstrated that this can occur with social stereotypes as well; even when the co-occurrence of rare events is random and uncorrelated, people tend to perceive a correlation. In other words, even though members of Group A are presented as having trait Y in the same proportions as members of Group B are, because there are fewer As and Ys than Bs and Zs, perceivers will tend to develop an illusory correlation, thinking that As tend to have trait Y. This can happen with very abstract events, like the simultaneous presentation of letters, or very real events, like minority status and crime. The distinctiveness of the rare events causes them and their co-occurrence (which is even more unusual, and therefore distinctive) to be exceptionally noticeable and memorable, and this in turn leads to an overestimate of the prevalence of their co-occurrence ("I don't see criminals very often, but when I do they're usually Black").

The implications of illusory correlation are very clear for racial bias in polic-ing. Because minorities are, by definition, relatively rare in occurrence, and crime is unusual, the pairing of those two categories, in the news media in particular, likely leads to a general overestimation of their correspondence. Compounding this problem is the fact that crime tends to be overrepresented in television news reporting (Gilliam & Iyengar, 2000), and Blacks can be overrepresented in the news as crime perpetrators (Dixon & Linz, 2000, 2002), although this is not always the case (Dixon, Azocar, & Casas, 2003).

Stereotype Change

The same processes that promote the formation of stereotypes should be involved in changing them. If we learn stereotypes indirectly by hearing about them, or directly by perceiving correlations between group membership and traits, then can we not unlearn them by hearing they are untrue or by perceiving the absence of the correlation? Unfortunately, it seems that stereotypes are harder to change than they are to form in the first place. Perhaps they would not be very effec-tive heuristics if they were constantly in flux. Stereotypes have been shown to be resistant to change even in the presence of contradictory evidence (e.g., Kunda & Oleson, 1995; Rothbart & John, 1985; Weber & Crocker, 1983), and indeed to bolster themselves through self-fulfilling prophecies (Jussim & Fleming, 1996).

The rigidity of stereotypes in part reflects Abelson's (1986) insight that "beliefs are like possessions," that they are more than just passive reflections of mental associations and reinforced neural pathways, but they are something we come to value and defend. Also, perceptually, the absence of a co-occurrence is much less likely to be perceived than the presence of one. While we are prone to look for categories and patterns, and, due to illusory correlation effects, perceive relation-ships even where they do not exist, we are not nearly as good at keeping track of when things are unrelated. This is a limit of human information processing, but it is a practical necessity—there are just too many unrelated stimuli streaming through our senses for us to monitor and record. When things are related (or we perceive them to be), they pop out and are remembered better. Researchers have, in fact, shown repeatedly that information that matches stereotypes is perceived more effectively from the get-go (see von Hippel, Sekaquaptewa, & Vargas, 1995, for a review).

Layered on top of this information-processing limitation is the effect of more motivated biases. Specifically, to the extent that stereotypes sometimes serve the function of explaining inequality, or rationalizing our negative feel-ings toward groups, we are going to be reluctant to let them go, even in the pres-ence of countervailing evidence. This tendency to protect our prior beliefs is a well-documented phenomenon called *biased assimilation*. Psychologists Lord, Ross, and Lepper (1979; see also Hastorf & Cantril, 1954) demonstrated that, when presented with identical information, people evaluated it very differently depending on their prior conceptions about the topic. In their words, "[People] are apt to accept 'confirming' evidence at face value while subjecting 'disconfirming' evidence to critical evaluation, and as a result to draw undue support for their initial positions" (p. 2098). Stereotypes, as beliefs, serve as prior conceptions that give rise to biased assimilation.

One manner in which stereotypes are preserved is called *subtyping* (Weber & Crocker, 1983). Unless disconfirming evidence (i.e., behavior that violates stereotypes) is dispersed fairly evenly across many group members, people tend to recategorize those who violate stereotypes into subtypes (e.g., strong women, nurturing men, educated Blacks). The availability of subtypes helps to preserve the overall stereotype—"Yes, this individual violates the stereotype, but she is a different type from the rest." So, while stereotypes, like other beliefs, are subject to change, there are a number of factors that make them self-preserving.

Stereotype Content

When you think of a skinhead, what traits typically come to mind: White, male, young, tattooed, racist, aggressive, vulgar? Others? How about old people: slow, wise, cranky? Obese people? Gays? Women? African Americans? If you are like most people, including the students in my classes, you had traits pop into mind for each of these groups. You may not have endorsed them, but you knew what they were. You also probably got increasingly uncomfortable as we went from stereotyping skinheads to African Americans. Still, the traits came to mind. These are the contents, the actual substance of your stereotypes—the specific traits associated with some groups more than others.

Psychologists have examined the specific contents of people's stereotypes for nearly a century (e.g., Katz & Braly, 1933). Mostly, this has been done using questionnaire methods, asking people to list the traits they think are associated with different groups. Stereotypes, particularly negative stereotypes, are a sensitive subject, something that most of us are not generally comfortable acknowledging. In fact, surveys have shown a steadily decreasing tendency to report negative stereotypes of out-groups over a period of decades (Devine & Elliott, 1995; Karlins, Coffman, & Walters, 1969; Katz & Braly, 1933; Madon et al., 2001). These surveys have also shown that most stereotypes are based on little or no direct experience, and that there is considerable consensus between people about the specific contents of group stereotypes. These two findings reflect that stereotypes are conveyed through cultural media like literature, television, and film.

Whether the declining tendency for people to endorse negative stereotypes is due to real change in the content of our beliefs or just change in social norms about exhibiting bias is something of a false choice. It is no doubt a combination of the two, and they are mutually reinforcing—as people are less inclined to endorse and express negative stereotypes, others they come into contact with will be less likely to learn them; and the decline in prevalence of negative stereotypes will make it seem less normative, less acceptable, and so forth. Nevertheless, as research to be discussed in Chapter 4 has shown, most people are fully aware of the prevailing stereotypes of most groups, and the *mere knowledge* of stereotypes, even if they are consciously repudiated, is sufficient to bias behavior toward members of stereotyped groups (Devine, 1989).

Because of their unique place in American history, having been subjected to forced immigration and slavery, Jim Crow laws, segregation, and continuing discrimination across many domains of life (Council of Economic Advisers, 1998), African Americans have been the focus of much of the psychological research on intergroup bias, and this is true for stereotype content as well. It is easy to see how prevailing stereotypes of African Americans could promote racial profiling. African American stereotypes emphasize unlawfulness, with common references to harming others, through property theft and violent crime, and exploiting public resources through laziness and welfare receipt (Clarke & Pearson, 1982; Devine, 1989; Devine & Baker, 1991; Devine & Elliott, 1995; Gordon, 1986; Madon et al., 2001).

A particularly illuminating set of findings comes from work on race-crime stereotypes by Banaji and colleagues (Walsh et al., 1995; Park & Banaji, 2000). In these studies, research subjects were given a list of names and asked to circle those that they thought were criminals. The names varied in their race stereotypicality (e.g., Darnel Powell, Matthew Adams), but none of them were names of actual known criminals. In these experiments, participants were much more likely to circle Black-sounding names. More compelling, Walsh and colleagues went to great lengths to find a procedure that would eliminate this tendency, even instructing research subjects to not let race influence their judgments. When subjects were asked to circle names only if they had specific memories of where they learned that the people were criminals, they still wrongly identified more Black names. When asked to go back over the list and write down where they had learned of each person's criminality, subjects invented memories of news reports. A crucial aspect of these findings is that they address the argument that people are just acting "rationally," employing their knowledge of Black crime rates when judging the likelihood that someone is a criminal. Subjects in these experiments were not asked to say who they *thought* was *more likely* to be a criminal. They were asked to *recall* who they *knew* to be criminals, and in so doing they made real memory errors that were driven by a stereotype.

In addition to the specific race-crime association, more generally, African Americans appear to pose physical and material threats, being stereotyped as dangerous, violent, and hostile (Bargh, Chen, & Burrows, 1996; Devine, 1989; Devine & Baker, 1991; Devine & Elliott, 1995; Dovidio et al., 1986; Duncan,

1976; Jackson, Lewandowski, Ingram, & Hodge, 1997; Sagar & Schofield, 1980; Schaller, Park, & Mueller, 2003).

Latinos, who are also common targets of racial profiling, appear to share considerable stereotype content with African Americans, particularly with regard to being perceived as physically violent and criminal (Fairchild & Cozens, 1981; Jackson, 1995; Marin, 1984, Niemann Jennings, Rozelle, Baxter, & Sullivan, 1994). A study conducted in 2009 by the Consortium for Police Leadership in Equity (CPLE; 2010) for the Salt Lake City Police Department found that Whites dramatically overestimated and underestimated the proportion of drug-related and violent crime perpetrated by Latinos and Whites, respectively. In fact, according to police records, Latinos committed crimes at rates below those of Whites over the years studied.

Research has shown that police officers also hold the stereotypes of African Americans. Specifically, psychologists Eberhardt and colleagues (2004) had college students and police officers identify objects appearing on a computer screen as the images of the objects became less degraded and more recognizable. The objects were either crime related (guns, knives) or not. Prior to the objects being shown, participants were also exposed to faces of Black or White men subliminally (i.e., in a manner that precluded conscious recognition of the stimulus). Subliminal "priming" of this sort is an advantageous research method because participants' performance cannot be attributed to efforts to conform to presumed experimental hypotheses or social norms if they are unaware of the experimental condition brought about by the subliminal prime. Students and police officers were nevertheless faster to recognize the crime-related objects after seeing Black than White subliminal faces, indicating that the Black faces activated crime-related stereotypes that facilitated recognition of crime-related objects (see also Payne, 2001). In other words, the mere exposure to an African American face causes people, including police officers, to be more ready to think about crime-related concepts. Similarly, Eberhardt and colleagues also found that subliminal exposure to images of crime-related objects caused people to focus more on Black than White faces. In other words, the relationship is bidirectional—crime makes people think of Blacks, and Blacks make people think of crime.

Eberhardt and colleagues (2004) also found, in another study, that when police officers were asked outright to judge whether faces looked criminal, they chose Black faces more often than White faces, and they were especially likely to choose faces that were more stereotypically Black (e.g., darker skin).[4] Thus, police officers, like others, tend to associate Blacks with crime in both subtle and relatively overt ways.

---

4. In an even more alarming study, Eberhardt, Davies, Purdie-Vaughns, and Johnson (2006) found that among real capital defendants, those who looked (based on ratings from individuals blind to the study hypothesis and the outcomes of the trials) more stereotypically Black were more likely to be sentenced to death.

Are Stereotypes Inherently Accurate
or Inaccurate? A False Dichotomy

What if stereotypes associating Blacks and Latinos with crime and Muslims with terrorism are accurate? This question invokes a debate, over whether stereotypes are inherently accurate or inaccurate, that has played out in the social psychological literature (e.g., Jussim, Cain, Crawford, Harber, & Cohen, 2009; Judd & Park, 1993). The debate is, in my view, not a particularly productive one because stereotypes are beliefs (about the traits that are typical of groups), and beliefs vary in their accuracy from person to person and time to time. The accuracy of a belief is only as good as the information that gives rise to it.

Stereotypes, as *generalized* beliefs about a whole group, are based on necessarily incomplete information—we are unlikely to have direct information about more than a small proportion of any group. So, it is not likely that any one of us is going to have an accurate assessment of the prevalence of some trait (such as criminality or high intelligence) in a given group. We also know that inaccurate stereotypes can arise spontaneously, through illusory correlation (Hamilton & Gifford, 1976) or through efforts to justify inequality (Eagly & Steffen, 1984). But even nonillusory stereotypes, being beliefs about groups, will vary in their accuracy. And even those that may reasonably well reflect the *average* tendency for a group will be of limited utility in predicting *individual* behavior.

On virtually every measurable dimension, human categories (e.g., racial, ethnic, gender) have more variability within than between their groups.[5] Consequently, using a stereotype based on a group average is a crude strategy

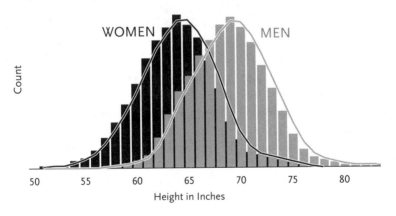

Figure 3.1
Overlapping frequency distributions for heights of men and women.

5. There are, of course, some characteristics that are unique to some groups, but these tend to be the very traits that *define* the groups. So, for example, men and women differ reliably with regard to certain anatomical structures. But this is the very thing that defines their gender, so it is not a "stereotype."

for making a prediction about an individual member of that group. For example, as illustrated in Figure 3.1, although men on average are taller than women, the difference in average heights between the groups is smaller than the overlap in the range of heights for both groups. Many women are taller than the average man, and many men are shorter than the average woman. So, even a relatively accurate stereotype like this, which reflects a real difference in *averages*, does not reliably predict what an *individual* will be like. A fire chief who chooses to not consider any women as firefighters because they are less likely to meet the minimum height requirement is, even if operating on a technically accurate stereotype, behaving irrationally—not to mention discriminatorily.

There is another problem with the application of "accurate" stereotypes. Some stereotypes may be "accurate" in a relative sense (e.g., this group tends to be heavier than that group). However, beliefs about the actual prevalence of some characteristic (e.g., being overweight) in some group are bound to be based on incomplete information (and imperfect memory). As a result, the likelihood that that belief will be *exactly* correct is virtually zero. In other words, while we might be able to detect a relative difference between groups (e.g., rural Americans tend to be heavier than urban Americans), calibrating the absolute level of some trait or the magnitude of difference between groups, is nearly impossible.[6] Furthermore, because not all members of a given group are identical, the likelihood that the stereotype will lead to an accurate prediction for a given individual is even lower. Even if you know that rural dwellers are relatively heavy, how heavy are they, and how much heavier than urban dwellers are they? What proportion of ruralites is heavier than the average urbanite?

If we are wondering about a trait that is either present or absent, such as a disease, or drug or weapon possession, as opposed to one that is a matter of degree, such as weight or height, the question becomes one of *prevalence*. Again, we may have an "accurate" stereotype that the trait is more prevalent in one group than others, but we should wonder, "How much more prevalent?" If the difference is small, the diagnostic value of the stereotype is low. Furthermore, if the base rate is low, meaning if the trait is rare in all groups, just less rare for the target group, then the stereotype will be of limited predictive value. For example, even if one group has 10 times as many terrorists in it as another group, if only 1 in 1,000,000 people in that group are terrorists, that information does not help you very much.

6. One might argue that there are some traits, including measurable physical characteristics like weight, for which there is in fact reliable information, based on epidemiological surveys. However, because most people do not read epidemiological studies, let alone commit their statistical results to memory, for practical purposes, this is not particularly relevant to understanding stereotyping. This reasoning has to, and will be, reconsidered in the case of racial profiling because, theoretically, law enforcement agencies and even individual agents may employ systematic data analysis to estimate crime prevalence for different groups.

Related to this base rate problem is the danger of committing the logical error of "affirming the consequent," discussed earlier in this chapter with regard to the pitfalls inherent in constructing criminal profiles based on criminal justice statistics. Just as it is foolish to infer that someone is pregnant because she is female (based on the knowledge that someone must be female if she is pregnant), it is problematic to assume that minorities are likely to be criminals based on the presumption that criminals are likely to be minorities. Minorities may be more likely to engage in criminal activity, but the vast majority of them do not.

Logical errors notwithstanding, it might be tempting to conclude that stereotypes of race and crime are different. After all, we have criminal justice statistics that show that Blacks and Latinos are dramatically overrepresented in prison, including for drug crimes, which are often the focus of racial profiling. However, we need to bear in mind that, as discussed in Chapter 1, stereotypes of race and crime are confounded by racial bias in criminal justice. Observational and experimental research has demonstrated that Blacks and Latinos are more likely to be stopped, searched, arrested, charged, convicted, and sentenced harshly, all else being equal. Accordingly, inferences about criminality based on conviction and incarceration rates are deeply flawed.

Stereotyping Process

During a lecture on the sources of stereotypes I was giving several years ago, I mentioned that food products seem to be most often associated with female symbols such as Betty Crocker, Aunt Jemimah, and Sara Lee. I asked for some counterexamples, some male figures in food products, like Cap'n Crunch. One student excitedly blurted out "Dr. Pepper!" To my credit, I noticed the error and just raised my eyebrows, saying nothing, letting silence fill the air for a few moments. Then some awkward laughter spread through the room as the students realized that they had all, at least for a moment, taken it for granted that Dr. Pepper was a man even though there is no "Dr. Pepper" character associated with the product. *Of course he's a man, he's a doctor!* This student probably was not a "sexist." He meant well. He was just racking his brain trying hard to answer his professor's question. He was having trouble finding an example, and so his handy heuristic stereotype pitched in. As he cross-referenced his memory for food products and males, Dr. Pepper seemed to match the search criteria. But he was wrong, just like people who assume that female doctors are nurses and male nurses are doctors are. What if these stereotypes are held by medical school admissions committee members?

In earlier historical periods (e.g., pre–civil rights movement America), the overt expression and application of stereotypes and prejudice may have been acceptable and commonplace. To be sure, there are some groups (e.g., obese people) who are still openly stereotyped. However, most stereotyping occurs more subtly in contemporary society. Perceivers rarely deliberately, let alone openly, invoke stereotypes to make judgments. However, stereotypes still influence their judgments and behaviors by incrementally influencing the inferences they make about the causes of, or motivations behind, ambiguous behavior. The effects of these stereotypes can be seen in memory biases (e.g., better memory for minority crime perpetrators in news reports; Dixon & Maddox, 2005; Oliver, 1999), and even in lethal behavior (e.g., Correll et al., 2002), to be discussed in Chapter 4.

The Darley and Gross (1983) experiment described at the beginning of this chapter offers a powerful demonstration of the process by which preconceptions like stereotypes influence judgments and behavior. After watching the same video (seeing the same girl behave the same way), those who believed she was poorer rated her as performing at a lower grade level than did those who believed she was from a high-SES background. Their preconceptions about how low-SES and high-SES children tend to perform colored their interpretations of her test responses. Ambiguous aspects of her performance were "disambiguated" by the stereotype. The resulting judgments were both inaccurate and discriminatory.

Similar results have been obtained across scores of experiments examining many different stereotyped groups, such as women, and racial and ethnic minorities (for a review, see Fiske, 1998). For example, Banaji, Hardin, and Rothman (1993) found that when people were "primed" with (made to think of) the concept of aggression (by unscrambling phrases like "never backs down"), they were more likely to rate the described behaviors of a person as aggressive, but only if he was a man (named Donald), not when she was a woman (Donna). The aggressive trait did not stick to Donna because it is not part of the female stereotype (it did not fit into the preexisting mental *schema*, or network of associated concepts). Similarly, in an earlier set of studies, subjects who were primed (subliminally) to think of Black people rated an individual (again, good old "Donald") as more hostile (Devine, 1989). Donald and Donna behaved the same in all of the descriptions but were judged differently as a consequence of the stereotypes associated with their respective groups.

In order for stereotypes to influence judgments and behavior, they must be engaged by two processes: activation and application. They are first activated in memory, usually by the presence of a member of the group or some indication of the group, like a name. Once activated, they are applied by helping to disambiguate some aspect of an individual or individuals (Gilbert & Hixon, 1991). Like other thoughts, stereotypes must first be triggered in our memories, then applied to understanding what we are perceiving or thinking about. This is the fundamental insight of social cognitive psychology—that cognition about people is like cognition about anything else, and so it involves attention, perception, and memory. Memory is basically mental associations constructed in a coherent way. Mental associations between social groups and traits are stereotypes.

To summarize, this is the process by which stereotypes often influence behavior: We try to understand other people, and predict what they will do, but have only partial information based on what we observe. Our observations often leave us without sufficient information and therefore with substantial room for interpretations. Stereotypes help fill in the blanks.

Stereotypes and Power

The basic process of stereotyping is of clear relevance to racial profiling. Like so many other domains of human judgment, policing involves making inferences based on incomplete information, and stereotypes can fill that void. There may, however, be a special relationship between stereotyping and policing because psychological scientists have identified a link between power and stereotyping (Fiske, 1993; Vescio, Gervais, Heiphetz, & Bloodhart, 2009). Specifically, studies have shown a tendency for those with high power to stereotype more than those with low power (Ebenbach & Keltner, 1998; Depret & Fiske, 1999; Goodwin, Gubin, Fiske, & Yzerbyt, 2000; Guinote, 2001; Richeson & Ambady, 2003), and that power (i.e., control over others) undermines thought suppression and thereby leads to bigger stereotype "rebound" effects (Guinote, 2007).

This tendency is not universal. In a laboratory experiment, Overbeck and Park (2001) found that those who were conferred high power were less likely to judge others stereotypically. As Vescio et al. (2009) note, power confers both authority (and the control, discretion, and flexibility inherent therein) *and* responsibility. To the extent that people with power embrace their obligations to those over whom they have power (due either to their personal values or to structural influences like accountability systems), power can have an equity-promoting effect.

While rank-and-file patrol officers (or security screeners) may not always *feel* powerful, at least not when interacting with command staff, they have considerable power at their discretion when interacting with citizens. The likelihood that this power differential could produce relatively strongly stereotypic judgments elevates the relevance of stereotyping to racial profiling in law enforcement and should give us additional cause for concern.

Stereotype Suppression

Most people do not want to be influenced by stereotypes, but, given that stereotypes can operate implicitly (to be discussed in Chapter 4), one does not need a conscious intent for them to bias judgments. One would have to attempt to actively suppress stereotypes to preclude their influence. However, stereotype suppression has been demonstrated to be a problematic strategy (Macrae, Bodenhausen, Milne, & Jetten, 1994). Specifically, Macrae and colleagues found that, when instructed to avoid using stereotypes in describing an individual, research subjects were able to reduce (although not generally

eliminate) stereotyping. However, once the instruction was no longer operative, they exhibited even stronger stereotyping than those given no suppression instruction. This is based on a more general phenomenon of thought
suppression brought to light by psychologist Daniel Wegner, who showed that
thoughts we try to suppress actually tend to become more active in our minds.
Wegner (1994) found, for example, that people are more likely to think of a
white bear when they are trying not to. (Try it yourself—close your eyes and
don't think of a white bear.) The very act of trying to suppress thoughts of
white bears (or stereotypes) requires that the construct be active in memory,
so it keeps triggering itself and related thoughts.

CONCLUSION

In sum, stereotypes are prevalent, they serve a cognitive shortcut function that
causes them to influence our judgments, and they are difficult to change or
suppress. As a result, their influence on judgments of people is commonplace.
Research discussed earlier in this chapter indicates that a prominent stereotype
associated with Blacks and Latinos has to do with criminality. Merely seeing a
Black face instantaneously causes people, including police officers, to think of
crime (and vice versa; Eberhardt et al., 2004). The implication is clear—people,
law enforcers included, are at risk of making discriminatory judgments of individuals based on stereotypes of groups. But surely most people are motivated to
avoid discriminating, and law enforcers are explicitly prohibited from doing so.
Might stereotypes influence us despite our best intentions? How could they? We
will consider these questions next.

CHAPTER 4

Unintentional Causes of Profiling

What's Under the Tip of the Attitude Iceberg?

A February 2007 Gallup survey of a national sample asked Americans, "If your party nominated a generally well-qualified person for president who happened to be Black, would you vote for that person?" Five percent of respondents said they would not (Jones, 2007). To be fair, hypothetical Jewish, female, Hispanic, and Mormon (relevant 4 years later) candidates fared even worse, but it was a Black nominee who ended up on the ballot. By the time late August 2008 rolled around, less than 3 months before the election, a Washington Post–ABC News poll found that 6% were still "entirely uncomfortable" (another 6% reported being "somewhat uncomfortable") with the idea that Barack Obama would be the first African American president (TNS Telecoms, 2008).

It is likely that that 5% or 6% is just the tip of the proverbial iceberg of people who were disinclined to vote for an African American for president. In addition to those who are willing to admit to a survey that they are prejudiced in this manner, there are more people who feel the same way but are not comfortable acknowledging it. There are others still who feel similarly but have not *recognized* it in themselves. Then there are probably a larger number of people who *could* vote for a Black candidate but are less likely to do so because of racial bias. Among this latter group, if they do not otherwise have a strong preference for one candidate or the other, candidate race could make the difference.

Because of this layering in attitudes, especially racial attitudes, icebergs are a helpful metaphor for understanding them. The tip, the part that sticks up above the water and can be seen with the naked eye, corresponds to the part of the attitude that we know we have and we are willing to express, to "show." But most of an iceberg is under the surface of the water. As any North Atlantic sailor knows, the part of the iceberg under the water, even though it cannot be readily seen, is very much real and consequential.

In the case of racial bias in the presidential vote, the attitude iceberg can describe the public attitude, with some people expressing their negative attitudes openly (above the surface), and others not. But the iceberg applies to us as individuals too, with parts of our attitudes being above the consciousness waterline where we can recognize them and possibly express them, and other parts being harder to identify.

The mass of the attitude iceberg that lies *beneath* the surface is composed of several layers. There is the layer that the attitude holder is aware of but is not inclined to express, so it cannot be "seen" from "above." It is in that murky area just below the surface where sometimes, when conditions are right (the sun is shining brightly, or a big wave and its trough roll by), it shows itself, however fleetingly. For attitudes, the conditions that may expose them could be a loss of self-control, maybe resulting from having a few beers, or being upset, or both— remember Mel Gibson's anti-Semitic tirade after being pulled over for driving under the influence?

As will be discussed later, people's responses to racial attitude questions are influenced by the circumstances under which they are asked (such as publicly vs. privately). The reluctance to express a racial attitude may come from sincere, internalized misgivings about the attitude (e.g., guilt), or extrinsic concerns about how others will react (e.g., shame), or both.

Farther down in the underwater part of the attitude iceberg are beliefs and feelings that the holder is not consciously aware of and therefore cannot deliberately and reliably express in response to a direct question. These are what psychologists call *implicit* attitudes. Extending the iceberg metaphor, there is now a kind of attitude *sonar* that helps us to detect what cannot be seen with the naked eye. These are commonly called *implicit measures*, and we will discuss their origins, uses, and implications later. Nowadays, we may even be starting to have something more literally like sonar for looking at attitudes that are not readily expressed. Specifically, researchers using electroencephalograms (EEG) and functional magnetic resonance imaging (fMRI) are comparing patterns of brain activities for people when they are thinking about members of different racial groups.

Much of this chapter will cover how implicit attitudes operate and are measured. They have been shown to be related to a range of important behaviors, including discriminatory behaviors. This too will be discussed.

To be sure, metaphors have their limits, and the attitude iceberg metaphor is no exception. It is especially apt for racial attitudes, which people are reluctant to express, so the tip may be a small part of the iceberg. But attitudes toward less sensitive topics, like sports teams or foods, may look more like inverted icebergs, with much of the attitude being out in plain sight. This is, however, what makes racial attitudes complicated and, like most icebergs, difficult to measure and potentially treacherous.

This chapter will cover the large and rapidly growing scientific literature on more subtle forms of bias—those that reside beneath the waterline of the mental iceberg—and how they can influence behavior despite our best intentions. Some of it will be technical, reflecting the nature of the research methods. Regardless of how arcane and technical all the experimental and data analytic procedures are, the fundamental insight is rather simple: *Because we can consciously manage only a fraction of the information constantly thrown at our five senses and sorted and stored in our memories, much of our mental life occurs outside of conscious awareness and control, and this includes how we react to people and the groups to which they belong.*

BIAS WITHOUT AWARENESS OR INTENT: THE CHANGING FORM, AND MEASUREMENT, OF PREJUDICE

In 1993, the prominent civil rights leader the Reverend Jesse Jackson stated, "There is nothing more painful to me at this stage in my life than to walk down the street and hear footsteps and start to think about robbery and then look around and see somebody White and feel relieved" (Johnson, 1993). Why would the most prominent living Black civil rights leader hold this negative stereotype of non-White Americans? Because he is exposed to the same information the rest of us are, indicating that Blacks and Latinos are criminally oriented and danger- ous. It is doubtful that Jackson *wants* to hold these beliefs, let alone be influenced by them. Yet he recognizes that he does hold them and that they influence him despite his strong intentions.

What separates Jesse Jackson from most others in this regard is that he used his recognition of the fear he felt of non-White men (or the absence of that fear in the presence of someone White) to *infer* a stereotype of which he might not otherwise have been aware. He realized that the stereotypes affect his thoughts, whether he likes it or not.

Social psychologists realized in the 1970s that prejudice tended to be mani- fested in a very different way than in the pre–civil rights period, when many Americans comfortably expressed beliefs that Blacks were morally and intellec- tually inferior to Whites. Because of the changing social norms of an increasingly egalitarian society, direct, questionnaire measures of racial attitudes became less reliable. Responses that people gave to questions about racial stereotypes, racial integration, and related attitudes have shown steadily increasing tolerance over the last century (Schuman et al., 1997; but see Devine & Elliot, 1995). For example, in 1942, 32% of White Americans surveyed favored racially integrated schools; by 1995, that number had risen to 96% (Schuman et al., 1997, Table 3.1A, pp. 104–105). Similarly, in 1958, almost no White Americans surveyed (4%) indi- cated approval of interracial marriage (Schuman et al., 1997, Table 3.1B, p. 106). By 2004, that number had risen to 76% (Krysan, 2011). This reflects dramatic increases in racial tolerance, though it should be noted that there is considerable room for improvement.

No doubt, much of this reflects real change in attitudes, specifically, increasing acceptance of minorities. This parallels increasing representation of minorities in positions of high status and power, even if they are still dramatically underrepresented. For most of the 20th century (not to mention the centuries that preceded it), no reasonable person would have expected an African American to be elected president. Barack Obama's election proves that in 2008, at least a slim majority of Americans were comfortable placing their trust in the competence of an African American.

Indirect Measures

The improvements in racial attitudes (pronounced continuing inequities notwithstanding) in the post–civil rights era were indisputable. However, social psychologists suspected that much of the reduction in prejudice reflected only changes in social norms for expressing these attitudes—that it had become taboo to exhibit prejudice, and so people were masking their real beliefs and feelings. This led researchers to explore *indirect* measures of bias. The significant proliferation of such studies in the 1960s and 1970s was reviewed by Crosby and colleagues (1980), who identified a new class of "unobtrusive" measures. For example, building on Darley and Latané's (1968) finding that people are *less* likely to help someone who is in peril if they believe they are not the only witness to the problem (an important phenomenon unto itself, called *diffusion of responsibility*), Gaertner and Dovidio (1977) found that White research subjects were less likely to help Black than White victims when there were multiple witnesses—when it was less clear what should be done. This is consistent with the discussions of stereotype function and process—that biases guide our judgments and behavior when circumstances are ambiguous.

Similarly, Donnerstein, Donnerstein, Simon, and Ditrichs (1972) took advantage of an established method for studying aggression (Buss, 1961) by putting people in the position of administering and receiving electrical shocks. Donnerstein et al. found that Whites administered higher levels of shocks to Blacks than to other Whites, *unless* they expected the other person to be in a position to "retaliate" (to be the shocker). In this latter condition, Whites did not administer stronger shocks to Blacks, but they did tend to hold the switch on longer for them.

Other researchers looked at more subtle manifestations of prejudice. Weitz (1972) and Word, Zanna, and Cooper (1974) found that nonverbal behaviors (eye contact, posture, proximity, etc.) of Whites were friendlier toward other Whites than toward Blacks. In a not-so-unobtrusive approach, Sigall and Page (1971) developed a "bogus pipeline" procedure. They hooked research subjects up to a polygraph like machine that they told them could detect their true attitudes. Subjects guessed that the machine would detect more negative racial attitudes than they indicated they had when not hooked up. These indirect measures of racial attitudes revealed that racial bias and discrimination were still prevalent, even though socially undesirable.

Modern Questionnaire Measures of Prejudice

Although the indirect measures described above were valuable for investigating prejudice, they had practical limitations, specifically in that they did not allow for a standardized *measure* and *index* (or score) of the magnitude of bias, like a questionnaire would. Questionnaire measures (surveys) are the stock and trade of many social psychologists for a number of good reasons. Through careful, empirical development they can be made to be very reliable, in the sense that people score consistently on them over time, and that they predict behavior. Questionnaires, when reasonably short, can be very practical tools that can be administered in almost any environment (train stations, shopping malls, classrooms, one-on-one meetings, and, these days, via the Internet). Scores from these questionnaires can be correlated with other measures to promote scientific understanding of psychological and social phenomena. So it posed a serious dilemma to social psychologists that scores on questionnaire measures of stereotyping and prejudice might be inaccurate gages of people's real dispositions.

The response was the development of new scales designed to tap negative racial attitudes without being subject to the distortions that result from direct questions about such taboo subjects. In contrast to surveys of "old-fashioned racism," measures of "modern racism" (aka "symbolic racism") were developed by social psychologists Sears and McConahay (1973; McConahay & Hough, 1976). Because of the unique role of anti-Black prejudice in American history (slavery, lynchings, and the continued denial of basic rights like voting and equal access to education), the social psychological study of prejudice has focused on attitudes toward Blacks, and the contemporary racism measures, too, were specific to Blacks. The underlying principle of measures of modern racism was that direct questions about the character, quality, and intellect of Blacks would no longer be answered genuinely by most Whites. Accordingly, scholars of modern racism sought to tap the underlying "anti-Black affect" (i.e., feelings) by asking about attitudes toward situations and policies that bear on Black American life.

The Modern Racism Scale (MRS; McConahay, 1986), the most widely used measure, asked respondents to indicate how strongly they agreed or disagreed with statements like "Over the past few years, the government and news media have shown more respect to Blacks than they deserve," and "Blacks are getting too demanding in their push for equal rights." It proved effective at picking up a meaningful range of attitudes and policy preferences.

And yet, even the *Modern* Racism Scale has proven, since its creation in the 1980s, to be antiquated, now reactive to respondents' concerns about appearing racist. For example, Fazio and colleagues (Fazio, Jackson, Dunton, & Williams, 1995) found that people's scores on the MRS varied as a function of the race of the survey administrator and the anonymity respondents felt during administration. Recognizing these limitations, one of the originators of symbolic racism theory has developed an updated, less reactive (i.e., less prone to make people react defensively) version of the scale (Henry & Sears, 2002).

Having made the case for the limitations of explicit questionnaire measures of racism, I hasten to add that they continue to have considerable value, and even very overt questions yield troublingly high levels of intolerance. This is evident in the nontrivial number of Americans who recently indicated they could not vote for a Black person for president. Furthermore, as noted earlier, as recently as 2002, 35% of White Americans surveyed indicated disapproval of interracial marriage (Krysan, 2011). This reflects more than just idle survey responding—in 2000, the state of Alabama held a public referendum to repeal a defunct antimiscegenation law that remained in state law. Antimiscegenation laws—those criminalizing interracial marriage—had been ruled unconstitutional by the U.S. Supreme Court in 1967 in *Loving v. Virginia* (388 U.S. 1 (1967)). In 2000, Alabama voters overturned the statute outlawing interracial marriage, but only by a three-to-two margin. More than 40% of Alabama voters preferred to keep the law on the books. Questionnaire measures, some more blatant than others, continue to reveal that, although racial bias in America has declined steadily and dramatically (Schuman et al., 1997), it is still overtly evident in a nontrivial proportion of the population.

Nevertheless, most people are disinclined to express anti-Black attitudes, even on the most modern of questionnaire measures, and yet racial discrimination persists. In recent decades, newer methods have been developed to measure implicit stereotypes and prejudice that may not show up in a questionnaire score but can still influence behavior. We will learn about these shortly but first will consider some background on psychological scientific methods in order to understand the rigor and significance of the implicit methods.

THE PSYCHOLOGICAL SCIENCE OF THINKING

More than half a century ago, Scott M. Smith and colleagues (Smith, Brown, Toman, & Goodman, 1947) sought to end a long-standing debate among scholars of human thought. One camp argued that in order for humans to think, we had to move our lips, or "subvocalize." It seems like a preposterous, even insulting theory now, but it held some sway at the time. Obviously, it was easily disconfirmable that people had to move their lips *visibly*—anyone can conduct the experiment of thinking without moving his or her lips. But the belief, influenced by the theory that language and thought were inextricably linked, maintained that thought was accompanied by at least tiny, imperceptible movements corresponding to speech.

Smith engaged in a radical and dangerous experiment, on himself, to falsify this hypothesis. He poisoned himself with a powerful paralytic drug, curare, and then, while on a ventilator, observed in himself whether he was able to think while no part of his body could move. A poorly calibrated dose of the drug could have caused brain damage or death. Smith survived and reported that he had indeed been able to continue thinking throughout his paralysis.

Now this is not exactly a great experiment by most standards. The sample size (one) was very small (would this generalize to other people?), and the one subject knew the hypothesis and had a stake in the outcome. But it illustrates two important things for our purposes: (1) how ingenious and adventurous scientists can be in pursuing knowledge; and (2) how far science has come in understanding human mental processes, shedding absurd, unempirical theories like phrenology (inferring personality traits and aptitudes based on bumps on the cranium) and the idea Smith was testing about thought and speech. Psychology has become hyperempirical—it places a premium on the scientific method of hypothesis testing and rigorous statistical procedures—and, with technological advances like computers and brain imaging, very sophisticated and cutting edge. No doubt, 50 years from now we will look back and view many of today's research paradigms as crude, but the scientific rigor is unlikely to be questioned.

Smith's experiment illustrates something else that is very important—how far psychology has come in the last century in terms of understanding consciousness. The field has gone from entertaining the seemingly silly (in retrospect) idea that we have to move our lips to think, to a modern understanding that, in a way, we do not really even have to "think" in order to think. Specifically, based on a steady progression of research on nonconscious mental processes (e.g., Hilgard, 1977; Kihlstrom, 1987; Bargh, 1997), we now know that much of our thoughts and feelings occur with little if any mental effort and without conscious (subjective) awareness, let alone lip movements.

IMPLICIT MEMORY AND AUTOMATIC ACTIVATION

Implicit memories are mental associations that we are not consciously aware we possess.[1] *Automatic activation* is the rapid, spontaneous, unintentional, virtually effortless triggering of mental processes, such as memories. Cognitive

1. In addition to distinguishing between implicit and explicit memory, cognitive psychologists have also distinguished between *semantic* and *episodic* memory. The former involves knowledge that we have but cannot necessarily trace to a source. The latter involves memory we can attach to a specific *episode*, as in, "I know that I finished reading this chapter because I remember the moment I slammed the book shut." Episodic memory is very *explicit* in that there is a consciously accessible trace of the memory.

psychologists have demonstrated, using a number of very careful experimental paradigms, that implicit memories can be stored and automatically activated (Kihlstrom, 1987). For example, experiments have involved showing people stimuli (words, images) *subliminally* (i.e., so briefly or peripherally that the research subject has no conscious awareness of having seen the stimulus), and then shown that the concept represented by a given subliminal stimulus was nevertheless stored in memory because it influenced a subsequent judgment. For example, some research subjects would be exposed to a subliminal image (e.g., a hat) and then, not even knowing they had seen anything, were asked to fill in the blank in a word like H_T. Those who saw the hat were more likely to fill in the blank with an *A* than an *O* or *I* or *U*, compared with those who saw something else.

Cognitive psychologists have shown that the retrieval of memories (the activation of mental associations) happens automatically, meaning that it happens without conscious effort or intent. Although you may sometimes deliberately search your memory, you have probably noticed that most memories pop up very spontaneously—you see a friend, and her name just comes to mind. Then there are new acquaintances whose names have not yet been rehearsed enough to be automatically activated, and you have to think hard to remember them.

Being exposed to a single stimulus (a word, an image, a sound, a smell, a feeling) instantaneously triggers many associations. Only when we effortfully and deliberately think about our own thinking can we trace the trail of associations back to an origin. The automatic processing of implicit memories allows us to handle a lot of information, which is, in fact, what we are confronted with on a continual basis.

To better understand how implicit memory and automatic processing operates, you need only consider your own experience learning to drive. This is a common metaphor for understanding automaticity because it is apt and easy to relate to. But if you never learned to drive, similarly useful metaphors include learning to ride a bicycle, read, or type. You may remember that at first it was difficult (especially if you started on a standard transmission!) coordinating the steering, accelerating, and braking while at the same time scanning the terrain in front of and around the car and keeping in mind the rules and knowing when to go and when to stop, how much to turn the wheel to avoid the curb and other cars and pedestrians. It took a lot of concentration. But as you practiced, it became easier and smoother, to the point where you did not really have to think about it anymore—not consciously, anyway. Now when driving you can spend most of your mental energy focusing on your surroundings, possibly adjusting climate controls and the stereo, or holding a conversation (not on a hand held phone, please). You may even have had the experience of arriving somewhere you have driven to many times and not really remembering all the steps that went into getting there, realizing you were on "autopilot."

Learning to drive is an example of the process of *automatization*—repeating a process until it becomes fluid and requires little conscious thought and effort. And implicit, well-learned memories for how to drive and how to get places allow us to move around efficiently and conserve most of our mental resources for more complicated, novel, and interesting topics. This is true for much of our daily thinking and behavior. Automatic processing and implicit memory are utterly essential for human survival. Without these capabilities we would be constantly bogged down in the minutiae of every thought and action.

Priming

Cognitive psychologists interested in memory, categorization, and automaticity (e.g., Hasher & Zacks, 1979; Meyer & Schevaneveldt, 1971; Posner & Snyder, 1975; Shiffrin & Schneider, 1977; Rosch, 1975) developed reliable methods for studying *priming* (the activation of a memory or association) and how primed thoughts can automatically contaminate responses to other stimuli. They have utilized *semantic priming* procedures wherein people are presented with a series of words that appear in pairs—a *prime* and a *target*—usually one right after the other. The primes will come from different categories (e.g., having to do with birds [*feather, wing,* etc.] or buildings [*brick, concrete,* etc.]) that are either associated with the target or not. The primes are presented very briefly, in some experiments subliminally. The research subject's job is to respond to the target (the second word), either by placing it in a category (e.g., bird vs. building) or, in some experiments, by identifying it as a word as opposed to a nonword (random string of letters). For example, a single trial of such an experiment may involve having the word *feather* followed by the word *sparrow,* and the research subject presses a button to indicate that *sparrow* is a real word. Or, *feather* may be followed by *wprrsoa,* and the subject hits the button that indicates it is not a word. The words are paired randomly, with equal numbers of every type of combination, and each research participant will get dozens or even hundreds of word pairs to respond to.

The tasks tend to be pretty easy, and so subjects rarely make errors. It is the speed with which the subjects respond, measured to the millisecond, that is taken as an index of the strength of the association between the prime and the target. The logic here is that, when we see (consciously or not) something (a word, an object), it instantaneously triggers thoughts about that thing, which trigger more thoughts about other things related to it (psychologists call this *spreading activation*).

If the prime and target are semantically related (i.e., if they share meaning), thoughts about the target will be "primed" before it even appears. Consequently, targets that are responded to more quickly after certain primes (e.g., *sparrow* after *feather*) are probably semantically related to those primes. In this manner, we can make inferences about mental associations based on speed of response to word pairs; if people respond faster to *sparrow* when it is preceded by *feather* than by *brick*, we infer there is a stronger association between *feather* and *sparrow* than between *brick* and *sparrow*.

It may not be surprising or even interesting that people think of birds when they see words like *feather*. The important insight here is that this happens not only without conscious awareness but also *without conscious intent*. We have these thoughts whether we want to or not. Neely (1977) demonstrated compellingly that this type of semantic activation and categorization happens automatically, even when people try to stop it, provided the target appears very soon after the prime.

Studies of subliminal perception/cognition support the notion of implicit memory and automatic thought activation by showing that semantic priming effects occur even when research subjects have no conscious experience of seeing the priming stimulus (e.g., Greenwald, Draine, & Abrams, 1996; Greenwald, Klinger, & Liu, 1989). Specifically, subliminal priming studies involve showing the prime (usually a simple word or image) so rapidly (e.g., for less than 30 milliseconds) and/or peripherally (in an unpredictable corner location in the field of vision) that the subject cannot recognize it (and may not even realize she saw anything at all).[2] In these studies, even though people are not consciously aware of the primes, responses to the targets are nevertheless influenced by the nature of the primes (e.g., positive targets are responded to more quickly when preceded by positive than negative primes). This necessitates that the meaning of the primes was derived and related thoughts activated, even though there was no conscious, subjective experience of perceiving them, and therefore demonstrates compellingly that human mental processes operate in part outside of conscious awareness or control.

Our Efficient Minds

Really, this ability—to process information nonconsciously—is a necessity. Imagine life if we weren't able to automatize processes or store knowledge in implicit memory, if driving a car required as much conscious attention every day as it did the first day. But there is a downside to this efficiency. It may seem totally benign, even beneficial, that memory activation is largely uncontrollable when we're talking about feathers and birds and driving. But when we get in the domain of interpersonal judgments and behaviors, and group-based stereotypes, it becomes problematic.

---

2. The ability of humans to perceive and recognize subliminal stimuli (i.e., those they do not consciously recognize) has been firmly established by cognitive psychologists employing strong tests that allow ample chance to disconfirm the hypothesis (Merikle, Smilek, & Eastwood, 2001).

IMPLICIT STEREOTYPES AND AUTOMATIC DISCRIMINATION

An explosion of social psychological research in the last several decades has shown convincingly that, like other mental processes, much of stereotyping and prejudice occurs outside of conscious awareness or control. This leads to unintentionally discriminatory judgments and behaviors. Social psychologists have adopted and modified cognitive psychology's effective methods for studying implicit memory to demonstrate that gender, racial, ethnic, age, and other stereotypes are rapidly activated in the mere presence of a stimulus (an image, a name, a word) related to the group, and this can elicit stereotype-consistent, biased judgments.

Watershed Studies in the Application of Automatic Processing and Implicit Memory to Social Phenomena

It's not just car driving that we automatize. And it's not just birds and buildings that we categorize and store in implicit memory. It's also people that we categorize, and traits (stereotypes) and feelings (prejudice) that we associate with them, implicitly, in our memories.

Implicit Stereotyping

In the early 1980s, multiple social psychological laboratories started simultaneously applying implicit memory and automaticity theories and research methods to *social cognition*—beliefs and attitudes about social groups like women and racial minorities. The view was that stereotypes, being associations in our memories between groups (e.g., minorities) and traits (e.g., criminality), can and are also stored implicitly and activated automatically. Social psychologists Gaertner and McLaughlin (1983) as well as Dovidio, Evans, and Tyler (1986) in separate studies used semantic priming methods to show that stereotypes (group-trait associations) are activated similarly to other memories. Using semantic priming procedures, they found that White research subjects were faster to categorize targets stereotypically associated with Blacks (e.g., aggressive) and Whites (e.g., intelligent) after being primed with the words *Black* versus *White*, respectively. Subsequent studies have shown that this occurs when the primes are words or names associated with the groups, not just the labels (e.g., Blair & Banaji, 1996; Banaji & Hardin, 1996), and when the primes and targets are presented in such rapid succession as to preclude controlled processing. Studies have also shown that this occurs even when the group primes are presented subliminally (e.g., Wittenbrink, Judd, & Park, 1997), so that it is impossible that the stereotypes are being activated consciously or deliberately.

While others were studying implicit social beliefs (stereotypes), Fazio and colleagues (Fazio, Sanbonmatsu, Powell, & Kardes, 1986), applying the procedures established by Neely (1977) to tease apart automatic and controlled processes, demonstrated that attitudes can be activated automatically, without conscious intent. Fazio aptly defined attitudes as associations between objects and evaluations, simply how positively or negatively oriented we are toward something. Fazio et al. (1986) presented research subjects with a series of word pairs (a prime followed by a target), composed of clearly positive or negative words (e.g., *heaven, hell, life, death*), instructing them to ignore the prime and categorize the target as good or bad as quickly as possible. When the target followed the prime after a very short interval (300 milliseconds), subjects could not preclude the influence of the prime—they categorized good and bad targets faster when they were preceded by good and bad primes, respectively. The implications of this, as Fazio and colleagues noted, were serious—*people evaluate things as good or bad even when they do not mean to, and they do it very rapidly, and it influences their responses to other things.*

Bargh, Chaiken, Raymond, and Hymes (1996) showed this kind of automatic attitude activation even when the task was simply to *read* the target word aloud, indicating that people do not even have to be thinking consciously about whether things are good or bad to automatically evaluate them. This makes sense when we consider what a fundamentally essential ability it is to be able to decide quickly how good or bad things are, and, consequently, how we should act toward them. Greenwald and colleagues (1996) subsequently showed that such automatic evaluation occurs even for primes that are presented subliminally. Many other studies have provided similar evidence for the ubiquity of automatic attitude activation (see Glaser, 2002, 2007, for reviews).

Automatic Prejudice

Fazio and colleagues (1995) extended the evidence of automatic attitude activation to automatic prejudice, prejudice being an attitude toward a group.[3] Replacing the positive and negative prime words with briefly presented pictures of Black or White men's faces, but still having research subjects categorize the target words as good or bad, Fazio and colleagues found that White subjects were faster to categorize positive words as good when they were preceded by White

---

3. The term *implicit prejudice* is more common than *automatic prejudice*. Technically, *implicit* refers to lack of *awareness*, whereas *automatic* refers to lack of *control*. Implicit associations (e.g., between groups and traits or evaluations) can be automatically activated.

faces and faster to categorize negative words as bad when they were preceded by Black faces.[4] In order for people to respond faster to bad and good words after seeing Black and White faces, respectively, they *must* have evaluated the Black and White faces relatively negatively and positively, respectively. Given the rapid presentation of the stimuli, this happened *automatically* (i.e., spontaneously and unintentionally). It is noteworthy that Fazio and colleagues' motivation for conducting this experiment was not to provide evidence of nonconscious racial bias (Fazio, personal communication, ca. 1994). Rather, Fazio's career-spanning interest in attitudes and their relations to motivation and behavior led him to test his theories of automatic attitude activation in a domain—racial attitudes—where people should be resistant to expressing negative attitudes. A demonstration of automatic preference for Whites over Blacks, and the absence of a correlation between the automatic measure and a parallel questionnaire measure, would be strong evidence of a disassociation between automatic and controlled expressions of attitudes.

Fazio and colleagues' experiment and the many similar demonstrations that have followed illustrate that people have nonconscious, automatic biases for and against racial and other groups. One widely used method for studying implicit stereotyping and prejudice is the Implicit Association Test (IAT; Greenwald, McGee, & Schwartz, 1998). The IAT is a highly adaptable and sensitive computerized measure of implicit beliefs and attitudes. It requires subjects to categorize words or images on two dimensions simultaneously, using only two response keys. In the case of a racial prejudice IAT, that would involve categorizations of Black versus White and Positive versus Negative. One stimulus appears at a time. Essentially, the average amount of time (in milliseconds) it takes to make the categorizations when Black is paired on the same response key with Negative and White with Positive is subtracted from the average amount of time it takes when Black is paired with Positive and White with Negative to yield an implicit racial preference index. Visit www.projectimplicit.org for demonstrations and explanations. Project Implicit has now used Web-based IATs to collect data from literally millions of people from all over the world, allowing for statistically powerful tests and careful refinement of scoring algorithms.

Decades of research on implicit bias, including hundreds of published studies using methods like semantic priming and IATs, have yielded a large body of evidence allowing for a high degree of confidence that implicit bias is commonplace and relates reliably (i.e., has "predictive validity") to conceptually similar and relevant variables such as questionnaire and behavioral measures of

---

4. Black subjects showed the opposite pattern of results. In a similar experiment run on Yale undergraduates (Fazio et al.'s study was conducted on Indiana University undergraduates), Mahzarin Banaji and I found the same result for White students, but no in-group preference for Black students (Glaser & Banaji, 1999).

bias, as well as other implicit measures of the same attitudes. Such findings have been reviewed and meta-analyzed, revealing the effects to be quite robust (e.g., Greenwald et al., 2009; Hofmann, Gawronski, Gschwendner, Le, & Schmitt, 2005; Nosek, 2005).

The Effects of Implicit/Automatic Biases on Judgments of Others

It is certainly interesting that our minds have stored in them racial, ethnic, gender, and other group-based stereotypes and prejudices that we are not even aware of, and that they can be activated without our conscious intent. But this would truly be cause for concern if these biases affect our judgments of and behaviors toward others. If we do not consciously endorse these beliefs and attitudes, can they still influence our judgments? The answer, from scores of careful experiments, is a clear yes.

In 1989, Patricia Devine published an influential study investigating the automatic and controlled aspects of stereotyping. Devine found that, while few of her research subjects were willing to endorse (i.e., indicate agreement with) negative stereotypes of African Americans (e.g., lazy, violent), when asked what they thought were the prevailing stereotypes that *other* Americans held of Blacks, almost everybody knew what they were. In a separate experiment, Devine asked people to rate the behavior of a man named Donald, who was depicted in a short story. People who were subliminally primed with Black stereotypes prior to reading about Donald subsequently rated his behavior as more hostile (but not more negative on other, stereotype-irrelevant, dimensions). These same people had explicitly disavowed the very racial stereotypes that they were applying to Donald. Devine's work and that of others who have followed (e.g., Augoustinos, Ahrens, & Innes, 1994; Hense, Penner, & Nelson, 1995; & Lepore & Brown, 1997) demonstrate that the mere *knowledge* of a stereotype, which most people possess, makes the application of it to a group member very likely.

Implicit racial biases can cause people to react to minorities in a manner that can lead to altercations. Hugenberg and Bodenhausen (2003) showed research subjects videos of carefully matched Black and White faces changing from hostile to happy expressions and vice versa. People tended to perceive hostility sooner and happiness later in the Black faces. Importantly, the extent to which people showed this bias was correlated with the strength of their implicit (but not explicit) negative attitudes toward Blacks. Because even subliminal perceptions of African Americans have been shown to trigger automatic hostile responses (Bargh et al., 1996), implicit racial bias has the potential to "complicate" interracial interactions, to say the least. In policing, where tense interracial interactions as well as physical contact are common, and concerns over use of force are serious, the implications are very real.

Applying Stereotypes Even to Ourselves

There is a separate line of research that compellingly demonstrates that stereotypes influence our thoughts and behaviors *despite* our intentions. Claude Steele's (1997) research on "stereotype threat" has shown that people for whom there is a stereotype about their group's ability perform in a manner consistent with the stereotype when they are caused to think about their group membership and/or the stereotype. For example, stereotype threat research has shown that women and Blacks perform more poorly on math tests after merely checking a box to indicate their gender or race (Nguyen & Ryan, 2008; Spencer, Steele, & Quinn, 1999; Steele & Aaronson, 1995). White males even show a small "stereotype lift" effect under these circumstances, performing better than White men in the control condition where they do not check a box (Walton & Cohen, 2003). Stereotype threat has been shown to be influential across a range of behaviors, even affecting athletic performance (Stone, Lynch, Sjomeling, & Darley, 1999).

The relevance here is that Black and female college students (and White basketball players) obviously do not *want* to underperform. The stereotype effect is almost certainly unintentional. Similarly, the effects that stereotypes have on our outward behaviors toward others, such as judging their performance or suspiciousness, can happen in spite of our best, most egalitarian intentions.

The Effects of Implicit/Automatic Biases on Discriminatory Behavior

Stereotype threat effects are certainly troubling, as are effects of implicit biases on judgments of others. Even greater concern would arise if there were compelling evidence linking implicit biases to discriminatory *behavior*. Early evidence for this was provided in Fazio and colleagues' initial study of automatic racial attitudes discussed earlier (Fazio et al., 1995). Fazio et al. found that the magnitude of their implicit racial bias measure (as indexed by the differential speed of categorizing positive and negative target words after White and Black face primes) was correlated with the friendliness research subjects exhibited toward a Black experimenter after the task (see Amodio & Devine, 2006; Dovidio et al., 1997; Dovidio, Kawakami, & Gaertner, 2002; Richeson & Shelton, 2005, for subsequent, similar findings). After decades of research examining the nature of implicit stereotypes and prejudice, a growing literature has in fact examined a wide array of discriminatory behaviors across a range of populations, finding implicit biases to reliably relate to biased treatment of minorities, women, and other stigmatized groups (see Jost et al., 2009, for a review). For example:

- Rudman and Ashmore (2007) found that student subjects who showed relatively negative implicit racial or ethnic bias on IAT measures were more likely to (based on their own reports) have used racial/ethnic slurs against, socially excluded, and even physically harmed minorities. They were also more likely to recommend cutting the budgets of relevant minority student groups.

- Swedish hiring managers were more likely to grant job interviews to applicants with ethnic Swedish than Arab-Muslim backgrounds in a carefully designed hiring audit study. The tendency for managers to favor Swedes in granting interviews was correlated with an IAT measure of implicit preference for Swedes over Arab-Muslims (Rooth, 2010).
- Medical researcher Alexander Green and colleagues (Green et al., 2007) found that medical residents who scored higher in anti-Black/pro-White bias on an IAT were less likely to recommend an essential medical treatment (thrombolysis) for an ostensible Black patient described as presenting with symptoms of myocardial infarction warranting that treatment.
- Arcuri, Castelli, Galdi, Zogmaister, and Amadori (2008) found that undecided Italian voters' implicit attitudes toward candidates predicted their self-reported votes in elections held one month later (see also Galdi, Arcuri, & Gawronski, 2008), and Roccato and Zogmaister's (2010) undecided Italian voters' vote choices were predicted by an IAT measure better than by an explicit measure of candidate preference.
- Palfai and Ostafin (2003) found that excessive drinkers' implicit attitudes toward alcohol were correlated with self-reported rates of binge drinking.
- Similarly, Dutch researchers (e.g., Thush, Wiers, Ames, Grenard, Sussman, & Stacy, 2007) have used the IAT to measure implicit attitudes toward addictive substances like cocaine and alcohol, finding them to relate to past, and to predict future, abuse of these substances.
- When given an (admittedly distasteful) implicit measure of the association between children and sex, convicted pedophiles scored positive, whereas a non-pedophile sex offender comparison group did not (Gray, Brown, MacCulloch, Smith, & Snowden, 2005).
- Nock, Park, Finn, Deliberto, Dour, and Banaji (2010) found that an IAT measuring the association between self and death/suicide was a strong predictor of subsequent suicidal attempts, stronger than well-established predictors like depression.

These findings and others like them (see Jost et al., 2009 and Greenwald et al., 2009, for reviews) indicate across a variety of ages, cultures, and professions that implicit biases are predictive of actual, consequential behaviors, such as medical treatments, hiring, voting, and substance abuse. Some of these studies have been comprehensive enough to allow analysts to statistically control for other explanatory variables, indicating that implicit biases are likely to have direct, *causal* effects on these behaviors.

Because implicit biases are commonplace and influence our behaviors, and because stereotypes relating minorities (particularly African Americans) to aggression and crime are widely known, if not always consciously endorsed, and because law enforcement agents are normal human beings with normal human information processing, there is a very high likelihood that implicit biases cause discriminatory effects in policing, including racial profiling.

"SHOOTER BIAS"

Seated in front of a video monitor with your hand on a control stick, you are instructed that you will see a series of photographs of men. Each will hold either a gun or a harmless object like a cell phone. Your job is to "shoot" by squeezing the trigger on the stick as quickly as possible whenever there is a gun and to pull back as quickly as possible whenever there is no gun. Partway through the task you realize that some of the men are Black and some are White. Would you let their race influence how quickly you "shoot"? Would you shoot the Black men faster? Would you allow yourself to accidentally shoot more unarmed Black men than unarmed White men?

Of course not! Well, not intentionally, at least. But people as well-intentioned as you are, in actual experiments like this, *do* tend to shoot Black men faster and erroneously shoot more unarmed Black men (Correll et al., 2002; Correll, Park, Judd, Wittenbrink, Sadler, & Keesee, 2007; Glaser & Knowles, 2008; Greenwald, Oakes, & Hoffman, 2003; Park, Glaser, & Knowles, 2008; Plant & Peruche, 2005; Peruche & Plant, 2006; Plant, Peruche, & Butz, 2005; see also Payne, 2001, for conceptually similar demonstrations).[5] This tendency is called *shooter bias* (Correll et al., 2002). The experiments are carefully designed and executed to allow for strong tests of racial bias in decisions to shoot. For example, half of the guns are light metal, and half are dark, so that results cannot be attributed to perceptual contrast.

What Causes Shooter Bias?

Surely, there are very few people who would exhibit this behavior intentionally, even in a simulation. Racial discrimination is taboo in America, and shooting Blacks is an undesirable behavior for most people, made especially potent by highly publicized, tragic wrongful police shootings of unarmed Black men.

---

5. In the original shooter bias experiments (e.g., Correll et al., 2002; Correll, Park, Judd, & Wittenbrink, 2007; Correll, Park, Judd, Wittenbrink, Sadler, & Keesee, 2007), "shoot" responses were indicated with a button press. My colleagues and I (Glaser & Knowles, 2008; Park et al., 2008) have obtained similar results with more behavior-like procedures, replacing the button press with a trigger squeeze on a control stick device. "No shoot" responses are made by pulling back on the stick, as if pointing a gun upward.

Given the emphasis in the preceding chapters, it may not surprise you to learn that racial stereotypes are at least partly to blame.

In their initial demonstrations of shooter bias, Correll and colleagues (2002) gave participants questionnaire measures meant to tap racial prejudice (the emotional part) and questions about the stereotype of Blacks as violent and dangerous. The prejudice measures did not relate to the magnitude of subjects' shooter bias scores. Nor did a question asking whether the subjects personally endorsed (believed) the stereotype that Black men are violent and dangerous. However, Correll found that subjects' reports of whether or not violence and dangerousness were part of the American cultural stereotype of Blacks (not necessarily a stereotype that the subjects endorsed) did correlate significantly with shooter bias. This result is reminiscent of Devine's (1989) finding that people's reports of their own attitudes are often skewed by a desire to be or at least to appear unprejudiced; but mere awareness of a stereotype, even if it is personally (consciously) rejected, is sufficient to cause discriminatory behavior.

Correll, Park, Judd, and Wittenbrink (2007), in a follow-up study to their original demonstration of shooter bias, provided evidence that stereotypes *cause* shooter bias. In one experiment, subjects who were randomly assigned to read news stories about White criminals subsequently exhibited weaker shooter bias, although this was manifested in a greater tendency to shoot unarmed Whites, not a decrease in the tendency to shoot unarmed Blacks. In another experiment, Correll and colleagues manipulated the strength of the association between Blacks and guns by having subjects carry out the shooter procedure with different proportions of armed Blacks and Whites. On subsequent trials of the task, they found that shooter bias was stronger among those who had seen more Black men with guns.

Eric Knowles and I (Glaser & Knowles, 2008) preceded our measure of shooter bias with implicit measures of racial prejudice and stereotypes. Paralleling Correll et al. (2002), who used questionnaire measures, we found that an implicit measure of racial prejudice (a Black/White–good/bad IAT) was *not* related to shooter bias. However, a measure of an implicit race-weapons stereotype—an IAT measure of the strength of associations between Blacks or Whites and weapons or tools—was a good predictor of shooter bias. Whether we like it or not, the implicit stereotypes our culture feeds us, associating Blacks with aggression, danger, and weapons, put all of us at risk of committing discriminatory acts like racially biased, wrongful shooting.[6]

6. Further evidence for the causal role of stereotypes in shooter bias comes from work by Unkelbach, Forgas, and Denson (2008), who extended the finding to Muslim-appearing men (comparing turban-clad vs. bareheaded targets). Unkelbach et al. found that the bias against Muslims was even greater than usual when subjects were induced to be in a happy mood. Prior research has consistently shown that positive mood causes more "heuristic" processing, like stereotyping (e.g., Forgas, 1998).

Research on shooter bias has obvious and profound implications for policing. Although most officers never discharge their firearm in the field, when it does happen, there are often jarring ramifications for the officer, department, and community. Furthermore, high-profile cases of fatal shootings by police of unarmed Black men, like Amadou Diallo in New York City in 1999, and the more recent fatal shooting of a subdued (face-down) man, Oscar Grant, by a Bay Area Rapid Transit officer in Oakland have, in addition to the tragedy inherent in a wrongful death, proven to be profoundly disruptive for the affected departments.

Perhaps most disturbing to departments are shootings of plainclothes or off-duty police officers by other officers, such as the recent fatal case of NYPD officer Omar Edwards, in East Harlem. In the wake of the Edwards shooting, New York's governor commissioned a task force to investigate mistaken-identity shootings of police officers by police officers. The task force found a clear racial component, with 9 out of 10 off-duty officers shot by on-duty officers since 1982 being Black or Latino (New York State Task Force on Police-on-Police Shootings, 2010, as cited in Baker, 2010). These off-duty officers who get shot typically have their guns drawn in an attempt to intervene in a crime; their innocence is indisputable. Subsequent to the task force's report, a Black, plainclothes officer, William Torbit Jr., was fatally shot in January 2011 by fellow Baltimore police officers while working to manage an unruly crowd at a nightclub. The dramatic racial disproportion in these shootings is compelling evidence of shooter bias in the field, and the effects are devastating.

The implications of shooter bias need not be constrained to shooting incidents. Rather, the phenomenon is likely representative of the potential for a much broader class of troubling forms of unintended discrimination, including more commonplace uses of nonlethal force as well as judgments of suspicion, decisions to search, and so forth. That racially discriminatory responses are evident even in a task as sensitive and potent as the use of lethal force (i.e., shooting) makes it all the more likely that they occur in less controversial behaviors, such as pat-downs and forms of physical restraint that can lead to a range of consequences, from denial of dignity to injury to physical altercation that puts suspects, officers, and bystanders at risk.

If the types of unintended discriminatory behaviors shooter bias likely reflects were limited to the civilian populations represented by research samples typically employed in social psychological experiments (college students, community members, and, increasingly, general population members participating through the Internet), they would raise concern over racial discrimination and conflict in general. But their implications for policing are more convincing because actual police samples exhibit similar biases.

Stereotype-driven discriminatory judgments and behavior are normal human experiences, and police officers, being normal human beings, are therefore susceptible to them. Nevertheless, direct evidence of shooter bias and/or related biases being exhibited by samples of police officers is useful for those interested in promoting fairness as well as compliance with fundamental law enforcement principles of nondiscrimination.

Before discussing experiments that have directly measured shooter bias in police samples, it is worth considering a powerful set of studies that examined the associations (i.e., stereotypes) police officers hold linking Blacks with crime. As noted in Chapter 3, Eberhardt et al. (2004) subliminally primed subjects with crime-relevant objects like guns and knives (or, in a control condition, other objects) and then assessed the extent to which they focused their attention on Black or White faces.[7] Subjects exposed to the crime-relevant objects focused more on the Black faces. Eberhardt and colleagues replicated this finding with a sample of police officers, using crime- and enforcement-related words (e.g., *violent, crime, stop, investigate*) as the subliminal primes. Police in this sample were more likely to focus their attention on Black faces after being made to think about crime, even though they did not know they had been exposed to the crime-related words. After the attention task, subjects were shown a series of Black and White faces, some of which they had seen previously, some of which they had not. These faces had been rated on how racially stereotypical they were (how "Black" or "White" they looked). Police officers in the crime-priming condition of the experiment were more likely to indicate that they remembered seeing more stereotypically Black faces. In another study, Eberhardt et al. asked one group of police officers to rate the racial stereotypicality of Black and White faces, and another group to indicate whether each face looked "criminal." The officers in this latter group were more likely to indicate that faces looked criminal when they were Black, and this was especially the case for the more stereotypically Black faces; the most stereotypically White faces were identified as criminal the least often.

In sum, the work by Eberhardt and colleagues indicates that racial stereotypes linking Blacks with crime are common, robust, and present in police officers. The research discussed next reflects how these stereotypes can influence police behavior, making it racially biased, even in highly sensitive and consequential tasks like the decision to shoot.

Testing for shooter bias using a Floridian police sample, Plant and Peruche (2005; see also Peruche & Plant, 2006) found that officers were significantly more likely to shoot unarmed Black than unarmed White men in the shooting simulation. Working with police and a citizen comparison group in Denver,

---

7. Eberhardt et al. (2004) cleverly appropriated a "dot-probe" task from cognitive psychological studies of attention and perception. Presented with a pair of faces (one Black, one White), subjects have to identify on which face a dot appears. Faster identification of a dot on one type of face or the other indicates that the subjects were already inclined to look at that face.

as well as a nationally representative sample of officers, Correll, Park, Judd, Wittenbrink, Sadler, and Keesee (2007) found that all three groups exhibited shooter bias as measured by reaction times—they were significantly faster to shoot armed Blacks than armed Whites and to not shoot unarmed Whites than unarmed Blacks. In terms of errors (shooting more unarmed Black than White targets or failing to shoot more armed White than Black targets), the community sample exhibited this in addition to the bias in reaction time. The Denver police sample was more likely to shoot unarmed Blacks than unarmed Whites, but this effect was only "marginally" statistically significant. In a second study, a Denver police sample did not exhibit this bias. The national police sample did not exhibit shooter bias in error rates.

That Correll, Park, Judd, Wittenbrink, Sadler, and Keesee (2007) did not reliably find shooter bias among police officers in the error rates measures is encouraging. In fact, police officers were less inclined than the community sample to shoot overall. This may reflect their training and/or the seriousness with which they take such a task, given its relevance to their jobs. It would be premature, however, to be sanguine about shooter bias among police officers. The consistent presence of the bias in reaction time measures indicates that police officers possess the same stereotypes and that those stereotypes do indeed influence the nature of their shooting responses. That the bias sometimes does not translate into racial disparities in errors (wrongful shootings) in the experiments may be a function of the relative ease and simplicity of the task. In the field, under dramatically more stressful and distracting conditions, the association evidenced in the response speeds may well translate into errors. Historically, we know, this has indeed happened.

Reducing Shooter Bias

Sang Hee Park and I (Park & Glaser, 2011) have found that giving people experience with a shooter task where a smaller proportion of Black targets are armed serves to reduce shooter bias on subsequent experiment trials. Replicating a finding from a nonpolice sample (Plant et al., 2005), Plant and Peruche also found that shooter bias by police was essentially eliminated after extensive practice with the task when the trials contained equal proportions of armed and unarmed Blacks and Whites. It should be noted, however, that after the extensive practice, shooting errors (shooting unarmed targets) were reduced to a very low level overall. It may be that part of the elimination of the racial bias was due to a compression of errors in general (a "floor effect"). This is not irrelevant. Police officers *do* get practice of this sort. To the extent that such practice reduces errors in the field (a difficult premise to test, given the rarity of actual shootings), it is likely to reduce the potential for race-based wrongful shootings.

However, we should bear in mind that Correll, Park, Judd, and Wittenbrink (2007) found that shooter bias can *increase* if people are exposed to stereotype-consistent trials (more Blacks with guns). In fact, Correll, Park, Judd, Wittenbrink, Sadler, and Keesee (2007) also found that the magnitude of the shooter bias effect in their national police sample was positively correlated with the percentage of African Americans in the communities in which they served. So unless practice and experience consistently involve stereotype-neutral (if not counterstereotypic) pairings, shooter bias and other forms of racial discrimination are likely to persist.

Just as a subliminal picture of a hat will cause people to fill in the blank in H_T with an A instead of an I or an O or a U, believing someone is poor will cause people to unintentionally judge them as less intelligent (Darley & Gross, 1983). Similarly, people will spontaneously interpret ambiguous behavior as more aggressive if they are told the person being described is named Donald instead of Donna (Banaji, Hardin, & Rothman, 1993).

These implicit stereotypes can lead to subtle and not-so-subtle discriminatory behaviors. In my own research, for example, my colleagues and I have found that an implicit association between Blacks and weapons predicts shooter bias (Glaser & Knowles, 2008). Nobody in our experiments *wants* to shoot Blacks faster than Whites, but they do. This has been shown to generally be the case—implicit stereotypes and attitudes can bias our judgments and behaviors, especially the quick and spontaneous ones, despite our best conscious intentions.

Many researchers have been excited about the advent of implicit measures of stereotyping and prejudice because they get around people's efforts to avoid looking biased. The implicit measures have been seen as tapping the hidden, underlying attitudes. This is, in fact, a useful application of the methods. But there is much more to it than that. Implicit biases are not the same as explicit biases. Yes, they tend to be correlated, but by no means perfectly. They predict different kinds of behaviors (Dovidio et al., 1997). It is the very *implicitness* of these biases that makes them particularly likely to cause discrimination even for people with egalitarian motives. For the very reason that we are not subjectively *aware* of implicit beliefs and attitudes, it is difficult to recognize, let alone inhibit, the influence they have on our judgments and behaviors.

The impact of implicit biases on judgments and behavior has significant relevance for policing. Police officers do not want to behave in a biased manner, yet they, like the rest of us, possess implicit stereotypes that skew their perceptions of individual citizens.

THE IMPORTANCE OF MOTIVATION IN CONTROLLING BIAS

In her seminal study of automatic stereotype activation and application, Devine (1989) provided evidence that stereotypes are activated automatically in memory even for people who score low in prejudice on questionnaires. One important factor that differentiates those who score low in explicit prejudice is that they exert control over the *expression* of their biases. Devine and other researchers have in recent decades made substantial progress in better explaining the role of *motivation to control prejudice* in the expression of bias (e.g., discrimination).

The Fazio et al. (1995) study was an important milestone in this line of research. As described earlier, Fazio and colleagues employed a sequential priming procedure, using Black and White faces as primes, to develop a measure of automatic attitudes toward Blacks and Whites. They found that those who scored higher in automatic anti-Black attitudes behaved more negatively toward a Black experimenter. Fazio and colleagues also found that the scores on the implicit measure did not correlate with scores on an explicit questionnaire measure of prejudice, the MRS. At first blush, this seems to indicate that the implicit measure is not a reliable predictor of bias. In fact, it may be that it is the explicit questionnaires that are unreliable; scores on the MRS were sensitive to context—they tended to be lower when the questionnaire was administered by a Black experimenter in a nonanonymous setting.

To further explore this possibility, Fazio and colleagues administered a new scale designed to assess people's desires to behave in an unprejudiced manner, the Motivation to Control Prejudiced Reactions (MCPR) scale. The MCPR asked subjects to indicate how much they agreed or disagreed with statements like "In today's society it is important that one not be perceived as prejudiced in any manner," and "I get angry with myself when I have a thought or feeling that might be considered prejudiced." They found that those who scored low in MCPR (i.e., were not particularly concerned about being or appearing prejudiced) showed a positive correlation between implicit prejudice (their automatic attitude index) and explicit prejudice as measured by the MRS questionnaire—the stronger they associated Blacks with negative and/or Whites with positive on the priming task, the higher their anti-Black prejudice score on the MRS. In other words, how we express our prejudice is a function of both our underlying implicit biases *and* our more conscious, egalitarian motives with regard to how we want to behave.

Fazio and colleagues (Dunton & Fazio, 1997), as well as Devine, Ashby Plant, and their colleagues (e.g., Devine, Plant, Amodio, Harmon-Jones, & Vance, 2002; Plant & Devine, 1998), have pursued questionnaire measures of motivation to control prejudice with considerable success, finding them to reliably explain relations between implicit bias and more deliberate behavior. Psychological research has consistently shown that people think and react to things on multiple levels, usually involving more rapid, basic responses, followed sometimes by slower, more effortful, thoughtful responses (Srull & Wyer, 1988). When we have sufficient time and cognitive resources (i.e., when we are not rushed, tired, or distracted), our conscious goals and efforts can override more spontaneous, superficial responses. Much of the time, our spontaneous responses are adequate and, in fact, efficient. In the realm of racial interactions, given the pervasiveness of racial biases, they become problematic, and so conscious motivations to control prejudice serve as an important check on discrimination and conflict.

Many of our behaviors, however, are relatively spontaneous, or occur under conditions of time pressure or distraction. The shooter task is a good example, where well-meaning people tend to exhibit discriminatory behavior that could have deadly consequences. Conscious motivation to control prejudice will have only limited efficacy for mitigating behaviors like shooter bias. Accordingly, my colleagues and I (Glaser & Knowles, 2008; Park et al., 2008) have begun exploring the possibility of an *Implicit* Motivation to Control Prejudice (IMCP). This is based on the idea that, in addition to thoughts and feelings operating outside of consciousness, goals and motives can and do as well (Chartrand & Bargh, 1996; Glaser & Kihlstrom, 2005; Moskowitz, Gollwitzer, Wasel, & Schaal, 1999; Shah & Kruglanski, 2003). In fact, we have found that those who score high in our measure of IMCP (assessed using reaction time procedures like the IAT) show a weaker relation between their implicit stereotypes and their spontaneous behavior. Specifically, we (Glaser & Knowles, 2008) measured an implicit race-weapons stereotype (an IAT linking Blacks and Whites with weapons or tools) and shooter bias in the same sample. We also gave them our IMCP measure. While most subjects showed a positive relation between the implicit race-weapons stereotype and shooter bias, those high in IMCP showed no such relation—they *possessed* the stereotype, but they appear to have short-circuited its effect on their spontaneous behavior. These findings offer hope that even spontaneous discriminatory behaviors like shooter bias can be controlled.

IMPLICIT BIAS, THE ATTITUDE ICEBERG, AND THE PRESIDENCY

I started this chapter by noting that a nontrivial proportion of eligible American voters indicated that they could not vote for a Black person for president. This was based on surveys, where people were asked to state their attitude. Because it is generally taboo in modern society to admit to this kind of racial bias, it is surprising that so many people indicated they would not vote for a Black candidate. There is almost certainly another group, perhaps larger, that would not vote for a Black person, but will not admit it, either to themselves or to the survey taker. And there is no doubt an even larger group that, while not ruling out voting for a Black person, are disinclined. The survey respondents who overtly indicated that they would not vote for a Black candidate were just the tip of the proverbial iceberg of racial bias.

Based on social psychological research on *implicit* bias, we now know that there is another racial attitude iceberg—the one that floats *within our individual minds*. The tip if this iceberg is the explicit attitude each of us is willing to express, and it tends to be a pretty tolerant, accepting attitude. Beneath that is the attitude we may be aware we hold but are not comfortable expressing, at least not exactly as we feel it. And beneath that, still, is the implicit part of our attitude, the part that we are not even consciously aware we hold. The implicit attitude is often out of sync with the explicit attitude, especially when there are pressures (like social norms, including those against prejudice) influencing the expression of the attitude.

Even these submerged, implicit attitudes are influential on behavior that is as seemingly careful and deliberate as voting for president. This is not just a theoretical presumption. Several studies have provided empirical evidence that implicit racial bias had a significant effect on the 2008 presidential election (Finn & Glaser, 2010; Greenwald, Smith, Sriram, Bar-Anan, & Nosek, 2009; Payne, Krosnick, Pasek, Lelkes, Akhtar, & Tompson, 2010). In the 2008 election, recognizing with Barack Obama's candidacy the potential for a racial component, the American National Election Studies (ANES) added a measure of implicit racial bias to its large, national survey of eligible voters. For many decades, the ANES has been conducting extensive, highly rigorous longitudinal studies of voters in the periods surrounding national elections, asking respondents about their backgrounds, preferences, voting intentions, and, after the election, who they voted for. In 2008, ANES added a new measure, the Affect Misattribution Procedure (AMP; Payne, Cheng, Govorun, & Stewart, 2005).

The AMP, like other implicit measures, assesses people's attitudes not by *asking* them directly but by inferring the attitudes from how the people respond to a series of symbols paired with racial stimuli. With the racial bias AMP, people are asked to indicate whether they find a Chinese character (letter) to be pleasant or unpleasant. Each character is preceded by a very brief presentation of a Black or a White face, with which it has been randomly paired. The name—Affect Misattribution Procedure—derives from the logic that people doing the task *misattribute* to the neutral stimulus (the Chinese character) the *affective* (evaluative) response they have to the racial stimulus. The extent to which a person is more likely to rate characters as pleasant when they are preceded by White rather than Black faces, and more likely to rate characters as unpleasant when they are preceded by Black faces, provides an index of implicit preference for Whites (obviously, the task will not work well for people who already know the meanings of Chinese letters).

What Chris Finn and I found, analyzing the ANES data for 2008, was that scores on AMP tasks taken in September and October were a reliable predictor of voting for John McCain or Barack Obama in November. Specifically, those who showed more anti-Black/pro-White bias on the AMP were significantly less likely to vote for the Black candidate, Obama, and more likely to vote for the White candidate, McCain. The size of these effects was approximately the same as the size for the explicit racial attitude measure. Most compellingly, the AMP measure of implicit bias was a reliable predictor of voting against Obama and for McCain even after statistically controlling for historically important vote choice variables like political party identification and ideology as well as voter race and explicit racial bias. Similar results were obtained by Payne, Krosnick, and colleagues (2010) using the ANES data and by others using IAT measures of implicit racial bias (Greenwald et al., 2009). The implicit bias may help to explain why, in an election year with a severe economic crisis, a deeply unpopular incumbent from the opposing party, an opponent who ran, at best, an inconsistent campaign, and a large voter registration advantage, Obama did not win by a larger margin.

Even with something as important and deliberative as presidential vote, and in a time that some have described as "postracial," prejudice appears to be operative on multiple levels. The racial attitude iceberg, with some bias clearly above the waterline, and more lurking in the murkier depths below, is still a problem. If people cannot put aside their racial biases in something as loaded with the functioning and symbolism of a free society as the election of a president, how can they be expected to do so reliably in their day-to-day and moment-to-moment interactions with others?

In conclusion, implicit stereotypes and prejudice have been well documented across many different experiments with a variety of samples. These biases have been shown to predict a range of discriminatory behaviors (see Greenwald et al., 2009; Jost et al., 2009, for reviews), although they are most likely to cause the most spontaneous types of behavior (Dovidio et al., 1997), like shooting under time pressure (Correll et al., 2002; Glaser & Knowles, 2008).

Implicit stereotyping is normal human cognition, and police are normal humans who have been demonstrated to exhibit spontaneous discriminatory behaviors (e.g., Correll, Park, Judd, Wittenbrink, Sadler, & Keesee, 2007; Eberhardt et al., 2004; Plant & Peruche, 2005). Police operate under conditions of uncertainty, dealing with people whose level of suspiciousness is ambiguous. This is reflected in the fact that the overwhelming majority of pedestrian stops result in no arrest or warning (e.g., Jones-Brown et al., 2010; OAGSNY 1999; SJPD, 2007). Police also often work under conditions of stress and pressure, which have been demonstrated to promote the use of stereotypes. Accordingly, police are no doubt influenced by racial, ethnic, age, gender, class, and other stereotypes in their judgments of suspiciousness and decisions to stop and search civilians. *Even if it is not being done deliberately, this is racial profiling—prior conceptions about race and crime are causing minorities to be regarded with greater suspicion.*

This is not to say that profiling caused by "explicit" stereotypes (i.e., those the holder has conscious awareness of) is necessarily *deliberate*. Police and others may be fully aware of stereotypes that they hold, work hard to not discriminate, but nevertheless have their judgments subtly influenced by their stereotypes. Having conscious awareness of a stereotype does not prevent it from influencing you, nor does it necessitate that you will act on it deliberately.

But *implicit* stereotypes are undetectable (through conscious introspection) and therefore all the more likely to have unintended effects, as demonstrated in the shooter research. It is the very *implicitness* of the stereotypes—the fact that they are not consciously accessible—that makes them particularly hard to avoid using. Like the bottom of an iceberg, they are hard to see, but they influence our movements and cause us to "bump" into others in a manner that can be destructive. Using our new sonar-like methods to "see" under the surface is a good start. We now better understand what we are dealing with and can start to take corrective measures. Such approaches will be discussed in Chapter 8, after we consider the effects of racial profiling, the case of profiling in counterterrorism, and the policy landscape.

CHAPTER 5

The Effects of Racial Profiling

Benefits and Costs

In 1999, when asked about racial profiling, Chief Bernard Parks of the Los Angeles Police Department gave a response that exemplifies the belief that using race as a basis for suspicion is rational: "It's not the fault of the police when they stop minority males or put them in jail. It's the fault of the minority males for committing the crime. In my mind, it is not a great revelation that, *if officers are looking for criminal activity, they're going to look at the kind of people who are listed on crime reports*" (Goldberg, 1999, emphasis added). Parks is African American. Some might argue that this gives his argument greater weight. However, my point is not to contend that Parks's comment reflected racial bias but rather that he subscribed to the view that police officers' use of race or ethnicity in deciding who to stop and search is a rational application of knowledge derived from crime reports. Implicit in this statement, "if officers are looking for criminal activity," is the belief that stopping minorities is an efficient and therefore effective way for police to spend their time because it will lead to the capture of more criminals (and seizure of more contraband).

The idea that racial profiling is efficient and effective has strong intuitive appeal and is the primary rationale offered to justify it. Targeting police attention and resources on those who are presumed to be most likely to be engaged in criminal activity (e.g., possessing weapons or drugs for use or sale) should lead to greater *incapacitation* of criminals, as well as disruption of drug trade and violent crime.

A related rationale is that profiling will have an enhanced *deterrent* effect on crime. The argument holds that the most likely offenders, detecting an increased probability of apprehension and sanction because their racial group is targeted, will cut back on their criminal activity. This belief is exemplified by Homer,

Louisiana, police chief Russell Mills's statement: "If I see three or four young black men walking down the street, I have to stop them and check their names. I want them to be afraid every time they see the police that they might get arrested" (Witt, 2009). To be fair, Chief Mills's statement is extreme and probably not one that would be widely endorsed. But it reflects a way of thinking.

The theory that racial profiling will deter crime effectively is less compelling on its face than the incapacitative theory. If one group has a higher offending rate and they are policed at a higher rate, that will almost certainly lead to more criminal captures, at least in the short term (but see mathematical simulations below for long-term effects). This relationship is simple. Deterrence, on the other hand, is a messy criminological concept both in theory and in practice, with expert estimates of its magnitude varying considerably (Levitt, 2002). Nevertheless, it is generally accepted that increases in enforcement cause decreases in offending for many crimes.

The problem with the application of deterrence theory to racial profiling, as will be discussed at greater length below, is that *racial profiling represents a special case of deterrence because there is no actual increase in enforcement, just a shift.* Consequently, if more attention is paid to one group, less will be paid to others. Unless the crime of interest is heavily concentrated in the targeted group, racial profiling could end up causing more crime.

With regard to both incapacitation and deterrence, the logic used to support racial profiling is grounded in the same resource constraint premise: Police have finite time and resources; if they can concentrate them on populations most likely to offend, they will more effectively mitigate crime. This chapter will confront the assumptions underlying this rationale.

ASSUMING THE EFFECTIVENESS OF RACIAL PROFILING

The effectiveness rationale is not confined to practitioners like Chief Parks. One of the world's most renowned criminologists, James Q. Wilson, used a *Wall Street Journal* column to go on the record in favor of profiling on the basis of its efficiency, asking rhetorically: "Black men are six to eight times more likely to commit violent crimes than are white men. When the police patrol the streets trying to prevent crime, should they stop white and black men at the same rate?" (Wilson & Higgins, 2002). As discussed in Chapter 1, the application of violent crime statistics to the kinds of crimes typically involved in racial profiling is problematic. But the quote illustrates the perception, even among criminological elites, that profiling is efficient.

The efficiency argument has also been made with regard to profiling in counterterrorism. In a *New York Times* op-ed titled "Let Them Profile Me," Indiana University professor of humanities and law Fedwa Malti-Douglas (2002) made the following argument, noting the seeming conflict of interest due to her Middle Eastern ethnicity: "There will be more Richard Reids and John Walker Lindhs, who will not be found through profiling. Yet it is a fact that the particular terrorist group sworn to our destruction, Al Qaeda, is made up largely of Middle Easterners. It is not unreasonable to direct increased attention to passengers with some connection to the Middle East." The logic of this argument with regard to the wisdom of focusing counterterrorism efforts primarily on Middle Eastern terrorist groups will be discussed further in Chapter 6. For the present purposes, this statement illustrates the support for the notion that it makes sense to focus enforcement resources on a particular ethnic group.

More formally, academic economists who study racial profiling (e.g., Borooah, 2001; Knowles et al., 2001) operate on theories and models that assume the stopping of people from groups with higher offending rates to be efficient. They refer to racial disparities in police stops and searches arising from accurate stereotypes as "statistical discrimination." This approach is based on Becker's (1957) influential theory that markets will reward rational actors—employers who hire the most effective staff, even if making those selections based on group stereotypes; and, by extension, police who stop those most likely to be guilty, even if making those selections based on group stereotypes, will be most effective.

Economists working in this area make the assumption that if minorities are stopped at a higher rate, but hit rates (e.g., contraband finds or arrests) are equal, then this is only "statistical discrimination" (and it is rational and acceptable). If hit rates are lower for minorities, economic theory holds that it reflects racial animus (prejudice)—minorities who are stopped are less likely to be arrested because they were stopped for the wrong reason (racial bias instead of reasonable suspicion). This is a reasonable and powerful insight, but it is incomplete. Hit rates could be lower not due to animus so much as an *inaccurate* stereotype—a stereotype that may be fully wrong, or directionally right while proportionally wrong. The stereotype with regard to the actual prevalence of some trait within a group is almost certain to be incorrect because of lack of complete information, the human tendency to overlook base rates, and illusory correlation (see Chapter 3). A "nonracist" (one with no ill feelings toward the minority group) could have overestimated the prevalence of the trait (criminality) and end up looking like a racist. Conversely, a "racist" (a bigoted person) could, by coincidence, behave in a fashion that is coincidentally calibrated to the "correct" stereotype (the proportional rate of offending) and not look like a racist.

Becker's theory also holds that markets will punish those who discriminate *irrationally*, or have a "taste for discrimination" (aka racial animus), because they will miss out on qualified talent. It is not clear that police who irrationally profile (i.e., profile based on inaccurate stereotypes) will be "punished" in the same way, so the extension of Becker's theory to racial profiling is problematic. The "costs" and "benefits" of discrimination in law enforcement are not the same as those in competitive business markets. In employment discrimination, it could be argued that when employers miss out on hiring a qualified minority applicant, the cost of this is offset for them because they are reaping the "benefit" of not having to interact with someone they are likely to find relatively unpleasant (because of their bigotry toward that person's group). In policing, the bias causes the police to have *more* interaction with minorities; if it is based on animus, it is a particularly oppressive variety. It is more likely that it is caused by the cognitive biases—stereotypes—described in the preceding chapters. This is why the social psychological distinction between the cognitive, affective, and motivational components of attitudes is valuable in understanding discrimination. To explain discrimination, we need more to choose from than rationality and bigotry. There is also unbigoted irrationality—judgments based on purely cognitive biases (stereotypes) that are inaccurate.

IT'S EFFECTIVE? ESTIMATING THE EFFECTIVENESS OF RACIAL PROFILING

In 1999, Harvard law professor Randall Kennedy published a cogent indictment of racial profiling, arguing in *The New Republic* that profiling violates basic American constitutional tenets and contributes to Black disenfranchisement and resentment. Notably, like others, Kennedy stipulated that racial profiling made sense on efficiency grounds. It was Kennedy's excellent essay that sparked my interest in the subject. His legal and moral arguments, like those of many of his colleagues (e.g., Alschuler, 2002; Banks, 2001, 2003), were compelling. But his readiness to concede that profiling is efficient caught my attention.

My initial insight was that if police are already profiling, it would be difficult, if at all possible, to determine its effectiveness because they would have systematically altered the criminal justice landscape. Specifically, profiling would, regardless of any actual differences in offending rates, cause minorities to be overrepresented in the criminal justice system (including prison); if minorities are stopped more *because* they are minorities (and Whites are therefore stopped less because they are White), more minority (and fewer White) criminals will be caught.

This distortion will have two effects that may result in a self-perpetuating cycle: Stereotypes of minorities as criminals will be reinforced by their overrepresentation in the criminal justice statistics; and those stereotypes will be used to further rationalize continued racial profiling. At the time of this insight, without yet having given the subject much thought, it was only vaguely donning on me that another effect was that, as more minority criminals and fewer White criminals were caught and incarcerated, their proportions in the *unincarcerated* populations would change—there would be fewer minority and more White criminals at large. Consequently, profiling would lead to a double distortion of the stereotype; it would be driving up the perception while driving down the reality (at least among those at large).

Because of this potential for distortion, I questioned the accuracy of the stereotypes that promoted the conclusion that profiling is efficient, and I worried that profiling would lead to a self-fulfilling prophecy, where police operate on a stereotype that they are continuously bolstering through that operation. I crafted a longish letter to this effect and sent it to the editor of *The New Republic*. Much to my surprise, the magazine published it.

Empowered by my letter-writing success, not satisfied with the solely rhetorical nature of my argument, and persistently nagged by the logical and empirical puzzle of the effectiveness of racial profiling, I set about trying to estimate the effect that profiling would have on incarceration rates for targeted groups and others. My primary objective was simply to illustrate how profiling itself can create racial disparities in incarceration rates. My secondary objective became to test the effectiveness claim. This may seem like a relatively simple and straightforward study to conduct, but that is not the case.

The basic premise of the claim that racial profiling promotes police effectiveness requires that the effectiveness is achieved through efficiency gains. Police have finite resources, so they cannot stop and search everyone for contraband—not that that would be acceptable to anyone. Accordingly, police normally use indicators of suspiciousness in deciding whom to stop and search. To the extent that the indicators are accurate (i.e., they really are related to and predictive of crime), a greater proportion of stops and searches will lead to arrests and seizures. In the absence of the ability to stop and search *more* people, stopping and searching people who are genuinely more suspicious is the best way to increase desired outcomes. If a particular minority group has a higher rate of offending, targeting that group for more stops and searches will yield more arrests and seizures, without an increase in resources expended.

In 1999, I set out to test these two possibilities: (1) that profiling *causes* racial disparities in criminal justice, and (2) that profiling is effective (leads to more captures given fixed resources). The obvious approach was to obtain criminal justice data on (a) different groups' offending rates; (b) the rates at which the groups are stopped and searched by the police, perhaps for a particular, manageable geographical region for which data were available; and (c) the rates at which they are arrested, convicted, and punished. From this I could calculate how many arrests (and/or convictions and sanctions) are achieved as a function of rates of criminality and profiling. Easy.

In fact, this was not achievable. The last item—rates at which different racial and ethnic groups are arrested, convicted, and punished—is attainable because our criminal justice system records and reports such data fairly reliably. The FBI and Bureau of Justice Statistics collect arrest data from virtually all local, state, and federal law enforcement agencies. The BJS also collects conviction and parole/incarceration data. But such data are not sufficient for the analyses I hoped to do. I also needed criminality rates for different groups and profiling rates.

Estimating criminality rates is much more problematic. As indicated previously, offending rates for typically profiled crimes like drug possession are not generally known. Arrest data are available, but those are confounded by racial profiling.[1] In other words, if minorities are already being stopped and searched at rates disproportionate to their offending—and we know this to be the case in many jurisdictions—then arrest rates will be inflated for them and therefore will not serve as accurate indices of offending. Survey data (Substance Abuse and Mental Health Services Administration, 1999) indicate similar rates of drug use among Whites and Blacks, but it remains possible that minorities are involved in more drug transportation and sales. Still, it is not feasible to generate reliable estimates of differential drug crime rates for different racial or ethnic groups to be used as parameters in a statistical model.

I also needed to have an estimate of the rate at which police were profiling, meaning the extent to which officers were making decisions to stop and search individuals based on their race or ethnicity, *above and beyond the direct indicators of suspiciousness or traffic violations.* The rates at which police stop and search members of different groups is increasingly available. In 1999, some, but few, departments systematically collected and reported data on the demographics of everyone who was stopped and searched. In the time since, and in part due to concerns and lawsuits over racial profiling, more departments have employed increasingly rigorous methods, including computer-aided dispatch (CAD) reporting systems wherein a computer file is opened automatically when a stop is registered by an officer, and all data fields, including the driver's (and often passengers') ostensible race/ethnicity, must be filled in. There are no guarantees that such systems will be consistently and reliably implemented, and there still appears to be a great deal of discretion in the reasons officers can provide for stops, as well as the dispositions of the stops, but this is a big step in the right direction.

However, merely knowing how many people from a given group are stopped is not sufficient for estimating the "rate" at which they are stopped, let alone the rate at which they are stopped on the basis of race. This is the *benchmark problem* discussed in Chapter 2, also known as a *base rate problem.* To calculate the rate of profiling, we need a denominator with which to divide the number of people stopped. This denominator would reflect the number of opportunities the police had to stop people from this group, and that can be defined in a number of ways with varying degrees of validity. The crudest denominator would be the number of people from that group in the population, and that would be decreasingly crude

---

1. We must also bear in mind that racial profiling applies to officer-initiated encounters, not calls for service (i.e., complaints or reports). Racial disproportions resulting from calls for service are more likely to result from either different offending rates or differences in tendencies by civilians to report people from one group or another.

if one could meaningfully limit that population to the geographical location in which the stops are made, assuming (and this is a problematic assumption) that people from outside of that location do not travel through it. Some analysts will use registered driver statistics to establish a base rate, if focusing on vehicle stops, and if data on race and ethnicity of licensed drivers in a given area are available.

A much less crude approach to establishing a base rate would be a survey of people transiting through the area of interest (possibly an interstate highway corridor). This in fact can be and has been done (Lamberth, 1994) but is extremely labor-intensive. Less crude still would be to have such a survey include precise information about the vehicles (year, make, condition, presence of tinted windows, observable violations like broken taillights—a common pretext for traffic stops), the drivers (presumed[2] race/ethnicity, gender, approximate age), passenger numbers and demographics, and, importantly, *behavior*. Behavior would include driving factors like speed and recklessness, but also driver and passenger actions, like frequent mirror glances. One can imagine how expensive a survey of this sort would be—it would require vehicle-based, moving survey takers, working in pairs, repeating circuits hundreds of times in multiple locations. The purpose would be to establish the rate at which drivers from different groups are present in the areas of study, but also to provide other information (like driving behavior) that should be taken into account when determining whether racially disproportionate stop rates are due to bias.

Information technology has made substantial gains since 1999, and so it is likely that roadside cameras could facilitate and standardize driver (and pedestrian) benchmarking procedures. A growing number of cities are using publicly placed crime surveillance cameras.

Even if roadside camera–based data had been available in 1999 for assessing driver characteristics and behaviors, this would not have allowed for an accurate assessment of the effects of racial profiling because offending rates (e.g., drug possession) are unknown, and group-based differences are also unknown. To know if profiling is effective, we would need to know if it is occurring in the context of real differences in offending or not, and how big those differences are.

In sum, in the absence of reliable estimates of offending rates and profiling rates, an assessment of the effects of profiling was not feasible. Other analysts had experienced the same frustration. The U.S. Congress's General Accounting Office (GAO, 2000a; now called the Government Accountability Office) and California's Legislative Analyst Office (LAO, 2002) reached similar conclusions about the inadequacy of available data to properly assess the state of racial

---

2. Observers cannot definitively ascertain a driver's "real" race or ethnicity, which may be multifaceted (e.g., biracial) or hard to discern. They can, however, do their best to report a category that patrol officers are likely to infer, which would be sufficient for the purposes of assessing profiling.

profiling, reflected even in the title of the GAO report: *Racial Profiling: Limited Data Available on Motorist Stops.*

SIMULATING THE EFFECTS OF RACIAL PROFILING

Without being able to calculate the real effects that real profiling had had on real criminal captures—in terms of both increasing captures and creating disparities—I set about to do the next best thing, to mathematically *simulate* what the effects would be. Simulation has an obvious disadvantage relative to working with real data—results of the analyses cannot be said to directly describe what has already happened in the real world. But this approach had a major advantage; it allowed for more precise examinations because I was able to test a broad array of scenarios, manipulating the degree to which police were profiling, and the magnitude of the difference in offending rates between groups.

These simulations and their results are described in detail in a report published in the *Journal of Policy Analysis and Management* (Glaser, 2006), but I will summarize the methods and findings here. The basic approach is to develop a reasonable mathematical formula (or formulas) to describe the presumed relationship among variables (e.g., profiling rate, criminality rate, and criminal capture rate) and then to use that formula to calculate the results, in this case, in terms of how many criminals are incarcerated

The point of the simulations was to project the percent of the population that is incarcerated as a function of the percent of that population that is stopped by the police in a given time period and the percent of that population that is engaged in criminal activity (e.g., carrying illicit drugs). I focused on incarceration because it most directly relates to the intended incapacitative goal and common effect of drug interdiction—catching the criminals and taking them out of commission by incarcerating them. Not all captured drug criminals get incarcerated, but millions in the United States do (Western, 2006). Drug treatment alternative programs could be a different outcome of arrest, but they are still rare. Some convicts receive probation, but this dramatically raises their probability of future incarceration.

Before describing the math behind this simulation approach, it is important to note that I will represent this in a very abstract, stripped-down way, recognizing that the real world is not so simple. For example, all stops of criminals do not result in incarcerations; all criminals are not always doing something illegal when they are stopped and searched. The purpose of the simulation is to derive a best approximation of what could actually happen.

This approach is also not meant to imply that police are wantonly stopping and searching citizens without any race-neutral basis for suspicion. When police decide to stop and search drivers and pedestrians in pursuit of contraband, they make those determinations based on multiple factors. When race is one of those factors, that is racial profiling. To the extent that a suspect's race (or ethnicity) pushes him or her above a threshold of suspicion, triggering a stop and/or search, that has the functional effect of race *causing* the intervention. Put another way, *if race is part of the profile*, given two individuals, one White and one Black, who are otherwise identical in possessing attributes in the profile (e.g., young, male, wearing sunglasses, driving 1 mile per hour under the speed limit), the Black individual is more likely to get stopped and searched. In this sense, the simulation to be described is meant to represent *only the probabilistic part of policing with regard to suspect race*—the extent to which a suspect's race *raises the probability* that he will be stopped or searched. In practice, a higher probability of satisfying the profile translates into more stops for minorities.

The Math

The formula I developed was deliberately simple and straightforward, and I will present and describe it shortly. In presenting this formula, I run a substantial risk of losing a big part of my audience; some people (maybe some of my colleagues) will find it too simplistic, and others will find it intimidating and alienating. To the former group, all I can say is that, in mathematical modeling, parsimony is a virtue. The model is not meant to describe the totality of profiling or policing, only the effect of race being a basis of suspicion. To the latter group, I say, please bear with me; I will try to explain it clearly. You do not need to follow the math to follow the basic idea and to understand the results of the simulation.

The purpose of the formula is to calculate how many people in a given population (e.g., a racial group) will be incarcerated at a given time as a function of the following: (1) what proportion of that group was already incarcerated before that time; (2) what proportion of that group is engaged in crime (e.g., carrying illicit drugs or weapons at a given time); and (3) what proportion of that group the police stop in a given time period. This relationship can be stated mathematically as follows:

$$I_t = I_{t-1} + \sigma(C - I_{t-1}) - \rho I_{t-1}$$

In this formula, I_t represents the proportion of the population that is incarcerated at time t.[3] That is what we are solving for. This will of course first and foremost be a function of how many people from that group were already incarcerated prior to that time (I_{t-1}). Then we will want to add to that everyone who got captured since time $t - 1$. So, to I_{t-1} we add the criminals who have been captured

---

3. Time t can just be thought of as any time of interest, but the model usually treats it as a point after which a new rate of profiling (or, in some scenarios, no profiling) has begun.

since. That will be a function of how many people in the population at large are criminals and how many are stopped (simplistically, the model assumes that criminals who are stopped are incarcerated—see description of assumptions, below). To calculate that, we need a variable for the *stop rate* (the proportion of the population that is stopped during a given time period). For that we use σ (the Greek letter sigma), and we allow it to range from zero (nobody stopped) to one (everybody stopped). The stop rate (σ) is then multiplied by the proportion of the population that is "criminals" (C), in this case, the proportion who would be carrying contraband (drugs, weapons) at a given time.[4] For example, if 10% of a population is carrying contraband and 5% of the population is stopped, half a percent (0.5%) of that total population will get caught.

However, before we calculate the number of new captures, we need to acknowledge that some of the criminals have already been incarcerated, and so they are not "available" to be captured until they are released from prison. I_{t-1} is the proportion of this group who have already been incarcerated, so we will subtract that from C to get the *at large* criminal population ($C - I_{t-1}$). That is the quotient by which we will multiply σ.

Finally, we have a "re-entry rate," ρ (rho). This is the rate at which prisoners from the group leave prison and re-enter the at-large population (or die in prison and are replaced). We multiply it by I_{t-1}, the incarceration rate from the previous period, because that is the pool from which prisoners will re-enter. The re-entry rate is always set to be the same for both groups in the simulation, and to be the same as the overall stop rate. The re-entry rate serves as a sort of release valve. Without it, incarceration rates could continue to accumulate until they met the criminality rate, a very unrealistic condition.

This gives us the equation we use to simulate the effect of stop rates on incarceration rates: Incarcerations now are a function of incarcerations to date plus the rate at which at-large criminals are stopped minus the rate at which previously incarcerated criminals re-enter the at-large population.

What does this have to do with racial profiling? So far, this just sounds like a simulation of what happens when you stop a population at a particular rate. The profiling part of the simulation comes in when I execute this equation for two different groups simultaneously and add up their incarcerations. Specifically, we consider that there are two subpopulations: a minority group and everyone else.

---

4. It is tempting to think of C as the *offending* rate instead of the *criminality* rate because even those who are criminally inclined are unlikely to be offending at all times, and so will not necessarily be caught if stopped and searched. However, offending rate, like *crime* rate, is a different variable—it represents how many offenses are committed. Offending rate could therefore be higher for one group not because a higher proportion of the group is criminally inclined, but because a small number each commit many offenses. Criminality rate reflects the proportion of the population who are inclined to commit crime, but for the sake of this simulation, it can be thought of as the proportion at any given time who are engaged in a crime that would be detectable in a traffic or pedestrian stop.

In the simulations, the minority group is typically 20% of the population. I ran a wide array of simulations assuming many different criminality and stop-rate scenarios. The two groups are linked in the sense that the overall stop rate is fixed at 5% per time period (1 out of every 20 people are stopped). Therefore, if one group is stopped more, the other group has to be stopped less. For example, if the minority group is being stopped at a higher rate, such as 15%, the majority group has to be stopped at a lower rate, 2.5% (15% of 20% + 2.5% of 80% = 5%).

This interdependence of the two groups' stop rates is the crux of the efficiency test. To test whether profiling, by targeting high-crime groups, is efficient, we have to assume that there is no overall increase in police resources. Accordingly, the overall number of stops (percent of the total population) has to be held constant. If stops of one group go up, stops of others have to go down.

Assumptions of the Model

Before discussing the results of the simulations, it is important to lay out the assumptions of the model used. Inherent in the equation presented above are a number of obvious assumptions. But there are some additional assumptions that must be made to use the equation to simulate the effects of racial profiling. For the most part these assumptions are made in order to keep the model clear and parsimonious—explaining as much as possible with as few variables as possible. I will explain why these assumptions are necessary and why, even though they may be unrealistic, they do not undermine the validity of the findings.

The model is not meant to depict actual criminal justice statistics. It is intentionally simplistic and idealized in order to isolate the effects of profiling in its simplest form—police stopping people on the basis of race.

Assumption 1: Every criminal who is stopped gets incarcerated. This is obviously not the case in reality. "Criminals" are not engaged in crime at all times, so they may not be carrying contraband or other evidence of crime at the time of the stop. Nevertheless, we can view variable C as representing not so much the proportion of the group that is *always* criminal but rather the proportion that would be engaged in detectable crime (e.g., possessing illicit drugs) at any given moment. Still, even people who get caught do not always get arrested, let alone convicted and incarcerated. I could have added to the model another variable that reflects the rate at which criminals who are stopped are arrested, but any racial differences in this rate were not the purpose of the analysis. By assuming all stops of criminals lead to incarcerations, this can just represent the proportion of stops that do lead to incarcerations, without addressing other sources of racial disparities in incarceration rates. In sum, making this assumption allows us to generate projections of incarceration rates that, while not intended to be real, do serve to depict how racial profiling can affect, if only partially, incarceration rates.

Assumption 2: There are no other racial bias effects in the criminal justice sequence from stop to incarceration and release. This assumption, like assumption 1, is not meant to imply that this is the case in the real world. There is ample correlational and experimental evidence, discussed in previous chapters, that minorities receive harsher treatment. However, in order to *isolate* the effects of the use of race in the decision to stop on efficiency and disparities in criminal captures, this assumption is necessary. To be sure, racial biases in other stages of criminal processing are not irrelevant—they will cause disparate outcomes that will reinforce the stereotypes that promote racial profiling. That too, however, is beyond the scope of this analysis.

Assumption 3: Police do not update their profiles over time based on changing hit rates. As police capture and deter more minority criminals because of racial profiling, the crime rate among the at-large minority group should go down. Consequently, hit rates (finding contraband) would go down among minorities stopped. This could cause police to reassess their stereotypes and change their stop rates. This would be consistent with economic theories that expect "markets" and other human systems to equilibrate. Economists operating in the general equilibrium modeling framework (e.g., Knowles, Persico, & Todd, 2001) argue that such trends will seek an equilibrium—that police and criminals, being rational actors seeking to minimize costs and maximize gains, will adjust their behaviors to adapt to these changing realities. Specifically, if police detect (somehow) that minorities commit more crime, they will pay more attention to minorities (racial profiling). If police target minorities, minority criminals will commit less crime (deterrence). If police detect that fewer minorities are committing crime, they will adjust their beliefs and their behavior accordingly. The system will continually seek an equilibrium wherein police are acting in a manner that will maximize captures. However, given the social psychological understanding of how stereotyping works (e.g., resisting change), and recognizing that stereotypes are likely reinforced by the disproportions in incarceration rates that result from profiling, I think it is unlikely that police and criminal behavior would equilibrate effectively, let alone promptly. Furthermore, psychologists have demonstrated that people are not particularly sensitive to real base rates (Kahneman & Tversky, 1973) and tend to better remember information that is consistent with their prior beliefs (Lord et al., 1979), so stereotypes are unlikely to change. To the extent that profiling, even if having diminishing returns, continues to focus on minorities, minorities will continue to be overrepresented among those arrested and incarcerated, helping to perpetuate the stereotype.

Assumption 4: Police in these simulations are stopping people at random, but at varying rates depending on their minority or majority status. This is, fortunately, not the case in most policing, with the exception of security screening, but even in that case, searches are not *solely* random. Police stop people based on a number of factors, including responding to a call for service, responding to a "be on the lookout" call or "all points bulletin," traffic violations, and race-neutral bases for suspicion based on their own discretion, such as age, gender, time of day and location, type of car or dress, furtive movements, and so forth. The present simulations are intended to model only the *probabilistic* component of decisions to stop arising from driver or pedestrian race, above and beyond all these other reasons for stops. In this sense, the simulations depict the effect of just the racial component of the decision, even if it is part of a compound profile, on incarceration rates. The simulations should not be taken to imply in any way that police are arbitrarily stopping people solely on the basis of race.

Police in some jurisdictions may end up stopping members of some racial or ethnic groups at higher rates than others without it reflecting any racial bias whatsoever. If one group has a higher offending rate, and its members exhibit the relevant race-neutral indicators (bases for suspicion) in a manner proportional to their offending, they will be stopped at a higher rate. But this alone will not cause them to be captured in a manner that is disproportional to their offending rate.

Running the Simulations

In order to simulate the effects of different rates of profiling as a function of different rates of criminality, I applied the relationships in the above equation (solving for incarcerations at a given time; I_t) to a computer spreadsheet, which allowed me to readily calculate the total incarceration rate (combined for the two groups, meant to represent the whole population). The next step was to generate many iterations of this to simulate the effect of different policing scenarios *over time*. In each iteration, the spreadsheet drew a new starting incarceration rate (I_{t-1}) from the previous iteration's resulting incarceration rate. In this manner the simulation reflected that the criminality rate in the at-large population changes as a result of how many criminals were captured in the preceding period. This was iterated repeatedly, until the trends reached a steady state—the groups' incarceration rates hit their asymptotes, and further iterations did not change the results.

In the initial simulations, I set total stop rate per epoch as 0.05 (5% of the population is stopped during that period). *Profiling* is simulated by changing the proportions that are stopped between groups, so that it is always 5% of the *total* population that is stopped. Therefore, if the stop rate for the minority group goes up, the stop rate for the majority group must go down—to keep the total rate at 5%. Similarly, I kept the overall criminality rate constant, at 10%, and varied the relative rates. Holding *total* criminality rate and *total* stop rate constant allowed for meaningful comparisons across scenarios, isolating the effects of changes in *relative* criminality rate and *relative* stop rate. Specifically, if *overall* criminality and stop rates are always 10% and 5%, respectively, then any differences in capture rates across scenarios will be a function solely of the *relative* rates of criminality, the *relative* rates of stops (profiling), or the interaction of the two. Consequently, we can test if profiling (stopping one group at a higher rate) promotes efficiency (more captures, holding total stops constant). We can also test if profiling causes disproportionate minority incarcerations regardless of differences in criminality.

To be more concrete, with this approach we could compare capture rates when the minority group is stopped at a rate of 12.5% (12,500 out of every 100,000 individuals are stopped per period) and the majority group is stopped at a rate of 3.125% (3,125 out of every 100,000) with a scenario where both groups are stopped at a 5% rate.[5] Or, we could compare scenarios where the stop rates are the same (5%), but the criminality rates vary (e.g., both at 10% vs. a 4:1 ratio of 25% and 6.25%). The actual simulations looked at these and many other scenarios, including those where there are criminality differences *and* stop rate differences. The goals of the simulations are to look for general trends in terms of overall criminal captures as well as group-based disparities, but also to conduct a "sensitivity analysis" to determine the conditions under which captures are greatest and discrepancies are least.

SIMULATION RESULTS

The primary finding from the simulations is that profiling (i.e., different rates of stops for the two groups), regardless of criminality rates (even when they are equal), in and of itself exacerbates (or creates) disparities in incarceration rates that exceed any disparities in criminality rates. In other words, if the police are stopping members of different groups at different rates, *based on their group membership,* the group that is stopped at a higher rate will represent a share of the incarcerated population that is greater than their share of the general and criminal populations. This is depicted in Figure 5.1, which represents a scenario in which the minority and majority groups have the same criminality rate (10%), with half of the criminals (5% of the total population) already incarcerated prior to the beginning of profiling. The police stop minority group members at a rate four times that of the majority, 12.5% and 3.125%, respectively, for a total stop rate of 5%. Even though the two groups have the same offending rate, the profiling creates a disparity in their incarceration rates that grows over time until the trends level off to a steady state.

In addition to the disparity becoming increasingly pronounced, the overall capture rate is being affected too. While the minority capture rate goes up due to the increased attention from the police, the majority capture rate declines from the 5% (50% of all criminals) status quo, due to decreased police attention. Because the majority, by definition, makes up a larger share of the population, their trend is most influential, pulling the overall trend downward. The result is

5. With the 20%/80% minority/majority split, these stop rates yield the requisite total stop rate of 5%.

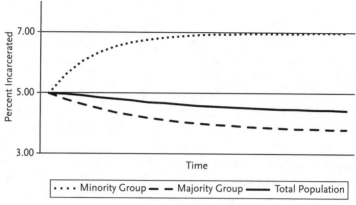

Figure 5.1

Effects of profiling on incarceration rates over time, when groups have equal criminality rates.

Note: Adapted from Glaser (2006). The minority group is 20% of the total population, and the majority group is the remaining 80%. In this scenario, both groups have the same criminality rate (10%), and half of the criminals have been incarcerated at the start (reflecting no profiling in the prior period), but the minority group is stopped at a rate (12.5% per epoch) that is four times the stop rate (3.125%) of the majority. The overall stop rate is 5%.

that, because a relatively small share of majority group criminals are being caught, the overall capture rate suffers, with approximately 44% of criminals being incarcerated at steady state, relative to 50% prior to profiling. The numbers chosen for these simulations are somewhat arbitrary, so they should not be taken literally, but they do represent the general trend that one should expect if profiling occurs. It has the potential to undermine effectiveness by reducing criminal captures, in addition to having the discriminatory effect of creating racial disparities. This is on top of the discriminatory effect of interfering with the lives of a disproportionate number of *innocent* minorities.

If the police are stopping members of the two groups at equal rates, all else being equal, they will be incarcerated at rates that are proportional to their criminality. If they have the same criminality rate, equal proportions of them will be incarcerated consistently over time. If one group is stopped at a higher rate (let us say double), that group will be incarcerated at that higher rate (double the rate of the other group), but overall captures will be lower than they would be if no profiling were occurring. This is a general case, not just limited to the simulation shown here. *Profiling in the absence of criminality differences undermines criminal incapacitation and creates criminal justice disparities.*

How does Profiling Reduce Capture Rates?

If police divert time and resources to stopping (and searching, etc.) members of a minority group, given that such resources are finite, they will stop fewer members of other groups. As greater numbers of minorities are incarcerated (as a function of stopping more of them), their *at-large* criminal population will decline, while the at-large criminal population for the majority will increase, because those re-entering from prison are not being taken off the streets at the same rate. If police persist in profiling the minority, their hit rates (contraband finds or arrests per stop) will decline. Hit rates will increase for the majority group. Over time, police will be stopping more people from a group with declining offending rates while stopping fewer people from a group with increasing offending rates. That is inherently inefficient.

A useful analogy is to think of a family that goes fishing. There are two fishing places near their home. They have heard that people catch more fish at Duck Pond than at Mountain Lake. So they fish every day of the summer at Duck Pond. They fish Duck Pond so much that they catch fewer and fewer fish. Why? Because they are "fishing the pond dry." They are depleting the fish population in the pond. Meanwhile, at Mountain Lake, the relatively neglected fish population is flourishing. Like all analogies, this one is imperfect for a number of reasons. It does, however, capture the core reason that profiling can be inefficient; the very behavior of the police (or fishermen) affects the population they are seeking to capture and renders their future outcomes different. At the same time, the behavior may be reinforced. The family did, after all, catch a lot of fish at Duck Pond. They just did not know how many fish they were missing out on at Mountain Lake. Because people are wired to perceive, construe, and remember information that is consistent with their prior beliefs, all the caught fish at Duck Pond probably reinforced the belief that it was the best place to fish. This may be true of outcomes of stops of minorities as well.

We have seen that racial profiling can have counterproductive effects on criminal capture rates if the stereotype is wrong—if both groups have the same criminality rate. What if profiling occurs in the presence of unequal criminality rates—what if police are more frequently stopping a minority group that actually has a higher criminality rate? This is a more direct test of the efficiency hypothesis because that hypothesis is, after all, based on the presumption that those targeted for profiling have a higher offending rate. Only true racist authoritarians would advocate profiling a group they do not believe to be offending at a higher rate.

I ran hundreds of simulations, representing hundreds of different combinations of profiling and criminality rates. Results from a small but informative selection of scenarios are presented in Table 5.1. In this table, all scenarios involve a 4:1 minority-to-majority criminality ratio, in order to show what happens when the minority's criminality rate is dramatically higher than the majority's. These are conditions under which racial profiling would have the potential to be justified on efficiency grounds.

The first row of statistics in the table indicates what would happen if there was no profiling—both groups are stopped at a rate of 5% per epoch. Assuming they had been, to that point, incarcerated at rates that were proportional to their criminality—four times as many minorities per capita (12.5% of the minority population) than majority group members (3.125%)—that will continue to be

Table 5.1 SIMULATED EFFECTS OF PROFILING RATES
ON INCARCERATION RATES

Profiling Rate			Outcomes[c]				
Percent Stopped per Cycle		Stop Rate Ratio (Min: Maj)	Percent of *Group* Incarcerated (% of *Criminals* Incarcerated)				Ratio of Percents Incarcerated (Min:Maj)
Minority[a]	Majority[b]		Minority	Majority	Total		
5.00	5.00	1:1	12.50 (50.0)	3.13 (50.0)	5.00 (50.0)		4.0:1
8.33	4.17	2:1	15.62 (62.5)	2.84 (45.5)	5.40 (54.0)		5.5:1
10.71	3.57	3:1	17.04 (68.2)	2.60 (41.7)	5.49 (54.9)		6.6:1
12.50	3.13	4:1	17.86 (71.4)	2.40 (38.5)	5.49 (54.9)		7.4:1
13.89	2.78	5:1	18.38 (73.5)	2.23 (35.7)	5.46 (54.6)		8.2:1
15.00	2.50	6:1	18.75 (75.0)	2.08 (33.3)	5.42 (54.2)		9.0:1
16.67	2.08	8:1	19.23 (76.9)	1.84 (29.4)	5.32 (53.2)		10.5:1
20.00	1.25	16:1	20.00 (80.0)	1.25 (20.0)	5.00 (50.0)		16.0:1
20.83	1.04	20:1	20.16 (80.6)	1.08 (17.2)	4.89 (48.9)		18.7:1
25.00	0.00		20.83 (83.3)	0.00 (0.0)	4.17 (41.7)		

Adapted from Glaser (2006). Scenarios represented in this table assume 4:1 criminality ratios and 1:4 population ratios (minority-to-majority ratios).
a. The minority group constitutes 20% of the total population and has a criminality rate of 25%.
b. The majority group constitutes 80% of the total population and has a criminality rate of 6.25%.
c. The "percent of group incarcerated" statistics reflect the percent after repeated cycles and the trends have reached their steady states. Numbers in parentheses are the percent of the *criminal* population that would be incarcerated.

the case for as long as the 1:1 stop rate ratio persists.[6] This will result in 5% of the total population being incarcerated and 50% of the criminal population being incarcerated. This scenario offers a good baseline (no profiling) against which to compare results from other profiling scenarios.

We see, looking down the rows of the table, that if greater attention is paid to the minority group (given that it has a higher criminality rate), higher capture rates are obtained, *to a point*. A 2:1 profiling rate yields a total criminal capture rate of 54% (compared with 50%), and 3:1 and 4:1 profiling rates yield almost 55%. While these are not dramatically higher rates (a 10% increase in captures), they do reflect some real gains. However, there is a troubling cost: Even at a relatively "moderate" profiling rate of 2:1, the ratio of group populations *incarcerated* is disproportionate to the criminality rate ratio. Specifically, after profiling at a 2:1 rate, 15.62% of minority and 2.84% of majority group members become

6. This relies on the use of a re-entry that is equal to the stop rate, which, as described earlier, is necessary to compare the different scenarios because under these conditions only criminality rates and stop rates will affect incarceration rates.

incarcerated, for a 5.5:1 ratio, outstripping the 4:1 criminality ratio. As the profiling ratio increases, this disparity gets even more pronounced. At the seemingly "optimal" (in terms of overall captures) profiling rate of 4:1, the minority-to-majority incarceration rate ratio is 7.44:1, nearly double the actual criminality rate ratio.

This pattern poses a nuanced moral quandary. Some might say, "If it's criminals who are being caught, it's their problem." It is, indeed, difficult to argue that the rights of the guilty minority criminals who are caught are being infringed—they are guilty, after all. There is, however, another side to this coin: There is a clear, and unjust, privilege afforded to majority-group criminals, who are able to commit crime with relative impunity. Furthermore, as will be discussed later in this chapter, the destabilizing effects on the minority community arising from a high proportion of its population being incarcerated, and all of the disadvantages attendant to that, pose a profound problem.

Returning to Table 5.1, we find that, in addition to the criminal justice disparities that profiling creates, it is evident that the gains in criminal captures from profiling diminish and can even become losses when the profiling is disproportionate to the criminality, just as they are counterproductive in all cases when there is no criminality difference (e.g., as shown in Figure 5.1). At the extreme, if only minority group members are stopped (25% per epoch, to achieve the required 5% overall stop rate), then 20.83% of minority and 0% of majority group members would be incarcerated, but *only 41.7% of criminals would be incarcerated*. Similarly, a 20:1 profiling rate yields an overall capture rate of 48.9% of criminals (below the 50% achieved without profiling) but a minority-to-majority incarceration ratio of 18.7:1, a greater than fourfold distortion of the criminality ratio. Employing a somewhat different mathematical approach, Press (2008) reached similar conclusions, that "strong profiling" is suboptimal.

One of the surprising generalities of the simulations is that police can attain the same overall capture rates with a more moderate profiling regime. For example, in the case where the criminality ratio is 4:1, overall criminal captures reach 54.9% with a profiling rate of 4:1 but also with a rate of 3:1. In the latter case, it takes a few more cycles to reach the peak, but there is less distortion of incarceration disparity (6.6:1 vs. 7.4:1). This more moderate regime would also result in fewer stops of innocent minorities—although still at a higher rate than for the majority. While this conclusion is interesting, and may serve to help law enforcement agencies encourage moderation, it should not be taken as an endorsement of racial profiling. Even the more moderate approach yields troubling racial disproportions in incarceration rates.

The simulation results presented in Table 5.1 are limited to scenarios in which the minority group (20% of the population) has a criminality rate (25%) four times that of the majority group (6.25%). They are also limited to scenarios in which the minority group is profiled, as well as the one, baseline scenario in which both groups are stopped at the same rate. It is entirely possible that, in reality, minorities who have a lower criminality rate will get profiled. This was clearly the case, for example, in the disproportionate stops of Black women by U.S. Customs agents in the late 1990s (GAO, 2000b). Nevertheless, no mathematical simulations are necessary to demonstrate the obvious—that profiling a group that has a lower criminality rate will (1) be inefficient and (2) cause disparities in incarceration rates that are disproportionate to the criminality rates.

That profiling *causes* racial differences in criminal justice outcomes that are disproportionate to racial differences in offending is what Harcourt (2004, 2007) refers to as a "ratchet effect." Harcourt, in his 2007 book critiquing "actuarial" methods in criminal justice, developed mathematical models to illustrate that, even

> [u]nder normal conditions, the use of accurate prediction instruments will have a distortive effect on the target population, a distortion that operates as a ratchet. The distortion occurs when successful profiling produces a supervised population that is disproportionate to the distribution of the offending population. (p. 28)

These disproportions then cause the kinds of instability that promotes more crime among minorities, and the kinds of stereotypes that further promote profiling, thus *ratcheting* up the problem. Harcourt argues, and I agree, that ratcheting occurs beyond decisions to stop and search, all the way through sentencing and parole. But we can see from the simulations presented here that profiling alone, even if we assume an absence of bias in subsequent phases of criminal justice, causes racial disproportions in outcomes and can serve to undermine criminal incapacitation by reducing overall capture rates.

WHAT ABOUT DETERRENCE?

Law enforcement is intended to do more than just incapacitate criminals; it is also meant to *deter* them. Deterrence theory holds that criminals are sensitive to changes in the "cost" of crime; to the extent that those inclined to commit crime perceive an increase in the cost of crime, they will commit fewer crimes—they will be deterred. The cost of crime is, for the most part, a function of the severity of punishment and the likelihood of being apprehended. Accordingly, a complete analysis of the effects of racial profiling would include consideration of deterrent effects. Advocates of racial profiling would argue that, if a particular group is responsible for more than its share of crime, targeting that group will have an especially potent deterrent effect. Like the incapacitation hypothesis, this has strong intuitive appeal.

I have to admit that when I was first working on simulations of racial profiling, I was resistant to including deterrence in the model. My reasoning was that racial profiling poses a *special case* with regard to deterrence because it is not simply that there is greater enforcement but that there is a shift in enforcement. If that shift is toward one group, and the police resources are held constant, that means fewer resources (e.g., fewer stops) dedicated to other groups. My naive sense was that, if deterrence was operative, this would be a wash—targeted groups would commit less crime, and untargeted groups would commit more. Fortunately, I added deterrence to the model anyway, and the results were illuminating.

In order to include deterrence in the model, I first needed to establish a reasonable estimate of the strength of the deterrent effect. Without capture and punishment being a certainty, deterrence will not be complete, so we know that a deterrent effect is only going to be partial. In fact, police can typically patrol only a fraction of a given population at any given time, so deterrence is necessarily limited. Furthermore, the assumption that criminals are perfectly "rational actors," dispassionately calculating the costs and benefits of their actions relative to alternatives, is problematic, at best (Caulkins & MacCoun, 2003; MacCoun, 1993). Consequently, estimates of the magnitude of deterrent effects will necessarily be rough.

Careful attempts to tease apart the incapacitative and deterrent effects of enforcement (e.g., Kuziemko & Levitt, 2004; Levitt, 1998; Spelman, 1994, 2005) have revealed that estimates vary considerably across crime types, populations, and study methods. Nevertheless, in consultation with leading experts, I triangulated on a deterrence parameter of –0.2. This coefficient—what economists call a *supply elasticity*—indicates that for a single unit increase in cost of crime (e.g., probability of capture), there will be a one-fifth reduction in offending. For the present model, that could be thought of in the following terms: A 10% increase in stops would yield a 2% decrease in offending. Whether the specific elasticity coefficient employed in this model is a precise representation of the real world is not crucial, as long as it is negative (more enforcement leads to less crime), and within the ballpark of well-documented estimates.

In order to incorporate deterrence in the simulations, I allowed the criminality (C) coefficients to be sensitive to the stop rate (σ) so that, as the stop rate increased for a given group, the criminality rate decreased.[7] The general

---

7. This adjustment to the criminality rate (C) had to reflect the *change* in probability of capture *relative to the prior stop rate*. Accordingly, a new, deterrence-affected criminality rate (C_i) was calculated using the following formula: $C_i = C_1 + e(\sigma_i - \sigma_1)$, where C_1 represents the criminality rate when both groups are stopped at the same rate, e is the elasticity rate, σ_i is the profiling stop rate (the rate tested for that group in that scenario), and σ_1 is the stop rate when both groups are stopped at the same rate. In this way, if there is no profiling, then $\sigma_i = \sigma_1$ and $C_i = C_1$. But if there *is* profiling (if $\sigma_i > \sigma_1$), then, because e is negative, that group's criminality rate is reduced. Because the stop rates are inversely related for the two groups in the simulation (as one goes up, the other has to go down, to maintain an overall stop rate of 5%), when the profiled group's C_i goes down, the other group's goes up—they commit more crime.

result was that, across all scenarios in which there was profiling, criminal capture rates were lower than they were without deterrence included in the model. Table 5.2 provides some examples, building on the results shown in Table 5.1 with regard to the total percent of criminals captured as a function of profiling rate.

As can be seen in Table 5.2, when deterrence is incorporated as a factor in the simulations, the percent of criminals who are incarcerated (incapacitated) is, with one exception, always lower than when deterrence is not factored in. The one exception is, unremarkably, when there is no profiling, and so there is no differential deterrent effect. The second and third columns of the table report the percent of the total (both groups combined) criminal population incarcerated as a function of varying degrees of profiling (column 1) for the 4:1 criminality ratio presented in Table 5.1. This is where the minority group is specified to have a criminality rate four times that of the majority group. The results in the third column of Table 5.2 show that the gains of profiling would be even more modest if criminals are responsive to stop rates (i.e., if deterrence is operative). Furthermore, the counterproductive effects (capture rates lower than without profiling) are evident at more moderate rates of profiling.

The fourth and fifth columns of Table 5.2 represent the effects of profiling with and without factoring in deterrence for a less extreme difference in offending

Table 5.2 SIMULATED EFFECTS OF PROFILING RATES (STOP RATE RATIO) ON INCARCERATION RATES *WITH* VERSUS *WITHOUT* DETERRENCE

	Percent of Criminals Incarcerated			
	4:1 Criminality Ratio		2:1 Criminality Ratio	
Stop Rate Ratio (Min:Maj)	*Without* Deterrence	*With* Deterrence	*Without* Deterrence	*With* Deterrence
1:1	50.0	50.0	50.0	50.0
2:1	54.0	53.8	51.1	50.9
3:1	54.9	54.3	50.5	49.9
4:1	54.9	54.0	49.5	48.5
5:1	54.6	53.3	48.3	47.0
6:1	54.2	52.5	47.2	45.6
8:1	53.2	51.0	45.3	43.0
16:1	50.0	46.4	40.0	36.4
20:1	48.9	44.9	38.4	34.4
25:0	41.7	35.0	27.8	21.1

Note: Scenarios represented in this table assume 1:4 minority-to-majority population ratios. The deterrence coefficient used in these calculations was −0.2. The "percent of criminals incarcerated" statistics reflect the percent incarcerated out of all criminals in the population, after the trends have reached their steady states.

(2:1 instead of 4:1). Here we see that including deterrence has a more dramatic downward pressure on criminal capture rates, yielding mostly counterproductive (inefficient) effects.

Why would deterrent effects render profiling less efficient? Deterrence usually causes people to not commit crime, thus reducing criminality. But racial profiling is a special case with regard to deterrence because it involves not a net increase of enforcement but a redistribution of enforcement. As minorities are targeted, sensing a greater risk in committing crime, their criminality (at least the rate-of-offending part of it) goes down.[8] Likewise, as majority group members are overlooked, they sense a decreased risk and commit more crime. Because more attention is being paid to a group (minority) whose offending has declined, and less attention is being paid to a group (majority) whose offending has gone up, the net effect is that fewer offenders are caught.

We can call this *reverse deterrence*—the dilution of law enforcement for non-profiled groups causes them to commit *more* crime. Because nonprofiled groups tend to be majority groups, the net effect of reverse deterrence can be a decrease in captures and an increase in crime.

REVERSE DETERRENCE: THE HIDDEN COST OF RACIAL PROFILING

In my models, I have assumed that the size of the deterrence elasticity would be the same for minority and majority groups. Because the two groups' stop rates are interdependent (they must yield an overall stop rate of 5% per period), and because the majority group is larger, the deterrent (or reverse deterrent) effect will be more diffuse on the majority group. As a result, reverse deterrence causes an overall drop in capture rates, and thereby more criminals *at large* and more crime, but it does not (in my models) raise the overall *criminality rate*. However, Harcourt, in his analyses (2004, 2007), notes that the efficiency of profiling is dependent on the relative elasticities of the two groups; more specifically, if "the targeted population is less responsive to the change in policing, then the profiling will *increase* overall crime in society" (Harcourt, 2007, p. 123). Persico (2002) articulated a similar thesis, stating, "If the elasticity to policing is lowest for the group which is policed more intensely, moving the system towards a more fair allocation *increases* the effectiveness of policing" (p. 1474).

Harcourt (2007), in fact, makes a compelling argument that minorities typically targeted for profiling probably are less elastic:

---

8. Crime rate is a function of criminality (the proportion of the population that commits any crime) and offending (how many crimes they commit).

If they do in fact offend more, there is every reason to believe that they may be *less* elastic to policing....If their offending is different, then why would their elasticity be the same? If they are, for instance, offending more because they are socioeconomically more disadvantaged, then it would follow logically that they may also have less elasticity of offending to policing because they have fewer alternative job opportunities. (p. 123)

On the other hand, Persico (2002) noted that targeted minorities may also expect harsher punishments, and this would make them *more* responsive to changes in intensity of enforcement.

Whether or not minorities' offending is less responsive to policing, because profiling leads police to pay more attention to groups who are offending less and less attention to groups who are offending more, deterrence theory points to a very practical problem with sustained profiling.

Furthermore, both Persico (2002) and Harcourt (2004, 2007) point out that the objective of policing is to mitigate crime and its effects. Merely obtaining higher arrest rates, which profiling, when targeted at higher-offending groups, may accomplish, is not sufficient. If profiling causes crime to increase, via either fewer captures or more offending, it is counterproductive. On deterrent and incapacitative grounds, the crime-reducing effects of racial profiling are questionable at best.

Reverse Deterrence: An Experimental Demonstration

I have previously speculated (Glaser, 2006), as have Harcourt (2004, 2007) and Persico (2002), that deterrence may, in the case of racial profiling, be a double-edged sword. Specifically, if the profiled group commits less crime, nonprofiled groups would likewise commit more. Because nonprofiled groups tend to be the majority of the population, this could lead to a net increase in crime. Until recently, however, this was only a theoretical postulation. Now there is some experiment-based evidence that racial profiling can *cause* increased transgressions by members of nonprofiled groups.

The challenges in testing the reverse deterrence thesis empirically are manifold. First, to determine if it happens in the real world, we would need to know when and where profiling is happening, but we would also need to have good estimates of the base rates of offending for the different groups against which to compare offending rates when profiling is happening. It would not be enough to show that, for example, Whites offend more when Blacks are profiled, because both the high White offending and the profiling could be caused by some other factor, like a higher sense of White privilege. An experiment would be a powerful way to determine causality—that the profiling *causes* reverse deterrence (more offending by the nonprofiled group). But we cannot conduct an experiment that involves real crime—that would not pass federal guidelines protecting human subjects, nor would it be politically tenable for any law enforcement agencies involved.

Several years ago, I received an e-mail from a fellow social psychologist, Amy Hackney, saying that she had read my 2006 paper, thought the reverse deterrence idea was interesting and important, and had an insight into how it could be tested. Dr. Hackney had read about an experiment in which the researchers were able to measure the rate at which people *cheated* on an ostensible "cognitive skills" test (Vargas, von Hippel, & Petty, 2004). She thought, and I agreed, that cheating could be a reasonable proxy for crime that we could measure under controlled conditions in the laboratory. Sure, cheating on a test is not the same thing as possessing illicit drugs or weapons, but it is a violation of rules, ethics, and strong social norms, especially in an academic setting, where we would conduct the study. Our primary purpose in the study was to test whether merely scrutinizing members of one group would cause members of another group to transgress more. Dr. Hackney and I set about designing an experiment using the Vargas et al. cheating paradigm that would test the effects of racial profiling on illicit behavior.

In the Vargas et al. study, research subjects were given a list of 15 very difficult anagrams (word jumbles) to solve in a short period of time. Twelve of the anagrams (e.g., recsnapa, ngliebapaar, rkaihscb) were so difficult as to be almost never solved legitimately in such a short span. Subjects were instructed that when they were finished they should score their own results with the answer key on the page underneath the testing page, and they could then leave. Words among the 12 most difficult that were solved correctly, without any scratch work (e.g., checked off letters) on the page, were scored as cheats.[9]

In our experiment (Hackney & Glaser, 2013), we had people carry out the same "cognitive skills test," but we embedded it within a racial profiling manipulation. Specifically, we varied whether the test administrator seemed to be giving extra scrutiny to Black or White or no students with regard to cheating. At the beginning of the test, the administrator told the students (all Georgia Southern University undergraduates) that she wanted to make sure there was no cheating, and then she called on two students to move near her desk where she could keep an eye on them, and she watched them throughout the testing period. Unbeknownst to the research subjects, these two were always "confederates," part of the staff of the study, posing as subjects. We varied whether the confederates both were White or Black. We also had a no-profiling control condition wherein nobody was moved or scrutinized.

The results (summarized in Figure 5.2) were very clear and were consistent with the idea of reverse deterrence. In the control condition, where nobody was

---

9. Vargas et al. (2004) validated this measure of cheating by showing, for example, that scores on the test were not correlated with students' grade point averages but *were* correlated with an implicit measure of dishonesty.

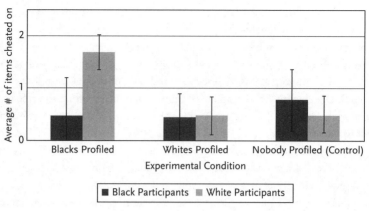

Figure 5.2
Average number of items cheated on as a function of participant race and experimental manipulation of racial profiling. Error bars represent 95% confidence intervals. Total $N = 278$. (Reprinted with permission from Hackney & Glaser, 2013.)

singled out, the cheating rate was low, fewer than one word per person, on average, and Black and White subjects cheated at about the same, statistically indistinguishable rate. In the condition where White confederates were singled out (the "Whites Profiled" condition), there was again no difference in cheating. It was in the critical condition where Black confederates were singled out (the "Blacks Profiled" condition) that behavior was affected. While Black participants cheated at the same low rate, White participants in this condition cheated statistically significantly more than did any other group in the experiment. *This is evidence of reverse deterrence—Whites transgressing more when Blacks are targeted.*

In this experiment, we did not see reverse deterrence operating the other way; Black students did not cheat more when White students were profiled. It is likely that, being members of a chronically *suspect race*, Black students were careful to avoid cheating no matter what. It is also likely that neither Black nor White students had a preexisting schema for Whites being profiled. When Black confederates were being targeted, this probably activated the stereotype that Blacks are more suspect, and thereby caused students to infer that Blacks were being subjected to greater scrutiny. In contrast, when White confederates were targeted, this was less likely to be construed as *race-based*. It seems plausible that this would happen in real crime profiling as well, if there were circumstances under which majority groups were profiled.

Racial Profiling could Increase Crime

The implications of reverse deterrence go beyond mere inefficiency. Because of reverse deterrence, racial profiling could cause more crime to be committed. First, if transgressors from a larger group (e.g., Whites) are being motivated to transgress more, while those from a smaller group (e.g., Blacks) are being motivated to transgress less, the net effect could be more crime, simply by virtue of the size of the groups. This will depend, of course, on the rate of offending within the groups—if the minority group has a much higher offending rate, deterring it could yield a net decrease in crime. Layer on top of that, however, the possibility that minorities may be less responsive to changes in the expected cost of committing crime (Harcourt, 2007), and you have a real potential for a net increase in crime as a function of racial profiling—the profiled group commits moderately *less* crime, whereas the majority group shows a more dramatic *increase*.

The Hackney and Glaser (2013) experiment yielded results consistent with profiling causing a net increase in crime. Because the only change in cheating was an increase for Whites when Blacks were profiled, the net effect was more offending overall when Blacks were profiled. If, in real crime, White offending rates are substantial and minority elasticities are smaller, racial profiling of minorities could, in addition to exacerbating racial disparities in incarceration rates, actually increase crime.

PROFILING DEPARTMENTS MAY CATCH FEWER CRIMINALS: SOME REAL-WORLD EVIDENCE

Legal scholar David Harris has attempted to assess the effects of racial profiling on criminal captures. Examining statistics from a number of departments for which data were available, Harris (2002a, Chapter 4) compared hit rates (percent of searches that result in arrests) across racial/ethnic groups as a function of their rates of stops of Whites and minorities. He found that minorities who were stopped tended to be considerably less likely to be arrested.

Similarly, Ramirez, Hoopes, and Quinlan (2003, p. 1212) reviewed studies that examined contraband hit rates as a function of the race/ethnicity of the suspect searched. In almost all cases, although minorities were more likely to be searched, those searched were no more likely than Whites to be found in possession of contraband, and in several cases Blacks and Latinos were less likely than Whites.

If minorities are being stopped and searched at relatively high rates, but yielding contraband at lower rates, departments may be missing large populations of offenders among non-minority populations.

IT'S NOT JUST ABOUT CRIMINALS: EFFECTS OF PROFILING ON INNOCENT CIVILIANS AND COMMUNITIES

As has been discussed at length, racial profiling can have the effect of undermining criminal justice objectives in terms of both distorting the proportionality of who is incarcerated and compromising crime mitigation. Those are causes for serious concern for law enforcement officials from rank-and-file to top brass, for policymakers, and for the broader public.

We would be sorely remiss, however, if we did not consider another set of very serious problems that racial profiling poses. *Profiling, whether or not efficient in terms of criminal captures and crime mitigation, has a disproportionate and therefore discriminatory effect on innocent members of the targeted groups.* This is the case because profiling necessitates that a larger proportion of innocent minorities will be stopped and searched. This is just a simple mathematical necessity. For example, let us say that a minority group that represents one fifth of the population has a criminality rate of 10%, and the remaining four fifths of the population has a rate of 2%. If the police stop and search more people from the minority group, they will catch more criminals than if they stop the two groups at the same rate, at least in the short term (recall Figure 5.1). However, a larger share of the 90% of innocent minorities will also be stopped and searched.

To be more concrete, if these two groups lived in a city of 1 million people, there would be 200,000 minorities. Twenty thousand (10%) of them would be "criminals" (i.e., engaged in some detectable, prosecutable activity). Among the remaining majority of 800,000 people, 16,000 would be criminals. If police randomly[10] stop 10% and 2% of minority and majority group members, respectively, this will lead to 18,000 (10%) and 15,680 (2%) of their innocent populations being stopped as well. Innocent minorities would have five times the likelihood of experiencing the disadvantages (inconvenience, humiliation, stigma, risk of altercation, and even potentially wrongful arrest) of being stopped. In fact, analyses of police department data indicate that the vast majority of stops and searches lead to no arrest. The San Jose Police Department, for example, reported that in 2006–2007, 2.2% of 65,355 vehicle stops led to arrests. Of course, there are many reasons for vehicle stops. But even among stops that led to searches (implicating suspicion of crime), only 7.1% resulted in a finding of contraband or other evidence of crime (SJPD, 2007). Similar proportions are seen in the data on the millions of stops resulting from NYPD's pedestrian stop and frisk program.

The preceding example involves a pronounced disproportion in the criminality rates. The same general pattern—more minority innocents being stopped—will occur regardless of differences in criminality rates, as long as more minorities are stopped at least partially on the basis of race or ethnicity. If the profiling practice continues, an increasingly large share of the innocent minority population will

---

10. Except in DUI and security screening checkpoints, police do not generally stop or search people on a *random* basis. The random aspect of this simulation is meant to represent the *racial profiling component* of the decision to stop. It is the part of the decision to stop that is above and beyond any race-neutral basis of suspicion and would therefore lead to stops, searches, and arrests above and beyond those that would occur otherwise.

be subjected to these unnecessary intrusions. This is certainly consistent with what African Americans have reported to survey takers (e.g., Newport, 1999).

Mere Inconvenience?

To some, these stops and searches of innocent civilians are benign—a mere "inconvenience" (e.g., Wilson & Higgins, 2002) that should be tolerated by members of the suspected group for the sake of others. Others argue that the consequences of innocent minorities being stopped and searched are significant. First, it represents a violation of the due process and equal protection clauses in the Fourth and Fourteenth Amendments to the U.S. Constitution. More practically, these stops represent time lost for the civilian. Because racial and ethnic minorities tend to be lower in socioeconomic status with relatively tenuous employment, the resulting cost of being late for work or for a job interview could be substantial.

Police stops are also stressful. Anyone who has been pulled over has experienced an accelerated heart rate accompanying the feelings of disappointment and concern. It is an anxiety-provoking experience. For Black men, this stress may be a chronic feature of their driving experience, compounded by concern that they may be treated with extra suspicion. Psychological research on stress has shown that it tends to cause profound, lasting physiological harm (e.g., McEwen, 1998). Research has even specifically demonstrated that the psychological stress resulting from racial, ethnic, and gender discrimination has severe emotional and physiological consequences (e.g., Clark, Anderson, Clark, & Williams, 1999; Flores, Tschann, Dimas, Pasch, & de Groat, 2010).

One cause of this stress is social stigma. People who are consistently treated differently become stigmatized, and belonging to a group that is stigmatized can have that effect indirectly. If one belongs to a group that has an undesirable stereotype associated with it, such as criminality for Blacks, situations like interactions with police that signal that stereotype are especially unpleasant and threatening. Whites who are stopped by the police may experience frustration and embarrassment when they reflect their circumstance in the eyes of bystanders. Blacks, who are stigmatized by crime, are likely to experience far more intense negative emotions as a result of attention from the police. David Harris (1999) and Kathryn Russell (1998, 1999) cite numerous cases of prominent, upstanding Black Americans (including celebrity athletes, musicians, and actors, as well as prominent lawyers, businesspeople, and professors) who report having been stopped for "driving while Black," as well as accounts of more anonymous Black Americans who have experienced humiliation, exasperation, and even despair as a result of unnecessary traffic stops.

All of the negative psychological and logistical effects that minorities experience when being stopped by the police, particularly when the stops are unjustified, are likely to lead to a sense of alienation and disenfranchisement. If one belongs to a group that is consistently treated unfairly by government authorities, one's faith in public institutions is bound to suffer. Psychologists Tom Tyler and Yuen Huo discuss such problems in their book *Trust in the Law* (2002). They argue that when communities (e.g., racial or ethnic minority groups) do not trust police, they are less inclined to help with law enforcement activities—less likely to report crimes, provide information, or cooperate in investigations. In addition to creating an uncivil environment, this can undermine police effectiveness in solving crimes and keeping the peace. This trust-eroding aspect is therefore further basis for concern about the effectiveness of racial profiling.

SELF-FULFILLING EFFECTS OF RACIAL PROFILING RESULTING FROM DISPROPORTIONATE INCARCERATION

So far we have noted that racial profiling can be counterproductive in a number of ways. It can, under excessive conditions, actually lead to fewer criminal captures. It can, through reverse deterrence, cause a net increase in crime. Additionally, by affecting *innocent* minorities who will inevitably be subjected to a disproportionate amount of unnecessary law enforcement attention, it can alienate communities, eroding their trust in law enforcement and thereby undermine effective policing.

There is yet another manner in which racial profiling can be counterproductive, and that is through the destabilizing effects that result from incarcerating a substantial proportion of minority men. This destabilization can lead to a self-fulfilling prophecy in the sense that minorities whose lives and opportunities have been disrupted by criminal punishment (incarceration or probation) become less able to be productive members of society and more likely to commit more crime in the future. There are a number of causal pathways to this unfortunate outcome. Additionally, the negative effects on the incarcerated individuals reverberate throughout their communities.

As the Bureau of Justice Statistics (2003) has estimated, approximately 32.2% of African American men alive in 2003 would be incarcerated during their lifetimes. Western (2006) documented that millions of these incarcerations will be for drug offenses (the most commonly profiled crime). Needless to say, these high rates of incarceration destabilize minority communities, at the very least depriving them of wage earners and parents, and costing legal fees.

In addition to the direct costs (e.g., lost wages) during incarceration, there are other ways that high rates of minority incarcerations harm and destabilize minority communities, including some very fundamental civic practices. All but two U.S. states disenfranchise voters who have a criminal conviction, at least during their sentence or parole. Twelve states permanently disenfranchise convicts, five of these with no mechanism for lifting the ban (Legal Action Center, 2004). This disenfranchisement, combined with disproportionate incarceration of minorities, causes minority communities to have a weaker voice in electoral outcomes. One must bear in mind that, as discussed earlier, even if minorities have a higher offending rate, racial profiling will cause them to be convicted at rates that are out of proportion with their offending rates. In this way, racial profiling serves to disproportionately erode the ability of minority communities to participate and thereby be represented in basic democratic processes. This lack of voice can further alienate minorities, who will feel less adequately represented. More fundamentally, however, their constitutional right to representation is violated.

High minority conviction rates also have profound implications for the future prospects of those convicted. Sociologist Devah Pager (2003) has compellingly demonstrated how having a criminal record undermines one's ability to obtain employment. Conducting an audit study experiment with a large sample of real employers, where Black and White men presenting identical qualifications applied for jobs, Pager investigated the effects that a criminal record would have on job prospects. Some of the applicants indicated having a felony conviction for cocaine possession with the intent to distribute. Pager found that the felony conviction dramatically reduced the rate at which applicants were called back, and that this effect was especially pronounced for the Black applicants. White applicants had their prospects cut in half by a criminal record, from 34% to 17% getting callbacks. Black applicants fared worse with or without a criminal record, but their prospects were reduced nearly threefold, from 14% to 5% getting called back. In other words, Black job applicants, already handicapped by the stigma of race, face particularly bleak employment prospects if they have a criminal record. This finding jibes with those obtained from analyses of real criminal justice and labor statistics (e.g., Raphael, 2006). African Americans, therefore, face a double jeopardy: Their employment prospects are excessively diminished by having a criminal record, and they are obtaining criminal records at disproportionately high rates *because of racial profiling* and other biases in the criminal justice system. These severe barriers to employment no doubt promote higher levels of criminal activity (Raphael & Winter-Ebmer, 2001), reflecting a vicious cycle—a self-fulfilling prophecy.

In addition to financial and psychological harms, disproportionate criminal justice outcomes can also visit harms to the *physical health* of minority communities. Specifically, Johnson and Raphael (2009) have found that incarceration rates of Black men are strongly predictive of subsequent AIDS incidence rates among Black women, even when statistically controlling for a host of known predictors. The high rate of HIV exposure in prison is carried out to the most proximal members of the general population, contributing substantially to the relatively high rates of infection among Black Americans. It seems plausible that other infectious diseases would exhibit similar patterns. That a significant part of the African American HIV/AIDS problem could be attributable to the distortions in incarceration rates resulting from racial profiling is deeply troubling.

Straightforward mathematical reasoning indicates that racial profiling inevitably causes targeted communities to receive more than their share of investigation and criminal sanctions. Consequently, concerns about the impact of racial profiling extend well beyond its unconstitutionality and potential to increase crime rates (via reverse deterrence), to disturbing negative effects on minority communities: lost wages and human capital; stigma and stress; psychological and civic disenfranchisement; and even disease.

CONCLUSION

While it is true, and therefore intuitively appealing, that targeting groups known to have higher offending rates will lead to more captures in the short term, a longer, broader view of the problem yields a different conclusion. Consequently, even in the "best case" (where profiled groups really do offend at relatively high rates), racial profiling is deeply problematic. The research discussed in this chapter has shown that profiling tends to yield very modest efficiency gains that diminish over time; that profiling may have reverse deterrent effects that actually increase crime; and that racial profiling, by causing minorities to bear an excessive criminal justice burden, visits upon their communities a host of serious negative consequences, including economic, psychological, physiological, and democratic.

As Persico (2002) and Harcourt (2004, 2007) have poignantly noted, controlling crime and promoting public safety are the primary purposes of policing. To the extent that profiling can increase crime while harming communities, it runs a high risk of contravening those core objectives. Although racial profiling is generally formally prohibited in law enforcement, evidence considered in Chapter 2 reveals that it is fairly widespread. As law enforcement officials and policymakers consider what to do going forward, they should bear in mind that the costs of doing little or nothing (stated bans lacking enforcement mechanisms, included) are considerable and strike at the core of American values of equality, fairness, and humaneness. Along these lines, the policy landscape regarding racial profiling will be discussed in Chapter 7, after a consideration in Chapter 6 of a particularly controversial domain of racial profiling: counterterrorism.

CHAPTER 6
Flying While Arab

Racial Profiling in Counterterrorism

A massive explosion has just destroyed half of a U.S. government building, killing and injuring as yet untold hundreds of workers and visitors, mostly civilians. In the moments after the explosion, as shocked rescue workers arrive at the scene and begin the overwhelming task of extracting victims from the flames and rubble, law enforcement officials begin their search for the cause. Judging from the blast, it is soon apparent that the explosion originated from just outside the front of the building. It was most likely a bomb, and the nature of the target indicates that this was a terrorist attack. Federal, state, and local agents quickly scramble to collect clues and, maybe, identify suspects, who have not yet had long to flee the scene.

Within hours of the blast, investigators have a few leads. Several Middle Eastern men who were in the city at the time of the bombing are sought for questioning. Conventional wisdom holds that the longer it takes to identify a suspect or suspects, the less likely they are to be found, as the trail goes "cold." The authorities may have caught a break that could shut this case down quickly, maybe even provide leads to terrorist collaborators.

No such luck. The Middle Eastern men prove to be innocent: random individuals, like hundreds of others, who happened to have been near the attack that morning. In the days that follow, investigators identify the real perpetrator, a White, American-born army veteran...

...named Timothy McVeigh. As he fled the scene on the interstate, McVeigh was pulled over by a state trooper because his car did not have a license plate. He was arrested for possession of a concealed weapon and taken into custody. The trooper found in his cruiser a card McVeigh had tried to hide that had written on it "TNT at $5 a stick. Need more." Meanwhile, parts of the truck used for the bombing were traced by the FBI to a rental agency whose employees helped construct a composite sketch that closely resembled McVeigh. In other words, Timothy McVeigh did not cover his tracks well and was apprehended as a result, and he was convicted because of excellent, meticulous investigative work and astute policing. But he might have gotten away and faded into hiding, perhaps waiting to commit another terrorist attack another day, had he just driven a car with a license plate.

The bombing of the Murrah Federal Building in Oklahoma City in 1995 was, at the time, the most deadly and destructive act of terrorism ever perpetrated on American soil. McVeigh was an antigovernment extremist, inspired by White separatist writings. With the help of his friend Terry Nichols and two other co-conspirators, he planned and executed the attack with a fertilizer-based bomb loaded in a rental truck. He confessed to the crime, never expressed regret, and was executed by the federal government in 2001.

What does this have to do with racial profiling? First, ask yourself, how did you react when you read that Middle Eastern men were being sought? Was it surprising, or did it seem right? Were you surprised, before it became clear that this was a description of Oklahoma City, to hear that the perpetrator was White? Did it occur to you that the law enforcement and media attention paid to the initial suspects may have been a distraction? Did you wonder how many other people had been seen near the blast, and why they were not suspects?

We do not want to make too much hay out of this initial misdirection in the Oklahoma City investigation. Law enforcers got their man, and pretty swiftly. It was an extreme circumstance, and things were happening quickly. Furthermore, there was a known terrorist threat from Arab Muslim groups who had attempted to destroy the World Trade Center two years earlier. But one lesson is very clear: Despite the prevailing stereotype of terrorists as Muslim Arabs, the second-most deadly and destructive terrorist act on American soil, to this day, was perpetrated by White, Christian Americans who hated the U.S. government and sought to weaken it by killing innocent civilians.

The corollary lesson is that a terrorist profile including "Middle Eastern" could make it easier for future Timothy McVeighs to slip through by diverting law enforcement attention. While the September 11, 2001, attacks were perpetrated by Muslim extremist foreign nationals from the Middle East, White domestic terrorists could have perpetrated similar attacks.

Nevertheless, in the wake of the 9/11 attacks, the follow-on attacks in London, Madrid, Bali, Mumbai, and other locales and the known existence of al-Qaeda and other anti-Western, Muslim terrorist groups, it would be psychologically impossible, and strategically foolhardy to ignore this information about a very real and persistent threat. The question is, what are the right ways to use the information, and how do we avoid having it undermine national security and civil rights?

RACIAL PROFILING IN COUNTERTERRORISM

To this point, the discussion in this book has focused almost exclusively on the type of profiling that has been prevalent in drug law enforcement. In that case, the targets are primarily Black, but also Latino, and in some cities Asian. The stereotypes are well known. Although the targeted groups are minorities, they represent substantial segments of the population—Blacks constitute approximately 12.6% and Latinos 16.3% of the U.S. population. The crime of primary interest, illicit drug possession for use or sale (and, secondarily, illegal weapons possession), is committed by members of all ethnic groups at comparable, if not equal, rates. The crime is widespread but tends to have small individual consequences, although it arguably results in great aggregate harm to society. As documented in Chapter 2, there is ample evidence that racial profiling of African Americans and Latinos, particularly in drug law enforcement, is a very real phenomenon throughout the United States.

Counterterrorism is a domain of racial profiling that is of considerable public interest. Much less research has been conducted on profiling in counterterrorism than in drug law enforcement, but because of its importance, it warrants consideration here.

Terrorism has some similarities with drug crime and some stark differences, and these need to be considered when applying knowledge of drug interdiction profiling to counterterrorism profiling. In a sense, terrorism and drug crime are mirror images. Drug crimes are relatively widespread (thousands occur every day) but relatively low impact (each drug sale affects mostly those involved in the transaction). In contrast, terrorist acts are extremely rare, especially in the United States, but have immense impact, by design. Even hapless, failed terrorist attacks, like the "Underwear" and Times Square bombing attempts in early 2010, sparked widespread anxiety, substantial allocations of governmental resources, and debates over U.S. foreign policy. As constitutional lawyer Jonathan Turley (2002) put it in congressional testimony on counterterrorism and airport screening, "Quite frankly, society can live with a couple of nickel bags of narcotics making it through the law enforcement net. The costs of failure to detect criminality at an airport are far more immediate and deadly."

A crucial difference between terrorism and drug crime is the motivation underlying them. Drug crime is motivated primarily by economic factors—drugs are a product that is produced, transported, and sold on an identifiable market for profit. It is an illicit, "black" market because drugs like cocaine, methamphetamines, heroin, and, with some recent exceptions, marijuana, are illegal. But it is a market nonetheless, and the primary motive is financial gain. Terrorism is, with few exceptions, motivated by ideology and group conflict. It stems from disdain for others and their beliefs and a desire to hurt and/or change them. Al-Qaeda's stated goals, for example, are to force the United States and its allies out of the Muslim world. The prevalence of suicidal terrorism proves that, at least for those who actually carry out the acts, it is not motivated by material self-interest.

The implications of this dramatic motivational difference are, first, that drug crime and terrorism will react differently to practices aimed at deterring them. Specifically, people motivated by extreme ideology will be especially difficult to deter. More discussion on this will follow. Second, the ideological nature of terrorist motivations raises the likelihood that there is a real, lasting, predictable link between ethnic (specifically, religious) identification and the type of crime. In contrast, there is no reliable, instrumental link between race and drug crime. If there is a correlation (higher rates for some groups), it is mostly caused by economic factors (Blacks and Latinos are, on average, substantially poorer and less educated and have less access to employment in licit markets).

Regardless of these stark differences, both types of crime have been addressed with racial profiling. And in both cases, profiling appears to be a flawed strategy, for some of the same and also for some different reasons. The problems with drug war racial profiling have been described in Chapter 5. A consideration of counterterrorism racial profiling will follow. Because failures to deter and detect terrorist attacks can have catastrophic consequences, understanding the promise and perils of racial profiling in counterterrorism is imperative.

DEFINING TERRORISM

Terrorism, being a complicated phenomenon that has taken many forms over many centuries, has been defined in a variety of ways. Kruglanski and Fishman (2009) offer a practical "working definition" of terrorism "as the symbolic use of violence by nonstate actors with social and political (hence not purely criminal) objectives intended to intimidate, frighten, or coerce a wider audience than the direct (instrumental) targets of the attack" (p. 3). This definition captures the central feature of terrorism, that it is, in fact, intended to *terrorize* a citizenry that is larger than the direct targets, with the objective of changing the behavior of that citizenry and/or its government. Kruglanski and Fishman (2009) and other terrorism experts limit the definition to "nonstate actors." There is a long and brutal history of governments enacting reigns of terror on their own and other nation's citizenries, in some cases even to achieve ideological objectives. However, nonstate terrorists terrorize in part *because* they lack the power of a state and so resort to drastic, violent, and destructive means. For practical purposes, it is necessary to separate terrorism from violence against civilians by states if for no other reason than the means to combat it will be very different. In this sense, it is important to recognize that "counterterrorism" is only a subset of the larger policy realm of "national security," which includes defense against hostile nations.

TERRORIST PROFILING ≠ RACIAL PROFILING

Part of the history of counterterrorism involves the extension of criminal profiling to terrorist profiling. As with other crimes, like serial murder, the FBI took a lead role in promoting terrorist profiles, wherein profilers, often psychologists or psychiatrists, would construct a demographic sketch of the presumed perpetrator based on available evidence (e.g., crime scene evidence or any communications from a perpetrator).

Terrorism expert Andrew Silke (2001) investigated the history of terrorist profiling, finding it, like criminal profiling, to have had minimal success, while perceptions among law enforcement tended to overestimate its effectiveness. One "eerily accurate" (Schauer, 2003, p. 157) terrorist profile was that developed by James Brussels describing the "Mad Bomber," George Metesky, who set off at least 37 explosives in public places in New York City throughout the 1940s and 1950s. Although not the cause of his capture, Brussels's profile ended up fitting Metesky with remarkable precision, down to his clothing and cohabitants. Schauer (2003) gives credit to the celebrated success of this case for the subsequent rise of criminal profiling. But the Mad Bomber case, memorable as it may be, appears to be the exception, not the rule. Silke (2001) concludes, "While [offender] profiling has been used in terrorist cases, its impact has tended to be either negligible or detrimental to the investigation" (p. 256).

Although the history of terrorist profiling is an important part of any background discussion of counterterrorism, we need to bear in mind that there are fundamental differences between *terrorist profiling* and *racial profiling in counterterrorism*. This distinction is the same as that between "criminal profiling" and "racial profiling" in general. The former involves efforts to narrow a pool of suspects for an already perpetrated act or series of acts (as was the case with the Mad Bomber and the Unabomber); the latter involves using race or ethnicity (most often national origin) to identify likely perpetrators of, and prevent, *future* crimes (as is done in port security screening). What criminal and terrorist profiles have in common with racial profiles is that they are often based on very subjective inferences by the profilers.

THE AMERICAN EXPERIENCE WITH TERRORISM

Although it might seem otherwise to a generation of Americans, terrorism was not invented on September 11, 2001. There is a long history that some scholars trace back thousands of years. In modern times, long, destructive terror campaigns have been perpetrated by groups such as the Irish Republican Army (IRA) in the United Kingdom; the Palestine Liberation Organization (PLO) in Israel and Europe, with successor groups like the currently active Hamas; and the Basque separatist group ETA in Spain. In the United States, the Weather Underground perpetrated antigovernment destructive acts in the late 1960s and early 1970s, although it avoided human targets. The Oklahoma City bombing in 1995 and the Atlanta Olympics bombing, perpetrated by White, Christian extremist Eric Rudolph in 1996, as well as the series of attacks by the Unabomber, Ted Kaczynski from 1978 to 1995, were all motivated by antigovernment ideology.

Attacks on American targets by Muslim terrorists began in earnest in the 1990s. Americans had been passengers on hijacked international flights as early as the 1970s, but these were not anti-American attacks per se. The murder by the PLO of an elderly American, Leon Klinghoffer, on a captured cruise ship in 1985 may mark the beginning of the new era, at least in terms of Americans' perceptions of the phenomenon. Soon after, the first attempted bombing of the World Trade Center by al-Qaeda in 1993, the 1998 bombings of U.S. embassies in Tanzania and Kenya, and the bombing of the USS *Cole* docked in a Yemeni port in 2000, as well as untold failed attacks, brought America into a new era of terrorist threat.

It is, however, because of 9/11, as well as follow-on attacks abroad and attempts in the United States, that terrorism has for the first time become a significant, lasting part of the American psyche and a major influence over policy, both domestic and foreign. The attacks of 9/11 triggered assertive counterterrorism efforts, including trillion-dollar wars, aggressive detention and interrogation of suspects, intensive passenger screening procedures, and racial profiling at airports, borders, and other locations.

In November 1999, nearly 2 years before the 9/11 attacks, a Gallup poll found that 81% of a large, national sample of adults reported believing that racial profiling is wrong (Newport, 1999). Prior to September 11, 2001, such questions inevitably evoked thoughts of drug war profiling of Black and Latino motorists, a subject that was very much in the news in that period. After September 11, 2001, questions about counterterrorism profiling evoked a different public sentiment. A large survey of Americans conducted by National Public Radio, The Kaiser Family Foundation, and the Kennedy School of Government in November 2001 found that 66% approved of profiling "people who are Arab or of Middle Eastern descent" (NPR, 2001). However, Americans' support for profiling at that time seems to have been limited to profiling of Middle Easterners. In fact, in the same NPR/Kaiser/KSG survey, when respondents were asked a more generic question about racial profiling, with a reference to motorist stops, only 21% approved, a rate very similar to the 1999 Gallup result.

The level of acceptance of racial profiling in counterterrorism is not limited to groups that expect to be unaffected. Fifty-four percent of Arab Americans asked in an Arab American Institute survey on October 10, 2001 (a month after the attacks) agreed that it is "justified for law enforcement officials to engage in extra questioning and inspections of people with Middle Eastern accents or features" (Arab American Institute, 2001).

Support for profiling of Arabs and Middle Easterners seems to have endured for at least some time after the immediate aftermath of the September 11, 2001, attacks. A June 2002 survey of registered voters by the Fox Broadcasting Company (2002) found that 54% approved of "using racial profiling to screen Arab-male airline passengers." Later still, an August 2006 Quinnipiac University Polling Institute survey found that 60% of U.S. voters supported profiling of Middle Eastern–looking people at airports and train stations.

It appears that many Americans are able to hold somewhat conflicting attitudes toward drug war profiling and counterterrorism profiling, likely reflecting concerns over personal and public safety and security. This ambivalence is reflected in the statements of individuals asked about profiling of Arabs, such as, "It's not right, but it's justified" (quoted in Verhovek, 2001).

Part of the tolerance for racial profiling in security screening is due to a more pragmatic sense of the need to trade off freedoms not just for security but also for personal convenience. Along these lines, Viscusi and Zeckhauser (2003) surveyed college students to ask how much time they would need to be able to save during airport screening in order to support profiling of passengers. Not surprisingly, respondents were more likely to support profiling the longer the screening time would be without profiling. Non-White respondents were much less supportive.

Part of the support for racial profiling in counterterrorism appears to stem from, or at least be spurred on by, negative attitudes toward and beliefs about Arabs and Muslims (Panagopoulos, 2006; Rowatt, Franklin, & Cotton, 2005). Anecdotally, extremely intolerant views of Muslims have been expressed, even by members of Congress: Representative John Cooksey of Louisiana stated, specifically in reference to racial profiling: "If I see someone [who] comes in that's got a diaper on his head and a fan belt wrapped around that diaper on his head, that guy needs to be pulled over." In 2006, then CNN Headline News show host, Glenn Beck interviewed Representative Keith Ellison, the first Muslim ever elected to the U.S. Congress. Ellison, by the way, is an African American who was born and raised in Detroit. Beck felt compelled to start the interview as follows:

I have been nervous about this interview with you, because what I feel like saying is, "Sir, prove to me that you are not working with our enemies." And I know you're not. I'm not accusing you of being an enemy, but that's the way I feel, and I think a lot of Americans will feel that way.

Beck, 2006

Most American views are, hopefully, more moderate and less bigoted. But Cooksey's and Beck's expressions likely represent the tip of the proverbial iceberg (see Chapter 4) of anti-Muslim attitudes. Such attitudes do not promote a clearheaded, rational evaluation of the merits of racial profiling in counterterrorism.

EVIDENCE OF RACIAL PROFILING IN COUNTERTERRORISM

With an estimated 1,271 government organizations and 1,931 private firms engaged in counterterrorism and national security efforts in roughly 10,000 locations throughout the United States (Priest & Arkin, 2010), it is difficult to speak in generalities about counterterrorism practices. Airport screening is the most common domain of counterterrorism in terms of the sheer number of individuals involved, as well as the relevant history of terrorism, and it is widely acknowledged, and not particularly controversial, that passenger profiling is used in airport security screening (Subcommittee on Aviation, 2002). This results from a consensus that weapon detection technology, while extremely valuable in preventing hijackings and bombings of airplanes, is insufficient to prevent attacks (Ron, 2002). This conclusion was powerfully reinforced by the September 11, 2001, attacks, which involved previously unsuspected weapons (box-cutters) and using the planes themselves as lethal and highly destructive missiles.

Formal methods of terrorist profiling have their roots in the Israeli government's response to the 1968 hijacking of an El Al passenger jet (Ron, 2002). The first formal system used in the United States to profile airline passengers (the Computer-Assisted Passenger Pre-screening System; CAPPS) was developed in 1994 by Northwest Airlines with the support of a grant from the Federal Aviation Administration (FAA), and interest in it became widespread after the 1996 crash of TWA Flight 800, and based on recommendations from the federal government (Subcommittee on Aviation, 2002). CAPPS is known to have included at least 40 passenger variables (e.g., passenger's address, method of payment, time of purchase, origin, and destination), but the specific list of factors is a carefully kept secret (Corrigan, 2002) for the obvious reason that knowledge of the profiling factors would help terrorists circumvent the system. Nevertheless, the FAA and the Department of Justice (DOJ) have asserted that race, ethnicity, and national origin were not included in CAPPS (DOJ, 2003a).

In recent years, a second-generation program, CAPPS II, has been developed by the Office of National Risk Assessment (ONRA) of the Transportation Security Administration (TSA). CAPPS II has been succeeded by a program called Secure Flight, which has a focus on constructing, disseminating, and promoting the use of "no-fly" lists, prohibiting air travel by those suspected of involvement in terrorism.

Anecdotal Evidence of Racial Profiling in Passenger Screening

Aviation officials' denials notwithstanding, anecdotal evidence of Middle Eastern passengers (and those mistaken for them) getting subjected to extra scrutiny indicates that racial profiling is happening. It is either the case that systems like CAPPS *have* included ethnic variables; that other variables, such as origin and destination, alone or in combination, correlate so highly with ethnicity as to serve as a close proxy; that discretionary judgments on the part of individual screeners is leading to *informal* racial profiling; or that some combination of these possibilities is operative.

Some of the anecdotal evidence, which is abundant, is quite stunning. Respected journalist Fareed Zakaria, for example, stating that he has no particular objection to using national origin as one of multiple factors, asserted in 2002, "As a swarthy young man with an exotic name, trust me, we're being checked....I've taken more than 50 flights all over the country since September 11, and I've been searched about 60 percent of the time. Either they are checking me out or I'm the unluckiest man alive."

In August 2009, Bollywood megastar Shahrukh Khan was detained for questioning in Newark, New Jersey, for more than an hour and a half. Khan is described as "one of the biggest movie stars in the world," whose "fame merited a wax figure at Madame Tussauds [wax museum] in London, England" (Bhatnagar, 2009). Bhatnagar, noting how "prominent Indian travelers including former Indian president Abdul Kalam and Indian Nobel laureate Amartya Sen have also been victims of racial profiling at airports," argues:

> What makes Khan's case particularly stinging, however, is that he had just completed filming "My Name Is Khan," a movie that deals with discrimination against Muslims in the United States in the post-9/11 environment. Yet, there he was, a famous movie star, experiencing a poignant example of life imitating art imitating life.

One man, Ashraf Khan, who was removed from an airplane without cause in the weeks following the 9/11 attacks and had to miss his brother's wedding as a result, described the effect on him: "I am really depressed about the whole situation, the way they've treated me, like I'm some sort of criminal" (Verhovek, 2001).

Higher on the evidentiary hierarchy, although still technically anecdotal, are reports from the Sikh Coalition, an advocacy organization that has collected and documented complaints of hundreds of Sikh individuals who report having been subjected to secondary screening at airport security checkpoints (Sikh Coalition, 2010). Sikhs are not Muslims, but they are often mistaken for them. Male Sikhs wear turbans, and the Sikh Coalition, having received hundreds of complaints, believes that Sikhs are asked by TSA officers to submit to pat-downs of their turbans at a rate that far exceeds that for others wearing clothes that could just as easily conceal something. Sikh turbans are tight fitting and cannot conceal anything as large as a pair of loose-fitting pants or a dress can. Early complaints held that TSA screeners were asking Sikh travelers to remove their turbans, an act that, when done publicly, is strictly forbidden in Sikh tradition. The TSA now has a stated policy allowing head coverings through checkpoints (TSA, 2007), but this does not preclude pat-downs, to which Sikh travelers claim they are subjected at disproportionate rates.

The Sikh Coalition's 2010 civil rights report offers a telling case of air passenger profiling:

> Gurinder Singh Ahluwalia, President & CEO of Genworth Financial Wealth Management, has been traveling through Oakland International Airport about three times a month for business since the summer of 2006. Ahluwalia believes he is profiled 100% of the time by TSA officers at Oakland International Airport because of his turban. He says, "It has gotten worse over time. When I first started traveling it was happening about 80% of the time. Now it's 100% of the time....As an individual, I am frustrated by the haphazard process. As an American, I don't feel safe because of a TSA officer's flawed logic, and as a business person, I feel very limited. I can't just teleconference all my meetings to avoid this wastage of time, embarrassment and disrespectfulness." (p. 22)

Evidence of Racial/Ethnic Profiling in Post-9/11 Immigration Programs

In the years immediately following the 9/11 attacks, the DOJ, and then the newly created Department of Homeland Security (DHS), engaged in an aggressive immigrant registration program that was ostensibly designed to help improve records in the service of keeping better track of *all* noncitizens residing within the United States. The program started with a subgroup. According to a report in *The New York Times* (Swarns, 2004), the DOJ and then the DHS "required male noncitizens from 25 mostly Arab and Muslim countries to register with immigration authorities between November 2002 and April 2003. None of the Arab and Muslim men who came forward has been charged with crimes related to terrorism." Through this program more than 83,000 immigrants registered, and although about 13,000 were found to lack legal immigration status, "officials now say there is little evidence to suggest that it succeeded in capturing suspected terrorists." Whatever the result, this is evidence that U.S. national security agencies were using national origin to systematically screen individuals, including approximately 70,000 legal immigrants.

In addition to voluntary registration, a smaller number of immigrants have been subjected to interviews by national security agencies. *The New York Times* reported in October 2008 that the DHS interviewed more than 2,500 immigrants from Muslim countries (Lichtblau, 2008). *The Times* article further reported that of a sample of 300 cases turned over by the federal government, none were charged with terrorism-related offenses. *The Times* (Firestone & Drew, 2001) also reported that in the months following the 9/11 attacks, of the more than 1,200 people who were arrested on terror-related charges, most had been released from custody, 104 had been charged with federal crimes, and "Senior law enforcement officials said today that of the group, only 10 or 11 were believed to have any relationship to the terrorist group Al Qaeda." According to *The Times* article:

> One former senior FBI official described the investigation this way: "When you send a whole lot of agents out after a whole lot of people, they're going to find some who committed various crimes. It's just inevitable. And when they find criminal activity, even if it's not the crime they were looking for, they're going to make an arrest." Since mid-October, in fact, the number of people who the authorities believe have any connection to the Sept. 11 attacks has grown only slightly, even as the F.B.I. and the Immigration and Naturalization Service have continued to round up and hold hundreds of people.
>
> Firestone & Drew, 2001

Profiling expert David Harris (2002b) notes that approximately 8,000 young Arab men were subjected to "'voluntary'" questioning by the DOJ in the months following 9/11. Notably, Harris reports that "law enforcement professionals reacted by quietly refusing to take part in the questioning and commenting that this tactic differed markedly from established methods for conducting antiterrorism investigations" (p. 40).

Another program in which the DOJ was clearly using national origin to profile suspected terrorists is the Absconder Apprehension Initiative (AAI). Absconders are "noncitizens who willfully fail to depart the United States after receiving a final order of deportation from an immigration judge" (Eldridge, Ginsberg, Hempel, Kephart, & Moore, 2004, p. 154). The National Commission on Terrorist Attacks Upon the United States (the "9/11 Commission") looked into the DOJ's absconder program and found that, although the department claimed that it was not intended to target terrorists, "The first phase would focus on several thousand priority absconders 'who come from countries in which there has been al Qaeda terrorist presence or activity...because some of them have information that could assist our campaign against terrorism'" (Eldridge et al., 2004, p. 154, quoting Deputy Attorney General Larry Thompson's official memo providing guidance on the AAI), and the National Security Unit of the Immigration and Naturalization Service was tasked with carrying out the initiative. As pointed out by Hussain (2008), the commission's analysis revealed that of the 5,932 priority absconder cases pursued in the first phase of the initiative, only 14 were referred to the FBI for terrorism-related investigation, but "no absconders who were removed as part of Phase 1 were deported under a terrorism statute or prosecuted for terrorism-related crimes" (Eldridge et al., 2004, p. 155). It should be noted that, as of the commission's 2004 report, 1,858 cases were still open, so it remains possible that some of these alleged absconders would be found to be connected with terrorism.

It is not at all clear that any further phases of the AAI, beyond the initial Phase 1 targeting aliens from countries with al-Qaeda presence, were carried out:

> The Commission believes the remaining absconders who were not apprehended in the first phase of the program no longer receive special attention from immigration enforcement personnel. Indeed, DHS has absorbed Phase 2 of the AAI into its current fugitive operations unit.
>
> Eldridge et al., 2004, p. 155

The effect of this sequence of actions appears to be that the federal government has used national origin to single out aliens for deportation in the name of counterterrorism.

Federal Law Enforcement Does Not Racially Profile . . . Except When It Does

Federal officials have been careful to disavow racial or ethnic profiling, but sometimes their own words belie their assurances. For example, in 2003 the DOJ announced a sweeping ban on racial profiling, fulfilling a campaign promise by President George W. Bush. However, the DOJ carved out an explicit exception for "national security," stating that "federal law enforcement officials who are protecting national security or preventing catastrophic events (as well as airport screeners) may consider race, ethnicity, alienage, and other relevant factors" (DOJ, 2003a). Ironically, while this was the first formal federal ban on racial profiling, it also served, through this exception, to be the first formal allowance for racial profiling in federal law enforcement. Because federal officials and agents already condemned racial profiling, the net effect of the new policy may have been to promote it. While only formalizing an already de facto ban, it served to *institutionalize* racial profiling in counterterrorism.

A similar example of paradoxical reasoning can be seen in testimony by Michael Chertoff (then assistant attorney general, Criminal Division; later director of the DHS) before the Senate Judiciary Committee (November 28, 2001):

> We have emphatically rejected ethnic profiling.... On the other hand, we do know certain things about what terrorists themselves have chosen to do. We know that, for example, bin Laden has chosen to recruit people from certain countries, or to train people in certain countries.... And we'd be foolish not to look at those criteria as a way of culling through the pool of people who have come from overseas and deciding who might have useful information.

This approach may be perfectly rational given the context, but it is nonetheless ethnic profiling.

The trend seems to have persisted long after 2001. In July 2008, the Associated Press reported in a well-sourced[1] article, "The justice department is considering letting the FBI investigate Americans without any evidence of wrongdoing, relying instead on a terrorist profile that could single out Muslims, Arabs or other racial and ethnic groups" (Jakes, 2008). At the same time, FBI official investigatory guidelines became determinedly projective: "The guidelines are the latest step in moving beyond a reactive model (where agents must wait to receive leads before acting) to a model that emphasizes the early detection, intervention, and prevention of terrorist attacks and other criminal activities" (FBI National Press Office, 2008). The appeal of this kind of approach is clear for counterterrorism, to the extent that it does lead to early detection. However, in the absence of "leads," investigations will most likely involve the kind of demographic culling that gives rise to racial profiling. The only check on profiling indicated by the FBI was that the guidelines "prohibit opening an investigation based solely on an individual's race, ethnicity, or religion" (FBI National Press Office, 2008). As discussed earlier, the "sole factor" prohibition is an empty one because a *profile* is inherently multifaceted, and it is easy to circumvent with the addition of a single additional factor, such as gender or age.

The merits of racial profiling in counterterrorism will be discussed later. A compelling argument can be made that it is rational and perhaps effective to consider national origin and religion in seeking to identify those involved in terrorism. Constitutional considerations are another matter. And there are good reasons to be concerned that racial profiling is counterproductive, diverting resources from real threats while promoting the very radical views that cause terrorism. What is evident at this point is that, U.S. officials' protestations notwithstanding, racial profiling (based largely on national origin and

---

1. "More than a half-dozen senior FBI, Justice Department and other U.S. intelligence officials familiar with the new policy agreed to discuss it only on condition of anonymity" (Jakes, 2008).

presumptions about religion) has indeed happened, and likely continues to happen in U.S. counterterrorism efforts.

WHY PROFILE IN COUNTERING TERRORISM?

If you asked the typical American on September 10, 2001, what he or she thought of racial profiling, that person would think of Blacks and Latinos being pulled over on an interstate, and the answer you would get would be a pretty emphatic condemnation. In the days, months, and years following the 9/11 attacks, attitudes toward racial profiling became more complicated, as people were faced with the highly salient ethnic identity (Arab Muslim) of the hijackers and the terrorist network (al-Qaeda) to which they belonged. Soon, public calls mounted for racial profiling in counterterrorism, particularly in airport security screening. The general reasoning held that "the particular terrorist group sworn to our destruction, Al Qaeda, is made up largely of Middle Easterners. It is not unreasonable to direct increased attention to passengers with some connection to the Middle East" (Malti-Douglas, 2002). As Debra Saunders (2001) of the *San Francisco Chronicle* bluntly put it, "The nation is under attack from noncitizens who have entered the country. Visitors from countries with hostile populations should expect some extra scrutiny and inconvenience."

Similarly, criminologists Wilson and Higgins (2002; see also Krauthammer, 2005) have argued that racial profiling of Middle Eastern travelers in airport screening makes sense. Surprisingly, some of these commentators (e.g., Wilson & Higgins, 2002) have subscribed to a false dichotomous choice between random searches and racial profiling, implying that one precludes the other when, in fact, they are complementary. Even thoughtful scholars who are critical of profiling (e.g., Turley, 2002) have been known to succumb to what I call "the old lady fallacy," believing that if old ladies get subjected to secondary screening (as these observers have witnessed, with alarm), the process must be flawed. This fails to recognize that a *truly random* system, by definition, means that *everyone* has an equal probability of being selected. If the system is not truly random, people (perhaps careful terrorists) will notice, and they may exploit its nonrandomness, seeking recruits or unwitting accomplices who fall outside the pool.

Random selection for extra screening may serve a powerful deterrent effect. To my knowledge, there is no direct evidence of the deterrent effect of random search protocols on terrorism. However, it is a reasonable proposition that deterrence would result relatively directly from random searches because, although nobody can predict who will be searched, it is very concrete to would-be perpetrators that *somebody* will definitely get searched. Terrorists who plan attacks for years and are prepared to sacrifice their lives, but are not keen to languish in prison, wish to maximize their probability of success and minimize their probability of being apprehended. The random chance of a more thorough screening reduces their likelihood of success and therefore is likely to have a deterrent effect. It is most important to emphasize that random selection and profile-based selection are *not mutually exclusive*. They can be, and are, done in concert.

DESPERATE TIMES CALL FOR DESPERATE MEASURES

One legally oriented argument in favor of racial profiling in counterterrorism invokes extreme measures taken by the U.S. government in times of war, such as Abraham Lincoln's suspension of habeas corpus and Franklin Roosevelt's internment of Japanese Americans and noncitizen residents. The argument, as articulated in a law journal article by R. Spencer Macdonald (2002), holds that "our judicial system has recognized that extremely urgent situations—such as wartime—may require restrictions on civil liberties that would normally be facially unconstitutional" (p. 119). The argument manages to acknowledge the fundamental problems with the Supreme Court rulings on Japanese internment and simultaneously embrace the precedent:

> *Hirabayashi* and *Korematsu* have since been harshly criticized by both the courts and civil liberties groups (footnote omitted). Yet the underlying concept—that an emergent and genuine threat to the United States as a whole can supersede even important and fundamental rights—seems particularly relevant to considerations of airport security in light of September 11. (p. 124)

In fact, the Supreme Court precedent Macdonald invokes (*Schenck v. U.S.*, 249 U.S. 47, 52 (1919)), a free speech case, held that constitutional rights may be suspended "when a nation is at war." The United States was never technically "at war" with terrorist groups; only Congress has the power to declare war, and it did not. But even if it were, that the terrorism problem existed long before September 11, 2001 (even including an attack on the World Trade Center in 1993), and persists more than a decade later—a period longer than any war in U.S. history—begs the question: *How long should the country allow the suspension of constitutional protections?* Another problem with this argument is that the precedents—the Alien and Sedition Acts, Lincoln's suspension of habeas corpus, internment of Japanese Americans—are generally reflected upon with regret, as low points in American history. Whether or not one can claim that the desperate measures were constitutionally permissible because the courts acceded to them, it is also unlikely that the country would have suffered significantly without these infringements on liberties, particularly in the case of Japanese internment, which passed Supreme Court scrutiny but is universally regarded as a travesty.

There are some obvious logical flaws (e.g., the false choice between profiling and random searches) in the reasoning of racial profiling advocates. Furthermore, the constitutionality of the practice is highly suspect. Even if it may pass judicial scrutiny in the exigent circumstances, like its constitutionally questionable predecessors it is likely to be judged harshly by history. Nevertheless, the fundamental argument—that racial profiling in counterterrorism is efficient and effective—warrants consideration.

VERY LARGE AND VERY SMALL NUMBERS

The kind of crime that is usually targeted by racial profiling is very common. It is a conservative estimate to say that drug crimes—possession for use or sale— number in the thousands per day in the United States and span every region of the country, occurring in urban, suburban, and rural settings. Considering counterterrorism requires us to think about profiling under conditions where the targeted behavior is very rare and the targeted group is very large. Specifically, there have probably been somewhere in the ballpark of 200 (Beutel, 2012)[2] known terrorism attempts in the United States since 2000; most of them failed, and one was devastatingly successful. It is worth noting that more than two thirds of those plots were by non-Muslims (Beutel, 2012).

If we are to consider the utility of profiling Arabs and Muslims, meaning, as commentators like Malti-Douglas and others have advocated, targeting them for greater scrutiny in places like airports, we need a sense of how many of them there are to sift through. There are well over 1 billion Muslims in the world. Pakistan and India have very large Muslim populations, as do many Arab and North African countries and Iran. Several hundred million Muslims live in Asian countries like Indonesia, Malaysia, and the Philippines, where there is less anti-American sentiment, but terrorist groups are operative nonetheless. Estimates of the number of Muslims in the United States vary, but the U.S. census puts the number at 1.2 million *adult* Muslims, which should translate to more than 2 million total. The organization Muslim Advocates puts the estimate at "about six million" as of June 17, 2010 (Khera, 2010).

Perhaps the most relevant population statistic, for a consideration of racial profiling in U.S. air transit safety, is the number of Muslims traveling to and within

2. Beutel's (2012) analysis for the Muslim Public Affairs Council drew on multiple media, nonprofit, and government sources to catalog known plots, finding 52 Muslim and 117 non-Muslim plots between September 11, 2001 (not inclusive), and January 2012. Most reached operational phase, and most were prevented prior to implementation.

the United States over a given period of time. A reliable estimate of this number is not readily available, but we can get a sense of the order of magnitude by considering that there were approximately 811,000 visitors to the United States from the Middle East in 2011 (International Trade Administration, 2012). However, the world and U.S. population estimates are not irrelevant, because these are the numbers from which Muslim extremist terrorist groups would ostensibly recruit. Furthermore, in estimating the probability that a given air traveler who fits the ethnic profile is a terrorist, we must consider the probability that a given person (whether traveling or not) from that group is a terrorist.

This is the classic Bayesian probability issue (see Chapter 3). We must acknowledge that, even though Muslim *terrorists* planning to commit a hijacking are almost certain to try to board a passenger jet, Muslim nonterrorists also have a greater than zero probability of trying to board a passenger jet, and the more there are of them (Muslim nonterrorists), the lower the probability that any one traveling Muslim is a terrorist.

To be more concrete, let us assume that 10% (an obviously high estimate) of Muslim terrorists (i.e., Muslims intent on committing a terrorist act) plan to board a passenger jet bound for a U.S. destination, presumably with the intent to commit a hijacking; and that only 1% of Muslim nonterrorists plan to board a passenger jet bound for a U.S. destination. Let us also assume that of the more than 1 billion Muslims in the world, 10,000 are terrorists.[3] Working with these assumptions that certainly overestimate the number of terrorists and underestimate the number of nonterrorists with the intent, resources (i.e., funds, paperwork), and wherewithal to board a passenger jet bound for a U.S. destination, a simple calculation reveals that the probability of a Muslim attempting to board a passenger jet being a terrorist is just under 1 in 10,000. That means that even if all (identifiably) Muslim travelers were subjected to careful, secondary screening that was capable of detecting their intent, the hit rate would be virtually indistinguishable from zero.

Of course, even at 1 in 10,000, if any of these attempts were successful, it would be a disaster and would certainly be worth preventing, even at great cost. But this analysis illustrates what a weak indicator Muslim identity is of terrorist threat, even under generous assumptions. In comparison to other known indicators of suspicion, such as the method used to pay (e.g., cash) for tickets, whether

3. These numbers are obviously very rough, intended not to generate an actual prediction but to illustrate, with reasonable, even generous, proportions, what the probability of a given Muslim passenger being a terrorist is. The number of terrorists intent on hijacking a U.S.-bound passenger jet (and with any plausible ability to even attempt that) is surely much lower than 10,000, while the rate of flying among nonterrorist Muslims is likely higher than 1%. We know from history that the number of attempts has been only a handful over the last decade, not close to the 1,000 specified by this scenario, while there have been far more than 10 million flights by Muslim passengers.

luggage is checked, nervousness, and other behaviors, this 1 in 10,000 (and likely much lower) indicator is hardly reliable.

The Worst of the Worst

The large number of Muslims in the United States and the world and the relatively small number of terrorists render Muslim identity a poor indicator of threat. Bolstering this notion is a consideration of those Muslims seen as the greatest threat. With regard to those who have been detained at the U.S. military prison at Guantanamo Bay, Cuba, the evidence seems to indicate a low rate of involvement in terrorism. Those detained at Guantanamo—those that former defense secretary Donald Rumsfeld termed "the worst of the worst"—include fighters captured on Afghanistan battlefields, but they also include foreign nationals picked up on U.S. soil, categorized as "enemy combatants," and deprived of basic criminal defendant rights. However, despite being "the worst of the worst," most of the Guantanamo detainees have been released, either back into the United States or, more commonly, to other countries, without charge. If there were credible evidence that these individuals were involved in terrorist plots, it is hard to imagine that they would be released. For example, *The Washington Post* (White, 2007) has reported that, of approximately 140 Saudi Arabian detainees, about 90 had been returned (as of 2007) to Saudi Arabia. Although Saudi Arabia is an ally of the United States, as profiling proponents have pointed out, all 19 of the 9/11 hijackers came from that country. This indicates that it should at the very least not be taken for granted that Saudi Arabia will effectively neutralize anti-Western terrorist threats, such as those arising from repatriated terrorists. In other words, it seems unlikely that these 90 or so repatriated detainees (64% of Saudi Guantanamo detainees) posed a real terrorist threat—if they had, they would not have been returned.

AND THEN THERE ARE THE OTHER TERRORISTS...

Setting aside that Muslim identity is an extremely weak indicator of terrorist threat, if the only terrorist threat to America and its allies came from Muslim groups, it might make some sense to focus attention on those groups. But that is hardly the case. In fact, the history of terrorism in the United States is replete with White and, for the most part, Christian perpetrators. These include Timothy McVeigh, but also Eric Rudolph, who bombed the Olympic Village at the 1996 Atlanta Olympics, as well as several abortion clinics. The Unabomber, Ted Kaczynski, carried out 16 bombings between 1978 and 1995 (one of them happened in the building next to the one I was in when I was a graduate student at Yale University in 1993). The anthrax attacks, some fatal, that occurred in the weeks following the 9/11 attacks were, it is now believed, carried out by former FBI scientist Bruce Ivins, who died of an apparent suicide in 2008 when he learned he would soon be charged with the crimes. The Mad Bomber, George Metesky, perpetrated at least 37 bombings in New York City in the 1940s and 1950s.

There is also a long and well-populated history of White separatist militia groups bent on antigovernment terrorism, including, most recently, the Hutaree, a Midwestern Christian militia that was allegedly planning the execution of a police officer and bombing of a funeral in April 2010 in order to "[touch] off an uprising against the U.S. government" (Williams & Barrett, 2010). The plot was broken up with the arrest of nine members by the FBI in March 2010. And it should not be forgotten that one of the most destructive terrorist groups in American history was the Ku Klux Klan, the White supremacist group that, over a period of more than a century, perpetrated thousands of killings and acts of brutality and intimidation, mostly against African Americans (and their supporters), in order to promote their ideological goal of White hegemony.

These historical cases clearly falsify the hypothesis that terrorism in America is exclusively a Muslim-caused problem. The statistics, however, are even more compelling. The Muslim Public Affairs Council (MPAC) compiled a list of known terrorist plots in the United States since September 11, 2001. More than two thirds were planned or perpetrated by non-Muslims. This ratio requires careful interpretation. Indeed, there are many non-Muslim groups, and there are relatively few Muslims in the United States. Based on the number of Muslims who reside in or visit the United States annually, we would predict far less than one third of terrorist plots to be carried out by Muslims, if they were evenly distributed. Nevertheless, the notion that most (let alone almost all) terrorism is perpetrated by Muslims is forcefully contradicted by these simple statistics.

Also telling in the MPAC analysis are the proportions of plots that became operational (i.e., moved beyond mere aspiration) and were implemented (i.e., attempted). A greater proportion of Muslim plots (21.2%) than non-Muslim plots (5.1%) never reached an operational stage, and a greater proportion were prevented prior to implementation (90.4% vs. 61.5%). This may be a reflection of greater scrutiny of Muslim groups; their plots are more likely to be interdicted earlier because they are more likely to be monitored. On the one hand, this can be seen as reflecting the success of law enforcement attention to Muslim suspects; on the other, it can be seen as a relatively high failure rate regarding prevention of plots by non-Muslim groups. These statistics are consistent with the notion that a significant cost of profiling is the failure to deter and prevent crimes by nonprofiled groups.

The extensive and continuing history of White Christian terrorism has not stopped commentators from viewing contemporary terrorism as a purely Middle Eastern, Muslim phenomenon, especially in the wake of 9/11. For example, in his otherwise thoughtful legal arguments in favor of racial profiling in airport screening (but not other domains of law enforcement), Macdonald (2002) asserts that "all nineteen terrorists involved in the September 11 attacks belonged to [al-Qaeda]," and that "these hijackers were exclusively adult males of Middle Eastern ethnicity" (p. 120, citing Taylor, 2001). While this is certainly true, and may well reflect a real correlation between terrorism and Middle Eastern ethnicity, Macdonald has exhibited the *converse accident fallacy*, otherwise known as the "hasty generalization" fallacy. Based on the one terrorist event, he presumes that all (or most) other such events will be the same. This presumption, already flawed based on the past, has been falsified by the intervening history with terrorist attempts by a Briton of European and African descent (the Shoe Bomber), an African (the Underwear Bomber), and a Latino American (the Dirty Bomber), to name a few of the better-known cases. All were, in fact, Muslim, but this cannot be said of Andrew Joseph Stack III, who flew his private airplane on a suicide mission into an Internal Revenue Service building in Austin, Texas, on February 18, 2010, killing several people and destroying the building. Nor can it be said of the Christian extremist Hutaree, whose terrorist plot was foiled by the FBI in 2010.

Predicting that all future terrorist attacks will be perpetrated by Middle Eastern Muslims is more than just a hasty generalization problem. It is a result of confirmatory bias that can have a circular effect. For instance, Macdonald sites as an example of successful, "rational" profiling the apprehension of Millennium Bomber suspect Ahmed Ressam at the Port Angeles, Washington, inspection point in December 1999. However, thorough accounts of the case indicate that Ressam was already on international watch lists, including Canadian (he was entering the United States from Canada when caught). Traveling under an alias (Benni Noris), Ressam aroused the suspicion of an astute customs agent because he was acting nervous, his travel route did not jibe well with his stated travel purpose, and his answers were inconsistent (Bernton, Carter, Heath, & Neff, 2002). Furthermore, the customs agent searched his trunk with the expectation of finding illicit drugs, if anything. Accordingly, the search *may* have resulted in part from a drug courier profile, although it is not evident that this was a *racial* profile. Nevertheless, that lucky coincidence hardly makes it evidence of the effectiveness of racial profiling *in counterterrorism*. What is particularly interesting is that Ressam's apprehension *is* taken as evidence of a racial profiling success. It suggests that his Muslim identity, while not causing his apprehension, is nevertheless seen as the cause. This fallacy takes the following form: Racial profiles of terrorists include Muslim identity; Ahmed Ressam is Muslim; Ahmed Ressam was caught; therefore Ahmed Ressam must have been caught through profiling.

Focusing on Muslim terrorists can be seen as a mistake akin to the "drunkard's fallacy." This logical error alludes to the parable of the drunkard who is looking for his lost keys under a lamppost at night. When asked, "Is this where you think you lost them?" he replies, "No, but it's where I can see." In the case of looking for terrorists among Muslims, it is not that there are no terrorists to be found there, but part of the motivation for looking only at Muslims is that it is something we can do—we have a schema for Muslim terrorists, and we think we know what they look like (misguided screenings of Sikh travelers notwithstanding). To try to find White American terrorists might be like groping around in the vast darkness outside the ring of light cast by the lamppost.

But, Really, What if All Terrorists Were Muslims?

As noted previously, racial profiling in counterterrorism is complicated by the fact that the history of domestic terrorism in the United States is, while psychologically dominated by Muslim extremist groups because of 9/11, nevertheless rife with acts perpetrated by White Christians. Many of these terrorists are active today. But what if current terrorism were perpetrated almost exclusively by Middle Easterners? Would it then be rational to focus counterterrorism resources on them? Results of profiling Arabs and Muslims, as well as views expressed by high-ranking counterterrorism experts, indicate that it might well be ineffective and possibly counterproductive.

As noted earlier, roundups of immigrants from Muslim countries have been unproductive, resulting in few if any terrorism prosecutions. Also troubling is the likelihood that they have actually done more harm than good. Regarding the registration program conducted by the DOJ and the DHS in 2002–2003, "Some officials say this sweeping roundup of illegal immigrants diverted resources from more pressing counterterrorism needs, strained relations with some Arab and Muslim nations and alienated immigrants who might otherwise have been willing to help the government hunt for terror cells in this country" (Swarns, 2004). In fact, the DHS scrapped the program after it inherited it from the DOJ, "saying resources could be better used on other counterterrorism initiatives" (Swarns, 2004).

In addition to just the mere dilution in effectiveness caused by diversion of resources to only one type of suspicious group, it is possible that Arab/Muslim profiling will have the kind of reverse deterrent effects discussed in Chapter 5. In fact, terrorist groups do appear to adapt to profiles, as evidenced by the use of female suicide bombers in Israel and Iraq. Four female suicide attacks were reported in Iraq between November 2007 and January 16, 2008, leading the Associated Press to report that "extremists have been using women more frequently in recent months" (Chester, 2008).

In 1986, a Palestinian group placed explosives in the luggage of a terrorist's unwitting, pregnant Irish girlfriend, bound from London to Tel Aviv. El Al security discovered the bomb during a thorough baggage check that was, obviously, not triggered by a racial profile. The increasing numbers of Somali Americans being recruited by Muslim extremists (Hsu & Johnson, 2009) may also reflect a desire to exploit, by defying, the extant profile.

Even if we persist in assuming that it is rational to profile Arabs and Muslims, how do screeners even identify the "right" populations? As discussed previously, airport screeners appear to have a hard time telling Sikhs from Muslims. Other South Asian populations (including the other billion or so Indians who are not Sikhs or Muslims) are also mistaken for Arabs. If the profile is expanded to Somalis or Yemenis, who have large Muslim populations with significant radicalized subsets, will screeners be able to tell them from Ethiopians or other North African groups? How do screeners tell Muslim Arabs from Christian Arabs, or Muslim from Christian or Buddhist Filipinos and Malaysians? As RAND Corporation profiling experts Riley and Ridgeway (2006) put it,

> Even if the goal of security were mistakenly limited to identifying Muslims, the task would be complicated by the fact that Muslims come from nearly all countries in the world, and from every racial group. Many have identifiably Muslim names, but others do not—and names can be changed, legally or with fake identification documents.

Riley and Ridgeway proceed to list four known Muslim *converts* who have become involved in extremism and terrorist activities: White American Adam Gadahn, who joined al-Qaeda; the British Shoe Bomber, Richard Reid; the Dirty Bomber, Jose Padilla; and "American Taliban," John Walker Lindh. They further note:

> To enter Israel for terror attacks, Hamas suicide bombers have disguised themselves as Israeli soldiers, Hasidic Jews and elderly people. Arab terrorists have dyed their hair blond to look like German tourists, and are known to be recruiting women, older people and converts to Islam to join terrorist ranks.

Former CIA counterterrorism head Vincent Cannistraro is on record as criticizing the effectiveness of racial profiling in counterterrorism: "It's a false lead. It may be intuitive to stereotype people, but profiling is too crude to be effective. I can't think of any examples where profiling has caught a terrorist" (Zakaria, 2002). Similarly, Doris Meissner, commissioner of the Immigration and Naturalization Service during the Clinton administration, has criticized the extensive registering and detention of Middle Eastern immigrants, stating, "If it was really important to get cooperation from these communities in the war against terrorism, the worst way to do that was to hang the immigration swords over their heads" (Hendricks, 2003, A5).

FBI Sacramento Office head, Drew Parenti, who has been reaching out to Muslim groups, laments that law enforcement scrutiny of American Muslims contributes to the radicalization of some: "We want to keep the forces of hatred and evil overseas. The Muslim community wants the exact same thing as everyone else—a safe community and freedom to pray" (Stapley, 2010).

Another concern is that America's hostile stance toward Middle Eastern and South Asian immigrants has discouraged many students and scientists from those regions from coming to the United States to study, teach, and conduct research. Indeed, the years following 2001 saw marked declines in foreign student visa applications and issuances (Institute for the Study of International Migration, 2005), but recent years have seen a reversal of that trend (e.g., Institute of International Education, 2011). The decline of foreign students represents the loss of thousands of person units of brain power that the country traditionally harnesses to promote science, medicine, and technology. In sum, the alienation of millions of Muslims, whether Americans or foreign nationals, that results from their discriminatory treatment can lead to a host of harmful unintended consequences, including increased terrorism.

Confusion Over Race and Nationality

In February 2010, former Speaker of the House Newt Gingrich, appearing on *The Daily Show*, was asked by host Jon Stewart why he thought it was wrong for the FBI to treat the Underwear Bomber, Umar Farouk Abdulmutallab, as a criminal (Mirandizing him, etc.), but that he considered it acceptable when the previous administration handled the Shoe Bomber, Richard Reid, the same way. Gingrich responded that, unlike Abdulmutallab, Reid was a U.S. citizen.[4] Gingrich was wrong—Reid was a natural-born British citizen of European and African descent. What caused that error? Perhaps in part it was caused by a need to rationalize a position in the moment. But why that particular error? A series of fascinating psychological experiments provides a telling insight into how race and ethnicity get confused with nationality and therefore complicate efforts to identify terrorists.

Social psychologists Thierry Devos and Mahzarin Banaji (2005) employed the Implicit Association Test (IAT) to investigate the connections people have in their minds between race and nationality. As you may recall from Chapter 4, the IAT indexes the strength of people's implicit (nonconscious) associations between concepts by measuring the relative facility with which they are able to categorize words or images representing those concepts when they are paired. In Devos and Banaji's study, research subjects were asked to categorize people as

---

4. U.S. citizenship has not been, it should be noted, a guarantee of constitutional rights for terror suspects, as evidenced in the case of the American-born suspected Dirty Bomber, Jose Padilla. Nor is citizenship a requirement for the conferral of basic criminal suspect protections, such as Mirandizing.

Black or White (or Asian)[5] using the same response keys they used to categorize symbols as either American (e.g., the American flag, the U.S. Capitol) or foreign (a foreign flag, foreign buildings). The results revealed that, on an implicit level, people had a stronger association between White and American than between Black (or Asian) and American, even though on explicit questionnaire measures the same samples did not differentiate between Blacks and Whites in terms of their Americanness.

Devos and Banaji tested the robustness of this tendency to identify Whites more strongly than Blacks with America. In one study they used Black and White U.S. Olympic athletes as their stimuli, finding that, although on explicit questionnaire measures subjects reported associating Black athletes more strongly with America and even being more familiar with those athletes, on the implicit measure they associated Whites more strongly with America. Devos and Banaji showed similar effects for Asian Americans, even showing that well-known foreign White celebrities (e.g., Elizabeth Hurley) were more strongly associated with being American than well-known Asian *American* celebrities (e.g., Lucy Liu).

The confusion between race and nationality documented by Devos and Banaji implicates another danger for security officials and screeners seeking to prevent terrorism. If foreigners are seen as more likely perpetrators of terrorism, the tendency to perceive racial and ethnic minorities as less *American* and more *foreign* could cloud the judgment of screeners. The tendency to perceive Whites as more American, regardless of their nationality, could also cause agents to overlook a whole class of foreign (European) terrorists. Simultaneously, the tendency to perceive racial minorities as less American, in a climate of fear of foreign-born terrorism, could further undermine race relations in America.

DO RATCHET EFFECTS APPLY TO THE "WAR ON TERROR"?

Harcourt (2007; see description in Chapter 5) argues compellingly that racial profiling in drug law enforcement can have a deleterious "ratchet effect"—by causing targeted minorities to be overrepresented in the criminal justice system, and to bear a disproportionate share of punishment, profiling harms minority communities, disenfranchises and alienates them, and creates a vicious cycle. If this is true in counterterrorism, too, profiling of Muslims could have the effect of making terrorism more likely to occur and harder to investigate.

5. Devos and Banaji (2005) compared implicit national identities for African, Asian, and White American categories, pairing them against each other in all three combinations.

The application of the ratchet thesis to counterterrorism is complicated. First, the base rate of crime may be too low to have the effect in terms of disproportionate incarcerations. Thousands of drug crimes occur daily, while terrorist acts are rarely attempted. While millions of Black Americans have been incarcerated for drug law violations, a much smaller number of Muslims have been incarcerated for terror-related activities, even including the hundreds who have been held without trials in federal custody. As a result, even though Muslims are overrepresented in the counterterrorism system, the absolute numbers may be too small to have a significant impact (e.g., economic) on the communities.

However, because individual terrorist acts can have large effects even if they rarely occur, the relatively small number of individuals who have been detained and possibly tortured by the U.S. government may pose a substantial threat if they end up becoming radicalized by the process. Hundreds of Guantanamo Bay detainees have been released into countries with active terrorist networks. Even if they were not terrorists before they were captured, they may become so after. In this sense, the small numbers may be irrelevant because terrorism is a small numbers phenomenon.

Profiling may Undermine Investigative Efforts

In addition to the potentially radicalizing effects of wrongful and inhumane detention of terror suspects, the more widespread scrutiny of people of Muslim, Middle Eastern, and South Asian descent, particularly in passenger and border screening, likely serves to disenfranchise and alienate many members of these groups. Additionally, the conspicuous detentions may have indirect alienating effects on other members of the groups (i.e., Muslim, Middle Eastern, South Asian) from which detainees tend to be drawn, causing them to distrust law enforcement officials and possibly their neighbors. Investigators often rely on community involvement to identify terrorism suspects. Beutel (2012), in fact, provides a substantial list of terrorist plots that were broken up with the assistance of (e.g., tips from) Muslim community members. The trust-eroding and alienating effects of discriminatory enforcement could undermine community involvement.

With regard to the more daily, mundane effects of profiling, people of Middle Eastern and South Asian descent (and others who are often presumed to be Muslim) suffer indignities in air travel ranging from suspicious looks to extra searches to insulting comments to prohibition from flying to removal from airplanes. In one relatively dramatic incident in July 2002, a U.S. domestic flight was escorted by a military plane because Indian passengers were seen passing notes and changing seats. The Indian passengers were held for questioning but released.

The specter of this kind of treatment causes many people to alter their behavior and forgo normal functions. Foss (2002), for example, reported cases of Middle

Eastern Americans who have avoided talking on flights, sitting near the front, and even getting up to use the restroom, and some others have avoided flying altogether. One Arab American flyer (and writer) even debated whether or not to take a pen on a flight. Another reported feeling "heartsick about a decision he made the other day: not to take his father-in-law, who is German, to the airport for his flight home" because he would have drawn too much attention (Verhovek, 2001).

In the words of Muslim Advocates Executive Director, Farhana Khera, in congressional testimony, providing specific examples of Muslim Americans who, without cause, have been surveilled, detained, interrogated, searched, and denied basic rights, like boarding flights:

> Muslims have also embraced our nation's promise of life, liberty and the pursuit of happiness. But since 9/11, these hopes and dreams have been dashed, and fundamental rights infringed. Today we face government discrimination in our everyday lives—whether we enter a mosque to pray, get on a plane, cross the border, or log onto the Internet. We worry that we will be interrogated by government agents, or worse, arrested and detained, for no reason at all.
>
> Khera, 2010, p. 2

The indignity, frustration, anxiety, and fear that many Muslim Americans, residents, and visitors experience due to enhanced scrutiny, disrespect, deprivation of rights, and detention are likely to have a marginalizing and disenfranchising effect. For those who may be prone to extreme views and behavior, these offenses may be sufficient to push them over to radicalism. For the vastly larger number of moderate people, this treatment may at least serve to undermine their sense of belonging and therefore their enthusiasm for cooperating with law enforcement. In this sense, racial profiling in counterterrorism may have a harmful ratchet effect.

TERRORISM ≠ DRUG CRIME

The Special Case of Islamic terrorism?

In understanding racial profiling in the context of counterterrorism, it is worth considering a structural difference between counterterrorism profiling and drug crime interdiction profiling. Specifically, there is, in the former case, an *instrumental* (and therefore causal) connection between the group and the behavior. Islamic terrorism (which appears to be the primary focus of U.S. counterterrorism efforts) is perpetrated because of a cultural conflict and with the purpose of achieving a group-based objective. That purpose is, ostensibly, getting the United States and Europe out of Middle Eastern affairs, but perhaps also merely to exact vengeance and undermine Western power and influence more generally. This could mean that Muslim identity (particularly fundamentalist Muslim identity) is *causally* related to terrorism and therefore a legitimate diagnostic factor, if not a strong one.

In contrast, any higher drug crime rates among African Americans or Latinos do not reflect any group psychology or strategic act on the part of the criminals. In other words, there is nothing inherent in being Black or Latino, aside from socioeconomic factors that are correlated with minority status, that *causes* people to commit drug crimes.

However, it should be remembered that the vast majority of Muslims do not endorse terrorism and may not even support the terrorists' goals. Because such a minute fraction of Muslims are involved in terrorism, the causal connection between Muslim identification and terrorism may be moot; as discussed previously, the predictive power of *being Muslim* is too low to be useful.

Perhaps more important, the instrumental connection between being Muslim and engaging in terrorism is of potential use if we are concerned only with Islamic terrorism. As discussed earlier in this chapter, the history of terrorism in the West is rife with acts perpetrated by White Christians and other non-Muslims. Although Islamic terrorism is understandably salient in the minds of Americans and Europeans in the period after the September 11, 2001, attacks, counterterrorism officials would be remiss if they neglected other populations.

Undeterrable

Another crucial difference between terrorism and drug crime is that terrorists are difficult to deter, and *suicidal* terrorists are virtually undeterrable, in the sense that they are less sensitive to the costs of getting caught. Perhaps it is more nuanced than that—they do not want to get caught and imprisoned, but they are prepared, in fact determined, to die for the cause and so are willing to take great risks. Psychologist Arie Kruglanski and his colleagues (Kruglanski, Chen, Dechesne, Fishman, & Orehek, 2009) contend that suicidal terrorists' primary motivation is a "quest for significance" that transcends their own physical existence. In this sense, the costs and benefits that they weigh in their contemplation may be hard to influence. Nonsuicidal terrorists (e.g., those who aspire to plant and remotely detonate bombs) should also be more difficult to deter than other types of criminals because they are ideologically motivated; the costs and benefits that are important to them are not monetary or even personal but rather relate to a larger cause for which they are willing to make personal sacrifices.

Suicidal terrorists are prepared to make the ultimate sacrifice. As a result, the success of their operation is more important to them than their own lives. In this sense, it may be more appropriate for counterterrorism officials to think in terms of *deferrence* than *deterrence*. Specifically, when security agencies make particular targets (e.g., "high-value" targets like skyscrapers and airplanes) especially difficult to successfully attack, the targets become less appealing. For example, the use of scanners, reinforced cockpit doors, new requirements for carry-on objects, and the presence of armed air marshals make even suicidal hijackings nearly impossible. Accordingly, terrorists will likely seek other approaches that may be less effectively terrorizing than blowing up airplanes or using them as missiles. In this sense, they are not ultimately deterred but are "deferred" to lower-value targets.

If security agencies can defer terrorists low enough, the targets (and the magnitude of impact) may be too low to be deemed worth attacking. Of course, such deferrence will only be temporary, until terrorists can figure out a new way to attack a sufficiently high-value target or until they become desperate enough to attempt a low-probability-of-success, high-value target attack.

Consistent with the idea of deferrence, Harcourt (2006) cited analyses of trends in terrorist targeting to demonstrate that when counterterror security procedures have hardened targets (e.g., antihijacking methods imposed in the 1970s), terrorists shifted to other types of attacks entirely (e.g., assassinations). Harcourt argued that this should apply to terrorists' reactions to racial profiling as well. Targeting certain demographic groups will likely lead terrorist organizations to recruit outside the profile. In this way, the profile itself can become a counterterrorism liability because surveillance resources will be focused away from the new perpetrators.

Detecting Counterterrorism Profiling?

Another manner in which counterterrorism and drug crime interdiction differ is in how we can study them. As discussed in Chapters 2 and 5, one of the most promising methods for detecting racial profiling is "outcome testing," wherein hit rates for different groups are compared. Among those who are stopped and searched by the police, if minorities have lower hit rates (a smaller proportion are found to be carrying contraband), that is evidence of racial profiling in the decisions to stop and search. Unfortunately, this approach cannot be effectively applied in counterterrorism because the hit rate for all groups is effectively zero. Thankfully, even failed attempts at terrorism are extremely rare. And, as discussed earlier, even among the "worst of the worst" few hundred terror suspects held at Guantanamo Bay Cuba, few have been found to be tied to terrorism.

However, in the absence of hit rate differences between groups, discrepancies in who gets stopped and searched (e.g., in airport screening) *are evidence of racial profiling*. If essentially nobody is being caught, but one group (or really a "group" composed of disparate ethnic groups often perceived as Muslim) is being stopped and searched at higher rates, then we know the searches are due not to actual differences in suspiciousness but to ethnic stereotypes. However, it should be acknowledged that, because individual terrorist acts by design have widespread, societally destabilizing effects, deterring (or *deferring*) them through aggressive, targeted screening may be a more legitimate strategy than it would be in drug crime interdiction.

THE REAL STORY OF THE SHOE BOMBER: THE DISTRACTION OF RACE/ETHNICITY; THE MOVING TARGET PROBLEM; AND THE VIRTUES OF BEHAVIORAL PROFILING

On December 22, 2001, not long after the September 11 attacks, while Americans and our allies were still profoundly unsettled, an airliner bombing attempt came close to success. The terrorist, Richard Reid, was a natural-born British citizen of mixed-race descent (his mother is White, and his father is Jamaican) who had converted to Islam, become radicalized, and apparently got connected with al-Qaeda. Reid attempted to detonate plastic explosives built into the heel of his shoe during an American Airlines flight from Paris to Miami. The widely reported story is well known, if for no other reason than we all now have to remove our shoes during airport screening. When Reid tried to ignite his explosives with a match, a flight attendant noticed and interceded. After struggling with the flight attendants, Reid was subdued by passengers before he could detonate the bomb. The flight was diverted to Boston, where he was taken into custody. He pleaded guilty to eight criminal counts of terrorism and is serving a sentence of life without the possibility of parole in a super-maximum security prison in the United States. For obvious reasons, Reid came to be known as the Shoe Bomber.

Had Richard Reid succeeded in taking down American Airlines Flight 63, given the prevailing agitation of the American public in the wake of 9/11, he would very likely have had a devastating effect on the United States (and many other countries). In addition to the deaths suffered that day, nerves would have been deeply rattled, air travel would likely have declined significantly for an extended period, and national security resources and attention would have been scrambled at a time when agencies were working to coalesce around a coherent infrastructure and strategy.

The Reid story has multiple lessons. First, it is widely acknowledged that his Anglo-sounding name and British citizenship helped him slip through security with less suspicion than he may have aroused with a Muslim name and Middle Eastern origins. This points to the limits of racial profiling because, as discussed earlier, terrorists can confound profiles by changing names and appearance, recruiting outside the profile, or even exploiting unwitting accomplices who are outside the profile.

Second, Reid's method—an explosive built into his shoe—represented an innovation that had not been anticipated, or at least not been the focus of much concern, prior to his attempt. Before 9/11, nobody was looking for box-cutters as weapons (although, anyone who has used a box-cutter knows how dangerously sharp and potentially lethal they are). Screening was primarily focused on bomb and gun detection. Reid may have been exploiting the post-9/11 shift in focus to small objects that could be used as hand-to-hand weapons. The terrorist technique is a moving and adapting target, shifting from armed hijacking to bombing to suicide hijacking back to bombing, and so forth. And the bombing techniques also shift, for example, from suitcases to shoes to liquids. Focus on race and ethnicity may be a distraction for screeners from the actual threats.

Third, even though techniques shift and evolve over time, bombing with plastic explosives was not a new approach. The failure of mechanical devices to detect the explosives represents a significant and serious gap in air transit security. The good news is that it is a gap that can be closed with technological modifications that should be relatively noninvasive and nondiscriminatory.

The final and most important lesson of the Shoe Bomber is based on an aspect of the case that is surprisingly not well known. This lesson is crucial to any discussion of national security or racial profiling. It is that *race-neutral, behavioral profiling can be effective*. A behavioral terrorist profile actually *did* identify Reid as a threat *before* he boarded the flight. In testimony before the U.S. House Committee on Transportation and Infrastructure Subcommittee on Aviation, Turley (2002, citing Specaro, 2002, and *Air Safety Week*, 2001) reported that Reid was in fact flagged by a security subcontractor to American Airlines at de Gaulle Airport in Paris and subjected to extensive questioning because he lacked a verifiable address, had purchased a one-way ticket, purchased it with cash, had no clear travel plan, and brought no luggage. As a result, Reid missed his first flight on December 21 and was rebooked on the same flight the next day. Had security personnel used the occasion to physically search Reid more carefully, his conspicuously malformed explosive shoe could have been discovered, and the airline would not have had to rely on luck and the astuteness and toughness of its flight staff and passengers. There has also been some speculation that the extra 24 hours of wear may have caused the shoe and fuse to dampen, thus interfering with Reid's attempts to detonate the bomb.

BEHAVIORAL PROFILING/SCREENING

The type of behavioral profiling that first triggered concern over Reid focuses on what the traveler *does* rather than what he *is*. Terrorism expert Andrew Silke (2011) reports that behavioral profiling (also called *behavioral screening*) systems of this sort, based on an Israeli model, have been in place in the United Kingdom and United States since at least 2003, and no doubt they are being used in other countries as well. Silke writes that "behavioral screening … works on the premise that terrorists on missions act in certain ways and that their behavior while engaged in illegal activity will unintentionally betray their presence" (p. 7).

In explaining the advantages of behavioral profiling/screening, Silke and others note that there is an intuitive appeal to the idea that terrorists suffer from mental illness or personality disorders. This idea may lead one to assume that terrorists, as sociopaths, might not experience the kind of emotions or exhibit the kinds of behaviors one would expect from a normal person under those circumstances. However, careful, empirical research on terrorists, even suicidal terrorists, indicates that they tend to be psychologically normal (e.g., Kruglanski & Fishman, 2009; Kruglanski et al., 2009; Silke, 1998; Victoroff & Kruglanski, 2009), and certainly more normal than other types of violent criminals. Consequently, they are likely to show the trappings of a normal response while doing something extremely abnormal and dangerous (possibly suicidal)—they will be visibly anxious.

Silke (2011) describes the behavioral screening programs employed by the United Kingdom and the United States, which are, respectively, the Behavioral Analysis Screening System (BASS) and the Screening Passengers by Observation Technique (SPOT). According to Silke, SPOT may be more effective because it focuses primarily on anxious behavior, whereas BASS makes "more esoteric claims" about more general attributes of suicidal terrorists. Silke expresses healthy skepticism about both systems, given the lack of empirical evidence of their effectiveness. Specifically, he cites statistics from TSA reports indicating that SPOT is used in 161 American airports, more than 3,000 security officers working in these airports have been trained in the system, and more than 200,000 passengers have been identified by SPOT for greater scrutiny. Yet, of all these cases, "the system has not been credited yet with even one clear terrorist detection" (p. 9).

Silke reports that SPOT *has* led to approximately 2,000 arrests, for nonterrorism crimes detected under questioning. But as far is its record with regard to its primary objective, mitigating terrorism, it has no known hits. However, we must bear in mind that, as discussed previously, the behavior it is trying to detect is extremely rare. A hit rate of zero certainly represents an absence of affirmative evidence for its effectiveness, but zero is not far below the actual prevalence of the crime. If terrorist attacks on American airliners occurred with any frequency in the years since airports began using SPOT, the zero hit rate would be a better indicator of poor effectiveness. However, terrorist attempts in that period (the Shoe Bomber, the Underwear Bomber, the 2006 multi-aircraft liquid explosives plot) have all involved perpetrators boarding or planning to board planes in foreign airports. So the effective rate of attempts is zero, as far as we know, and the SPOT hit rate is the same, by Silke's accounting. Even if there have been a few attempts that have resulted in attackers successfully boarding planes, with the millions of passenger-flights in the United States per year, that rate is effectively zero.

This all leaves us in a state of high uncertainty about the utility of programs like SPOT, not necessarily due to any flaw in the program itself. Silke notes, however, that the program is relatively low in cost—several million dollars per year in total—and so involves little risk. He adds that it must be considered as just one part of a multifaceted terrorist detection and deterrence program, including, for example, technology, random searches, and onboard security measures.

LESSONS LEARNED FROM CUSTOMS ENFORCEMENT

The low base rate problem we have with SPOT renders an evaluation of its effectiveness very difficult, if at all possible. But we may be able to generalize to it from experiences in similar domains that have higher rates of offending. Specifically, the experience of the U.S. Customs Service between 1998 and 2000, as described in Chapter 5, is telling. After 1998, and in the wake of concerns about high search rates of minority travelers, the Customs Service prohibited the use of race or ethnicity in stops and searches and mandated an emphasis on traveler behavior. As a result, searches declined by about 75% and hit rates shot up, the net result being roughly the same number of contraband hits with far fewer false alarms (unnecessary intrusions) and far less racial disparity. In the customs case, the rate of carrying contraband is much higher than zero, and so it allows for a test of the effectiveness of behavioral profiling. The results are very promising.

The contrast and tension between racial profiling and sound investigative work are evident in the investigation of the Oklahoma City attack discussed earlier. Several Middle Eastern men were immediately investigated. In retrospect, we now know that the Middle Eastern suspects proved to be bad leads, and sound investigation was the key to catching McVeigh and preventing him from carrying out any more attacks. A piece of the axle from the truck used in the bombing was traced to the rental company, and the staff there provided a description of McVeigh that matched his appearance well. McVeigh was already in custody after being pulled over for driving without a license plate and the weapons possession charge that resulted from that stop. Investigators connected the dots *inductively*, building up from hard evidence at the crime scene until they came to McVeigh.

In contrast, a reliance on terrorist profiles, including the prevailing Middle Eastern stereotype, would not have led to McVeigh. The specific information arising from the crime scene and other actual details of the crime provide a basis for investigation that is so much more diagnostic of the perpetrator than broad generalizations like racial or ethnic stereotypes that the utility of the former swamps that of the latter.

It is fair to ask, however, what if there is no crime scene, because the crime has not occurred yet? This is where *the use of ethnicity in terrorist profiling* contrasts with *ethnic profiling in counterterrorism.*[6] When investigating a terrorist act that has already been committed, just as with other crimes, offender profiles are rarely helpful and can be counterproductive (Silke, 2001). In the absence of direct evidence emerging from a crime scene, when security officials are trying to apprehend or deter perpetrators *before* they strike, perhaps racial or ethnic profiles will be more valuable. But it should first be acknowledged that counterterrorism is not conducted in an information vacuum. Solid investigative and human intelligence work has led to the capture of numerous terrorists and the prevention of attacks. In other words, racial profiling is not the only detection tool in the counterterrorism arsenal, and other tools have track records of effectiveness.

As discussed previously, if the security goal is to prevent *Islamic extremist* terrorism, then focusing on Muslims certainly could make sense. But just as using a racial profile to catch drug couriers will divert attention from White couriers, focusing on a narrower population of terrorists will also divert attention away from other types. Imagine a soccer goalie whose intention is to guard only one portion of his goal. He may end up with a perfect record of repelling goals from that section, but the other team will nevertheless be able to score, and more easily, especially if it figures out what he is doing.

CONCLUSION

Journalist Fareed Zakaria (2002) relayed a telling, cautionary tale:

> In 1942, eight Nazi agents—all German-Americans or Germans who had lived in the United States for long stretches—landed on New York's Long Island with instructions to destroy American power plants, factories and bridges. They were captured by the FBI, President Roosevelt declared them enemy combatants and they were tried and convicted by a military tribunal. This case—Ex parte Quirin—is the model often cited to explain how we should fight the war on terror bluntly and robustly. But it leaves out one part of the story. The FBI had no idea that these men had landed and knew nothing of their plans. The terrorists were discovered only because one of the eight men was an American patriot. He had set off on the mission with the intention of divulging the plot to the authorities.

This early case of attempted sabotage by members of a minority group bears some resemblance to current circumstances. The minority group is defined by a national origin they share with a wartime enemy. They walk among us, and many are tempted to deprive them of basic rights and to subject them to harsh

---

6. In the case of terrorism, because the prevailing stereotype is Arab/Middle Eastern/ Muslim, I use the term *ethnic* instead of *racial*, but, as discussed when defining *racial profiling* in Chapter 1, it is the same phenomenon.

treatment. But blunt and robust counterespionage techniques did not foil the attack; rather, the robustness of American democratic principles, and their appeal to the double agent, did.

Because of the very low rate of terrorism among Muslims, profiling them reflects the logical error of affirming the consequent (i.e., *terrorists are Muslims; therefore Muslims are terrorists*). Worse, profiling can lead to alienating the group and perhaps thereby promoting radicalization and terrorism while undermining efforts to combat terrorism. At the same time, most security experts agree that focusing profiles on *behavior* is more effective than focusing on race, ethnicity, and national origin, which are generally regarded as distractions from valid indicators of suspicion.

Terrorism expert Andrew Silke (2011) contends that one of the central goals of terrorists is "provocation"—to get their enemies to "suspend or sideline the normal methods and operation of law and order" (p. 4). Racial profiling in counterterrorism, by compromising individuals' Fourth and Fourteenth Amendment rights, has this effect. In this sense, the implementation of racial profiling in counterterrorism, and the disparate treatment of classes of individuals that it necessarily results in, can be seen as a capitulation to terrorists, helping them to achieve their objective. It is not just the inherent insult to the principles of a free society and constitutional liberties that profiling represents, nor the direct harms to those innocent civilians who get tangled in the profiling web, but a very real threat to security resulting from the alienation and radicalization of individuals who may support, if not become, terrorists.

CHAPTER 7

The Policy Landscape

Racial profiling is wrong, and we will end it in America.

President George W. Bush, February 27, 2001

Given the incalculably high stakes involved in [counterterrorism] investigations, federal law enforcement officers who are protecting national security or preventing catastrophic events (as well as airport security screeners) may consider race, ethnicity, alienage, or other relevant factors....there can be no expectation that the information must be specific to a particular locale or even to a particular identified scheme.

Department of Justice fact sheet issued in 2003 to clarify the policies set in place following President Bush's February 2001 declaration

The use by police officers of race, ethnicity, religion, or national origin in deciding which persons should be subject to traffic stops, stops and frisks, questioning, searches, and seizures is improper.

End Racial Profiling Act [ERPA], Senate version, 2004, Section 2(a)(2), as yet not passed by Congress

We think these [past Supreme Court rulings] foreclose any argument that the constitutional reasonableness of traffic stops depends on the actual motivations of the individual officers involved.

U.S. Supreme Court majority in *Whren v. United States*, 1996

The first question we need to ask in any policy analysis is, simply, "Is there a problem?" (Bardach, 2005). And, if there is, we need to define that problem carefully—the more precise the definition, the more likely the chosen solution will solve the core problem. If there is a problem, and it rises to a level that warrants remediation, then we can talk about policy changes.

Most policy analysis involves relatively micro-level problems that can be addressed by a single agency. Racial profiling is a more macro-level problem, extending nationally, even internationally, and operating at multiple levels (i.e., local, state, and federal). Consequently, a problem definition and set of proposed solutions will be a relatively ambitious undertaking, and individual agencies will do well to define their problems carefully and consider solutions that are appropriate for their unique circumstances. That said, there are commonalities across agencies, particularly with regard to overriding laws (constitutional protections) and principles (e.g., fairness and civility), as well as concerns about effectiveness and efficiency in terms of crime mitigation and public safety.

Part of the thorniness of defining the racial profiling problem is that it invokes a classic policy tension between individual liberties and public safety. This trade-off rubs many people the wrong way. Benjamin Franklin famously declared, "They who can give up essential liberty to obtain a little temporary safety, deserve neither liberty nor safety." But in reality these trade-offs are ubiquitous. Free speech, for example, is permitted but only up to the point where it harms others. Speed limits and seat belt requirements restrict our choices but save lives and medical costs. Law enforcement necessitates some intrusion into people's free exercise of their lives, even innocent people. We, as a society, with the ultimate adjudication of the Supreme Court, draw lines about what are acceptable infringements on liberty. It is not sufficient that a law or enforcement strategy will make people safer; there is a moral, legal, and pragmatic calculus about how much safety is worth a given increment of lost liberty. Courts are continuously refining the threshold, even with such sacrosanct concepts as free speech.

There have been times in American history where dramatic infringements were imposed on basic liberties in the name of public safety and national security, including the Alien and Sedition Acts, Abraham Lincoln's suspension of habeas corpus, the internment of Japanese Americans during World War II, blacklisting of citizens by Joseph McCarthy's House Committee on Un-American Activities in the early days of the Cold War, and recent practices like the required registration of South Asian immigrants, "extraordinary rendition" of terror suspects to other countries for interrogation, and torture (aka "enhanced interrogation techniques") employed in counterterrorism. Maybe these examples represent only extremes. Most, if not all, of these practices have been judged harshly by history, once ostensibly imminent threats subsided (or proved exaggerated or unfounded). And yet, they recur because, in the words of Supreme Court justice Thurgood Marshall, "History teaches us that grave threats to liberty often come in times of urgency, when constitutional rights seem too extravagant to endure" (dissenting *Skinner v. Railway Labor Executives' Ass'n*, 489 U.S. 602, 635 (1989)).

The safety-liberty trade-off may, in some cases, be a false choice. There are certainly increases in public safety that do not require a sacrifice in liberties (e.g., securing airplane cockpit doors, improved road surfaces). Furthermore, there is reasonable disagreement about what reflects a tolerable loss of liberty (e.g., the privacy that is sacrificed by traffic enforcement cameras, gun registration requirements). It is clear, however, that racial profiling, because it necessarily leads to disproportionate criminal justice outcomes, involves a sacrifice, and one that is borne by the targeted minority communities. This raises serious civil rights concerns.

The analyses laid out in Chapters 1, 2, 5, and 6 should make it clear that racial profiling is real and that it poses a number of problems, both for targeted communities and for police effectiveness. Furthermore, legal scholars tend to agree, despite the judiciary's forbearance, that racial profiling is a constitutionally impermissible form of discrimination (e.g., Harris, 2002a; Kennedy, 1999; Turley, 2002; Alschuler, 2002). In particular, it violates the Fourth Amendment (unreasonable searches and seizures) and Fourteenth Amendment (equal protection) of the U.S. Constitution, as well as Title VI of the Civil Rights Act of 1964, which bars discrimination based on race, color, or national origin by recipients of federal support. Similarly, racial profiling violates the public's basic sense of fairness and individual liberty, and this has been reflected consistently in public opinion polling. The violation of constitutional and basic fairness principles is felt most acutely by those who belong to targeted groups; as a consequence, members of these communities may be less likely to cooperate with police, in terms of both reporting crimes and cooperating with investigations. Policymakers, including police command staff, oversight boards, national security officials, executives, and legislators, are likely to conclude, as many have already, that the limited utility, not to mention the potential for counterproductive effects, makes racial profiling not worth the violation of civil liberties.

If these arguments strike you as exclusively liberal or "politically correct," consider a "conservative case against racial profiling"[1] offered by legal scholar Nelson Lund (2003). Lund rests his argument on three contentions. First, showing an unreferenced resonance with the vast psychological literature discussed in Chapters 3 and 4, he contends that stereotype-based judgments are ubiquitous but often erroneous. Second, Lund asserts that free markets will punish discriminators, and so discrimination will be self-regulated in the private sector—an apparent reference to Becker's (1957) influential economics theory. Lund's third point renders his second one moot; government agencies do not have to compete in free markets, so when they discriminate, Lund contends, it is less likely to be checked and more likely to be out of control and abusive. The implications of this third point are that profiling by counterterrorism agents could lead to widespread violations of civil rights, and that unchecked reliance on stereotypes in counterterrorism will serve to distract officials from real threats, a point discussed in Chapter 6, and to which we will soon return.

1. Lund's article is specific to, as its title indicates, "racial profiling in the war on terrorism", but his arguments hold well for racial profiling across domains.

The application of economic theories of discrimination to racial profiling (Lund's second point) is, as noted in Chapter 5, problematic because police who rely on racial stereotypes will not be "punished" in the same way that businesses that fail to hire from the best pool of applicants will. Even in competitive markets, however, if discrimination is the norm (i.e., if most employers, lenders, and so forth, are discriminating), the market will not "punish" discriminators because they will not be at a disadvantage. Furthermore, discriminators are unlikely to attribute any competitive cost to their discriminatory practices, let alone correct for them. Consequently, even if markets are self-regulating vis-à-vis discrimination, the process would be slow and evolutionary in the sense that the discriminators might be gradually selected out through attrition. In counterterrorism, the insensitivity of discriminators to the costs of discriminating is especially acute because hit rates are virtually zero, so agents are unlikely to detect whether their stereotype-based judgments are helping or hurting. But this is essentially Lund's point—that government agents who profile will not be held accountable for poor performance that results from it.

Lund's argument is not all about efficiency; it is also about government violation of civil rights. He, like many others, points out that the internment of Japanese Americans during World War II was rationalized, even for years after the war, on the grounds of national security, but this was based on grossly inaccurate stereotypes. Lund (2003) concludes, pragmatically, "In light of the constitutionally dubious nature of this technique, the burden should be on those who advocate its use to show that it actually works and that it is necessary. So far, that burden has not been met" (p. 341).

As discussed in Chapter 5, racial profiling's effectiveness is, at best, modest, and it can be counterproductive in terms of reducing criminal captures, possibly increasing crime, and harming police-community relations. Law enforcement experts agree that the "gold standard" of good policing (and counterterrorism) is good intelligence and direct observation of behavior (i.e., *suspicious* behavior; Silke, 2011). Even in the case of the September 11, 2001, terrorist attacks, which are often invoked as a justification for racial profiling, the hijackers' identities, in combination with their travel patterns, could have triggered additional scrutiny that might have prevented their boarding the planes or even led to their discovery. In fact, several of the hijackers were already under suspicion. Additionally, al-Qaeda trainee Zacharias Moussaoui, considered at one point to have been the "twentieth" accomplice in the September 11 attacks, had aroused suspicion with his unusual flight training behavior. Moussaoui was arrested, interrogated, and eventually tried and convicted. However, even though he was arrested weeks before the 9/11 attacks, and FBI field agents were desperately trying to have him investigated thoroughly, his knowledge and connections were not leveraged to yield an investigative breakthrough in time. As the 9/11 Commission determined, there was an intelligence failure in terms of interdepartmental information sharing and cooperation.

Many law enforcement executives agree that racial profiling does more harm than good, and this is evidenced by their opposition to profiling tactics even during the politically pressurized period in the months following the 9/11 attacks. Harris (2002b) notes that command staff in police departments resisted cooperating with Department of Justice (DOJ) efforts to question Middle Eastern men without reasonable suspicion, that senior U.S. intelligence officials collaborated on the production and dissemination of a memorandum advising against racial profiling and for a continued emphasis on observing behavior, and that "eight former FBI officials, including former chief of both the FBI and CIA, William H. Webster, went on record with [their] doubts about the law enforcement value of these tactics" (p. 41). The *Boston Globe* reported in October 2001 that five intelligence specialists from major law enforcement and security agencies had circulated a memo, titled "Assessing Behaviors," advising against the use of race or national origin in terrorist identification efforts. As one anonymous security official and author of the memo put it, "Security lies in the hard work of watching for suspicious behavior, not for suspicious people" (Dedman, 2001, as reported in Ramirez et al., 2003, p. 1227).

Considering all the pitfalls of racial profiling, as well as the moral, legal, and professional concerns, it is fair to say that many, if not most, relevant agencies and their governing bodies will want to mitigate it. Now we turn to the question of *how*. In so doing, we consider the major routes to policy change: judicial, legislative, and administrative. In this chapter, I will focus on the policy landscape to date—what has been done. As indicated earlier, racial profiling is a complex problem that manifests itself differently across geographical, jurisdictional, and crime domains. There is no one simple solution. Nevertheless, where possible, I will provide indications of how policies can be improved and implemented. Chapter 8 will lay out basic principles for ameliorating racial profiling, particularly with regard to mitigating the influence of race-crime stereotypes on law enforcement decisions.

JUDICIAL REMEDIES

Racial profiling can be adjudicated in the courts in two different ways: (1) as a civil action wherein citizens sue a law enforcement agency for violation of civil rights; or (2) in a criminal case, as a defense tactic to invalidate the admissibility of the results of a search. In a few civil cases the courts have agreed with legal scholars about the unconstitutionality of stops based on driver race or ethnicity. Such cases, however, tend to involve particularly egregious or patently unconstitutional behavior by police. Some of these cases, such as the Oakland, California, "Riders" civil rights lawsuit ended in court-administered consent decrees that included orders to cease and desist in biased practices and requirements of compliance with terms, including data collection by officers on all traffic (and in some cases pedestrian) stops. There is some empirical evidence that these actions result in reduced bias (Knowles et al., 2001), although it may be short-lived (Sanga, 2009). However, most civil suits alleging racial profiling have failed (Harris, 2002b). Even in civil cases, which require only a "preponderance of evidence" standard, the threshold for a finding of discrimination, which typically requires a demonstration of *intent*, is so high as to be prohibitive.

Judicial remedy for racial profiling has met even less success in criminal proceedings. U.S. courts have been very indifferent when racial profiling has been used as a defense. As summarized in Chapter 1 and covered at length in articles and books by legal scholars (e.g., Banks, 2001; Harcourt, 2004, 2007; Harris, 2002a, 2002b), the U.S. Supreme Court has laid out a series of decisions that, cumulatively, permit racial profiling. Harris traces the earliest court influence to *Robinson v. U.S.* (414 U.S. 218 (1973)), in which "the Supreme Court allowed police to perform a full search incident to a traffic arrest, despite the lack of any reason to fear the presence of weapons or the destruction of evidence....All that was important, the Court said, was that there was valid probable cause for the arrest" (Harris, 2002b, p. 38). In *Terry v. Ohio*, the Supreme Court ruled that police can detain and frisk (or "pat down") those they have stopped without warrant, based on reasonable suspicion. This decision resulted in the term *Terry stops*. *Whren v. United States* is probably the most influential court precedent giving rise to the tolerance of race-based stops and searches. *Whren* allows police to use "pretextual" stops, that is, "to stop any driver violating any observed traffic offense, even if the goal of the stop has nothing whatsoever to do with traffic enforcement" (from Harris congressional testimony, June 17, 2002, pp. 5–6). The quote at the beginning of this chapter, from the *Whren* majority opinion, conveys the essence of the Court's indifference to biased motives in officers' decisions and merits repeating here: "We think these [past Supreme Court rulings] foreclose any argument that the constitutional reasonableness of traffic stops depends on the actual motivations of the individual officers involved."

Constitutional law expert Jonathan Turley describes the Supreme Court's high-wire act, ruling on the validity of stops with a legal pretext without wading into the discriminatory perils they engender: "While the Court noted that the use of pretextual stops based on race could violate the Fourteenth Amendment, the Court stated that it would not delve into the subjective intent of an officer who can cite a valid pretext for a stop" (Turley, 2002). In the blunt words of the Court's majority, referencing previous decisions that support the *Whren* ruling, "We flatly dismissed the idea that an ulterior motive might serve to strip the agents of their legal justification" (*Whren v. U.S.*, 1996).

Harris has summarized the Court's disposition cogently:

In a series of decisions dating back more than a decade, the Supreme Court has created great police power and discretion to engage in traffic enforcement based on pretexts, and we have seen time and again, in state after state, how this discretion easily morphs into the tactic of profiling. These cases allow police to stop any driver violating any observed traffic offense, even if the goal of the stop has nothing whatsoever to do with traffic enforcement (*Whren v. U.S.*, 517 U.S. 806 (1996)); to order the driver (*Pennsylvania v. Mimms*, 434 U.S. 106 (1977)) and the passenger (*Maryland v. Wilson*, 519 U.S. 408 (1997)) out of any vehicle the police stop, without any evidence of danger or wrongdoing; and to ask for consent to a search of a driver's car without informing the driver that he or she has a right to refuse (*Ohio v. Robinette*, 519 U.S. 33 (1996)). In addition, the Court has allowed police to arrest drivers for traffic offenses even when the penalties for these infractions do not include imprisonment (*Atwater v. Lago Vista*, 532 U.S. 318 (2001)), and has decided that police do not violate the Fourth Amendment even if their search or seizure conduct violates state law. (*Virginia v. Moore*, 553 U.S. 164 (2008))

(Harris, House testimony, June 17, 2010)

Along with lenience toward driver and pedestrian profiling, the Supreme Court has allowed behavioral profiling of air passengers (*United States v. Sokolow*, 490 U.S. 1 (1989)).

Additionally, in *United States v. Vite-Espinoza* (342 F.3d 462 (2003)), a U.S. appeals court held that a suspect's ethnic appearance is permissible to warrant reasonable suspicion. While the court ruled that ethnicity *alone* is insufficient, this necessarily allows that race or ethnicity, as a component of a profile containing other characteristics, is a legal basis for suspicion.

In sum, the current jurisprudence allows for considerable latitude in profiling even though it is clear to most that racial profiling violates the U.S. Constitution. Except perhaps in the most extreme cases (e.g., overt expressions of intent to discriminate), legal challenge is not a practical solution to the racial profiling problem.

ADMINISTRATIVE APPROACHES

In the absence of an effective judicial remedy, one recourse for mitigating racial profiling would be administrative action by government executives (e.g., mayors, governors, and presidents). Law enforcement agencies report to these officeholders, who have governing authority over them. In fact, much of the policy action around racial profiling has occurred administratively. This action, however, has typically taken the form of blanket bans on racial profiling, and these prohibitions typically lack clear definitions, specific guidelines, and enforcement mechanisms. Perhaps this reflects the political nature of executive officeholders, whose policy actions often serve political purposes, especially with politically loaded issues like racial profiling.

The primary shortcoming of blanket prohibitions of racial profiling is that, due to general public condemnation of profiling, there is an effective ban on explicit, deliberate profiling anyway, particularly in standard policing (i.e., not counterterrorism). No agencies, and few if any officers, admit to currently doing it, although some are candid enough to acknowledge having done it in the past. Nevertheless, the evidence discussed previously indicates that profiling persists. This is most likely the case because, as the psychological research indicates, profiling occurs tacitly.

Banning . . . and Institutionalizing Racial Profiling

A case in point regarding the limited utility of blanket bans on racial profiling is the federal policy put in place in the early years of the George W. Bush administration. In February 2001, the newly inaugurated President Bush declared, "Racial profiling is wrong, and we will end it in America." In June 2003, the DOJ released a statement reasserting President Bush's declaration and providing some more specific direction (DOJ, 2003b). One limitation on the effectiveness of the DOJ's policy is that the department has direct authority over federal law enforcement agencies only, and while this represents thousands of agents, the vast majority of law enforcement is carried out by local and state departments. Highlighting the limitation of the policy, the DOJ's statement indicates that "the guidance provides that in making routine law enforcement decisions—such as deciding which motorists to stop for traffic infractions—consideration of the driver's race or ethnicity is absolutely forbidden." This clause, while forceful and unambiguous in its prohibition, is almost a non sequitur; traffic stops are rarely carried out by federal agents, being overwhelmingly the domain of state and local law enforcement, neither of which is bound by this ban. Nevertheless, it sets a standard that could perhaps be adopted by state and local departments.

The federal ban is far more ambivalent with regard to counterterrorism, stating,

> Since September 11, 2001, the President has emphasized that federal law enforcement personnel must use all available and legitimate tools to prevent future catastrophic terrorist attacks. . . . The racial profiling guidance, therefore, recognizes that race and ethnicity may be used in terrorist identification, but only to the extent permitted by the nation's laws and the Constitution.
>
> DOJ, 2003b

An accompanying fact sheet (DOJ, 2003a) is less ambiguous: "Given the incalculably high stakes involved in [counterterrorism] investigations, federal law enforcement officers who are protecting national security or preventing catastrophic events (as well as airport security screeners) may consider race, ethnicity, alienage, or other relevant factors" (p. 5). In case it is not clear from that language that the new DOJ policy is sanctioning racial profiling in counterterrorism, the following allowance reveals a clear intention to extend beyond imminent threats (i.e., "ticking timebomb" scenarios):

> Because terrorist organizations might aim to engage in unexpected acts of catastrophic violence in any available part of the country (indeed, in multiple places simultaneously, if possible), there can be no expectation that the information must be specific to a particular locale or even to a particular identified scheme. (p. 5)

As noted previously, the Constitution has generally been interpreted by the courts, though not typically by constitutional scholars, as permissive of, or at best indifferent to, racial profiling. Accordingly, the DOJ fact sheet (DOJ, 2003a) asserts that the ban "in many cases imposes *more* restrictions on the use of race and ethnicity in federal law enforcement than the Constitution requires" (p. 2, emphasis in original). However, if race or ethnicity "may be used in terrorist identification...to the extent permitted by the nation's laws and Constitution," in counterterrorism, racial profiling appears to be included. As a result, the DOJ's stated deference to constitutional protections is likely cold comfort to future targets of profiling.

As a result of these conditions, the otherwise emphatic ban on racial profiling in federal law enforcement appears to carve out an exception for counterterrorism. In that sense, it has the ironic effect of *institutionalizing* racial profiling in federal law enforcement. Given that there is a de facto ban on profiling (at least on overt profiling) to the extent that it is generally taboo and condemned and disavowed by law enforcement officials, it is possible that the construction of the federal ban, with its allowance for profiling in counterterrorism, has a net effect of making profiling more common.

Despite the serious problem with institutionalizing racial profiling in counterterrorism, the DOJ's 2003 policy does have some constructive elements. It is generally precise and recognizes that racial profiling involves the use of race or ethnicity "to any degree" (DOJ, 2003a, p. 2), not just as a sole factor. This is important because some definitions of racial profiling (as discussed in Chapter 1) require that race (or ethnicity) be the sole factor, but this renders the definition useless because it is rare and utterly impractical that officers would stop only minorities. Additionally, using race as the sole basis of suspicion amounts to racial *oppression*, not just racial profiling. Defining racial profiling in such a narrow and unrealistic manner can be an effective way to "define it away," but it is not helpful in addressing the real problem.

The DOJ directive is also precise and useful because it distinguishes between racial profiling and the permissible use of race or ethnicity in suspect descriptions. In addition, the accompanying fact sheet (DOJ, 2003a) provides highly illustrative, concrete examples of permissible and impermissible law enforcement behaviors with respect to suspect race. One such scenario is as follows:

Example: While parked by the side of the highway, a federal officer notices that nearly all vehicles on the road are exceeding the posted speed limit. Although each such vehicle is committing an infraction that would legally justify a stop, the officer may not use race or ethnicity as a factor in deciding which motorists to pull over. Likewise, the officer may not use race or ethnicity in deciding which detained motorists to ask to consent to a search of the vehicles. (pp. 2–3)

Again, vehicle stops are not a common federal law enforcement practice; virtually all of them are carried out by state and local police. However, to the extent that the example can be extended to other domains in which federal agents make decisions about who to detain and search, its standards are clear. Furthermore, to the extent that the policy may serve as a model for state and local agencies, its clarity is valuable.

Needing Teeth: Enforcement Mechanisms Would Make Bans More Effective

Although the federal ban is fairly strong on specificity, it provides no mandate or guidance for enforcement. This is, unfortunately, a more general pattern in racial profiling bans. Lacking enforcement mechanisms is a problem in prohibitions in any management or policy domain, but it is especially acute in this one because, as noted repeatedly, racial profiling is already widely condemned, and it is not carried out overtly in many, if any, agencies. Few if any law enforcement agents would admit to their superiors to using race or ethnicity as a basis for suspicion. Even if they did, without mechanisms for monitoring and sanctioning this behavior, it is unlikely to change.

Enforcement mechanisms would start with an effective monitoring process for detection of biased policing. This could include responsiveness to civilian complaints, peer reports (e.g., by other officers, such as partners), and supervisory oversight. More promising, in terms of reliability, would be systematic data collection and analysis. This will be discussed further later, but it is worth mentioning now that, because officers may be unwilling to admit to and/or unaware of suspect race influencing their judgments and behaviors, turning to more objective and comprehensive criteria—the proportionality of stops, searches, and arrests of people from different groups—should be effective.

Assuming that effective monitoring procedures are in place to *detect* biased policing, reasonable sanctions need to be available to supervisors. Without concern over consequences, officers may not be motivated to respect bans. This issue is complicated. First, most officers are likely intrinsically motivated to treat citizens fairly, do their jobs effectively, and follow rules. Given this assumption, it may be prudent for departments to structure sanction regimes hierarchically, meaning that, for example, first evidence of biased policing would trigger a supervisory meeting with the officer, perhaps including some training and/or counseling. Responses to subsequent occurrences (either complaint-based or data-based) would trigger more serious sanctions, including additional counseling and training, change in assignment, negative consideration in promotions, suspension, and even termination. For the more severe consequences, compelling evidence of biased policing would be warranted.

Departments will need to assess for themselves the appropriateness of various sanctions, perhaps in consultation with internal affairs departments and legal counsel. Regarding training procedures, many departments include training regarding biased policing at the academy and periodically thereafter, and it is no doubt prudent for cadets and veterans alike to be instructed on rules and procedures. There is, however, little empirical basis for having confidence in the effectiveness of "cultural sensitivity" or "diversity" training programs (Paluck & Green, 2009), which is what tends to come to mind with regard to remedial responses to biased behavior. Departments should also consider the benefits of *rewarding* officers for exhibiting consistently nonbiased behavior. Similarly, in the interest of promoting intrinsic motivation to police fairly, officers can be instructed on the threats to policing efficiency (undermining police-community relations; promoting offending by members of nonprofiled groups; obtaining low hit rates due to using low suspicion thresholds). Police officers, like other workers, are motivated to do their jobs well, whether or not there will be extrinsic rewards or sanctions.

Banning Specific Procedures Yields Specific Results

As discussed, blanket prohibitions on racial profiling may have limited utility because officers may not realize they are profiling, or are unlikely to admit it to others or even themselves. However, bans on specific procedures that tend to give rise to profiling may be more effective because they are more concrete and violations are more easily detected. In particular, procedures that allow for considerable discretion in judgments of suspicion are most likely to give rise to biased policing and therefore are good candidates for curtailment.

For example, the California Highway Patrol's (CHP) 2001 ban on the use of consent searches was made in response to an analysis of its drug interdiction program, Operation Pipeline, wherein minorities were stopped, and subjected to consent searches, at disproportionate rates. As discussed in Chapter 2, consent searches do not require probable cause and are therefore among the most high-discretion tactics police use; as a result, they are ripe for discriminatory application, and racial or ethnic disparities in rates of consent searches are compelling evidence of bias. By eliminating consent searches as an option, the CHP removed a major domain for racial discrimination. Such a ban, on a specific procedure, is more easily implemented and enforced than a more nebulous ban on something like racial profiling, which is a less concretely defined and understood practice, not to mention that it is already disavowed. It should be noted, however, that even if banning consent searches reduces racial/ethnic discrimination, it may be fairly characterized as treating the symptom rather than the "disease." If bias is affecting consent searches, it is likely affecting other procedures, like decisions to stop. Furthermore, banning consent searches removes an enforcement tool, albeit one that the CHP seems to have deemed more trouble than it was worth.

LEGISLATIVE APPROACHES

Although law enforcement is primarily overseen by executive and judicial branches of government, legislative bodies make rules that set boundaries on practices. In the case of racial profiling, "More than half the states have passed some kind of law against racial profiling or mandated some kind of study of the problem" (Harris, congressional testimony, June 17, 2010). Unfortunately, these laws often have little effect. They typically include the kinds of blanket bans described previously, similarly lacking monitoring and enforcement mechanisms. This may reflect that much of the motivation behind this kind of legislative action is political—primarily intended to convey disapproval of racial profiling, without analytic consideration of how best to achieve the stated objective. This political dimension is, of course, not unique to racial profiling. Furthermore, it is far from unusual for legislation in general, wherein it is often the case that only basic principles and preferences are laid out, with administrative agencies and courts expected to figure out, and sometimes wrangle over, implementation.

In addition to bans, state legislation often involves police training requirements and data collection requirements (i.e., mandating recording of demographic information including race/ethnicity of all citizens stopped by police), but these are often poorly specified, with unclear expectations for how training will occur (let alone how its effectiveness will be evaluated) and how the data will be analyzed and interpreted.

State legislatures have also had trouble passing laws addressing racial profiling (GAO, 2000a), in part because of opposition from law enforcement lobbying groups. In 1999, the California Assembly and Senate passed a law requiring demographic data collection on stops statewide, but it was vetoed by then governor Grey Davis, who was heavily reliant on political support from law enforcement groups. Other states have had similar experiences. The perception at the time was that mandatory data collection would be prohibitively onerous on officers, compromising their ability to do their jobs, as well as exposing them to liability for biased enforcement. There is also a perception among many officeholders that supporting policies that appear to tie the hands of police makes the elected officials look "soft on crime," which can be a political liability.

California did pass a law in 2000 prohibiting racial profiling in law enforcement and mandating relevant officer training (California Senate Bill 1102, Chapter 684). The new California law required that the state's Legislative Analyst Office (LAO) analyze data that are voluntarily collected and submitted by individual departments. Although it certainly is better than nothing, this approach is inadequate because it is likely that departments that voluntarily collect data will not be representative of the entire state. They may, in fact, be those departments most prone to independently take initiatives to mitigate profiling in the first place.

Other states have enacted laws relating to racial profiling. According to the Northeastern University Data Collection Resource Center, as of 2011, 28 U.S. states had enacted laws relating to racial profiling, all since 1997 and almost all since 2000. Of those, 19 states enacted bans, and 23 had at least one data collection requirement (some of them temporary). Only 10 states passed laws with training components aimed at remediating racial profiling. Data collection requirements are typically vague and lack guidelines for use (e.g., analysis) of data. Few states' laws specify enforcement mechanisms, save to prohibit retaliation against officers who disclose bias, and the vague exhortation to discipline officers in violation of the policy. Several states indicate that state funds will be withheld from departments found in violation of racial profiling laws. One state, New Jersey, criminalized racial profiling in 2003 and in subsequent legislation specified sanctions, including prison terms, for violators, although the latter has not been enacted. Because New Jersey was the seat of some of the most incendiary allegations and damning evidence of systemic racial profiling (in the mid-1990s), it is perhaps not surprising to see that there was the political will for aggressive legislation, but it should be noted that while the New Jersey legislature has considered many profiling policies, it has failed to pass most of them.

Although considerable effort has been spent on state legislation, the results are spotty. Many states have not passed any relevant laws, and those laws that have been passed tend to lack specificity or enforceability. This inadequate state of affairs could be rectified by comprehensive, overarching federal law.

Federal Legislation: The End Racial Profiling Act

At the federal level, despite years of effort, the long and dogged pursuit of a national policy on racial profiling has yet to reach its goal. First introduced in the House and Senate in June 2001, the End Racial Profiling Act (ERPA) has been proposed in almost every Congress since, but it has yet to receive a floor vote. The latest iteration, House Resolution 2851 and Senate Bill 1038, was introduced to the respective House and Senate committees by its primary sponsors, Representative Jon Conyers of Michigan, and Senator Benjamin Cardin of Maryland, with 54 House and 16 Senate cosponsors, in the summer of 2013. As with all previous attempts, ERPA has not yet been referred out of committees, nor is it expected to be.

Although of little effect unless it becomes law, ERPA represents a reasonably thorough and realistic model for addressing racial profiling, including clear regulatory language, provisions for data collection and reporting, grants to promote development of best practices, and enforcement mechanisms. ERPA would surely not live up to its name by literally *ending* racial profiling, but it could help to mitigate it substantially.

Declaring that "the use by police officers of race, ethnicity, religion, or national origin in deciding which persons should be subject to traffic stops, stops and frisks, questioning, searches, and seizures is improper," the 2004 Senate version of the bill went on to cite President George W. Bush's February 2001 declaration that "racial profiling is wrong, and we will end it in America" and his directive to the DOJ to implement policies to that end, which resulted in the 2003 statement discussed previously. ERPA noted, rightly, that the DOJ's response was inadequate:

> The Department of Justice Guidance is a useful first step, but does not achieve the President's stated goal of ending racial profiling in America: it does not apply to state and local law enforcement agencies, does not contain a meaningful enforcement mechanism, does not require data collection, and contains an overbroad exception for immigration and national security matters.
>
> (ERPA, Senate version, 2004, Section 2(a)(5))

The ERPA drafters have felt that state and local responses were also insufficient: "Current efforts by state and local governments to eradicate racial profiling and redress the harms it causes, while also laudable, have been limited in scope and insufficient to address this national problem. Therefore, Federal legislation is needed" (ERPA, Senate version, 2004, Section 2(a)(6)).

Calling for a "comprehensive national solution…to address racial profiling at the Federal, State, and local levels," ERPA offers a promising model because it includes the following elements: a clear definition; explicit prohibition and clear regulatory language; data collection requirements; funding for initiatives; and enforcement mechanisms.

ERPA (2013) defines racial profiling as follows:

> the practice of a law enforcement agent or agency relying, to any degree, on race, ethnicity, national origin, or religion in selecting which individual to subject to routine or spontaneous investigatory activities or in deciding upon the scope and substance of law enforcement activity following the initial investigatory procedure, except when there is trustworthy information, relevant to the locality and timeframe, that links a person of a particular race, ethnicity, national origin, or religion to an identified criminal incident or scheme.

This definition is clear and precise in terms of actors, targets, and activities. It is specific about the scope of the protected dimensions (race, ethnicity, national origin, and religion), and it recognizes that racial profiling involves the use of these categories "to any degree." Importantly, it specifies a clear exception for the use of race, ethnicity, and so forth in suspect descriptions and witness identifications.

The prohibition—"No law enforcement agent or law enforcement agency shall engage in racial profiling"—is unambiguous, especially considering the clear definition of racial profiling that precedes it. ERPA's language reinforces the prohibition by identifying civil (as opposed to criminal) remedies against agencies, agents, and/or responsible supervisors of those agents. The act goes so far as to provide a description of the nature of proof, although a somewhat nebulous one: "Proof that the routine or spontaneous investigatory activities of law enforcement agents in a jurisdiction have had a disparate impact on racial, ethnic, or religious minorities shall constitute prima facie evidence of a violation of this title" (ERPA, 2013). The criteria for findings of "disparate impact" are not provided and have been the source of considerable legal dispute in other domains of antidiscrimination law. Nevertheless, the specification of disparate impact, instead of "disparate *treatment*," signals a standard of evidence that does not require proof of *intent* to discriminate,[2] and this gives the law considerably more force. It also, by invoking disparate impact, which can arise in the absence of intent to discriminate, puts the onus on departments to affirmatively prevent racial profiling, as opposed to merely demurring to encourage it.

In addition to requiring that agencies have clear procedures for handling complaints of racial profiling, ERPA requires that departments collect data on "all routine or spontaneous investigatory activities," and that the data shall be "collected by race, ethnicity, national origin, gender, and religion, as perceived by the law enforcement officer." The use of officer perception, although prone to error, is not only the best available source but probably the most appropriate because it is, after all, officer perception that matters when it comes to racial profiling. That officers will be able to detect someone's religion is questionable, but this requirement helps in the domain of counterterrorism profiling, where perceived Muslims are targeted. Importantly, the data collection rules require that data "include detail sufficient to permit an analysis of whether a law enforcement agency is engaging in racial profiling," and to this end, ERPA mandates the establishment of (as yet

---

2. In employment discrimination jurisprudence, this impact versus treatment distinction is crucial. Disparate impact cases, although they represent a small fraction of suits, do not require evidence of intent but can involve "facially neutral" practices that nevertheless have a discriminatory impact on a class of individuals that can be demonstrated statistically and do not arise from a business necessity (i.e., the business outcome could be achieved without the discriminatory practice; Krieger, 1995).

unspecified) "guidelines for setting comparative benchmarks, consistent with best practices, against which collected data shall be measured."

To promote effective data collection and analysis, ERPA offers both federal support and oversight by requiring the DOJ to provide standardized data collection forms and to collect and analyze data, which local, state, and federal departments are required to submit to the DOJ. Providing further guidance and clarity, ERPA instructs that DOJ analysts would test for "disparities in the percentage of drivers or pedestrians stopped relative to the proportion of the population passing through the neighborhood," "disparities in the hit rate," and "disparities in the frequency of searches performed on minority drivers and the frequency of searches performed on non-minority drivers" (ERPA, 2013).

The task of analyzing the national database would fall to the Bureau of Justice Statistics (BJS), the DOJ's statistical wing. The BJS has demonstrated the capacity to effectively manage national data (as in the case of hate crimes data that are required to be submitted by all U.S. law enforcement agencies to the BJS under the Hate Crimes Statistics Act). However, it is far less clear that the BJS would have the capacity to provide agency-level evaluations that would promote compliance with ERPA's prohibition on racial profiling, especially given the challenges of quantifying racial bias in policing, a task that requires data on the demographics of the jurisdiction under study. ERPA's requirement that stop-rate disparities be analyzed in reference to rates of passage through neighborhoods is a valid, if imperfect, empirical approach, but it is a tall order to expect ongoing surveys of this sort. More promising is ERPA's call for analyses of disparities in hit rates. The outcomes of stops are either "hits" or what ERPA calls "false stops," and so this amounts to an outcome test.

ERPA further supports monitoring requirements by offering grants for the development of best practices, such as "the acquisition and use of technology to facilitate the accurate collection and analysis of data" (ERPA, 2013).

Recognizing legitimate concerns about confidentiality, and the limits of making inferences about individuals based on aggregate data, ERPA includes protections for individual officers, prohibiting the release of disaggregated information about any "officer, complainant, or any other individual involved in any activity for which data is collected and compiled under this Act."

Despite its strengths, as well as overwhelming public support for curbing racial profiling and strong rhetorical backing for that in most corners of Washington, ERPA has not passed. Opposition to policies like ERPA range from legitimate concerns about cost and time burdens placed on law enforcement agents and agencies to more dubious misgivings about preventing officers from being able to carry out their jobs effectively because of the loss of a useful tool. Some opponents conflate racial profiling with the use of race in suspect descriptions (as discussed in Chapter 5), expressing concern that prohibitions on profiling will prevent witnesses and police from describing and pursuing specific suspects effectively. This is an unfortunate and unproductive critique because racial profiling (wherein there is no known crime, let alone suspect) and use of race in suspect descriptions are obviously different tactics; furthermore, ERPA explicitly allows for the latter ("except when there is trustworthy information, relevant to the locality and timeframe, that links a person of a particular race, ethnicity, national origin, or religion to an identified criminal incident or scheme").

As noted previously, some lawmakers fear looking "soft on crime" if they vote to prohibit something that is perceived as an effective law enforcement practice, even if that perception is not accurate. American history clearly indicates that civil rights concerns are not always sufficient motivation for legislative action. As a case in point, the Civil Rights Act came a full decade after the landmark *Brown v. Board of Education* ruling. Legislators will factor political and pragmatic considerations into their decisions on civil rights legislation. Proponents of policies such as ERPA will therefore be well served if they make the case that racial profiling is of dubious crime-fighting value, can have ironic effects, creates criminal justice disparities, and undermines police-community relations.

From a historical perspective, it is possible that ERPA could have passed in an earlier era. It was first introduced in June 2001, when public condemnation of racial profiling was at a fever pitch. Before it came to a vote, however, the September 11 attacks occurred, and Congress's priorities shifted away from policies that would limit (or be perceived to limit) law enforcement powers. Although public attitudes toward racial profiling have continued to be preponderantly negative, surveys have found that majorities of Americans support profiling of Muslims in counterterrorism. Americans are therefore probably more ambivalent toward racial profiling than they were before 9/11. Furthermore, the political risks to elected officials of looking "soft on crime," now that the American schema of crime includes catastrophic terrorism, have become decidedly higher.

AGENCY-LEVEL ADMINISTRATIVE APPROACHES: A FRONT-LINES GROUNDSWELL?

Because courts have tolerated profiling given the slightest pretext, and legislatures have generally failed to act comprehensively, agency-level policies may be the most promising avenue for mitigating racial profiling. Executive administrative (e.g., presidential, mayoral) approaches were discussed earlier, but agency-level administrative approaches are another common domain for setting policy. Specifically, heads of police departments have wide latitude for making executive decisions about prohibitions, training, data collection and analysis, and enforcement. Like all managers, they have constraints. In addition to intrinsic motivations to mitigate bias, executives may be compelled by community activists and threats of court orders or legal liability. On the other side, budgetary constraints, staff objections to burdensome procedures and resistance to oversight, not to mention failure to recognize the potential for bias, militate against department-level policy action. Nevertheless, agency-level administrative rules have been shown to be effective in reducing problems in other areas and are therefore an important tool for mitigating racial profiling as well (White, 2011).

The reality appears to be that there is a substantial degree of action on racial profiling at the agency level. The perceptions about profiling and data collection have changed considerably among law enforcement executives in the last decade. Police and local officials are more likely to recognize that more information is better than less, and that preemptive efforts to monitor their own performance can both catch problems early and provide political and legal cover. From Iowa City to New York City, police departments throughout the United States have formally banned racial profiling. This is evidenced broadly among major city police departments, many of which are participating in the Center for Policing Equity (CPE),[3] a consortium of police departments and social scientists seeking to better understand equity issues in policing, including racial profiling. As of 2012, 26 law enforcement agencies are partners in the CPE, including large agencies like the Los Angeles County Sheriff's Department and police departments in Chicago, Houston, Toronto, Las Vegas, San Jose, Salt Lake City, Las Vegas, and Denver. Departments participating in the CPE venture commit to making their police-civilian encounter data available to researchers and to allowing researchers to collect additional measures, such as officer attitudes. In addition to the high participation rate of major city police departments in the CPE, the Association of Major City Police Chiefs (an organization representing the 60 largest police departments in the United States) voted in October 2010 to adopt the CPE-sponsored national research plan.

American law enforcement executives typically condemn profiling, often on moral and practical grounds. In the words of New York City police commissioner Raymond Kelly, "It's the wrong thing to do, and it's also ineffective" (Gladwell, 2006b). So there does appear to be the will to address profiling administratively, and this is evidenced in the many departmental policies across the United States that officially prohibit and monitor for racial profiling. It is beyond the scope of this book to attempt an accounting of the many thousands of agencies' programs to address racial bias in policing. What follows is a discussion of common themes in department policies that are evident from an informal survey, including bans, training, and data collection.

---

3. The CPE was formerly the Consortium for Police Leadership in Equity (CPLE). In full disclosure, the author is a member of the board of directors and an active researcher with the CPE.

Prohibition and Definition

Among departments that have a formal policy, it is common that they will have an explicit prohibition. The force of this prohibition depends in part on the definition of profiling that accompanies it. This is, of course, a general principle of policy analysis and setting—we must clearly and accurately define what we wish to regulate. If it is not clear what it is that is prohibited, agents will not know what behavior to change. Regrettably, departmental definitions of racial profiling will sometimes employ the "race as the sole basis" criterion. As discussed earlier, this definition is not useful because (1) using race as the sole basis of suspicion is more like full-blown racial oppression, is obviously illegal, and would require explicit departmental prohibition only for the most misguided of officers; and (2) using race as one of multiple components in a profile (the more useful definition) still has a discriminatory effect and therefore warrants prohibition. I believe that most officers in the United States would make this distinction and perhaps infer that any ban on "racial profiling" means race should not be used as a basis of suspicion, even if it is just one among multiple factors. Nevertheless, a clearer definition would be more effective, and there is a real risk that by prohibiting only the use of race as the *sole* basis of suspicion, departments are condoning using it as one among multiple factors. This could have the unintended effect of increasing profiling.

Training

As discussed previously, bans on profiling, even with enforcement mechanisms, will have only limited effect if officers do not fully understand what profiling is and how it comes about. Accordingly, departmental pronouncements would be more effective if accompanied by training to help officers understand the policy and how best to implement it. In addition to instruction on specific policies and procedures, many departments employ antidiscrimination or "cultural sensitivity" training. A popular option is Perspectives on Profiling, a computer-based, interactive program developed by the Tools for Tolerance for Law Enforcement program of the Simon Weisenthal Center. Perspectives on Profiling has won accolades from many department heads and has very useful components, such as clear definitions of terms, debunking of race-crime stereotypes, and distinctions between concepts like criminal profiling and racial profiling. However, it is not yet clear from any systematic evaluation that the program reduces profiling, and there is some preliminary evidence that programs of this sort can *increase* biases among police (Goff, 2010). As I have argued in Chapters 3 and 4, profiling results in part, perhaps in large part, from the unintentional application of stereotypes, some of which are implicit (i.e., not even known to those who hold them). Efforts to reduce profiling should address the implicit causes. Criminologist Lorie Fridell has begun developing just such a program, called Fair and Impartial Policing (www.fairandimpartialpolicing.com). General principles for addressing the effects of implicit stereotypes will be discussed in Chapter 8.

The CPE is developing training programs to help departments reduce racial bias in policing. The emphasis will be on empirically based methods for reducing bias and/or its influence on policing decisions and behaviors. There will also be rigorous evaluation components, involving multiple pretraining assessments of bias and linking training to outcomes such as racial disparities in use of force rates and in stop/search/arrest rates.

Data Collection and Analysis

It is an axiom (although one that is, regrettably, often forsaken) of public policy analysis that good programs need strong evaluation components. In order to determine to what extent a program is effective, assessments need to be made of the outcomes it is designed to affect. Preferably, these assessments would occur before and after the program is implemented; even better, there would be a comparison area or group where the program is not yet implemented—in this way, the experimental method of comparing randomly (or, the next best thing, quasi-randomly) assigned conditions allows for strong inferences of causality. The same is true for programs to mitigate racial profiling. In order to determine if prohibitions, incentives, or training procedures have reduced racial disparities, there have to be reliable methods in place for measuring disparities, both prior to the new procedures (at "baseline") and after.

The good news is that data collection on traffic and pedestrian stops is now a fairly widespread practice for many police departments throughout the United States. The bad news is that the methods are unstandardized, often allow for inconsistency on the part of reporting officers, and are rarely analyzed in a way that allows for valid inferences about disparities (GAO, 2000a; LAO, 2002). Some departments collect data voluntarily, and others do so in response to court action. Even in the latter case, it is often unclear what is to be done with the data. As a case in point, the Oakland Police Department is required to collect data on race, ethnicity, gender, and other variables as a result of the settlement in the Oakland Riders case, but it is not required to *analyze* those data in any meaningful way. (To that department's credit, it has proactively sought expert support for data analysis.)

Back on the plus side, all of these problems are remediable, and the passage of national policy (e.g., ERPA) with national standards, reporting requirements, and funding for development of best practices would put the United States on a fast track to effective monitoring of racial profiling. Furthermore, technologies like computer-aided dispatch (CAD) and dashboard- and body-mounted cameras are making reliable data collection and verification increasingly efficient and robust.

As discussed at length in Chapter 2, we still face challenges in how to determine whether there are in fact disparities. This is the old "benchmark" problem, and it has at least two layers: The first layer relates to whether stop rates for minorities are disproportionate relative to minorities' *presence* in the relevant population. The population benchmarks that are often used in police departments' internal analyses are based on U.S. census statistics, which say little about who is in a particular location at a particular time. This problem is complicated by the fact that police may be more extensively patrolling neighborhoods or traffic corridors with high minority representation or disproportionately stopping minority individuals when they are in predominantly White neighborhoods (Crawford, 2010; Meehan & Ponder, 2002). The second layer relates to whether the stop rates are disproportionate relative to minorities' *offending* rates. This presents an even bigger problem because, as discussed in Chapter 2, it is difficult, if at all possible, to know rates of offending in victimless crimes, given that the vast majority of drug and weapons possession crimes go undetected.

Describing these challenges is not meant to imply that racial profiling data collection and analysis is a hopeless enterprise. To the extent that minorities are being stopped at rates that are higher than their presence in the population may be a first sign of a problem and can be detected by analysis of police stop data. I say "first sign" because, as noted previously, if minority offending rates are relatively high, and police are responding to real indicators of offending, we would expect minorities to be stopped, searched, and so forth at higher rates. It should be noted that the *absence* of a disproportionate stop rate relative to the population cannot be taken as reliable evidence of the absence of racial profiling. If members of minority group offend at a rate *lower* than others and are stopped at a comparable rate, that would reflect a bias against them (they are getting stopped at a rate that is higher than their offending rate would justify). In this sense, disproportions relative to population benchmarks are neither necessary nor sufficient evidence of racial profiling. This is why an offending benchmark would be an ideal denominator in our racial profiling equation.

In the absence of a reliable benchmark for offending, the next best thing is the "outcome test" approach described in Chapter 2. Here we look at the hit rate among those stopped (the stop-arrest ratio). The best indicator available for hits is arrests, although we have to acknowledge that any biases in decisions to arrest will compromise the accuracy of these hit rates, and police do have and exercise discretion in that decision too. The logic of the outcome test is as follows: If police are using a lower threshold of suspicion for (i.e., are more inclined to stop or search) minorities, then they will be more likely to make "false positive" errors with minorities. This would have the effect that a smaller proportion of stopped minorities would be carrying contraband, and so a smaller proportion would be arrested. As long as police departments are collecting reliable data on who is stopped and searched (i.e., they are logging *all* stops and searches, and accurately recording suspect race/ethnicity), this approach will work because arrest data are reliable by virtue of standard procedures.

There are some important caveats about the outcome test approach. First, if minorities are offending at a higher rate, and the stop rate is proportional to that, the arrest rates among those stopped would be similar for Whites and minorities. This could, with a simplistic interpretation of outcome test results, look like the absence of profiling. Indeed, while it would represent an aggregate absence of bias and discrimination, it could still *result from* racial profiling. Specifically, police could be using race as a basis for suspicion in an accurate way. It is still racial profiling. The likelihood that the stereotype would be so perfectly calibrated to the relative offending rates is extremely low. More likely, the stereotype will be an under- or overestimate. If it underestimates, the outcome tests will yield higher arrest rates for minorities; if it overestimates, there will be higher arrest rates for Whites.

Another possibility is that minorities have a lower offending rate, but police are stopping and searching in a fairly arbitrary manner that is race-neutral. This would yield an outcome test result that looks like racial profiling because minorities would have a lower arrest rate among those stopped.

The point of these caveats is that even outcome test results are not perfect indicators of racial profiling. However, in most cases, a lower arrest rate (among those stopped and searched) for minorities is compelling evidence of racial/ethnic bias in the decisions to stop and search. Police departments have the capacity to collect and analyze these data on an ongoing basis, and outcome tests can be conducted at the unit and even the officer level. Consequently, outcome tests offer a promising metric for monitoring racial profiling.

A final caveat regarding the use of outcome tests: There is the risk that some officers, once they become aware of the use of the outcome test approach in their department, will alter their behavior to change the results. If they alter their behavior to stop using race as a basis for suspicion, that would be a desirable outcome. If, however, they start using differential standards for *arrests* for different racial or ethnic groups (e.g., letting more White offenders off with warnings in order to lower White hit rates), the effect would actually create greater disparities in criminal justice outcomes, thereby *compounding* the racial profiling problem the policy change was intended to reduce.

POLICIES RELATING TO PROFILING IN COUNTERTERRORISM

One important criterion policy analysts do well to consider in evaluating policy alternatives is *political feasibility* (Bardach, 2005). In order for a policy or program to work, it must, in addition to being effective, be able to survive political challenges and get enacted. This is true for racial profiling policies in general and has clearly been a factor in the many failed attempts to pass federal legislation.

Because of the understandable emotional charge of anything to do with terrorism and national security, political feasibility looms especially large in considerations of policies intended to address counterterrorism. Anything that may be construed as curbing counterterrorism efforts is likely to meet stiff political headwinds. Accordingly, it may be prudent to separate counterterrorism from other domains of racial profiling when analyzing, crafting, and attempting to pass policy.

Racial profiling in counterterrorism has many commonalities with more generic profiling (e.g., drug courier and day-to-day stop or search situations). In particular, it is based on stereotypes and all the pitfalls therein, it alienates members of the targeted groups, and it violates core constitutional principles. It differs, however, in several important ways, as discussed in Chapter 6. First, the type of crime targeted is very different, and although the cumulative negative effect of drug and weapons possession and sales on society may be greater than that from terrorism, the public psychological response is different—terrorism evokes widespread and lasting negative emotions, like fear, anger, anxiety, and despair, which, in turn, give rise to societal instability. Another way of thinking about this is that drug crimes are mostly inwardly focused, motivated by either a desire to use illicit drugs or a need to sell them for profit; terrorism is inherently outward, motivated by a desire to harm others and bring about political change. Most drug crimes are victimless; terrorism typically strives to maximize the number of victims. Second, counterterrorism profiling does not result in mass incarceration disparities because the terrorism offending base rates are so low. There are, in fact, incarceration disparities, with people of Middle Eastern or South Asian descent being more likely to be detained, but they number in the hundreds or thousands, not in the millions. Nevertheless, although terrorism is extremely rare, because of its inherently cataclysmic nature, government responses to it tend to include aggressive and controversial practices, including racial profiling.

The most relevant American government agency regarding racial profiling in counterterrorism is the Transportation Security Administration (TSA), which oversees the screening of more than 2 million airline passengers per day (TSA, 2012). The FBI, CIA, National Security Agency, Immigration and Customs Enforcement (ICE), and other agencies with national security responsibilities surely employ ethnic profiles to identify terror suspects, but the scale of agent-civilian contact in TSA activities is far greater.

As discussed in Chapter 6, the Federal Aviation Administration (FAA) regulates passenger screening protocols like the Computer-Assisted Passenger Pre-screening System (CAPPS), which was succeeded by CAPPS II and then Secure Flight. Secure Flight uses profiles and, presumably, specific intelligence about individuals to construct "no-fly" lists, which now contain an undisclosed but growing number of names (GAO, 2012). In addition to Secure Flight lists triggering extra screening or flight prohibition of individuals, every passenger is subjected to screening by TSA officers (TSOs). A certain percentage of passengers are subjected to random secondary screenings, but TSOs can also make discretionary decisions based on at least partially subjective assessments of suspiciousness.

In testimony before the U.S. House Transportation and Infrastructure Committee's Subcommittee on Aviation in 2002, legal scholar Jonathan Turley made an important observation regarding the potential for arbitrariness in passenger profiling: "Perhaps the most important protection is the continual review of criteria used for airport investigatory stops. Given the shifting intelligence on threats, a passenger [terrorist] profile is likely to evolve more than a drug or customs profile." Turley went on to argue that

> the greatest danger to citizens comes not in the brief investigatory stop but in their treatment after the stop. Congress is essential in guaranteeing that stops are limited in time and conducted in a respectful and non-threatening fashion by law enforcement.

This advice is understandable, but it also highlights the important difference between counterterrorism and other forms of racial profiling with higher-frequency crimes. Because in counterterrorism there are many stops (at airport security checkpoints) and very few (near zero) arrests, the concern is legitimately placed with process more than outcome.

In other policing domains, such as traffic stops, all the courtesy in the world will not change the fact that if police are stopping and searching minorities at disproportionate rates, they will be sanctioning and incarcerating them at disproportionate rates. Historically, the dramatic racial disproportions in incarcerations, and the sheer numbers (in the millions) require that concern, and the need for remedial efforts, be placed squarely on the processes leading to decisions to stop and search.

CONCLUSION

While policies to address racial profiling are variable and spotty, there are some common themes. One is that in a sense there is a de facto ban on most forms of racial profiling because, as a discriminatory practice, it runs counter to core Western values and guarantees of civil liberties. This was evident in the strong outcry against profiling when it came to public consciousness in the United States in the mid-1990s. However, this "ban" does not have a coherent enforcement mechanism, except for social disapproval. Even courts have been reluctant to penalize racial profiling. Furthermore, because much profiling occurs informally, even unintentionally, it is difficult to detect, let alone control.

In order for bans, be they de facto or de jure, to be effective, enforcement mechanisms must be in place. Enforcement, however, requires capacity for detection. To this end, many departments are now consistently collecting data on the demographics of civilians in all stops. But most departments are analyzing their data superficially or not at all, without reference to appropriate benchmarks. Fortunately, there is a promising trend for police departments to partner with social scientists who are more practiced in drawing valid inferences from complex data sets. ERPA's data collection and analysis goals are reasonably well aligned with this trend, and the passage of this act would help to standardize and promote effective methods, given that ERPA (as previously drafted) calls for standard data collection forms, requirements for reporting up to the DOJ, and grants to sponsor the development of best practices.

Police training regarding racial profiling is similarly unstandardized and heterogeneous. Additionally, the various programs' effectiveness is unknown. The coordinated development and assessment of training protocols would be helpful, and to this end, the CPE and other researchers are collaborating with multiple departments.

As with any policy domain, the available tools range across local, state, and federal, as well as judicial, executive, legislative, and agency, dimensions. And as with any policy domain, there is the risk of what social psychologists call *diffusion of responsibility*—the tendency to not take responsibility for dealing with a problem when it is believed that others might be doing so (Darley & Latané, 1968). As a result of the presumption of a de facto ban and the diffusion in the policy landscape, the response to racial profiling has been inadequate. There are no comprehensive federal policies, and state-level policies are mostly geared toward data collection, with little requirement for analysis, let alone enforcement. The local stratum, specifically police departments and sheriffs, sometimes acting in response to court orders, sometimes on initiative, is where the most action to monitor and remediate racial profiling has occurred. The local efforts, however, represent a patchwork of programs with little if any empirical basis or systematic evaluation.

Police departments can hardly be faulted for failing to take the initiative for putting in place comprehensive, rigorous counterprofiling policies and procedures. Their resources are strained, and their priorities are crime mitigation and public safety first and foremost. However, because racial and ethnic bias in policing can undermine effectiveness, in addition to violating core principles, mitigating it should be a widely shared priority.

In order for law enforcement agencies to remediate racial bias in policing, whether motivated by principle, court order, public or political pressure, or some combination of these factors, they must understand what gives rise to racial profiling. Similarly, they must operate on valid theories and practices for reducing discrimination. This brings us to the next and final chapter and its discussion of how to think about racial profiling in a way that will lead to effective mitigation.

CHAPTER 8

You Are Not a "Racist"

Destigmatizing Stereotyping and Profiling

I bet an awful lot of cops, if they looked at their own data, would be personally shocked that they had produced these statistics.... [Decisions to stop, search, and cite as a function of driver race are] either different for an objective reason, or somebody is consciously or unconsciously—and, I would offer, usually unconsciously—applying a different standard to those groups. And to be confronted with it is to take a big step toward changing it.

Edward A. Flynn, "the chief law enforcement officer in
Massachusetts"[1] according to the *Boston Globe* in 2003

Chief Flynn is not alone in his sentiments. In the words of racial profiling researcher (and former law enforcement agent) Brian Withrow, in congressional testimony:

> Nearly every day I meet with policing leaders, prosecutors and criminal justice policy makers who are concerned about the racial profiling controversy. Gone are the days when a police administrator merely scoffed at a racial profiling allegation as the musings of a malcontented citizen. I am encouraged by the fact that they take this issue very seriously. These leaders are making a difference, and these leaders are in the majority.
>
> Withrow, 2010

Withrow's impression is corroborated by the history of the Center for Policing Equity (CPE), a broad-based collaboration between North American police

---

1. Secretary of the state Executive Office of Public Safety.

executives and social scientists. At CPE meetings, racial bias in policing is generally the starting point of discussions, not a point of contention.

It is somewhat ironic that the first step to mitigating racial profiling may be to promote understanding that it is not as insidious as people think it is. Racial profiling is, for the most part, policing based on stereotypes. As discussed in Chapters 3 and 4, stereotyping is a normal cognitive process that serves the function of conserving finite mental resources (e.g., Bodenhausen, 1990; Fiske & Taylor, 1991; Macrae et al., 1994). Consequently, stereotyping is not a moral failing in and of itself. To the extent that stereotypes also operate outside of conscious awareness and control (e.g., Blair & Banaji, 1996; Banaji & Hardin, 1996), they can cause spontaneous discriminatory behavior despite our best intentions (e.g., Devine, 1989; Glaser & Knowles, 2008). Correspondingly, *unintentional* racial profiling—resulting from judgments of suspicion that are skewed by implicit stereotypes—is likely commonplace.

That stereotyping is normal human cognition, and that implicit stereotypes are ubiquitous, should not be taken as implying some kind of "rationalization" of racism. It is important to draw a bright line between the *holding* of stereotypic beliefs, implicit or explicit, and the conscious *endorsement* of those beliefs and willful acting on them. It is for this latter condition that I reserve the term *racism*. Most extreme are individuals who hold and accept racist ideologies—beliefs that some races (usually their own) are superior to others, morally, physically, intellectually, or otherwise. No doubt, some police officers are discriminating out of overt racist ideology, and there are likely still whole departments or units where racist cultures exist. Such cases, however, are categorically different from, and far less commonplace than, officers being influenced by stereotypes in the invisible manner born out in the research described earlier.

NORMAL ≠ DESIRABLE

Although unintentional discrimination resulting from stereotypes may reflect normal human cognitive processing and behavior, and should not be equated with "racism," this should not be taken as an *acceptance* of discrimination. There are many normal human tendencies, such as aggression, selfishness, and promiscuousness, that may have been adaptive for our ancestors but are generally undesirable today because they cause harms that violate our moral standards. In other words, *normal is not always desirable*. That is clearly the case with stereotype-based discrimination, which violates fundamental societal principles of equal treatment and due process hallowed in modern values and enshrined in the U.S. Constitution.

Still, some will argue that stereotype-based judgments are "rational" in the sense that (and only when) they take into account real differences—to ignore them would be to commit a *base rate error*. Base rate errors involve failing to factor in underlying probabilities, like the prevalence of a disease in a given population when interpreting a positive test result for an individual. Setting aside all the reasons for concern about the accuracy of stereotypes, we still must consider that stereotypes expose people to another kind of base rate error—the failure to account for the low prevalence of the trait in question, or the small difference in prevalence between groups. To be concrete, even if minorities have a higher rate of offending, if the overall rate of offending is low, using minority status to predict guilt is going to cause many errors. This is borne out in the very (and relatively) low rate of productive searches of minorities (e.g., GAO, 2000b; Jones-Brown et al., 2010; OAGSNY, 1999). Similarly, my (Glaser, 2006) and Harcourt's (2004, 2007) modeling research indicates that, barring dramatic group differences in offending rates (differences that are not, in fact, implicated by actual criminal justice or survey data), stereotype-based policing (aka racial profiling) is not particularly efficient and can have counterproductive effects, like reverse deterrence, increased crime, disenfranchisement, and undermined community cooperation.

So, racial profiling may reflect normal cognition, but it is undesirable on both moral and practical grounds. Nevertheless, it is commonplace because it involves ubiquitous stereotypes regarding race and crime. This poses a dilemma: How do we help law enforcement agents cease engaging in a behavior that they are unlikely to recognize in themselves, let alone own up to? The recognition of the unfairness of discrimination in general and profiling in particular, as well as the public outcry against profiling and law enforcement executives' disavowals of it, may cause police to be reluctant to acknowledge the possibility that it occurs within their ranks. Consequently, interventions to address racial profiling may be resisted by departments and individual officers.

This resistance to acknowledging racial bias in police decision-making is reinforced by the subtle nature of modern, implicit stereotyping; consistent with Chief Edward Flynn's prediction (see the quote at beginning of this chapter), officers are unlikely to experience subjectively the influence of implicit stereotypes on their judgments. In fact, people generally have a hard time accurately predicting how they will perform on measures of implicit bias. Consequently, even if confronted with their own data indicating a tendency to disproportionately stop, search, and arrest minorities, officers may attribute the outcomes to other factors (probably characteristics of the civilians they have stopped).

My view is that it is crucial to educate command staff and rank-and-file officers, as well as other law enforcement agents like Transit Security Officers, regarding the normalcy of stereotyping. Recognizing that stereotyping is normal, and in some ways adaptive, but has undesirable effects can open minds to (1) acknowledging that it happens and (2) working to prevent it. In essence, I am talking about *destigmatizing* stereotyping and racial profiling. This is an idea that is loaded with irony, given that stereotyping itself is a form of stigmatization.

CORE PRINCIPLES FOR POLICE TRAINING

As discussed in Chapter 7, there are multiple policy levers for mitigating racial profiling, but few have been pulled effectively. Legal prohibitions are of limited value because of the strong, prevailing de facto ban resulting from widespread condemnation of the practice—merely prohibiting something that is already taboo is unlikely to have much additional effect. Enforcement of bans is extremely difficult because of the challenges inherent in monitoring for profiling (e.g., establishing appropriate benchmarks). Judicial remedies have proven problematic because of the great latitude the courts have given officers in bases for stops and searches.

One area that holds promise is in officer training because many, perhaps most, police executives are concerned about profiling and so are amenable to agency-level interventions. However, merely talking to officers about the problem will not be sufficient, and there is good reason to be skeptical about the efficacy of the extant "cultural sensitivity" and "diversity" training programs (Paluck & Green, 2009). Few, if any, such programs have been subjected to even moderately rigorous evaluations such as those utilizing random assignment and control conditions, nor have they looked at real outcome variables like on-the-job performance. In the specific case of police training, after a thorough search for prejudice reduction program evaluations, Paluck and Green (2009) reported, "We were unable to locate a sensitivity- or diversity-training program for police that used more than a prepost survey of participating officers" (p. 343). In other words, at best these assessments have merely compared participants' self-reported attitudes before and after training. This is an approach that is empirically weak because many things, including expectations and desire to please program leaders, can cause people to report that their attitudes have been changed by the training, even if they have not. Furthermore, as social psychologists have known for a long time, there are no guarantees that changes in attitudes translate into changes in behavior (Ajzen & Fishbein, 1977).

Profiling reduction training will need to combine education about the nature and operation of implicit stereotypes and unintended discrimination with specific strategies for avoiding biased policing. In addition, monitoring and enforcement by supervisors will promote continued utilization of antibias strategies.

To start, training should include clear demonstrations of how stereotypes affect judgments and behavior—by helping us interpret, explain, and predict others' behaviors, the causes of which are often ambiguous, sometimes utterly mysterious. In conjunction with this, law enforcers should receive training on the nature of *implicit* stereotypes and how they cause *unintended* discrimination. Understanding that people are likely unaware of the stereotypes they possess will help to explain how these stereotypes can influence judgments and behaviors without their realizing it and despite their best intentions. Combining understanding of the normalcy of stereotypes, their ubiquity in implicit cognition, and the process by which stereotypes about groups contaminate judgments of individuals will help officers recognize that and how they are vulnerable to engaging in racial profiling.

To connect the dots: Most police do not want to discriminate, but they hold implicit and explicit stereotypes linking minorities, particularly Blacks, with crime. Whether motivated intrinsically to be unbiased or by extrinsic influences like social norms, monitoring, and sanctions, to the extent that officers cannot recognize when they are discriminating, they will not be effective at avoiding it. Stereotypes bias judgments, particularly when behavior is ambiguous. Civilian suspiciousness is inherently ambiguous, and standards for reasonable suspicion are low and woefully vague and variable, allowing for a lot of discretion. Police often act on gut feelings that they may attribute to real bases of suspicion but that could easily be spillovers from racial or ethnic stereotypes. Conscious efforts to control or "turn off" stereotypes are, at best, of limited utility and, at worst, can yield ironic, "rebound" effects (Macrae et al., 1994). Accordingly, interventions should involve education/training for police officers to better understand the process by which stereotypes might guide behavior, and the pitfalls therein, while making clear that holding a stereotype (and acting unintentionally on it) does not make one a "racist."

This approach also acknowledges the point made in Chapter 3, that sources of stereotypes are many, from direct experience to fictional media portrayals to completely spurious illusory correlations. Consequently, people typically cannot accurately identify, let alone verify, the sources of their stereotypic beliefs. Furthermore, people vary in their dispositions toward these stereotypes, with some readily endorsing them, others ambivalent, and others strenuously resisting them. Accordingly, it would be insufficient to merely provide information contradicting stereotypes, let alone to merely give instruction to resist their influence.

MEASURES OF IMPLICIT BIAS: POWERFUL AND PERILOUS

Antibias training would be bolstered by having officers experience having their implicit stereotypes measured. This would allow for direct and indirect feedback on their levels of bias. Indirect feedback can be provided by giving officers their implicit bias scores, but as with any psychometric measure, these scores are imperfect at the individual level, and it may be hard for officers to appreciate the meaning of a standardized bias score that will seem arbitrary in its magnitude (e.g., "You scored 0.5, which is 'moderate' bias").

More powerful would be the relatively *direct* feedback that many of the available procedures, most prominently the Implicit Association Test (IAT; Greenwald et al., 1998), afford. Such procedures, while tapping associations (e.g., stereotypes) that are essentially uncontrollable, nevertheless give rise to a *subjective* experience of the bias, even as it is evident to the test-taker that the expression of the bias cannot be controlled. Specifically, in the IAT, participants are asked to categorize many images, words, or names from four categories on two response keys.[2] For example, they may be asked to categorize words like *narcotics* and *obey* as relating to crime or lawfulness, while simultaneously categorizing intermixed photographs of Black and White men's faces. Because people have only two response keys available to group into four categories, they are forced to pair categories (e.g., Black with crime) on the same key and, consequently, in their minds. The speed and accuracy with which they make these categorizations are taken as an index of the strength of the association between the categories, and the two ways of combining them (Black + lawful and White + crime vs. Black + crime and White + lawful) are compared. The typical person finds it easier (and therefore goes faster and makes fewer errors) when pairings are compatible with the associations they already hold in their minds. In the race-crime example, people tend to respond faster when Black faces are paired with crime words and White faces paired with lawful words than vice versa. When the stereotype (group-trait association) is reasonably strong, one can feel the relative ease of doing the task when the groups are paired with their stereotypically compatible traits. More palpably, they can feel how difficult it is (it takes longer, and they make more errors) when the categories are paired counterstereotypically (e.g., White with crime and Black with lawful).

As noted, feedback could be provided to participants regarding their relative performance on the two configurations of the task. But the most powerful feedback is the palpable feeling that the task is harder with one pairing than the other. Specifically, most officers would experience having a harder time pairing Black with lawful and White with criminal than vice versa. They would take longer and make more errors. This would likely have the effect of opening their minds to the possibility that they hold implicit race-crime stereotypes. Implicit bias researchers sometimes call this, with tongues firmly planted in cheeks, *unconsciousness-raising*, and there is some early evidence that it works, at least in terms of changing explicit attitudes (Menatti, Smyth, Teachman, & Nosek, in press).

It has now been amply demonstrated that implicit biases (i.e., stereotypes and prejudices that operate outside of conscious awareness and control) affect our judgments of and behavior toward others. This has been submitted to rigorous empirical tests using meta-analysis (Greenwald et al., 2009). This research has also been reviewed with an eye toward behavioral correlates of implicit bias that are organizationally and societally impactful (Jost et al., 2009). As discussed in Chapter 4, measures of implicit bias have been found to correlate with, for example, hostile behavior toward minorities, employment discrimination, medical

2. The best way to understand how the IAT works would be to visit www.projectimplicit.org and try a demonstration task there.

decisions, and even psychopathology. Because police officers have been shown to possess implicit associations of race and crime (Eberhardt et al., 2004) and to exhibit spontaneous discriminatory behavior (Correll, Park, Judd, Wittenbrink, Sadler, & Keesee, 2007), and because of the established normalcy and ubiquity of stereotyping, there is little if any room for doubt that implicit stereotypes of race and crime influence police officers' decisions to stop and search. This helps to explain the discrepancy between the general formal and informal condemnation of profiling and the many findings of its occurrence. Consequently, it is important to factor implicit bias into our understanding of racial profiling.

What are the implications for the role of implicit bias in racial profiling? First and foremost, the likelihood that implicit stereotypes cause police to discriminate without intending to supports the notion that mere prohibitions on profiling will be inadequate. Second, training procedures can exploit implicit measures—having trainees take them—to raise awareness among officers of the potential for unintended bias. Third, implicit measures could be used in combination with other indices of bias (such as high stop and search rates for minorities, and low hit rates for minorities) to develop early warning systems to detect biased policing (by departments, units, or individual officers).

However, a strong caveat needs to be placed here with regard to the use of measures of implicit bias in any diagnostic fashion. Implicit measures are, like any psychometric, imperfect. They are good at detecting trends *in the aggregate*— they correlate with what you would expect them to, including explicit measures of the same attitudes, as well as consequential behaviors like those described earlier. The demonstration that most people, including police, hold implicit prejudice and stereotypes against minorities gives us good reason for concern about unintentional racial profiling being fairly widespread.

Using an implicit measure, however, to make a determination (an assessment or prediction) about an *individual* is something that needs to be done with extreme caution. At best, implicit measures account for about half of the variability in criterion measures, and less with sensitive topics like prejudice (Nosek, 2005). So there is a lot left over for other factors to explain and predict. Implicit bias, even if accurately assessed, will best predict only the most spontaneous, unintended aspects of behavior. People's behavior is multiply determined, with conscious and nonconscious, spontaneous and willful processes combining. Officers should not be punished or deprived of opportunities solely on the basis of nonconscious mental processes that they may well effectively override with motivations to control biases and act equitably.

If measures of implicit bias should not be used for hiring, promotion, or sanctioning decisions, what, if anything, should they be used for? First, as indicated previously, the testing process itself offers the potential for "unconsciousness-raising." When officers experience finding it harder to pair pictures of White than Black faces with words or images relating to crime, for example, they are likely to gain awareness and understanding of the presence and operation of this crucial bias. This, of course, would have to be accompanied by formal training on the meaning of implicit cognition and bias, and how they cause discrimination.

Second, while implicit measures should not be taken as unequivocal evidence of bias or the likelihood of discrimination, relatively extreme implicit bias scores could serve as red flags that would trigger further scrutiny. Most officers, like most undergraduates who have been studied and the hundreds of thousands of participants from all walks of life who have shown relatively negative attitudes toward Blacks on IATs on the Project Implicit website, will exhibit a stronger association between Blacks and crime than between Whites and crime. Consequently, the mere exhibition of an implicit Black-crime stereotypic association will not generally distinguish one individual from most others. In fact, the central finding of Devine's (1989) influential work on the automatic and controlled components of prejudice was that essentially everybody was aware of the negative stereotypes of Blacks, and so the stereotypes were likely to be automatically activated. What separated those who did not *exhibit* bias (on a questionnaire measure) from others was their motivation to behave without bias. Implicit bias scores, particularly those that are unusually high (i.e., "outliers"), can be used in conjunction with performance data or other indicators of bias. These other indicators would likely include questionnaire measures of explicit bias; questionnaire measures of motivation to control prejudice; civilian complaints; observations by peers and supervisors; and rates of stops, searches, arrests of, and/or use of force on minorities. This latter criterion, while potentially objective and compelling, would have to be handled carefully, taking into account the racial and ethnic breakdown of the beats the officers cover.

Taking into account the ethnic and racial composition of officers' beats serves multiple purposes. First, it provides denominators for the calculation of the stop rates, so that officers who patrol overwhelmingly minority areas are not penalized for stopping more minorities than officers who patrol Whiter areas. Second, it acknowledges the possibility that the ethnic composition of the beat can *cause* implicit biases. For example, officers patrolling a high-crime, largely Black area would likely have their race-crime stereotypes bolstered. In fact, officers in a national sample who reported higher percentages of Blacks in their communities exhibited significantly stronger "shooter bias"—the tendency to shoot armed Blacks faster than armed Whites in a computer-based simulation (Correll Park, Judd, Wittenbrink, Sadler, & Keesee, 2007)—which is a compelling index of unintended bias. In contrast to this finding, extensive research on the bias-reducing effects of "intergroup contact" (Pettigrew & Tropp, 2000, 2006) provides good reason to believe that officers working in relatively integrated areas could exhibit *less* bias, to the extent that they are having neutral or positive contact with minorities. Either way, it needs to be recognized that there will be multiple causes of racial disparities in stop and search rates, and that disparities alone, even when coupled with implicit stereotypes, do not necessarily implicate biased policing.

What's the Outcome?

Given the inherent ambiguity of police data, the outcome test approach described in Chapter 2 may be the most reliable (i.e., precise and valid) indicator of actual biased policing. As a reminder, the outcome test approach involves looking at the rate of successful searches—those yielding contraband or weapons—per stop and comparing the rate for different racial or ethnic groups. The fundamental insight of the outcome test is that if officers are deciding which people to stop and search without racial bias, but rather based solely on valid indicators of suspiciousness, different racial groups will yield similar hit rates—the outcomes of the stops or searches. This will be the case even if minorities are stopped and searched more, as long as they are offending at a commensurate rate. However, if officers are stopping and searching minorities at least in part because of racial stereotypes, hit rates will be lower for minorities because they will have had to meet a lower threshold of suspicion on legitimate indicators.

Importantly, the outcome test approach gets us around the benchmark problem because we do not need to know the actual offending rates or the rates at which different groups are being stopped and searched, both of which are extremely difficult to assess accurately. We need only know who is being stopped, not among whom they are being stopped. For an outcome test to be valid, however, the data have to be reliable. Every stop and its outcome need to be recorded, and recorded accurately. The proliferation of police stop data collection requirements and protocols, based on agency initiative, court order, or state law, aids this. But there is still the possibility of misreporting, intentional or not, on the part of officers. There is also considerable discretion available to officers with regard to verbal warnings, which often have no paper trail and therefore may not be reflected in data.

Some protocols require that officers contact their dispatcher whenever initiating a stop, and a computer file for the stop automatically gets opened. This increases the likelihood that stops will be recorded, but it does not guarantee the accuracy of the data. Dashboard-mounted cameras and the newer body-worn cameras will increase the likelihood that officers will record, and accurately so, their civilian encounters; they may even provide the opportunity for independent construction of stop and search data sets by other, neutral individuals (or software!) viewing and data coding the recordings.

Outliers

How would a department use implicit bias to identify officers who are at risk of racial profiling? Again, this should be done in conjunction with other indicators. Implicit measures, reflecting biases that are beyond the conscious awareness and control of the individual, should not be a basis for sanctioning. They could, however, be used to help identify officers who need additional training. As noted previously, because of the long-standing, prevailing, and media-transmitted race-crime stereotypes, most officers will exhibit a stronger association between minorities and crime than between Whites and crime, an association that will automatically trigger greater suspicion of minority subjects. But how strong is too strong?

In statistics, individuals who score (i.e., behave) in a manner that puts them outside the norm are called *outliers*. However, there is no one established standard for what makes an outlier. Most often outliers are identified based on how different their score is from the average score for their sample or population. For example, few people score under 70 or over 130 on IQ tests, and so those who do are often pegged as outliers. This necessarily raises the very valid question of why someone scoring 130 should be viewed any differently from someone scoring 129. This example is not entirely arbitrary; IQ tests are calibrated to achieve a mean of 100 and a standard deviation of 15 and to be normally distributed (bell curve shaped). As a consequence, about 2.5% of IQ test takers will score 130 or higher. About 0.13% (13 of 10,000) score 145 or higher, and fewer than 0.0000003% (3 of 10 million) score 160 or higher. Clearly 4 standard deviations above the mean is unusual, and we know "geniuses" can do things most of us cannot. Even 3 standard deviations above the mean is unusual, and so for many types of variables (e.g., income, height, speed), these are often treated as outliers, with statistical tests replicated after excluding them to ensure that the results are not skewed by a small number of people and consequently not representative of "normal" people.

Ideally, outliers can be identified as really *standing apart* from others. In statistical terms, this involves the presence of a *discontinuity* in the distribution of scores. In other words, there is a gap in the scores, with most people falling in one range, pretty smoothly spread out, and one or a few falling much higher or lower. An example that might resonate with most readers is in the domain of personal income. Most American adults earn incomes in the $20,000 to $200,000 range, and there are a lot of people in that range and a lot of very small gradations within it. Even among those who earn many hundreds of thousands of dollars annually, there is a smooth continuum of incomes, although there are many fewer of them, so the bell curve distribution is asymmetrical—it has a positive skew. Then come the billionaires, and the multibillionaires in particular. They are so rare, and they make so much more money than everyone else, that they are spread out, with big gaps between them. Warren Buffet and Bill Gates, for example, will be far out in the tail, with huge gaps between them and everyone else; they are like Pluto in our solar system. The essential point here is that when someone is an outlier, especially a discontinuous outlier, it often reflects that he or she is *categorically* different with regard to the variable of interest. Bill Gates is not just like the rest of us only more. He is in his own category. There are two important implications of this. First, we can learn a lot by understanding his story. Second, we should not expect that his experience will generalize to the rest of us. In fact, when economists talk about average income, they usually use the *median*, not the *mean*, for the very reason that people with very high incomes and outliers like Bill Gates can distort the mean as an estimate of the *typical* earner.

How does this relate to racial bias in policing? Because of the nature of human behavior and numbers, police officers will vary in their statistics, in terms of stops, searches, arrests, use of force, complaints, and racial differences in these variables, as well as implicit bias scores. Some of this will be due to qualities of the officers, and some will be random chance. And, of course, some will be due to the circumstances they are in, such as the characteristics of their beats, their shifts, their partners, and so forth. Accordingly, we cannot assume that an officer who has a higher rate of something than another officer is really more *prone* to that. To be more concrete, just comparing the arrest rates of two officers does not allow us to infer with certainty that the officer with the higher rate is more effective. He or she may be, but the difference could also be due to different work hours, beat, and simple chance.

One way to address this problem is to look at a lot of data (e.g., over many months or even years). In statistics, the *law of large numbers* dictates that the more data you have (e.g., the more respondents in the survey), the more likely the resulting statistics are to represent the real state of affairs accurately. So it will always behoove law enforcement agencies to look at as much data (outcomes over as much time or as many people) as they can. If someone is an outlier (e.g., making many more arrests than others do) one week but not the rest of the time, that probably says more about that week than it does about that officer. Inferring from that week's data that this person is exceptional would be a *false positive* error (concluding something is there when it is not). If, however, someone is pretty consistently outside the normal range, and particularly if there is a gap (a discontinuity) between his or her score and most others, that is cause for attention. He or she is probably functioning in a manner that is categorically different from others, perhaps operating under different assumptions or procedures.

In the case of monitoring for racial or ethnic bias in police officers, we would be looking for high, if not outlying, scores on multiple indicators: relative stop and search rates of minorities and Whites; relative arrest (hit) rates among minorities and Whites stopped and searched; civilian complaints; racial differences in rates of use of force; explicit racial attitudes assessed by questionnaire; and, ideally, implicit racial biases, including stereotypes associating minorities with crime and aggression. Outliers on any of these dimensions could warrant scrutiny. High scorers on multiple indicators should in particular because *the likelihood is low that multiple indicators would yield false positive errors on the same person.*

It should also be noted, however, that if an officer is patrolling a high-crime beat that is also largely minority-populated, both of these factors would likely cause the indicators to be high. This may not reflect a bias that the officer brings to the job, but it would still warrant concern and attention, lest the associations the officer is learning from the beat get generalized and turn into biased policing.

In the abstract, identifying outliers may sound straightforward, but it will require some care and nuance on the part of departments. Every department will have its own unique distribution of officers on a given dimension of interest. Some departments will be relatively invariant, some will be normally distributed (bell curve shaped), and others, perhaps most, will have a rightward (or positive) or leftward (negative) skew. Skews are common in variables that have "floors" or "ceilings." So, for example, variables like number of arrests (or income), which cannot have values below zero (a floor) but can vary upward quite a bit, will tend to be positively skewed, with a tail extending to the right, representing a diminishing number of people with high values. So, you will almost inevitably get a positive "tail" in the distribution that is simply a physical, mathematical consequence of the nature of the variable. The question becomes, how far out on that tail does one need to be to be considered outside the normal, acceptable range?

Outliers = Rotten Apples?

On undesirable outcomes, like high rates of use of force, a positively skewed distribution, with a small number of outliers at the high end, will be interpreted as a "rotten apples" problem—a high rate for the department is caused by a small number of extreme scorers (frequent force users) who are pulling up the departmental rate like Bill Gates pulls up the U.S. income average. In this sense, looking at the actual graphs of the distributions of data can be extremely helpful in defining the nature of the problem and generating solutions. A positively skewed distribution with a few "bad apples" at the high end implicates an intervention focused on the bad apples. A narrow, relatively symmetrical distribution with a high average indicates a more systemic problem that needs to be addressed systemically.

How to Interpret and Use Implicit Bias Scores Responsibly

As indicated previously, measures of implicit bias, while effective predictors of behavior in the aggregate, should be interpreted with caution at the individual level. Nevertheless, for an officer who has troubling scores on other measures, particularly performance measures like racial differences in use of force or hit rates, the *co-incidence* of a strong implicit antiminority bias is likely more than a *coincidence*. It may, in fact, offer valuable insight into the root cause of the disparities, specifically, mental associations that are biasing judgments of minorities.

In order to understand what high implicit bias scores mean, we must consider how they are calculated. Chapter 4 discussed extensively the theoretical and empirical bases for implicit bias measures—the lessons from cognitive psychology about the "associational" nature of memory and thought, and how that can be mapped with procedures measuring the speed with which stimuli (words, images) are categorized when paired with stimuli that share meaning. Social psychologists applied this to stereotypes because they, too, are mental associations, those between groups and traits. The general approach in implicit measures is to pair words or images that serve as exemplars of categories, such as racial categories (Black, White) and traits (criminal, lawful) or even just general evaluations (good, bad). People taking the measure respond to many (scores or even hundreds) of stimuli in sequence. The average speeds with which people respond when the categories are paired one way (Black with criminal, White with lawful) versus the other (Black with lawful, White with criminal) are compared. Based on the cognitive psychological research, we know that when people make these responses faster (or make fewer errors), it reflects that they have a stronger association between the paired categories. These speeds are measured in milliseconds.

The method for actually calculating a bias score is fairly complicated and varies some as a function of the specific measurement procedure, but the essential approach is to subtract the average reaction time for one set of category pairings from the average for the other and divide the difference by the standard deviation.[3] If we get a positive number when we subtract the average reaction time for Black-criminal/White-lawful pairings from the average for Black-lawful/White-criminal pairings, it indicates that the test-taker associated Blacks with crime (and/or Whites with lawfulness) more than Whites with crime (and/or Blacks with lawfulness). We would call this an *implicit race-crime stereotype*.[4]

As with any metric, there are several ways that we can identify high scorers.[5] One way would be to look for outliers, perhaps using the conventional use of 3 standard deviations from the mean, but this is not likely to be very helpful and is actually quite arbitrary. First, by definition, there will be very few people who score 3 standard deviations above the mean, so that procedure, which is usually employed to conservatively identify possibly misleading data, would

3. Dividing by the *SD* "standardizes" the implicit bias score, meaning that it gives us a difference score that is relative to how much that person tends to vary in reaction time. This is an important step because for a person who varies widely (e.g., has a standard deviation of 400 milliseconds), a 200-ms difference between means is not as meaningful as it would be for someone who varies in response time very little (e.g., has a 100-ms *SD*).

4. A fair amount of data treatment has to be undertaken before this subtraction can be done. For example, extreme reaction times will also be removed or replaced with the cutoff value. Data from test-takers who appear to be responding arbitrarily (e.g., by hitting the same response key every time) or in a fashion not appropriate for the task (e.g., by responding extremely slowly on most trials) need to be excluded.

5. Negative scores on an implicit race bias measure would indicate anti-White bias, and there is no reason why such scores, if strong, would not be valid triggers of concern, especially if accompanied by evidence of discriminatory behavior. However, it is the rare implicit test-taker, even among racial minorities, who reveals a pronounced anti-White bias.

be inappropriate. We are not necessarily looking for unusually extreme scores but rather simply high scores, indicating strong stereotypes. A lower threshold like 2 standard deviations could be employed, but this is also arbitrary; why treat someone who is 2.01 standard deviations above the mean differently from someone who is 1.99 above? Furthermore, if a department or unit has a systemic bias problem, the average implicit bias score for that department or unit will likely be high, so tagging only scores that are much higher than that average would overlook many cases of strong bias.

The discontinuity approach described earlier could be useful in the sense that it identifies people who appear to be *categorically* different from others, and it gets around the problem of the arbitrariness of the cutoff point (the discontinuity is where it is, and is a function of the unique qualities of the population being studied). The discontinuity approach has its shortcomings, however. First, in some populations, there is no discontinuity—the spread of scores is smooth. Second, it is still vulnerable to the problem of overlooking bias in departments with a systemic problem. While people scoring above a gap may well be in a different category than those below, this does not necessitate that those scoring below the discontinuity have levels of bias that warrant no concern.

In contrast to interpreting implicit bias scores, when looking at behavioral indicators, like arrest or use of force rates, the shape of a distribution of data (e.g., symmetrical or skewed) provides more inherently meaningful and readily interpretable information. For example, because use of force represents real, specific events, we can count them up and calculate the proportion of total events accounted for by those at the high end of the distribution. This allows for a fairly straightforward detection of "rotten apples," particularly if a small number of officers are responsible for a very large percentage of uses of force. If the distribution of rates of use of force is very positively skewed, with a small number of officers (in the right tail of the distribution) using force at much higher rates, this indicates a relatively isolated problem. In other words, most officers are behaving normally, and their range of frequency of use of force is reasonable; the outlying rotten apples are using force at such a high rate that they are responsible for most of the problem (see Gladwell, 2006a, for dramatic, policy-relevant examples).

Implicit bias scores have no such inherent, countable nature. They also differ in that they are not a behavior that matters in and of themselves. If 1% of a department is responsible for 50% of uses of force, it is pretty clear that those officers are doing something excessive, but no comparable calculation can be made for implicit bias. Nevertheless, implicit bias scores have been shown to predict discriminatory behavior (Jost et al., 2009). Consequently, implicit bias scores allow for reasonable inferences of the strength of bias, so we can predict who is *more likely* to discriminate. They are not, however, direct evidence of discrimination in the way that an excessive, racially disparate rate of use of force is. Nor should they be used that way.

Accordingly, high implicit bias scores should be used in conjunction with other indicators, such as those discussed previously (e.g., complaints; racial disproportions in stops, frisks, searches, use of force, and hit rates; supervisor evaluations). Departments could combine these scores in an additive (summing them up) or multiplicative (multiplying across them) manner to achieve a summary score. Both of these approaches have the advantage of being fairly intuitive and straightforward, but there are some problems to consider. On the one hand, adding scores on multiple indicators has the disadvantage of potentially undervaluing things, like implicit bias scores, that may have narrow ranges of scores, when added to factors, like use of force events, that will be counted in integers and could be in double digits. On the other hand, the multiplicative approach has the disadvantages of not handling zeros well (multiplying anything by zero yields a product of zero). Nor does it handle negative values well; implicit bias scores can be negative (indicating a "pro-minority" bias). Consequently, an officer with extremely high (undesirable) scores on other indicators with even the most slight, negative score on the implicit bias measure would appear to be favoring minorities.

There are some reasonable modifications that can be adopted for either the additive or the multiplicative approach, but all of them require making some arbitrary assumptions. For example, for the additive approach, the problem of the different scaling of the factors, and the consequent potential for implicit bias scores to be underweighted, could be addressed by standardizing and weighting the scores (multiplying them by a value to reflect their importance). The zero problem in the multiplicative approach could be addressed by adding a constant to all scores. The negative implicit bias score problem with the multiplicative approach is harder to handle in any valid way. One could set a floor of zero (plus the small constant that would be added to it), but this would be throwing away information.

Statistically Modeling the Importance of Different Factors

In the final analysis, the additive approach is more advantageous, and it turns out that the weightings need not be arbitrary. The statistical procedure *multiple regression* will allow for a data-driven calculation of weights that can be assigned to each factor, before adding them up, to best predict the likelihood of problematic policing. Regression will tell us how well, or poorly, each factor uniquely predicts the criterion variable, above and beyond the influence of the other factors. Some factors will be more strongly correlated with the outcome than others, and we want to assign the greatest weight to scores on those factors. A bonus benefit of this regression approach is that we can also include in the statistical calculations variables that might be beyond the officers' control but nevertheless likely to influence the outcome (e.g., the crime rate in the officer's beat; the racial/ethnic composition of the beat). Including *control variables* like this will make the prediction vis-à-vis any bias in the officer's own decision-making and habits more precise.

Constructing the regression model requires a number of pieces of information about each officer: data on all the variables of interest (e.g., complaints, performance, implicit bias) and, importantly, a valid criterion that we are trying to predict. This criterion variable would have to be something that is a first-order indicator of the problem—racial bias in policing—and something for which we have high confidence in the reliability of the data we have on it. In other words, this would be something that matters a lot (and is a source of concern) and that we can have confidence in the scores we have for it. The regression would be run on data from prior periods to identify how strongly related the factors of interest are with the criterion of interest, and the resulting weightings would be applied to the various factors' scores to estimate the risk that a given officer will engage in discriminatory behavior.

There is no objective score on "racial discriminatory propensity" handed down from on high that we could use as a criterion. Short of that, we need to identify the next best available thing. This could be one of the variables we have been considering already, most likely the outcome test score resulting from the analysis of relative (minority-to-White) rates of arrests per stop. Or, if a given department cares most about racial or ethnic disparities in use of force, that would be the best criterion. It would be tempting to use actual incidents of discipline for discrimination (i.e., have the variables in the model explain who has or has not be disciplined), but the frequency of disciplinary action is too low to be statistically useful, and the cases are probably highly idiosyncratic. What is crucial is that the criterion variable represents a reliable, high-consensus indicator of a problem.

Ideally, this statistical model, and the weights that would be derived from it, would be constructed using a very large, representative sample. Because the necessary resources (a sophisticated statistician and data for all the necessary variables) will not be available in most police departments, a broad-based effort will be needed to assemble and analyze a large database from a national sample representative of various regions, department sizes, and jurisdiction demographics. If this sample is large and heterogeneous enough, and if statistical tests indicate that departmental differences matter in terms of predicting the criterion variable, different models can be constructed for different types of departments. This undertaking is not unrealistic; it is within the capacity of the CPE, which is already implementing a national research program in collaboration with dozens of North American police departments, a program that was ratified by the Major Cities Chiefs Association.

Precision Helps Prediction

Generally speaking, when one is trying to make empirical (data-driven) predictions, the better the data, the better the prediction. This means that variables that are included in a statistical model should be carefully conceived and meticulously measured. Many of the variables discussed so far will come from police department records and will vary in their accuracy. Indicators of stops, the demographics of who is stopped, and the outcomes of the stops are only as accurate as the reports the officers provide. We will have more control over the quality of the data resulting from the attitudinal measures we will include in the analysis, and we should make the most of that.

It is an axiom of social psychology that measures of attitudes will predict behavior best to the extent that the attitude is matched to the behavior (Ajzen & Fishbein, 1977). For example, if you want to predict whether people will choose to eat apples, you could ask them how much they like fruit, or you could ask them how much they like apples. Both will probably work, but, not surprisingly, the latter will be a better predictor. Similarly, when measuring police attitudes, implicit and explicit, to predict if officers will engage in racial profiling, we should construct and adopt measures that are matched to the behavior.

While there are well-established measures of explicit and implicit attitudes toward Blacks, like the Symbolic Racism 2000 Scale (Henry & Sears, 2001) and the Black/White-Good/Bad Implicit Association Test (Greenwald et al., 1998), these are essentially measures of *prejudice* (i.e., positive or negative dispositions), and it is likely that *stereotypes* (beliefs about traits) will be more effective predictors. In fact, Correll et al. (2002) found that a measure of stereotyping, but not prejudice, predicted shooter bias, and Eric Knowles and I (Glaser & Knowles, 2008) found that an implicit race-weapons IAT, but not the standard prejudice IAT, correlated with shooter bias. Accordingly, departments wishing to employ psychological measures of racial bias, implicit and/or explicit, to estimate the risk of racial profiling would do well to utilize measures of relevant *stereotypes*. To that end, my colleagues and I have been developing implicit and explicit (questionnaire) measures of race-crime stereotypes, as well as measures of attitudes toward the use of race in judgments of suspicion. Our expectation is that officers who strongly associate minorities with crime will be more likely to engage in racial profiling, and this will be especially so for officers who think the use of race or ethnicity in judgments of suspicion is legitimate.

Ideally, the development of a reliable, multivariate (using a combination of multiple predictor variables) model for estimating officers' risk of racial profiling would be a nationwide collaborative venture between police leaders, legal experts, social scientists, and policymakers. The economies of scale that could be promoted by a national effort, perhaps facilitated by the eventual passage of an End Racial Profiling Act into law, could promote the development of a set of effectual national standards. Any such undertaking would have to reflect that different locales and the agencies that police them have different characteristics. One size will not fit all. The national approach would need sufficient flexibility to be adaptable to localities.

Watch the Hypocrisy

A crucial caveat here is that we do not want to commit the same type of error that we are critiquing by relying on aggregate statistics to make judgments about individuals. Any predictions about risk of discriminatory behavior must be used responsibly. The proposed data-driven approach will necessarily be imperfect and will lead to false positive identifications. Accordingly, it should be used cautiously and should never be the sole basis of sanction.

SHIFTING RESPONSIBILITY FROM "INTENT" TO "DUE DILIGENCE"

As I encountered more offended, defensive decisionmakers accused of discrimination, and as I counseled and consoled more embittered employees who knew they had been treated differently because of their race or gender or ethnicity but could not, as the law requires in such cases, prove that their employer harbored a discriminatory motive or intent, I became convinced that something about the way the law was defining and seeking to remedy disparate treatment discrimination was fundamentally flawed.

Krieger, 1995, p. 1164

In addition to implicit measures' utility in quantifying bias, perhaps more important is their value in revealing that these biases are the rule, not the exception. Because implicit biases are related to discriminatory behaviors, there is reason for concern that most people, including police officers, are at risk of discriminating on a regular basis. This raises a profound question about how to mitigate racial profiling: *How do we stop it when people do not even know they are doing it?* We need to acknowledge that officers may profile *in spite of* their conscious intent to be fair. As a consequence, proof of the *intent to discriminate* is not a useful standard for intervention because intentionality is rarely the cause of discrimination.

This is consistent with Krieger's (1995, 1998) groundbreaking legal thesis that the pervasiveness of *implicit* stereotyping and prejudice necessitates that employment discrimination jurisprudence move away from an *intent* model. In other words, because employers will likely discriminate not because they *intend* to but because stereotypes cause them to misjudge women and minorities, discrimination will not be effectively mitigated by punishing those who can be proven to have had the intent to discriminate. Spontaneous, unintended discrimination will be unchecked. Currently, for the vast majority of employment discrimination cases, as with racial profiling, the courts require a very high evidentiary bar, which includes evidence of intent.

Krieger (1995) argued that "the nondiscrimination principle, currently interpreted as a proscriptive duty 'not to discriminate,' must evolve to encompass a prescriptive duty of care to identify and control for category-based judgment errors and other forms of cognitive bias in intergroup settings" (p. 1166). In other words, the courts should shift from an *intent* model to one that holds employers accountable if they fail to execute reasonable measures to prevent discrimination. Krieger stopped short of advocating the adoption of a "negligence" model:

> Unlike other scholars who advocate a "negligence" approach to employment discrimination, I suggest that additional empirical and theoretical work must be done before the contours of such a duty can be precisely defined, let alone crafted into practical and effective legal rules. (p. 1166)

Krieger acknowledges that even just moving away from the intent doctrine would represent a tectonic shift in antidiscrimination jurisprudence—the courts are unlikely to deviate from their decades-old precedent.

Administrative License

So, it will probably be a long time before the judiciary is ready to modify its intent doctrine to hold institutions accountable for failing to take positive steps to prevent implicit bias from causing discrimination. In their management practices, however, administrative agencies like police departments need not adhere to the courts' standards of evidence in addressing discrimination. They are free to compel their employees to take affirmative steps to prevent discrimination like racial profiling. This could include training to raise awareness among supervisors and rank and file, but also the multivariate monitoring discussed earlier, combined with a system of incentives like promotion and, in extreme cases, sanction. The critical point here is that, as Krieger has argued, if we expect discrimination to arise only from conscious intent, we will fail to identify much, perhaps most, of it. If we hold people accountable only for intentional discrimination, we will address very little of it. In order to mitigate discriminatory practices like racial profiling in contemporary times, we need to shift the burden from a passive lack of intent to an affirmative due diligence to avoid the negligent act of allowing oneself or one's supervisee to discriminate.

The data collection and multivariate modeling described earlier would be pillars of a due diligence regime, allowing for an early warning system to detect biased policing before it becomes an enduring problem or a legal and political liability. Having valid and rigorous procedures in place will also signal a commitment to nondiscrimination and potentially provide legitimate political and legal protection in the event of a controversy. As a reminder of caution, this collection and analysis would have to be conducted conscientiously, and ideally in compliance with well-developed, national standards. This points again to the importance of passage of national legislation to provide guidance, resources, economies of scale, and legitimacy in support of these essential practices.

PRACTICAL STRATEGIES FOR MITIGATING
RACIAL PROFILING

If departments are going to hold themselves to something like a negligence standard, they will need tools for mitigating racial profiling. Many departments already engage in "diversity" and "cultural sensitivity" programs, but, as discussed previously, there is a lack of evidence that these programs actually reduce discrimination (Paluck & Green, 2009), let alone outcomes that result from *implicit* stereotypes. There are several classes of strategies that are promising, including altering discretionary practices that give rise to bias, providing training to change the biases, increasing officers' motivations to behave without bias, and promoting the kind of intergroup contact that has been definitively shown to reduce bias.

Reducing Discretion

Understanding that discrimination can and does occur in the absence of conscious intent implicates the necessity of policies and procedures that reduce the likelihood of racial profiling, beyond mere prohibition. In other words, because most officers will be unaware of the implicit stereotypes that cause them to stop minorities disproportionately, it will be difficult for them to avoid making biased judgments. Tactics like stop and frisk, wherein there is at least a tacit mandate to act with a low threshold of suspicion and high discretion, give rise to unjustified racial disparities (e.g., OAGSNY, 1999). Rules that standardize practices and remove discretion will help to reduce the impact of stereotypes. For example, the California Highway Patrol's discovery of ethnic bias in highway stops and searches led to the abolition of consent searches, which allow for great discretion.

Perhaps the most stunning demonstration of the benefits of reducing discretion comes from the experience of the U.S. Customs Service. As discussed in Chapter 2, an investigation by the General Accounting Office (GAO, 2000b) confirmed earlier findings and news media reports of racial disparities in passenger searches that were unsupported by contraband hit rates. Most strikingly, although Blacks and Latinos were searched at rates far beyond their representation in the traveling population, Blacks were no more likely than Whites to yield contraband, and Latinos were far less likely (1.4% vs. 5.8% hit rates). In 1998, Raymond Kelly, prior to becoming police commissioner in New York City, took the helm of the Customs Service and in 1999 instituted new policies that precluded the use of race or ethnicity in decisions to search, placing greater emphasis on observing passengers for suspicious behavior. The result was dramatically (75.4%) fewer searches (dropping from 32,857 to 8,099), but a steep increase in overall contraband hit rates, from 3.8% to 14.9%

between 1998 and 2000.[6] The net result was nearly the same number of contraband finds in the 2 years studied (1,251 in 1998; 1,204 in 2000),[7] but with far fewer passengers subjected to searches, and much smaller racial disparities under the new regime.

All in all, this policy change brought about a stunning increase in efficiency, while addressing equity and legality problems. At the directive's core were two strategies: perform fewer searches, and use a smaller number of more behavior-based indicators of suspiciousness. Gladwell (2006b) summarized the changes clearly:

> There had been a list of forty-three suspicious traits. [Customs commissioner Raymond Kelly] replaced it with a list of six broad criteria. Is there something suspicious about their physical appearance? Are they nervous? Is there specific intelligence targeting this person? Does the drug-sniffing dog raise an alarm? Is there something amiss in their paperwork or explanations? Has contraband been found that implicates this person? You'll find nothing here about race or gender or ethnicity, and nothing here about expensive jewelry or deplaning at the middle or the end, or walking briskly or walking aimlessly. Kelly removed all the unstable generalizations, forcing customs officers to make generalizations about things that don't change from one day or one month to the next. "We made them more efficient and more effective at what they were doing," Kelly said.

As indicated by the Customs Service experience, the proceduralization and standardization of profiles (e.g., terrorist, drug courier) itself may, in fact, reduce racial discrimination, provided race and ethnicity, and things that are correlated with them (e.g., clothing style) but not related to offending, are excluded from the profiles. In Turley's (2002) words, regarding airport security screening, "The benefit of a formal profiling system is that we can control the criteria and better monitor their use." Israeli security expert Rafi Ron (2002) agrees that a "professional procedure" will reduce the discretion of the screener and thereby mitigate the influence of bias.

We still need to bear in mind that "formal" profiling does not by any means preclude "informal" profiling. To the contrary, official use of perpetrator profiles could signal to agents that demographic factors are on the table. Nevertheless, because stereotypes tend to influence our judgments anyway, the employment of well-specified, empirically derived, formal profiles that do not include race and ethnicity could serve to squeeze out the influence of suspect race and ethnicity in favor of other, better indicators agents would be looking for.

---

6. Statistics derived from data table provided by Ramirez et al., 2003.
7. These numbers have to be compared with caution, given that crime rates change from year to year. Nevertheless, it is clear that a dramatic decrease in searches resulted in at most a very small decrease in captures.

Changing and/or Controlling Stereotypes

Eliminating or reducing the frequency of high-discretion stops and searches is a dependable method for mitigating discriminatory outcomes because bias is most influential under ambiguity and uncertainty, and discretion lends itself to subjectivity in decision-making. Eliminating discretion eliminates *opportunities* for bias to influence judgments.

Another obvious strategy is to change or control the beliefs that give rise to biased policing. As discussed in Chapter 3, however, stereotypes do tend to be resistant to change—we often "subtype" individuals who are counterstereotypic; we tend to seek and retain information that confirms our prior beliefs; we tend to see groups as more homogeneous than they are, and so forth. It should not, however, be conceded that the stereotypes that drive racial profiling cannot be weakened, if not permanently extinguished, or controlled. There are at least three promising avenues to effective stereotype remediation, even for implicit stereotypes that reside outside of consciousness and are triggered automatically. The first approach is through promoting motivation to control prejudice and stereotyping. The second is through training to alter the content of the stereotypes. The most established method is to promote personal contact with members of stigmatized groups.

Motivation to Control Prejudice

As discussed at length in Chapter 4, stereotype-based judgments are nearly inevitable even for those who do not endorse the stereotypes because mere knowledge of them is sufficient to trigger associations that will bias judgments. As Devine (1989) demonstrated a major factor that differentiates people who do not *exhibit* bias from those who do is acting on a goal to be egalitarian. Devine and her colleagues (e.g., Plant & Devine, 1998), as well as Fazio and his (e.g., Fazio et al., 1995; Dunton & Fazio, 1997), went on to develop and validate questionnaire measures of motivation to control prejudice. Devine, Plant, and colleagues have found that those high in intrinsic but low in extrinsic motivation (i.e., those for whom being egalitarian is motivated by personal conviction but not by concern over what others think) show less implicit stereotype activation.

My colleagues and I (Glaser & Knowles, 2008; Park et al., 2008; Park & Glaser, 2011) have developed a reaction-time measure of *implicit* motivation to control prejudice, which modulates spontaneous discriminatory behavior, specifically shooter bias. People appear to vary naturally, and quite a bit, on implicit, intrinsic, and extrinsic motivations to control prejudice, and this variability predicts their behaviors.

The first lesson of this line of theory and set of findings is that the effect of motivation to control prejudice on behavior indicates that prejudiced behavior *is controllable.* The highly motivated people still have the stereotypes in their minds, but they are better at not acting on them. The corollary lesson is that, to the extent that we can boost people's motivation to control prejudice, particularly the implicit and intrinsic types, we can cause a reduction in discrimination, even the spontaneous variety. This is a line of inquiry that is ripe for exploration. Some promising findings (e.g., Dasgupta & Rivera, 2006) suggest that it is possible. But as yet there are no established, validated methods for increasing implicit or explicit motivation to control prejudice.

Changing Stereotype Content

As discussed in Chapter 3, stereotypes tend to be resistant to change, but like any beliefs, they can be changed, with some effort. Attitude and belief change and persuasion constitute a vast area of social psychological research (Cialdini, 1984; McGuire, 1985; Zimbardo & Leippe, 1991), and there are many reasons for belief persistence and avenues for change that can be applied to stereotypes. Numerous studies have presented people with counterstereotypic information and observed the degree of change, typically finding resistance to change. One very basic model is based on learning theory, the fundamental idea that people (and animals) learn associations through repeated pairings (and learn behaviors through rewards). Accordingly, if stereotypes can be formed through associations (e.g., repeated pairings of the concepts of "Black" and "criminal" or "violent"), then they can be changed through repeated pairings of the opposite, or perhaps extinguished through repeated random, uncorrelated pairings.

One set of studies employed a relatively heavy-handed, blunt learning approach, having research subjects literally say "no" to repeated pairings of photographs of Black people with words representing Black stereotypes (e.g., *ignorant, aggressive*; Kawakami, Dovidio, Moll, Hermsen, & Russin, 2001). Kawakami and colleagues found that research subjects in their stereotype negation treatment condition subsequently exhibited weaker implicit stereotypes than those in the control condition, and that this difference was still evident a week after the intervention. Similarly, my colleague Sang Hee Park and I have exposed individuals to shooting simulations that include more armed Whites than armed Blacks, finding this to reduce their subsequent shooter bias relative to those in a neutral control condition (Park & Glaser, 2011). These procedures are, however, fairly labor-intensive, and it is not clear that the stereotype attenuation would be long-lived, considering that most people return to the same social environment and influences (e.g., news media) that formed the original stereotypes.

Furthermore, to the extent that stereotypes serve more than just an information-processing efficiency ("heuristic") function, mere exposure to counterstereotypic information will be inadequate. Because stereotypes also serve to rationalize inequities (e.g., Eagly & Steffen, 1984; Jost & Banaji,

1994), they will be both resilient and prone to reconstruction provided that the group-based inequities persist.

Stereotype Malleability

There is also evidence that immediate contextual factors can modulate racial stereotypes and prejudice, even those that are implicit (e.g., Dasgupta & Greenwald, 2001; Dasgupta & Rivera, 2006; Lowery, Hardin, & Sinclair 2001; Sinclair, Lowery, Hardin, & Colangelo, 2005; see Blair, 2002, for a review). For example, presenting an African American man in the context of a street scene elicits a more negative automatic response than presenting him in the context of a church does (Wittenbrink, Judd, & Park, 2001). Exposing people to a real African American person can reduce their automatic racial bias (Lowery et al., 2001), as can merely exposing them to a person wearing an antiracism T-shirt (Sinclair et al., 2005). Additionally, things that distract us from the category (e.g., racial) cues that activate stereotypes, such as other features of a person, can prevent such stereotypes from influencing judgments (Gilbert & Hixon, 1991). Consequently, there is considerable room for optimism that implicit biases are not as inevitably influential as was originally presumed.

The malleability of automatic stereotypes does not, however, render them unpredictable and uninfluential. Large, thorough, quantitative reviews (aka meta-analyses) of studies looking at the relations between implicit bias measures and discriminatory behaviors (e.g., Greenwald et al., 2009) reveal that the general trend is that those who have stronger biases exhibit more discrimination, just as they reliably exhibit more explicit bias (Hofmann et al., 2005; Nosek, 2005; Nosek & Smyth, 2007). All else being equal, we can expect implicit biases to cause discriminatory judgments and behaviors, unless proactive steps are taken to prevent that.

Contact

Perhaps the best-established method for reducing prejudice is *intergroup contact*. This refers to social (not necessarily physical) contact between members of different groups. It is an old idea (Allport, 1954) that has been tested hundreds of times and has been amply supported (Pettigrew & Tropp, 2000, 2006). Original formulations of the theory held that intergroup contact needed to meet four conditions to be effective: equal status between individuals; sanction by authority; common goals; and interdependence/cooperation. Pettigrew and Tropp's (2000, 2006) meta-analysis of hundreds of contact tests indicated that, although these conditions promoted greater prejudice reduction, none of them was a necessary condition. Mere contact (assuming it is not negative) is sufficient to reduce prejudice toward the other group, and not just the individuals with whom the contact took place. These effects tend to be middling in size. Most reassuring is that the higher the quality of the test (e.g., if it involves random assignment and a strong control condition), the greater the prejudice reduction effect tends to be. This indicates that the *real* effect is relatively reliable, so that when it is measured accurately, it shows up better.

A small number of studies have looked specifically at the effects of police-civilian contact on intergroup attitudes. Early studies examined the effects of police-civilian contact on civilian attitudes toward police (Rusinko, Johnson, & Hornung, 1978) and on attitudes between police and college students (Diamond & Lobitz, 1973). However, a few studies have looked at the effect of contact on police attitudes and behaviors. Peruche and Plant (2006) found that police officers who reported more positive personal contact with Black people in general and at work showed a more pronounced decline in shooter bias over the course of trials in their study. Dhont, Cornelis, and Van Hiel (2010) found in a Belgian sample that police who reported more positive and negative contact with immigrants reported more positive and negative attitudes toward immigrants, respectively.

Bringing about (as opposed to just measuring past) intergroup contact experiences for police officers may prove challenging, but there are several plausible opportunities. One would be to maximize interracial partner assignments, to the extent that department demographics allow. Departments that have some or most officers operating without partners may wish to consider looking for opportunities. Departments that do not have sufficient minority representation in their ranks will have difficulty arranging interracial partnerships for a significant portion of their staff. If minorities are underrepresented on the force, the value of interracial contact through partnering offers an additional incentive for remedying the underrepresentation.

Community policing approaches also hold promise for reducing bias through contact. After all, community policing has as a central tenet *positive* police-community personal contact. Community policing is designed to improve police-community relations and reap the benefits of increased public cooperation (Community Oriented Policing Services, 2012). That such contact could decrease bias in police could have reverberating benefits, with the quality of the contact improving because of the prejudice reduction it engenders, and community cooperation improving because of improving quality of contact, and so forth.

There are no guarantees that contact will weaken the race-crime stereotypes that most likely drive racial discrimination in policing. Nevertheless, given that it appears to be stereotypes, and not prejudice, that predict shooter bias (Correll et al., 2002; Glaser & Knowles, 2008), and that contact has been shown to facilitate a reduction in shooter bias in a police sample (Peruche & Plant, 2006; but note that Correll, Park, Judd, & Wittenbrink, 2007, found no direct relation between self-reported interracial contact and shooter bias in two large police samples), it is plausible that, under the right conditions, there would be a beneficial effect of contact on equitable policing.

Another mechanism by which intergroup partnering and community policing could reduce biased policing would be *recategorization*. As discussed in Chapter 3, one of the human cognitive processes most responsible for stereotyping, prejudice, and discrimination is *categorization*. We are hardwired to place objects and concepts we encounter into mental categories (e.g., Bruner, 1957; Rosch, 1975), and in the case of people, we spontaneously sort them into gender, racial, and other categories (Tajfel & Wilkes, 1963) onto which we attach stereotypes and feelings. *Recategorization* is the process by which we can, usually with some intentionality and effort, reduce prejudice by thinking about individuals in terms of different categories (Gaertner, Mann, Murrell, & Dovidio, 1989), ideally those to which we also belong and that are not stigmatized. In the case of reducing bias in policing, recategorization might take the form of moving from "suspect" to "citizen," from "African American" to just plain "American." Sometimes historical events, like foreign threats, can cause mass recategorization in this latter sense, although they can also cause a profiling-promoting recategorization toward those who share (or seem to share) the ethnicity of the enemy, as occurred in the treatment of Japanese Americans after the Pearl Harbor attacks, and of Middle Eastern and South Asian Americans after the September 11 attacks. To the extent that departments can promote helpful recategorization, through partnering, community policing, or more direct training, it has the potential to both reduce biased policing and improve community relations.

A Warning About "Credentialing."

Prejudice-reduction interventions like sensitivity training and intergroup partnering have obvious intuitive appeal. Why wouldn't greater cultural awareness reduce bias and discrimination? One reason for caution derives from an interesting and compelling line of social psychological research on what is called *moral credentialing* (Monin & Miller, 2001). Monin and colleagues have found that when people are given the opportunity to exhibit desirable attitudes or behavior, such as egalitarianism, they will subsequently behave, on average, in a less upstanding way than they would have. Apparently, the initial display of virtue can give people the "moral license" to flout these standards. Having received sensitivity training, or having a minority partner, could lead some officers to feel they had fulfilled their moral obligations ("I'm not biased, my *partner* is *Black*!") and to let down their guard. This credentialing phenomenon could elicit a sense of futility—why promote good behavior if it's going to lead to bad? Moral credentialing researchers, however, hypothesize that when positive behavior is viewed as a commitment to a goal (as opposed to progress toward the goal), credentialing effects are not likely (Merritt, Effron, & Monin, 2010).

ACCOUNTABILITY

Any efforts to reduce racial profiling would likely be bolstered by (and even heavily reliant on) the presence of appropriate accountability systems. But accountability turns out to be more complicated, and its benefits more tenuous, than most people presume. Lerner and Tetlock (1994) define accountability as "the implicit or explicit expectation of decision makers that they may be called upon to justify their beliefs, feelings, and actions to others" (p. 3098). Their extensive review of research on accountability indicates that decision-makers tend to conform their decisions to the presumed preferences of those who will evaluate them (Tetlock, 1983). However, when evaluators' preferences are unknown *and* they are perceived as having legitimate authority, and the accountability is anticipated *before* the decision-making occurs, decision-makers will be motivated to make more careful, thoughtful judgments that are less influenced by cognitive biases (such as racial stereotypes; Lerner & Tetlock, 1999). With these conditions met, accountability should be an advantageous component of any service provision program, including law enforcement.

Law enforcement agencies already have multiple systems of accountability and evaluators such as supervisors, promotions review committees, internal affairs divisions, and citizen review boards. In most departments, the primary evaluators will be supervisors up the chain of command. Clearly, they are going to be generally accepted as legitimate, and certainly as authoritative. But their preferences are likely to be known. If a formal antibias and/or discretion-reducing program has been instituted, officers will know that and will try to conform their behavior to that. In this case, the "conformity" effects that are seen as problematic in accountability research could prove an asset.

However, if officers do not believe their supervisors are committed to the goals of the program, or if the departmental culture transmits an acceptance of racial and ethnically based judgments of suspiciousness, this could contravene the purpose of the program. Additionally, if the evaluators are not seen as legitimate, accountability could backfire, with officers exerting effort to *rationalize* decisions instead of improving them. This could be the case with citizen review boards or even internal affairs divisions, if rank-and-file officers do not have or perceive good relations with them.

MAKE CATEGORIES EXPLICIT

When considering discrimination, there is a strong temptation in some ideological quarters to promote a "color-blind" view. This is a deeply problematic approach because, as discussed in Chapter 3, people are hardwired to categorize things, including people. Regardless of our intentions and philosophy, we will, starting at a young age, see people as falling into different groups even if we have not been told these groups exist, just as my 3-year-old son reinvented the category "Asian" and named it "Betty" after his Chinese babysitter. In fact, research has shown that when people are made conscious of the racial categories of the targets of their judgments, they are less likely to discriminate, even in legal decision-making (e.g., Sommers & Ellsworth, 2001).

You might be thinking, "But justice is blind." Think about that Lady Justice statue. She is not blind; she is blind*folded*. The relevance here is that justice cannot be expected to be unbiased because legal decision-makers are *un*biased but rather because they are *de*biased by a system of rules and procedures. Similarly, police cannot be blind to the color of citizens—they see them. Accordingly, they cannot expect to be color-blind, even if they want to be. Rather, they need to *behave* in a manner that is nondiscriminatory.

In some circumstances, blindfolding can really work. For example, research has found that female musicians are more likely to be hired by symphony orchestras when auditions are blind (i.e., auditioning musicians perform behind a screen; Goldin & Rouse, 2000). But in most cases, including policing, there is no comparable option. Because it is obviously unwise to literally blindfold officers, the next best thing is to make the racial categories explicit in their thoughts. Our minds will consider a person's race implicitly no matter what. By making the categories explicit, we can work to override the biasing effects of racial stereotypes.

VIGILANCE

Because of the implicitness and spontaneity of stereotyping, behaving in a relatively unbiased manner is an *active, not a passive*, venture. As discussed earlier, this means that it is not sufficient to merely *not intend* to discriminate; rather, it is necessary to *intend to not* discriminate. This will require vigilance on the part of decision-makers because, when judging others, we are processing a stream of information during which multiple opportunities for bias occur. Reviewing one's assessment at the end will likely not be sufficient to detect or correct for the influence of bias. Research has shown that people often form judgments of others in an "on-line" fashion, not a retrospective, "memory-based" fashion (Hastie & Park, 1986). In other words, we accumulate impressions as information accrues. Furthermore, we are most influenced by our earliest impressions, or preconceptions. As a consequence, if racial bias influences any impression along the way, it will be unlikely to be identified and expunged later. Rather, in all likelihood, it will contaminate subsequent impressions.

Consequently, people in positions of power, such as supervisors, jurors, and police officers, need to be mindful as they form impressions of others, maintaining vigilance for the influence of bias ("Would I think that behavior is suspicious if he were White instead of Black?"). But this could be exhausting, or simply unfeasible if one is trying to process a lot of information quickly. A simpler, more efficient, if not perfect, strategy might be to focus on information that is most relevant to the judgment at hand. This is consistent with Commissioner Kelly's instructions to customs agents to focus on fewer, more direct criteria for suspicion. The use of mental resources to evaluate appropriate behaviors (e.g., nervousness, evasiveness) carefully could serve to at least partially squeeze out the influence of racial or ethnic stereotypes. Having said this, truly implicit stereotypes can and will influence judgments automatically (i.e., with extremely little, some would argue virtually no, mental effort), so even when focusing all of one's cognitive resources on a prescribed set of features, there is hardly a guarantee that automatic thought will not react to other features, despite one's best intentions.

There is a thin line between the kind of cognitive distraction that can promote stereotype activation and the kind that can preclude stereotype application. Ultimately, intent focus on appropriate, legitimate features *and* vigilance for bias are complementary approaches that should both be employed.

CONCLUSION: FAIRER AND BETTER POLICING

Racial profiling poses a moral dilemma at the core of American (and, more broadly, Western) principles. How do we balance safety, security, and the rule of law with individual and civil liberties? Some may be interested solely in the constitutional questions with regard to reasonable searches and equal protection. Others may care solely about law enforcement efficiency and effectiveness. Probably most will wish to balance both concerns. And yet, a thorough policy analysis of racial profiling, considering logical, pragmatic, and constitutional criteria, reveals that the public safety–civil liberties question poses a false choice. The words of Benjamin Franklin ("They who can give up essential liberty to obtain a little temporary safety, deserve neither liberty nor safety") and others before him and since, express the philosophy that safety without liberty is not worth it; that security and liberty are intertwined by design in the U.S. Constitution. This is why the American system of criminal justice has a presumption of innocence, many due process protections, and a high, "beyond reasonable doubt" threshold for criminal sanction.

Nevertheless, throughout U.S. history, there have been severe lapses in the provision of liberty to certain groups. These have usually come in times of security crisis, as with the now infamous detention of Japanese Americans during World War II and the more recent rounding up of South Asian immigrants, use of "enhanced interrogation" and "extraordinary rendition," and other extralegal investigatory and prosecutorial procedures in the post-9/11 period.

One of these historical episodes is especially telling. Among the most notorious Supreme Court rulings is *Korematsu v. United States* (323 U.S. 214 (1944)), in which the Court majority ruled, in the aftermath of the Pearl Harbor attacks, that internment of Japanese American citizens like Fred Korematsu was constitutional. This case, although never overturned, has been widely and forcefully repudiated in the decades since. Lesser known is a companion case, *Hirabayashi v. United States* (320 U.S. 81, 100 (1943)). Gordon Hirabayashi was an American citizen who violated a curfew that was exclusive to people of Japanese descent. As with Korematsu, the Court sided with the U.S. government against Hirabayashi.

In its opinion, the Court reveals considerable ambivalence: First it states that "distinctions between citizens solely because of their ancestry are by their very nature odious to a free people whose institutions are founded upon the doctrine of equality." However, in the same opinion, the Court also holds that

> Because racial discriminations are in most circumstances irrelevant, and therefore prohibited, it by no means follows that, in dealing with the perils of war, Congress and the Executive are wholly precluded from taking into account those facts and circumstances which are relevant to measures for our national defense and for the successful prosecution of the war, and which may, in fact, place citizens of one ancestry in a different category from others.

Here the Court attempted to balance the inherent unfairness of treating one ethnic group as a suspect class, with rights suspended, against the desire for security in a time of war. The Court based its ruling in part on evidence that Japanese in the United States were engaged in anti-American espionage, thus allowing it to live with the paradox of the "irrelevance" of racial discriminations and the use of those very stereotypes by the government to deprive people of liberty.

What is most telling about *Hirabayashi* is that the Court's first instinct, to distrust the relevance of racial stereotypes, turned out to be correct. Hirabayashi's convictions were later overturned because it was revealed that prosecutors had suppressed evidence indicating that, in fact, very few Japanese Americans were actually suspected of, let alone caught engaging in, espionage. The stereotype was just as irrelevant as most, but given the exigencies of war, the Court was willing to accept that risk. It erred, and Gordon Hirabayashi and many others like him were wronged while the Constitution was unnecessarily affronted. War does not make stereotypes any more useful, just, apparently, more tolerable.

Racial profiling, be it in drug law enforcement or counterterrorism, is different from internment and curfews, at least in the eyes of the public. In addition to being less intrusive, there is a perception that it is efficient, and even that it is benign. It is perceived as being efficient because it involves targeting law enforcement resources where they are most likely to bear fruit—among populations with the highest offending rates. It is perceived as being benign because only criminals need to worry about it. The preceding analysis has revealed, however, that for logical, pragmatic, and legal reasons, racial profiling is of dubious rationality at best, and, far from benign, it is downright corrosive.

The logical problem involves an error akin to the fallacy of "affirming the consequent." Even if criminals are likely to be minorities, it does not follow that minorities are likely to be criminals. Consequently, the probative value of minority status for criminal suspicion is likely to be largely specious. Because the vast majority of minorities passing through any particular corridor are not engaged in criminal activity, using race as a basis of criminal suspicion is a dicey strategy, likely to distract one from more direct, and therefore efficacious, indicators. This is borne out by the relatively low contraband and weapons hit rates in stop and frisk regimes, even in the high-crime areas where they are concentrated.

The logical deficit in profiling is also borne out in a pragmatic analysis. My simulations (see Chapter 5) of the effects of various profiling regimes on criminal capture rates indicate that, except in cases of very extreme differences in offending, the gains in criminal captures arising from profiling are modest at best, and can be null or even counterproductive. Even when profiling is proportional to offending rates, returns tend to be unimpressive. More important, such profiling yields incarceration disparities that are in excess of offending disparities. Furthermore, any degree of profiling leads to higher proportions of *innocent* minorities being subjected to policing intrusion.

Returning to the assertion of benignity (i.e., "only criminals need be concerned"), profiling has collateral harmful effects on minority communities. We must bear in mind that profiling will necessarily lead to higher proportions of minority *criminals* being incarcerated than White criminals. In other words, White criminals and their relations are advantaged by profiling. It consequently causes minority communities to be economically destabilized through the loss of wage earners and the extra costs of legal representation, socially destabilized through the removal of family members, alienated through differential treatment (i.e., with greater suspicion and intrusion) of innocents, disenfranchised due to loss of voting rights, and even subjected to higher rates of disease contracted in prison and transmitted back to communities. In addition to all this, the disproportionate rates of criminal sanction that profiling engenders promote the very stereotypes that give rise to it in the first place.

Because of these many harms, the pragmatic analysis informs the legal/constitutional analysis because even Supreme Court decisions are influenced by practical considerations. In an idealized society, courts would be able to uphold constitutional principles in an absolute sense, without exception. Using race or ethnicity as a basis for suspicion that leads to a disparate rate of intrusion on minorities clearly violates Fourth and Fourteenth Amendment principles of due process and equal treatment. But more than one justice has expressed the sentiment that "the Constitution is not a suicide pact," meaning that the United States should not be bound to constitutional principles in circumstances where that will threaten its very existence.

More mundanely, courts have in some influential instances deferred to the putative public safety benefits of intrusions (i.e., search procedures that violate the spirit, if not the letter, of the Constitution) in domains such as traffic stops resulting in drug crime arrests that have little bearing on public safety, let alone national security. In fact, rulings relevant to the use of racial profiling as a criminal defense argument have given police wide latitude, allowing race-based searches, provided there is a legal pretext, unless their very purpose was to discriminate. Accordingly, the costs and benefits of racial profiling are valid and essential topics in the policy discourse, even in the judicial sphere. Judges, legislators, and executives will continue to weigh the loss of civil liberties that racial profiling levies on minorities against the potential benefits in terms of public safety. Judges will do so when deciding whether to throw out evidence as well as whether to sanction departments. Lawmakers will do so when considering whether to pass legislation that actively remediates profiling. And administrators will do so when setting departmental policies regarding officer conduct. All these policymakers, and the citizens they serve, will do well to consider the whole case, not just the intuitively appealing but empirically dubious theory that targeting groups with (putatively) higher offending rates will effectively mitigate crime.

These practical costs are substantial. Minority populations, particularly African Americans, are grossly overrepresented in prison and underrepresented in upward-mobility-promoting circumstances like college. This is due in considerable part to racial profiling, which causes the typical young, Black drug offender to have a dramatically greater chance of being incarcerated than the typical young, White drug offender. As discussed previously, the collateral harms to the wider community are dire. To make matters worse, because of reverse deterrence, profiling has the potential to actually increase crime rates. In sum, the presumptions that racial profiling is efficient, effective, and promotes public safety are highly questionable, to say the least.

If we accept that racial profiling does more harm than good and warrants intervention, we are still faced with a daunting challenge. As discussed in Chapter 4, a large body of research has demonstrated that stereotypes can and do operate outside of conscious awareness and control, and that they influence important behaviors despite one's best intentions. This is true for law enforcers, too. Consequently, a considerable amount of racial profiling is *unintentional*. This type of profiling will not be remediated by mere formal prohibitions. The absence of an intent to discriminate will not be sufficient. Affirmative steps will be needed to promote officers' active *intent to not discriminate* and, if possible, to weaken race-crime stereotypes. Increasing focus on legitimate bases of suspicion will complement these efforts.

Are there times when racial profiling is warranted? Perhaps. If credible intelligence indicates that a terrorist attack is imminent, shouldn't the national security apparatus and personnel use everything at their disposal to prevent it? If Islamic groups are responsible for most anti-American terrorism, shouldn't Muslims be targeted for greater scrutiny under these circumstances? That seems rational. Yet, even in this extreme, ticking time bomb–like scenario, the answer is not as obvious as it may first seem. Does the intelligence indicate that the plot is from an Islamic group? If not, profiling Muslims could be a deadly distraction. If so, wouldn't that be based on specific human intelligence about that group (e.g., intercepted communications)? Then are we really talking about profiling, or something more like acting on a suspect description? If the intelligence is more nebulous than that, how effective will focusing on Muslims (to the extent that they are reliably identifiable) be, given that there are millions in the United States and more than a billion in the world. What if the terrorist group has recruited outside the profile? Wouldn't it be most effective to follow the original strain of intelligence?

In practice, when there is "actionable intelligence," which would be needed to implicate an "imminent" threat, profiling is not utilized. It would be a distraction. Instead, investigators follow the actual trail of evidence. The very scenario that seems to provide a legitimate case for profiling turns out to be the exception that further disproves the rule.

Law enforcement is an inherently difficult and dangerous occupation. Police deserve to have at their disposal every means to deter, detect, and apprehend criminals and promote their prosecution—every means that qualifies as legitimate, that is. Because of the harms it visits on individuals, minority communities, and constitutional integrity, in addition to its counterproductive effects, including distraction, reverse deterrence, and deterioration of trust and cooperation, racial profiling does not qualify.

REFERENCES

Abelson, R. P. (1986). Beliefs are like possessions. *Journal for the Theory of Social Behaviour, 16*, 223–250.

Aboud, F. E. (1988). *Children and prejudice*. New York: Blackwell.

Ahmed, W., & Rezmovic, E. (2001). Racial profiling: A policy issue in need of better answers. *Chance, 14*, 40–41.

Air Safety Week. (2001, December 31). Terrorist with shoe bomb exposes shortcomings in aviation. *Air Safety Week, 15.*

Ajzen, I., & Fishbein, M. (1977). Attitude-behavior relations: A theoretical analysis and review of empirical research. *Psychological Bulletin, 84*, 888–918.

Allport, G. W. (1954). *The nature of prejudice*. Garden City, NY: Anchor.

Alschuler, A. W. (2002). Racial profiling and the Constitution. University of Chicago Legal Forum, 2002, 163–269.

Amodio, D. M., & Devine, P. G. (2006). Stereotyping and evaluation in implicit race bias: Evidence for independent constructs and unique effects on behavior. *Journal of Personality and Social Psychology, 91*, 652–661.

Antonovics, K. L., & Knight, B. G. (2004). A new look at racial profiling: Evidence from the Boston Police Department. *Review of Economics and Statistics, 91*, 163–175.

AP. (2001, June 1). *Report: Blacks searched more often.* Associated Press.

AP. (2002, July 30). Data show Nebraska Blacks searched more. Associated Press.

Arab American Institute. (2001, October 10). Survey of Arab Americans on racial profiling. Alliance of American Insurers.

Arcuri, L., Castelli, L., Galdi, S., Zogmaister, C., & Amadori, A. (2008). Predicting the vote: Implicit attitudes as predictors of the future behavior of decided and undecided voters. *Political Psychology, 29*, 369–387.

Atlanta City Auditor's Office. (2008). *Performance audit: Police computer aided dispatch data reliability.* Atlanta, GA: Atlanta City Auditor's Office.

Augoustinos, M., Ahrens, C., & Innes, M. (1994). Stereotypes and prejudice: The Australian experience. *British Journal of Social Psychology, 33*, 125–141.

Ayres, I. (2001). *Pervasive prejudice? Non-traditional evidence of race and gender discrimination.* Chicago: University of Chicago Press.

Ayres, I. (2002). Outcome tests of racial disparities in police practices. *Justice Research and Policy, 4*, 131–142.

Baker, A. (2010, May 27). Bias is seen in shootings of officers by colleagues. *The New York Times*, p. A21.

Banaji, M. R., & Hardin, C. D. (1996). Automatic stereotyping. *Psychological Science, 7*, 136–141.

Banaji, M. R., Hardin, C., & Rothman, A. J. (1993). Implicit stereotyping in person judgment. *Journal of Personality and Social Psychology, 65,* 272–281.

Banks, R. R. (2001). Race-based suspect selection and colorblind equal protection doctrine and discourse. *UCLA Law Review, 48,* 1075–1124.

Banks, R. R. (2003). Beyond profiling: Race, policing, and the drug war. *Stanford Law Review, 56,* 571–603.

Banks, R. R. (2004). *The story of Brown v. City of Oneonta: The uncertain meaning of racially discriminatory policing under the equal protection clause.* Stanford Law School Research Paper No. 81.

Bardach, E. (2005). *A practical guide for policy analysis: The eightfold path to more effective problem solving* (2nd ed.). Washington, DC: CQ Press.

Bargh, J. A. (1997). The automaticity of everyday life. In R. Wyer (Ed.), *Advances in social cognition* (Vol. 10, pp. 1–61). Mahwah, NJ: Erlbaum.

Bargh, J. A., Chaiken, S., Raymond, P., & Hymes, C. (1996). The automatic evaluation effect: Unconditional automatic attitude activation with a pronunciation task. *Journal of Experimental Social Psychology, 32,* 104–128.

Bargh, J. A., Chen, M., & Burrows, L. (1996). Automaticity of social behavior: Direct effects of trait construct and stereotype activation on action. *Journal of Personality and Social Psychology, 71,* 230–244.

Barstow, D., & Kocieniewski, D. (2000, October 12). Records show New Jersey police knew of racial profiling in '96. *The New York Times,* pp. A1, A29. Retrieved from http://www.nytimes.com/2000/10/12/nyregion/records-show-new-jersey-police-withheld-data-on-race-profiling.html.

Beck, G. (2006, November 14). CNN interview of Keith Ellison by Glenn Beck http://transcripts.cnn.com/TRANSCRIPTS/0611/14/gb.01.html.

Becker, G. S. (1957). *The economics of discrimination.* Chicago: University of Chicago Press.

Becton, C. L. (1987). The drug courier profile: "All seems infected that th' infected spy, as all looks yellow to the jaundic'd eye." *North Carolina Law Review, 65,* 417–481.

Berkovec, J. A., Canner, G. B., Gabriel, S. A., & Hannan, T. H. (1994). Race, redlining, and residential mortgage loan performance. *Journal of Real Estate Finance and Economics, 9,* 263–294.

Bernton, H., Carter, M., Heath, D., & Neff, J. (2002, June 23–July 27). The terrorist within: The story behind one man's holy war against America. *The Seattle Times.*

Beutel, A. J. (2012). Policy report: Data on Post-9/11 terrorism in the United States. Last updated January 2012. Los Angeles: Muslim Public Affairs Council.

Bhatnagar, C. S. (2009, August 31). Commentary: Time for America to ban racial profiling. *CNN.com.* Retrieved from http://www.cnn.com/2009/US/08/31/bhatnagar.khan/index.html

Blair, I. V. (2002). The malleability of automatic stereotypes and prejudice. *Personality and Social Psychology Review, 6,* 242–261.

Blair, I. V., & Banaji, M. R. (1996). Automatic and controlled processes in stereotype priming. *Journal of Personality and Social Psychology, 70,* 1142–1163.

Blakeslee, N. (2005). *Tulia: Race, cocaine, and corruption in a small Texas town.* New York: PublicAffairs.

Bodenhausen, G. V. (1990). Stereotypes as judgmental heuristics: Evidence of circadian variations in discrimination. *Psychological Science, 1,* 319–322.

Borooah, V. K. (2001). Racial bias in police stops and searches: An economic analysis. *European Journal of Political Economy, 17,* 17–37.

Breckler, S. J. (1984). Empirical validation of affect, behavior, and cognition as distinct components of attitude. *Journal of Personality and Social Psychology, 47,* 1191–1205.

Brown, R. (1995). *Prejudice: Its social psychology.* Cambridge, MA: Blackwell.

Bruner, J. S. (1957). On perceptual readiness. *Psychological Review, 64,* 123–152.

Bureau of Justice Statistics. (n.d.). *Correctional Populations in the United States, 1998.* Washington, DC: Department of Justice.

Bureau of Justice Statistics. (1995). *Correctional populations in the United States, 1993.* Washington, DC: Department of Justice. Retrieved from http://bjs.ojp.usdoj.gov/index.cfm?ty=pbdetail&iid=746.

Bureau of Justice Statistics. (1996). *Correctional Populations in the United States, 1994.* Washington, DC: Department of Justice.

Bureau of Justice Statistics. (1998). *Correctional surveys.* Washington, DC: Department of Justice. Retrieved from http://www.ojp.usdoj.gov/bjs/glance/tables/cpracepttab.htm

Bureau of Justice Statistics. (2000a). *Correctional Populations in the United States, 1997.* Washington, DC: Department of Justice.

Bureau of Justice Statistics. (2000b). *Prisoners in the United States, 1999.* Washington, DC: Department of Justice.

Bureau of Justice Statistics. (2003). *Prevalence of imprisonment in the U.S. population, 1974–2001.* Washington, DC: U.S. Department of Justice.

Bureau of Justice Statistics. (2008a). *Crime in the United States 2007.* Washington, DC: Department of Justice. Retrieved from http://www2.fbi.gov/ucr/cius2007/data/table_43.html

Bureau of Justice Statistics. (2008b). *Key facts.* Washington, DC: Department of Justice. Retrieved from http://www.ojp.usdoj.gov/bjs/glance/tables/corr2tab.htm

Bureau of Justice Statistics. (2008c). *National Crime Victimization Survey: Criminal victimization in the United States.* Washington, DC: Department of Justice.

Bureau of Labor Statistics. (2010, June 4). *Economic News Release: Table A-2. Employment status of the civilian population by race, sex, and age.* Washington, DC: U.S. Bureau of Labor Statistics.

Bureau of Justice Statistics. (2011a). *Correctional populations in the United States, 2010.* Washington, DC: Department of Justice. Retrieved from http://bjs.ojp.usdoj.gov/index.cfm?ty=pbdetail&iid=2237

Bureau of Justice Statistics. (2011b). *Prisoners in 2010.* Washington, DC: Department of Justice. Retrieved from http://bjs.ojp.usdoj.gov/content/pub/pdf/p10.pdf

Buss, A. H. (1961). *The psychology of aggression.* New York: Wiley.

Caulkins, J. P., & MacCoun, R. (2003). Limited rationality and the limits of supply reduction. *Journal of Drug Issues, 33,* 433–464.

Chapman, L. J. (1967). Illusory correlation in observational report. *Journal of Verbal Learning and Verbal Behavior, 6,* 151–155.

Chartrand, T. L., & Bargh, J. A. (1996). Automatic activation of impression formation and memorization goals: Nonconscious goal priming reproduces effects of explicit task instructions. *Journal of Personality and Social Psychology, 71,* 464–478.

Chester, C. (2008, January 16). Female suicide bomber kills 9 in Iraq. Associated Press.

Chronicle News Services. (2002, August 26). Police list those they believe will break laws. *The San Francisco Chronicle,* p. A7.

Cialdini, R. B. (1984). *Influence: The new psychology of modern persuasion.* New York: Quill.

Clark, K. B., & Clark, M. P. (1950). Emotional factors in racial identification and preference in Negro children. *Journal of Negro Education, 19,* 341–350.

Clark, R., Anderson, N. B., Clark, V. R., & Williams, D. R. (1999). Racism as a stressor for African Americans: A biopsychosocial model. *American Psychologist, 54,* 805–816.

Clarke, M. L., & Pearson, W., Jr. (1982). Racial stereotypes revisited. *International Journal of Intercultural Relations, 6,* 381–393.

Cole, D. (1999). *No equal justice: Race and class in the American criminal justice system.* New York: New Press.

Community Oriented Policing Services. (2012). *Community policing defined.* Washington, DC: U.S. Department of Justice. Retrieved from http://www.cops.usdoj.gov/Publications/e030917193-CP-Defined.pdf

Cordner, G., Williams, B., & Zuniga, M. (2000). *Vehicle stop study: Mid-year report.* San Diego, CA: San Diego Police Department.

Correll, J., Park, B., Judd, C. M., & Wittenbrink, B. (2002). The police officer's dilemma: Using ethnicity to disambiguate potentially threatening individuals. *Journal of Personality and Social Psychology, 83,* 1314–1329.

Correll, J., Park, B., Judd, C. M., & Wittenbrink, B. (2007). The influence of stereotypes on decisions to shoot. *European Journal of Social Psychology, 37,* 1102–1117.

Correll, J., Park, B., Judd, C., Wittenbrink, B., Sadler, M. S., & Keesee, T. (2007). Across the thin blue line: Police officers and racial bias in the decision to shoot. *Journal of Personality and Social Psychology, 92,* 1006–1023.

Corrigan, K. (2002, February 27). Remarks to U.S. House Transportation and Infrastructure Committee, Subcommittee on Aviation, hearing on aviation security with a focus on passenger profiling.

Cottrell, C. A., & Neuberg, S. L. (2005). Different emotional reactions to different groups: A sociofunctional threat-based approach to "prejudice." *Journal of Personality and Social Psychology, 88,* 770–789.

Council of Economic Advisers. (1998). *Changing America: Indicators of social and economic well-being by race and Hispanic origin.* Washington, DC: President's Council of Economic Advisers.

CPLE. (2010). *Deputizing discrimination? Causes and effects of cross-deputization policy in Salt Lake City, Utah.* Los Angeles: Consortium of Police Leadership in Equity.

Crawford, C. (2010). *Spatial policing: The influence of time, space, and geography on law enforcement practices.* Durham, NC: Carolina Academic Press.

Crosby, F. J., Bromley, S., & Saxe, L. (1980). Recent unobtrusive studies of Black and White discrimination and prejudice: A literature review. *Psychological Bulletin, 87,* 546–563.

Darley, J. M., & Gross, P. H. (1983). A hypothesis-confirming bias in labeling effects. *Journal of Personality and Social Psychology, 44,* 20–33.

Darley, J. M., & Latané, B. (1968). Bystander intervention in emergencies: Diffusion of responsibility. *Journal of Personality and Social Psychology, 8,* 377–383.

Dasgupta, N., & Greenwald, A.G. (2001). On the malleability of automatic attitudes: Combating automatic prejudice with images of admired and disliked individuals. *Journal of Personality and Social Psychology, 81,* 800–814.

Dasgupta, N., & Rivera, L. M. (2006). From automatic anti-gay prejudice to behavior: The moderating role of conscious beliefs about gender and behavioral control. *Journal of Personality and Social Psychology, 91,* 268–280.

Dedman, B. (2001, October 12). Memo warns against use of profiling in defense. *The Boston Globe,* p. A27.

Dedman, B. (2003). Detailed report of statistical analysis of Massachusetts traffic stop data for April and May, 2001. Boston: Boston Globe.

Depret, E., & Fiske, S. T. (1999). Perceiving the powerful: Intriguing individuals versus threatening groups. *Journal of Experimental Social Psychology, 35,* 461–480.

Devine, P. G. (1989). Stereotypes and prejudice: Their automatic and controlled components. *Journal of Personality and Social Psychology, 56,* 5–18.

Devine, P. G., & Baker, S. M. (1991). Measurement of racial subtyping. *Journal of Personality and Social Psychology, 17,* 44–50.

Devine, P. G., & Elliot, A. J. (1995). Are racial stereotypes really fading? The Princeton trilogy revisited. *Personality and Social Psychology Bulletin, 11,* 1139–1150.

Devine, P. G., Plant, E. A., Amodio, D. M., Harmon-Jones, E., & Vance, S. L. (2002). The regulation of explicit and implicit race bias: The role of motivations to respond without prejudice. *Journal of Personality and Social Psychology, 82,* 835–848.

Devos, T., & Banaji, M. R. (2005). American = White? *Journal of Personality and Social Psychology, 88,* 447–466.

Dharmapala, D., & Ross, S. L. (2004). Racial bias in motor vehicle searches: Additional theory and evidence. *Contributions to Economic Analysis and Policy, 3,* 1–21.

Dhont, K., Cornelis, I., & Van Hiel, A. (2010). Interracial public-police contact: Relationships with police officers' racial and work-related attitudes and behavior. *International Journal of Intercultural Relations, 34,* 551–560.

Diamond, M. J., & Lobitz, W. C. (1973). When familiarity breeds respect: The effects of an experimental depolarization program on police and student attitudes toward each other. *Journal of Social Issues, 29,* 95–109.

Dixon, T. L., Azocar, C. L., & Casas, M. (2003). The portrayal of race and crime on television network news. *Journal of Broadcasting and Electronic Media, 47,* 498–523.

Dixon, T. L., & Linz, D. (2000). Overrepresentation and underpresentation of African Americans and Latinos as lawbreakers on television news. *Journal of Communication, 50,* 131–154.

Dixon, T. L., & Linz, D. (2002). Television news, prejudicial pretrial publicity, and the depiction of race. *Journal of Broadcasting and Electronic Media, 46,* 112–136.

Dixon, T. L., & Maddox, K. B. (2005). Skin tone, crime news, and social reality judgments: Priming the stereotype of the dark and dangerous Black criminal. *Journal of Applied Social Psychology, 35,* 1555–1570.

DOJ. (2003a, June 17). *Fact sheet: Racial profiling.* Washington, DC: U.S. Department of Justice.

DOJ. (2003b). Press release: *Justice Department issues policy guidance to ban racial profiling.*

Donnerstein, E., Donnerstein, M., Simon, S., & Ditrichs, R. (1972). Variables in interracial aggression: Anonymity, expected retaliation, and a riot. *Journal of Personality and Social Psychology, 22,* 236–245.

Donohue, J. J. (2005). Fighting crime: An economist's view. *Milken Institute Review, 7,* 46–58.

Dovidio, J. F., Evans, N., & Tyler, R. B. (1986). Racial stereotypes: The contents of their cognitive representations. *Journal of Experimental Social Psychology, 22,* 22–37.

Dovidio, J. F., Kawakami, K., & Gaertner, S. L. (2002). Implicit and explicit prejudice and interracial interaction. *Journal of Personality and Social Psychology, 84,* 754–770.

Dovidio, J. F., Kawakami, K., Johnson, C., Johnson, B., & Howard, A. (1997). On the nature of prejudice: Automatic and controlled processes. *Journal of Experimental Social Psychology, 33,* 510–540.

Duncan, B. L. (1976). Differential social perception and attribution of intergroup violence: Testing the lower limits of stereotyping of blacks. *Journal of Personality and Social Psychology, 34,* 590–598.

Dunton, B. C., & Fazio, R. H. (1997). An individual difference measure of motivation to control prejudiced reactions. *Personality and Social Psychology Bulletin, 23,* 316–326.

Durose, M. R., Smith, E. L., & Langan, P. A. (2007). *Bureau of Justice Statistics special report: Contacts between police and the public, 2005.* Washington, DC: U.S. Department of Justice.

Eagly, A. H., & Steffen, V. (1984). Gender stereotypes stem from the distribution of women and men into social roles. *Journal of Personality and Social Psychology, 53,* 735–754.

Ebenbach, D. H., & Keltner, D. (1998). Power, emotion, and judgmental accuracy in social conflict: Motivating the cognitive miser. *Basic and Applied Social Psychology, 20,* 7–21.

Eberhardt, J. L., Davies, P. G., Purdie-Vaughns, V. J., & Johnson, S. L. (2006). Looking death-worthy: Perceived stereotypicality of black defendants predicts capital-sentencing outcomes. *Psychological Science, 17,* 383–386.

Eberhardt, J. L., Goff, P. A., Purdie, V. J., & Davies, P. G. (2004). Seeing Black: Race, crime, and visual processing. *Journal of Personality and Social Psychology, 87,* 876–893.

Eldridge, T. R., Ginsberg, S., Hempel, W. T., Kephart, J. L., & Moore, K. (2004). *9/11 and terrorist travel, staff report.* Washington, DC: National Commission on Terrorist Attacks Upon the United States.

End Racial Profiling Act. (2004, February 26). S. 2132 [108th]. Washington, DC: U.S. Senate.

End Racial Profiling Act. (2013, May 23). S. 1038 [113th]. Washington, DC: U.S. Senate.

Fairchild, H. H., & Cozens, J. A. (1981). Chicano, Hispanic, or Mexican American: What's in a name? *Hispanic Journal of Behavioral Sciences, 3,* 191–198.

Fazio, R. H., Jackson, J. R., Dunton, B. C., & Williams, C. J. (1995). Variability in automatic activation as an unobtrusive measure of racial attitudes: A bona fide pipeline? *Journal of Personality and Social Psychology, 69,* 1013–1027.

Fazio, R. H., Sanbonmatsu, D. M., Powell, M. C., & Kardes, F. R. (1986). On the automatic activation of attitudes. *Journal of Personality and Social Psychology, 50,* 229–238.

FBI National Press Office. (2008, October 27). New FBI guidelines. Washington DC: Federal Bureau of Investigation.

Federal Bureau of Investigation. (2011). *Uniform crime report, crime in the United States, 2010.* Washington, DC: U.S. Department of Justice. Retrieved from http://www.fbi.gov/about-us/cjis/ucr/crime-in-the-u.s/2010/crime-in-the-u.s.-2010/persons-arrested

Festinger, L., & Carlsmith, J. M. (1959). Cognitive consequences of forced compliance. *Journal of Abnormal and Social Psychology, 58,* 203–210.

Finn, C., & Glaser, J. (2010). Voter affect and the 2008 U.S. presidential election: Hope and race mattered. *Analyses of Social Issues and Public Policy, 10,* 262–275.

Firestone, D., & Drew, C. (2001, November 29). Al Qaeda link seen in only a handful of 1,200 detainees. *The New York Times.*

Fiske, S. T. (1993). Controlling other people: The impact of social power on stereotyping. *American Psychologist, 48,* 621–628.

Fiske, S. T. (1998). Stereotyping, prejudice, and discrimination. In D. Gilbert, S. T. Fiske, & G. Lindzey (Eds.), *The handbook of social psychology* (pp. 357–411). New York: Oxford University Press.

Fiske, S. T. (2001). Effects of power on bias: Power explains and maintains individual, group, and societal disparities. In A. Y. Lee-Chai & J. A. Bargh (Eds.), *The use and abuse of power: Multiple perspectives on the causes of corruption* (pp. 181–193). New York: Psychology Press.

Fiske, S. T., & Taylor, S. E., (1991). *Social cognition* (2nd ed.). New York: McGraw-Hill.

Flores, E., Tschann, J. M., Dimas, J. M., Pasch, L. A., & de Groat, C. L. (2010). Perceived racial/ethnic discrimination, posttraumatic stress symptoms, and health risk behaviors among Mexican American adolescents. *Journal of Counseling Psychology, 57,* 264–273.

Forgas, J. P. (1998). On being happy but mistaken: Mood effects on the fundamental attribution error. *Journal of Personality and Social Psychology, 75,* 318–331.

Foss, B. (2002, August 28). Arab-looking fliers expect scrutiny. Associated Press.

Fox Broadcasting Company. (2002, June 4–5). Survey.

Fredrickson, D. D., & Siljander, R. P. (2002). *Racial profiling: Eliminating the confusion between racial and criminal profiling and clarifying what constitutes unfair discrimination and persecution.* Springfield, IL: Charles C. Thomas.

Fridell, L., Lunney, R., Diamond, D., & Kubu, B. (2001). *Racially biased policing: A principled response.* Washington, DC: Police Executive Research Forum.

Gaertner, S. L., & Dovidio, J. F. (1977). The subtlety of white racism, arousal, and helping behavior. *Journal of Personality and Social Psychology, 35,* 691–707.

Gaertner, S. L., & Dovidio, J. F. (1986). The aversive form of racism. In J. F. Dovidio & S. L. Gaertner (Eds.), *Prejudice, discrimination, and racism* (pp. 61–89). San Diego, CA: Academic Press.

Gaertner, S. L., Mann, J., Murrell, A., & Dovidio, J. F. (1989). Reducing intergroup bias: The benefits of recategorization. *Journal of Personality and Social Psychology, 57,* 239–249.

Gaertner, S. L., & McLaughlin, J. P. (1983). Racial stereotypes: Associations and ascriptions of positive and negative characteristics. *Social Psychology Quarterly, 46,* 23–30.

Galdi, S., Arcuri, L., & Gawronski, B. (2008). Automatic mental associations predict future choices of undecided decision-makers. *Science, 321,* 100–1102.

GAO. (2000a, March). *Racial profiling: Limited data available on motorist stops.* Washington, DC: General Accounting Office.

GAO. (2000b, March). *U.S. Customs Service: Better targeting of airline passengers for personal searches could produce better results.* Washington, DC: General Accounting Office.

GAO. (2012, May). *Terrorist watchlist: Routinely assessing impacts of agency actions since the December 25, 2009, attempted attack could help inform future efforts.* Washington, DC: Government Accountability Office.

Gettleman, J. (2002, October 25). The hunt for a sniper: The profiling; A frenzy of speculation was wide of the mark. *The New York Times.* Retrieved from http://www.nytimes.com/2002/10/25/us/the-hunt-for-a-sniper-the-profiling-a-frenzy-of-speculation-was-wide-of-the-mark.html?ref=johnallenmuhammad

Gilliam, F. D., & Iyengar, S. (2000). Prime suspects: The influence of local television news on the viewing public. *American Journal of Political Science, 44,* 560–573.

Gilbert, D. T., & Hixon, J. G. (1991). The trouble of thinking: Activation and application of stereotypic beliefs. *Journal of Personality and Social Psychology, 60,* 509–517.

Gladwell, M. (2006a, February 13). Million-dollar Murray. *The New Yorker.*

Gladwell, M. (2006b, February 6). What pitbulls can teach us about profiling. *The New Yorker.*

Glaser, J. (2001, December 5). The fallacy of racial profiling. *The San Francisco Chronicle,* Op-ed.

Glaser, J. (2002). Reverse priming: Implications for the (un)conditionality of automatic evaluation. In J. Musch & K. C. Klauer (Eds.), *The psychology of evaluation: Affective processes in cognition and emotion* (pp. 87–108). Mahwah, NJ: Erlbaum.

Glaser, J. (2006). The efficacy and effect of racial profiling: A mathematical simulation approach. *Journal of Policy Analysis and Management, 25,* 395–416.

Glaser, J. (2007). Contrast effects in automatic affect, cognition, and behavior. In D. Stapel & J. Suls (Eds.), *Assimilation and contrast in social psychology* (pp. 229–248). New York: Psychology Press.

Glaser, J., & Banaji, M. R. (1999). When fair is foul and foul is fair: Reverse priming in automatic evaluation. *Journal of Personality and Social Psychology, 77,* 669–687.

Glaser, J., & Kihlstrom, J. F. (2005). Compensatory automaticity: Unconscious volition is not an oxymoron. In R. Hassin, J. S. Uleman, & J. A. Bargh (Eds.), *The new unconscious* (pp. 171–195). New York: Oxford University Press.

Glaser, J., & Knowles, E. D. (2008). Implicit motivation to control prejudice. *Journal of Experimental Social Psychology, 44,* 164–172.

Goff, P. A. (2010, November). The psychology of contemporary racial bias in policing. Invited address, Civil Rights Division, U.S. Department of Justice.

Goldberg, J. (1999, June 20). The color of suspicion. *The New York Times Magazine.*

Goldin, C., & Rouse, C. (2000). Orchestrating impartiality: The impact of "blind" auditions on female musicians. *American Economic Review, 90,* 715–741.

Goodwin, S. A., Gubin, A., Fiske, S. T., & Yzerbyt, V. Y. (2000). Power can bias impression processes: Stereotyping subordinates by default and by design. *Group Processes and Intergroup Relations, 3,* 227–256.

Gordon, L. (1986). College students' stereotypes of Blacks and Jews on two campuses: Four studies spanning 50 years. *Sociology and Social Research, 70,* 200–201.

Gordon, R. A., Michels, J. L., & Nelson, C. L. (1996). Majority group perceptions of criminal behavior: The accuracy of race-related crime stereotypes. *Journal of Applied Social Psychology, 26,* 148–159.

Gould, J. B., & Mastrofski, S. D. (2004). Suspect searches: Assessing police behavior under the U.S. Constitution. *Criminology and Public Policy, 3,* 315–362.

Gray, N. S., Brown, A. S., MacCulloch, M. J., Smith, J., & Snowden, R. J. (2005). An implicit test of the associations between children and sex in pedophiles. *Journal of Abnormal Psychology, 114,* 304–308.

Green, A. R., Carney, D. R., Pallin, D. J., Ngo, L. H., Raymond, K. L., Iezzoni, L., & Banaji, M. R. (2007). Implicit bias among physicians and its prediction of thrombolysis decisions for black and white patients. *Journal of General Internal Medicine, 22,* 1231–1238.

Greenwald, A. G., Draine, S. C., & Abrams, R. L. (1996). Three cognitive markers of unconscious semantic activation. *Science, 273,* 1699–1702.

Greenwald, A. G., Klinger, M. R., & Liu, T. J. (1989). Unconscious processing of dichoptically masked words. *Memory and Cognition, 17,* 35–47.

Greenwald, A. G., McGhee, D. E., & Schwartz, J. L. K. (1998). Measuring individual differences in implicit cognition: The implicit association test. *Journal of Personality and Social Psychology, 74,* 1464–1480.

Greenwald, A. G., Oakes, M. A., & Hoffman, H. (2003). Targets of discrimination: Effects of race on responses to weapons holders. *Journal of Experimental Social Psychology, 39,* 399–405.

Greenwald, A. G., Poehlman, T. A., Uhlmann, E., & Banaji, M. R. (2009). Understanding and using the Implicit Association Test: III. Meta-analysis of predictive validity. *Journal of Personality and Social Psychology, 97,* 17–41.

Greenwald, A. G., Smith, C. T., Sriram, N., Bar-Anan, Y., & Nosek, B. A. (2009). Implicit race attitudes predicted vote in the 2008 US presidential election. *Analyses of Social Issues and Public Policy, 9,* 241–253.

Grogger, J., & Ridgeway, G. (2006). Testing for racial profiling in traffic stops from behind a veil of darkness. *Journal of the American Statistical Association, 101,* 878–887.

Guinote, A. (2001). Lack of control leads to less stereotypic perceptions of groups: An individual difference perspective. *Analise-Psicologica, 19,* 453–460.

Guinote, A. (2007). Power and the suppression of unwanted thoughts: Does control over others decrease control over the self? *Journal of Experimental Social Psychology, 43,* 433–440.

Hackney, A., & Glaser, J. (2013). Reverse deterrence in racial profiling: Increased transgressions by non-profiled Whites. *Law and Human Behavior, 37,* 348–353.

Hamilton, D. L., & Gifford, R. K. (1976). Illusory correlation in interpersonal perception: A cognitive basis of stereotypic judgments. *Journal of Experimental Social Psychology, 12,* 392–407.

Hamilton, D. L., & Sherman, S. J. (1989). Illusory correlation: Implications for stereotype theory and research. In D. Bar-Tal, C.F. Graumann, A.W. Kruglanski, & W. Stroebe (Eds.), *Stereotyping and prejudice: Changing conceptions* (pp. 59–82). New York: Springer.

Harcourt, B. E. (2004). Rethinking racial profiling: A critique of the economics, civil liberties, and constitutional literature, and of criminal profiling more generally. *University of Chicago Law Review, 71*, 1275–1381.

Harcourt, B. E. (2006). *Muslim profiles post 9/11: Is racial profiling an effective counterterrorist measure and does it violate the right to be free from discrimination?* John M. Olin Law and Economics Working Paper No. 288. Chicago: University of Chicago.

Harcourt, B. E. (2007). *Against prediction: Profiling, policing, and punishing.* Chicago: University of Chicago Press.

Harding, J., Kutner, B., Proshansky, H., & Chein, I. (1954). Prejudice and ethnic relations. In G. Lindzey (Ed.), *Handbook of Social Psychology* (Vol. 2, pp. 1021–1061). Cambridge, MA: Addison-Wesley.

Harris, D. A. (1999). The stories, the statistics, and the law: Why "driving while black" matters. *Minnesota Law Review, 84*, 265–326.

Harris, D. A. (2002a). *Profiles in injustice: Why racial profiling cannot work.* New York: New Press.

Harris, D.A. (2002b). Racial profiling revisited: "Just common sense" in the fight against terror? *Criminal Justice, 17*, 36–41, 59.

Harris, D. A. (2010, June 17). Congressional testimony. U.S. House of Representatives Committee on the Judiciary Hearing of the Subcommittee on the Constitution, Civil Rights, and Civil Liberties. Ending racial profiling: Necessary for public safety and the protection of civil rights.

Hasher, L., & Zacks, R. T. (1979). Automatic and effortful processes in memory. *Journal of Experimental Psychology: General, 108*, 356–388.

Hastie, R., & Park, B. (1986). The relationship between memory and judgment depends on whether the judgment task is memory-based or on-line. *Psychological Review, 93*, 258–268.

Hastorf, A. H., & Cantril, H. (1954). They saw a game: A case study. *Journal of Abnormal and Social Psychology, 49*, 129.

Heider, F. (1946). Attitudes and cognitive organization. *Journal of Psychology 21*, 107–112.

Heider, F. (1958). *The psychology of interpersonal relations.* New York: Wiley.

Hendricks, T. (2003, June 27). Immigration policies called ineffective. *The New York Times*, p. A5.

Henry, P. J., & Sears, D. O. (2002). The Symbolic Racism 2000 Scale. *Political Psychology, 23*, 253–283.

Hense, R. L., Penner, L. A., & Nelson, D. L. (1995). Implicit memory for age stereotypes. *Social Cognition, 13*, 399–415.

Hernández-Murillo, R., & Knowles, J. (2004). Racial profiling or racist policing? Bounds tests in aggregate data. *International Economic Review, 45*, 959–989.

Hilgard, E. R. (1977). *Divided consciousness.* New York: Wiley.

Hilgard, E. R. (1980). The trilogy of mind: Cognition, affection, and conation. *Journal of the History of the Behavioral Sciences, 16*, 107–117.

Hoffman, C., & Hurst, N. (1990). Gender stereotypes: Perception or rationalization? *Journal of Personality and Social Psychology, 58*, 197–208.

Hofmann, W., Gawronski, B., Gschwendner, T., Le, H., & Schmitt, M. (2005). A meta-analysis on the correlation between the Implicit Association Test and explicit self-report measures. *Personality and Social Psychology Bulletin, 31*, 1369–1385.

Hsu, S. S., & Johnson, C. (2009, March 11). Somali Americans recruited by extremists. *The Washington Post*, p. A1.

Hugenberg, K., & Bodenhausen, G. V. (2003). Facing prejudice: Implicit prejudice and the perception of facial threat. *Psychological Science, 14*, 640–643.

Hussain, M. (2008). Defending the faithful: Speaking the language of group harm in free exercise challenges to counterterrorism profiling. *Yale Law Journal, 117*, 920–943.

Institute for the Study of International Migration. (2005). *Fact brief: Reason for concern? Trends in the numbers of foreign students in science and engineering through 2005.* Washington, DC: Georgetown University.

Institute of International Education. (2011). *Open doors 2011 regional fact sheet: Middle East.* New York: Institute of International Education.

International Trade Administration. (2012). *Office of Travel and Tourism Industries, 2011 market profile: Middle East.* Washington, DC: U.S. Department of Commerce.

Jackson, L. A. (1995). *Stereotypes, emotions, behavior, and overall attitudes toward Hispanics by Anglos.* Research Report No. 10. East Lansing, MI: Julian Samora Research Institute.

Jackson, L. A., Lewandowski, D. A., Ingram, J. M., & Hodge, C. N. (1997). Group stereotypes: Content, gender specificity, and affect associated with typical group members. *Journal of Social Behavior and Personality, 12*, 381–396.

Jakes, L. (2008, July 2). Racial profiling eyed for terror probes. Associated Press.

Johnson, M. A. (1993). Crime: New Frontier—Jesse Jackson Calls It Top Civil-Rights Issue. *Chicago Sun-Times*, 29 November 1993.

Johnson, R. C., & Raphael, S. (2009). The effects of male incarceration dynamics on acquired immune deficiency syndrome infection rates among African American women and men. *Journal of Law and Economics, 52*, 251–293.

Johnston, L. D., O'Malley, P. M., & Bachman, J. G. (2001). *Demographic subgroup trends for various licit and illicit drugs, 1975–2000.* Monitoring the Future Occasional Paper No. 53. Bethesda, MD: National Institute on Drug Abuse.

Jones, E. E., Wood, G. C., & Quattrone, G. A. (1981). Perceived variability of personal characteristics in in-groups and out-groups: The role of knowledge and evaluation. *Personality and Social Psychology Bulletin, 7*, 523–528.

Jones, J. M. (2007). Some Americans reluctant to vote for Mormon, 72-year-old presidential candidates. Washington, DC: Gallup News Service.

Jones-Brown, D., Gill, J., & Trone, J. (2010). *Stop, question and frisk policing practices in New York City: A primer.* New York: Center on Race, Crime and Justice, John Jay College of Criminal Justice.

Jost, J. T., & Banaji, M. R. (1994). The role of stereotyping in system justification and the production of false consciousness. *British Journal of Social Psychology, 33*, 1–27.

Jost, J. T., & Major B. (Eds.). (2001). *The psychology of legitimacy: Emerging perspectives on ideology, justice, and intergroup relations.* Cambridge, UK: Cambridge University Press.

Jost, J. T., Rudman, L., Blair, I. V., Carney, D. R., Dasgupta, N., Glaser, J., & Hardin, C. (2009). The existence of implicit bias is beyond reasonable doubt: A refutation of ideological and methodological objections and executive summary of ten studies that no manager should ignore. *Research in Organizational Behavior, 29*, 39–69.

Judd, C. M., & Park, B. (1993). Definition and assessment of accuracy in social stereotypes. *Psychological Review, 100*, 109–128.

Jussim, L., Cain, T. R., Crawfod, J. T., Harber, K., & Cohen, F. (2009). The unbearable accuracy of stereotypes. In T. D. Nelson (Ed.), *Handbook of prejudice, stereotyping, and discrimination* (pp. 199–227). New York: Psychology Press.

Jussim, L., & Fleming, C. (1996). Self-fulfilling prophecies and the maintenance of social stereotypes: The role of dyadic interactions and social forces. In N. Macrae, C.

Stangor, & M. Hewstone (Eds.), *The foundations of stereotypes and stereotyping* (pp. 161–192). New York: Guilford.

Kahneman, D., & Tversky, A. (1973). On the psychology of prediction. *Psychological Review, 80,* 237–251.

Karlins, M., Coffman, T. L., & Walters, G. (1969). On the fading of social stereotypes: Studies in three generations of college students. *Journal of Personality and Social Psychology, 13,* 1–16.

Katz, D., & Braly, K. W. (1933). Racial stereotypes of one hundred college students. *Journal of Abnormal and Social Psychology, 28,* 280–290.

Kawakami, K., Dovidio, J. F., Moll, J., Hermsen, S., & Russin, A. (2001). Just say no (to stereotyping): Effects of training in the negation of stereotypic associations on stereotype activation. *Journal of Personality and Social Psychology, 78,* 871–888.

Kennedy, R. (1997). *Race, crime, and the law.* New York: Random House.

Kennedy, R. (1999, September 13 & 20). Suspect policy. *The New Republic,* pp. 30–35.

Khera, F. (2010, June 17). Written testimony: Hearing on racial profiling and the use of suspect classifications in law enforcement policy. Washington, DC: U.S. House of Representatives, Committee on the Judiciary, Subcommittee on the Constitution, Civil Rights, and Civil Liberties.

Kihlstrom, J. F. (1987). The cognitive unconscious. *Science, 237,* 1445–1452.

King, M., Ruggles, S., Alexander, J. T., Flood, S., Genadek, K., Schroeder, M. B., Trampe, B., & Vick, R. (2010). Integrated Public Use Microdata Series, Current Population Survey: Version 3.0. [Machine-readable database]. Minneapolis: University of Minnesota.

Knowles, J., Persico, N., & Todd, P. (2001). Racial bias in motor vehicle searches: Theory and evidence. *Journal of Political Economy, 109,* 203–229.

Krauthammer, C. (2005, July 29). Give grandma a pass. *The Washington Post.*

Krieger, L. H. (1995). The contents of our categories: A cognitive bias approach to discrimination and equal employment opportunity. *Stanford Law Review, 47,* 1161–1248.

Krieger, L. H. (1998). Civil rights Perestroika: Intergroup relations after affirmative action. *California Law Review, 86,* 1251–1333.

Kruglanski, A. W., Chen, X., Dechesne, M., Fishman, S., & Orehek, E. (2009). Fully committed: Suicide bombers' motivation and the quest for personal significance. *Political Psychology, 30,* 331–357.

Kruglanski, A. W., & Fishman, S. (2009). Psychological factors in terrorism and counter-terrorism: Individual, group, and organizational levels of analysis. *Social Issues and Policy Review, 3,* 1–44.

Kruglanski, A. W., & Webster, D. M. (1996). Motivated closing of the mind: "Seizing" and "freezing." *Psychological Review, 103,* 263–283.

Krysan, M. (2011). *Data update to racial attitudes in America. An update and website to complement Schuman et al. (1997).* (http://www.igpa.uillinois.edu/programs/racial-attitudes/).

Kunda, Z., & Oleson, K. C. (1995). Maintaining stereotypes in the face of disconfirmation: Constructing grounds for subtyping deviants. *Journal of Personality and Social Psychology, 68,* 565–579.

Kunst-Wilson, W.R., & Zajonc, R.B. (1980). Affective discrimination of stimuli that cannot be recognized. *Science, 207,* 557–558.

Kuziemko, I., & Levitt, S. D. (2004). An empirical analysis of imprisoning drug offenders. *Journal of Public Economics, 88,* 2043–2066.

Lamberth, J. (1994). *Revised statistical analysis of the incidence of police stops and arrests of Black drivers/travelers on the New Jersey Turnpike between exits or interchanges 1 and 3 from the years 1988 through 1991.* (Report originally prepared as expert testimony in New Jersey v. Pedro Soto et al., 734 A.2d 350, 1996 (New Jersey)).

LAO. (2002, August 27). *An evaluation of racial profiling data collection and training.* Sacramento, CA: Legislative Analyst Office of California.

Legal Action Center. (2004). *After prison: Roadblocks to reentry—A report on state legal barriers facing people with criminal records.* New York: Legal Action Center.

Lepore, L., & Brown, R. (1997). Category and stereotype activation: Is prejudice inevitable?. *Journal of Personality and Social Psychology, 72,* 275–287.

Lerner, J. S., & Tetlock, P. E. (1994). Accountability and social cognition. In V. S. Ramachandran (Ed.), *Encyclopedia of human behavior* (Vol. 1, pp. 3098–3121). San Diego, CA: Academic Press.

Lerner, J. S., & Tetlock, P. E. (1999). Accounting for the effects of accountability. *Psychological Bulletin, 125,* 255–275.

Levitt, S. D. (1998). Why do increased arrest rates appear to reduce crime: Deterrence, incapacitation, or measurement error? *Economic Inquiry, 36,* 353–372.

Levitt, S. D. (2002). Deterrence. In J. Q. Wilson & J. Petersilia (Eds.), *Crime: Public policies for crime control* (pp. 435–450). Oakland, CA: Institute for Contemporary Studies Press.

Lichtblau, E. (2008, October 31). Inquiry targeted 2,000 foreign Muslims in 2004. *The New York Times.*

Lord, C. G., Ross, L., & Lepper, M. R. (1979). Biased assimilation and attitude polarization: The effects of prior theories on subsequently considered evidence. *Journal of Personality and Social Psychology, 37,* 2098–2109.

Lowery, B. S., Hardin, C. D., & Sinclair, S. (2001). Social influence on automatic racial prejudice. *Journal of Personality and Social Psychology, 81,* 842–855.

Lund, N. (2003). The conservative case against racial profiling in the war on terrorism. *Albany Law Review, 66,* 329–342.

MacCoun, R. J. (1993). Drugs and the law: A psychological analysis of drug prohibition. *Psychological Bulletin, 113,* 497–512.

MacDonald, H. (2001, Spring). The myth of racial profiling. *City Journal.* Retrieved from http://www.city-journal.org/html/11_2_the_myth.html

Macdonald, R. S. (2002). Rational profiling in America's airports. *Brigham Young University Journal of Public Law, 17,* 113–139.

Mackie, D. M., Hamilton, D. L., Susskind, J., & Rosselli, F. (1996). Social psychological foundations of stereotype formation. In C. N. Macrae, C. Stangor, & M. Hewstone (Eds.), *Stereotypes and stereotyping* (pp. 41–78). New York: Guilford.

Mackie, D. M., & Smith, E. R. (Eds.). (2002). *From prejudice to intergroup emotions: Differentiated reactions to social groups.* New York: Psychology Press.

Macrae, C. N., Bodenhausen, G. V., Milne, A. B., & Jetten, J. (1994). Out of mind but back in sight: Stereotypes on the rebound. *Journal of Personality and Social Psychology, 67,* 808–817.

Macrae, C. N., Milne, A. B., & Bodenhausen, G. V. (1994). Stereotypes as energy-saving devices: A peek inside the cognitive toolbox. *Journal of Personality and Social Psychology, 66,* 37–47.

Madon, S., Guyll, M., Aboufadel, K., Montiel, E., Smith, A., Palumbo, P., & Jussim, J. (2001). Ethnic and national stereotypes: The Princeton trilogy revisited and revised. *Personality and Social Psychology Bulletin, 27,* 996–1010.

Malti-Douglas, F. (2002, February 6). Let them profile me. *The New York Times,* Op-ed.

Menatti, A., Smyth, F., Teachman, B. A., & Nosek, B. A. (in press). Reducing stigma toward individuals with mental illnesses: A brief, online intervention. *Stigma, Research and Action.*

Marin, G. (1984). Stereotyping Hispanics: The differential effect of research method, label, and degree of contact. *International Journal of Intercultural Relations, 8,* 17–27.

McConahay, J. B. (1986). Modern racism, ambivalence, and the modern racism scale. In J. F. Dovidio & S. L. Gaertner (Eds.), *Prejudice, discrimination, and racism* (pp. 91–126). New York: Academic Press.

McConahay, J. B., & Hough, J. C., Jr. (1976). Symbolic racism. *Journal of Social Issues, 32,* 23–45.

McCorkle, R. C. (2003). *A.B. 500 Traffic Stop Data Collection Study: A summary of findings.* Carson City, NV: State of Nevada Office of the Attorney General.

McEwen, B. S. (1998). Stress, adaptation, and disease: Allostasis and allostatic load. *Annals of the New York Academy of Sciences, 840,* 33–44.

McEwen, T. (2002). *Computer aided dispatch in support of community policing.* Alexandria, VA: Institute of Law and Justice.

McGuire, W. J. (1985). Attitudes and attitude change. In G. Lindzey & E. Aronson (Eds.), *The handbook of social psychology* (3rd ed., Vol. 2, pp. 233–346). New York: Random House.

McGuire, W. J. (1989). The structure of individual attitudes and attitude systems. In A. R. Pratkanis, S. J. Breckler, & A. G. Greenwald (Eds.), *Attitude structure and function* (pp. 37–69). Hillsdale, NJ: Erlbaum.

Meehan, A. J., & Ponder, M. C. (2002). Race and place: The ecology of racial profiling African American motorists. *Justice Quarterly, 19,* 399–429.

Meer, N., & Modood, T. (2009). Refutations of racism in the "Muslim question." *Patterns of Prejudice, 43,* 335–354.

Menatti, A. R., Smyth, F. L., Teachman, B. A., & Nosek, B. A. (in press). Reducing stigma toward individuals with mental illnesses: A brief, online intervention. *Stigma Research and Action.*

Merikle, P. M., Smilek, D., & Eastwood, J. D. (2001). Perception without awareness: Perspectives from cognitive psychology. *Cognition, 79,* 115–134.

Merritt, A. C., Effron, D. A., & Monin, B. (2010). Moral self-licensing: When being good frees us to be bad. *Social and Personality Compass, 4/5,* 344–357.

Meyer, D. E., & Schevaneveldt, R. W. (1971). Facilitation in recognizing pairs of words: Evidence of a dependence between retrieval operations. *Journal of Experimental Psychology, 90,* 227–234.

Monin, B., & Miller, D. T. (2001). Moral credentials and the expression of prejudice. *Journal of Personality and Social Psychology, 81,* 33–43.

Moskowitz, G. B., Gollwitzer, P. M., Wasel, W., & Schaal, B. (1999). Preconscious control of stereotype activation through chronic egalitarian goals. *Journal of Personality and Social Psychology, 77,* 167–184.

Mustard, D. B. (2001). Racial, ethnic, and gender disparities in sentencing: Evidence from the U.S. federal courts. *Journal of Law and Economics, 19,* 285–314.

National Public Radio. (2001). Retrieved from http://www.npr.org/programs/specials/poll/civil_liberties/civil_liberties_results_1.html

Neely, J. H. (1977). Semantic priming and retrieval from lexical memory: Roles of inhibitionless spreading activation and limited-capacity attention. *Journal of Experimental Psychology: General, 106,* 225–254.

Nelson, T. D. (Ed.). (2009). *Handbook of prejudice, stereotyping, and discrimination.* New York: Taylor and Francis.

New Jersey v. Pedro Soto et al. 734 A.2d 350, 1996 (New Jersey).

Newport, F. (1999, December 9). *Racial profiling is seen as widespread, particularly among young Black men.* Gallup News Service.

New York State Task Force on Police-on-Police Shootings. (2010). *Reducing inherent danger: Report of the Task Force on Police-on-Police Shootings.* New York: New York State Task Force on Police-on-Police Shootings.

Nguyen, H. D., & Ryan, A. M. (2008). Does stereotype threat affect test performance of minorities and women? A meta-analysis of experimental evidence. *Journal of Applied Psychology, 93,* 1314–1334.

Niemann, Y. F., Jennings, L., Rozelle, R. M., Baxter, J. C., & Sullivan, E. (1994). Use of free responses and cluster analysis to determine stereotypes of eight groups. *Personality and Social Psychology Bulletin, 20*, 379–390.

Nock, M. K., Park, J. M., Finn, C. T., Deliberto, T. L., Dour, H. J., & Banaji, M. R. (2010). Measuring the suicidal mind: Implicit cognition predicts suicidal behavior. *Psychological Science, 21*, 511–517.

Norris, C., Fielding, N., Kemp, C., & Fielding, J. (1992). Black and blue: An analysis of the influence of race on being stopped by the police. *British Journal of Sociology, 43*, 207–224.

Northeastern University Data Collection Resource Center. (2011). *Legislation and litigation.* Retrieved from http://www.racialprofilinganalysis.neu.edu/legislation/index.php

Nosek, B. (2005). Moderators of the relationship between implicit and explicit evaluation. *Journal of Experimental Psychology: General, 132*, 565–584.

Nosek, B. A., & Smyth, F. L. (2007). A multitrait-multimethod validation of the Implicit Association Test: Implicit and explicit attitudes are related but distinct constructs. *Experimental Psychology, 54*, 14–29.

OAGSNY. (1999). *The New York City Police Department's "stop & frisk" practices: A report to the people of the State of New York from the Office of the Attorney General.* New York: Office of the Attorney General of the State of New York.

Oliver, M. B. (1999). Caucasian viewers' memory of Black and White criminal suspects in the news. *Journal of Communication, 49*, 46–60.

Ostrom, T. M. (1969). The relationship between the affective, behavior, and cognitive components of attitude. *Journal of Experimental Social Psychology, 5*, 12–30.

Overbeck, J. R., & Park, B. (2001). When power does not corrupt: Superior individuation processes among powerful perceivers. *Journal of Personality and Social Psychology, 81*, 549–565.

Pager, D. (2003). The mark of a criminal record. *American Journal of Sociology, 108*, 937–975.

Palfai, T. P., & Ostafin, B. D. (2003). Alcohol-related motivational tendencies in hazardous drinkers: assessing implicit response tendencies using the modified-IAT. *Behaviour Research and Therapy, 41*, 1149–1162.

Paluck, E. L., & Green, D. P. (2009). Prejudice reduction: What works? A review and assessment of research and practice. *Annual Review of Psychology, 60*, 339–367.

Panagopoulos, C. (2006). The polls-trends: Arab and Muslim Americans and Islam in the aftermath of 9/11. *Public Opinion Quarterly, 70*, 608–624.

Park, B., & Rothbart, M. (1982). Perception of out-group homogeneity and levels of social categorization: Memory for the subordinate attributes of in-group and out-group members. *Journal of Personality and Social Psychology, 42*, 1051–1068.

Park, J., & Banaji, M. R. (2000). Mood and heuristics: The influence of happy and sad states on sensitivity and bias in stereotyping. *Journal of Personality and Social Psychology, 78*, 1005–1023.

Park, S. H., & Glaser, J. (2011). Implicit motivation to control prejudice and exposure to counterstereotypic instances reduce spontaneous discriminatory behavior. *Korean Journal of Social and Personality Psychology, 25*, 107–120.

Park, S. H., Glaser, J., & Knowles, E. D. (2008). Implicit motivation to control prejudice moderates the effect of cognitive depletion on unintended discrimination. *Social Cognition, 26*, 379–398.

Parker, K. (2001, September 26). *All is fair in this war except for insensitivity.* Chicago Tribune. Retrieved from http://articles.chicagotribune.com/2001-09-26/news/0109260223_1_ingrid-mattson-islamic-terrorists-muslim-issues

Payne, B. K. (2001). Prejudice and perception: The role of automatic and controlled processes in misperceiving a weapon. *Journal of Personality and Social Psychology, 81*, 1–12.

Payne B. K., Cheng, C. M., Govorun, O., & Stewart, B. D. (2005). An inkblot for attitudes: Affect misattribution as implicit measurement. *Journal of Personality and Social Psychology, 89*, 277–293.

Payne, B. K., Krosnick, J. A., Pasek, J., Lelkes, Y., Akhtar, O., & Tompson, T. (2010). Implicit and explicit prejudice in the 2008 American presidential election. *Journal of Experimental Social Psychology, 46*, 367–374.

Persico, N. (2002). Racial profiling, fairness, and effectiveness of policing. *American Economic Review, 92*, 1472–1497.

Peruche, B. M., & Plant, E. A. (2006). The correlates of law enforcement officers' automatic and controlled race-based responses to criminal suspects. *Basic and Applied Social Psychology, 28*, 193–199.

Peterson, I. (2002, March 27). Racial study of speeders is released in New Jersey. *The New York Times*. Retrieved from http://www.nytimes.com/2002/03/27/nyregion/racial-study-of-speeders-is-released-in-new-jersey.html.

Pettigrew, T. F (1979). The ultimate attribution error: Extending Allport's cognitive analysis of prejudice. *Personality and Social Psychology Bulletin, 5*, 461–476.

Pettigrew, T. F., & Tropp, L. R. (2000). Does intergroup contact reduce prejudice? Recent meta-analytic findings. In S. Oskamp (Ed.), *Reducing prejudice and discrimination* (pp. 93–114). Mahwah, NJ: Erlbaum.

Pettigrew, T. F., & Tropp, L. R. (2006). A meta-analytic test of intergroup contact theory. *Journal of Personality and Social Psychology, 90*, 751–783.

Plant, E. A., & Devine, P. G. (1998). Internal and external motivation to respond without prejudice. *Journal of Personality and Social Psychology, 75*, 811–832.

Plant, E. A., & Peruche, B. M. (2005). The consequences of race for police officers' responses to criminal suspects. *Psychological Science, 16*, 180–183.

Plant, E. A., Peruche, B. M., & Butz, D. A. (2005). Eliminating automatic racial bias: Making race non-diagnostic for responses to criminal suspects. *Journal of Experimental Social Psychology, 41*, 141–156.

Plous, S. (2003). *Understanding prejudice and discrimination*. New York: McGraw-Hill.

Pope, C. E., & Feyerherm, W. (1995). *Minorities and the juvenile justice system: Research summary*. Washington, DC: Department of Justice, Office of Juvenile Justice and Delinquency Prevention.

Posner, M. I., & Snyder, C. R. R. (1975). Facilitation and inhibition in the processing of signals. In P. M. A. Rabbit & S. Dornic (Eds.), *Attention and performance* (Vol. 5, pp. 669–682). New York: Academic Press.

Press, W. H. (2008). Strong profiling is not mathematically optimal for discovering rare malfeasors. *Proceedings of the National Academy of Sciences, 106*, 1716–1719.

Priest, D., & Arkin, W. M. (2010, July 19). A hidden world, growing beyond control. *The Washington Post*.

Quinnipiac University Polling Institute. (2006, August 29). *Americans say 9/11 bigger than Pearl Harbor, Quinnipiac University national poll finds; voters back profiling in security checks, wiretaps*. Retrieved from http://www.quinnipiac.edu/institutes-and-centers/polling-institute/national/release-detail?ReleaseID=952

Ramirez, D. A., Hoopes, J., & Quinlan, T. L. (2003). Defining racial profiling in a post–September 11 World. *American Criminal Law Review, 40*, 1195–1233.

Ramirez, D. A., McDevitt, J., & Farrell, A. (2000). *A resource guide on racial profiling data collection systems: Promising practices and lessons learned*. Washington, DC: U.S. Department of Justice.

RAND. (2004). *Assessing racial profiling more credibly: A case study of Oakland, California.* Santa Monica, CA: RAND Corporation.

Rankin, J. (2010, February 15). Police ponder how best to collect race data. *The Toronto Star.*

Raphael, S. (2006). The socioeconomic status of Black males: The increasing importance of incarceration. In A. Auerbach, D. Card, & J. Quigley (Eds.), *Public policy and the income distribution* (pp. 319–358). New York: Russell Sage.

Raphael, S., & Winter-Ebmer, R. (2001). Identifying the effect of unemployment on crime. *Journal of Law and Economics. 44,* 259–283.

Rashbaum, W. K. (2010, February 7). Retired officers raise questions on crime data. *The New York Times.*

Richeson, J. A., & Ambady, N. (2003). Effects of situational power on automatic racial prejudice. *Journal of Experimental Social Psychology, 39,* 177–183.

Richeson, J. A., & Shelton, J. N. (2005). Brief report: Thin slices of racial bias. *Journal of Nonverbal Behavior, 29,* 75–86.

Ridgeway, G., & MacDonald, J. M. (2009). Doubly robust internal benchmarking and false discovery rates for detecting racial bias in police stops. *Journal of the American Statistical Association, 104,* 661–668.

Ridgeway, G., Schell, T. L., Riley, K. J., Turner, S., and Dixon, T. L. (2006). *Police-community relations in Cincinnati: Year two evaluation report.* Santa Monica, CA: RAND Corporation.

Riley, K. J., & Ridgeway, G. (2006, October 11). Racial profiling won't stop terror. *Washingtonpost.com.*

Risse, M., & Zeckhauser, R. (2004). Racial profiling. *Philosophy and Public Affairs, 32,* 131–170.

Roccato, M., & Zogmaister, C. (2010). Predicting the vote through implicit and explicit attitudes: A field research. *Political Psychology, 31,* 249–274.

Ron, R. (2002, February 27). Remarks to U.S. House Transportation and Infrastructure Committee, Subcommittee on Aviation, hearing on aviation security with a focus on passenger profiling.

Rooth, D. (2010). Automatic associations and discrimination in hiring: Real world evidence. *Labour Economics, 17,* 523–534.

Rosch, E. (1975). Cognitive representations of semantic categories. *Journal of Experimental Psychology: General, 104,* 192–233.

Rosch, E. (1978). Principles of categorization. In E. Rosch & B. B. Lloyd (Eds.), *Cognition and categorization* (pp. 27–48). Hillsdale, NJ: Erlbaum.

Ross, S. L. (1997). Mortgage lending discrimination and racial differences in loan default. *Journal of Housing Research, 7,* 117–126.

Rothbart, M., & John, O. P. (1985). Social categorization and behavioral episodes: A cognitive analysis of the effects of intergroup contact. *Journal of Social Issues, 41,* 81–104.

Rowatt, W. C., Franklin, L. M., & Cotton, M. (2005). Patterns and personality correlates of implicit and explicit attitudes toward Christians and Muslims. *Journal for the Scientific Study of Religion, 44,* 29–43.

Rudman, L. A., & Ashmore, R. D. (2007). Discrimination and the Implicit Association Test. *Group Processes and Intergroup Relations, 10,* 359–372.

Rusinko, W. T., Johnson, K. W., & Hornung, C. A. (1978). The importance of police contact in the formulation of youths' attitudes toward police. *Journal of Criminal Justice, 6,* 53–67.

Russell, K. K. (1998). *The color of crime: Racial hoaxes, White fear, Black protectionism, police harassment, and other macroaggressions.* New York: New York University Press.

Russell, K. K. (1999). "Driving while black": Corollary phenomena and collateral conse-quences. *Boston College Law Review, 40*, 717–731.

Sachdev, I., & Bourhis, R. Y. (1985). Social categorization and power differentials in group relations. *European Journal of Social Psychology, 15*, 415–434.

Sagar, H. A., & Schofield, J. W. (1980). Racial and behavioral cues in Black and White chil-dren's perceptions of ambiguously aggressive acts. *Journal of Personality and Social Psychology, 39*, 590–598.

Sanga, S. (2009). Reconsidering racial bias in motor vehicle searches: Theory and evidence. *Journal of Political Economy, 117*, 1155–1159.

Saunders, D. J. (2001, November 4). Ahsan Baig's molehill. *The San Francisco Chronicle*, Op-ed.

Saxe, L., Kadushin, C., Beveridge, A., Livert, D., Tighe, E., Rindskopf, D., Ford, J., & Brodsky, A. (2001). The visibility of illicit drugs: Implications for community-based drug control strategies. *American Journal of Public Health, 91*, 1987–1994.

Schaller, M., Park, J. H., & Mueller, A. (2003). Fear of the dark: Interactive effects of beliefs about danger and ambient darkness on ethnic stereotypes. *Personality and Social Psychology Bulletin, 29*, 637–649.

Schauer, F. (2003). *Profiles, probabilities, and stereotypes*. Cambridge, MA: Harvard University Press.

Schuck, P. (2002, January). A case for profiling. *The American Lawyer*, pp. 59–61.

Schuman, H., Steeh, C., Bobo, L., & Krysan, M. (1997). *Racial attitudes in America: Trends and interpretations* (Rev. ed.). Cambridge, MA: Harvard University Press.

Sears, D. O., & McConahay, J. B. (1973). *The politics of violence: The new urban blacks and the Watts riot*. Boston: Houghton Mifflin.

Shah, J. Y., & Kruglanski, A. W. (2003). When opportunity knocks: Bottom-up priming of goals by means and its effects on self-regulation. *Journal of Personality and Social Psychology, 84*, 1109–1122.

Shiffrin, R. M., & Schneider, W. (1977). Controlled and automatic human information processing: II. Perceptual learning, automatic attending, and a general theory. *Psychological Review, 84*, 127–190.

Sigall, H., & Page, R. A. (1971). Current stereotypes: A little fading, a little faking. *Journal of Personality and Social Psychology, 16*, 252–258.

Sikh Coalition. (2010). *Sikh Coalition Bay Area civil rights report 2010*. Fremont, CA: Sikh Coalition.

Silke, A. (1998). Cheshire-cat logic: The recurring theme of terrorist abnormality in psycho-logical research. *Psychology, Crime and Law, 4*, 51–69.

Silke, A. (2001). Chasing ghosts: Offender profiling and terrorism. In D. P. Farrington, C. R. Hollin, & M. McMurran (Eds.), *Sex and violence: The psychology of crime and risk assessment* (pp. 242–258). London: Routledge.

Silke, A. (2011). The psychology of counter-terrorism: Critical issues and challenges. In A. Silke (Ed.), *The psychology of counter-terrorism* (pp. 1–18). Abindon, Oxon, UK: Routledge.

Simmons, R. (2005). Not voluntary but still reasonable: A new paradigm for understanding the consent searches doctrine. *Indiana Law Journal, 21*, 773–824.

Sinclair, S., Lowery, B. S., Hardin, C. D., & Colangelo, A. (2005). Social tuning of automatic racial attitudes: The role of affiliative orientation. *Journal of Personality and Social Psychology, 89*, 583–592.

SJPD. (2007). *Vehicle Stop Demographic Study: Annual report: July 1, 2006–June 30, 2007*. San Jose, CA: San Jose Police Department.

Smith, S. M., Brown, H. O., Toman, J. E. P., & Goodman, L. S. (1947). The lack of cerebral effects of d-tubocuarine. *Anesthesiology, 8*, 1–14.

Sommers, S. R., & Ellsworth, P. C. (2001). White juror bias: An investigation of prejudice against Black defendants in the American courtroom. *Psychology, Public Policy, and Law, 7*, 201–229.

Specaro, P. (2002, January 7). France, U.S. probe CDG passenger screening, *Aviation Week and Space Technology*, p. 37.

Spelman, W. (1994). *Criminal Incapacitation.* New York: Plenum Press.

Spelman, W. (2005). Jobs or jails? The crime drop in Texas. *Journal of Policy Analysis and Management, 24*, 133–165.

Spencer, S. J., Steele, C. M., & Quinn, D. M. (1999). Stereotype threat and women's math performance. *Journal of Experimental Social Psychology, 35*, 4–28.

Srull, T. K., & Wyer, R. S. (Eds.) (1988). *Advances in social cognition, Volume 1: A dual process model of impression formation.* Hillsdale, NJ: Erlbaum.

Stapley, G. (2010, June 15). Federal agents extend hand to Modesto Muslims, hoping to get past distrust. *The Sacramento Bee.*

Steele, C. M. (1997). A threat in the air: How stereotypes shape intellectual identity and performance. *American Psychologist, 52*, 613–629.

Steele, C. M., & Aronson, J. (1995). Stereotype threat and the intellectual test performance of African Americans. *Journal of Personality and Social Psychology, 69*, 797–811.

Steward, D. (2004). *Racial profiling: Texas traffic stops and searches.* Austin, TX: Texas Criminal Justice Reform Coalition.

Stone, J., Lynch, C. I., Sjomeling, M., & Darley, J. M. (1999). Stereotype threat effects on Black and White athletic performance. *Journal of Personality and Social Psychology, 77*, 1213.

Subcommittee on Aviation. (2002, February 27). Hearing on aviation security with a focus on passenger profiling, staff summary. Washington, DC: U.S. House of Representative, Transportation Committee, Subcommittee on Aviation.

Substance Abuse and Mental Health Services Administration. (1999). *National Household Survey on Drug Abuse, 1999.* Rockville, MD: Department of Health and Human Services.

Swarns, R. L. (2004, December 21). Program's value in dispute as a tool to fight terrorism. *The New York Times.*

Sweeney, L. T., & Haney, C. (1992). The influence of race on sentencing: A meta-analytic review of experimental studies. *Behavioral Sciences and the Law, 10*, 179–195.

Tajfel, H. (1978). *Differentiation between social groups.* London: Academic Press.

Tajfel, H. (1981). *Human groups and social categories: Studies in social psychology.* Cambridge, UK: Cambridge University Press.

Tajfel, H., Billig, M. G. Bundy, R. P., & Flament, C. (1971). Social categorization and intergroup behaviour. *European Journal of Social Psychology, 1*, 149–178.

Tajfel, H., & Wilkes, A. L. (1963). Classification and quantitative judgement. *British Journal of Psychology, 54*, 101–114.

Tapias, M. P., Glaser, J., Vasquez, K., Keltner, D., & Wickens, T. (2007). Emotion and prejudice: Specific emotions toward outgroups. *Group Processes and Intergroup Relations, 10*, 27–39.

Taylor, S. (2001, September 25). The case for using racial profiling at airports. *The Atlantic.* Retrieved from http://www.theatlantic.com/past/politics/nj/taylor2001-09-25.htm.

Tetlock, P. E. (1983). Accountability and complexity of thought. *Journal of Personality and Social Psychology, 45*, 74–83.

Texas Department of Public Safety. (2001). 2001 supplement to the *Traffic Stop Data Report*.

Thush, C., Wiers, R. W., Ames, S. L., Grenard, J. L., Sussman, S., & Stacy, A. W. (2007). Apples and oranges? Comparing indirect measures of alcohol-related cognition predicting alcohol use in at-risk adolescents. *Psychology of Addictive Behaviors, 21,* 587–591.

TNS Telecoms. (2008, August 19–22). Washington Post–ABC News Poll. Washington, DC: The Washington Post-ABC News.

Tonry, M. (1995). *Malign neglect: Race, crime, and punishment in America*. New York: Oxford University Press.

TSA. (2007, August 28). Security screening of head coverings. TSA News Ticker. Retrieved from http://www.tsa.gov/press/happenings/head_coverings.shtm

TSA. (2012, June 4). Passenger screening. Retrieved from http://www.tsa.gov/what_we_do/screening/security_checkpoints.shtm

Turley, J. (2002, February 27). Testimony before the U.S. House Transportation and Infrastructure Committee, Subcommittee on Aviation, hearing on aviation security with a focus on passenger profiling. Retrieved from http://www.house.gov/transportation/aviation/02-27-02/02-27-02memo.html

Turner, J. C. (1975). Social comparison and social identity: Some prospects for intergroup behavior. *European Journal of Social Psychology, 5,* 5–34.

Turner, J. C. (1987). *Rediscovering the social group: Self-categorization theory*. Oxford, UK: Blackwell.

Tversky, A., & Kahneman, D. (1973). Judgment under uncertainty: Heuristics and biases. *Science, 185,* 1124–1131.

Tyler, T. R., & Huo, Y. J. (2002). *Trust in the law: Encouraging public cooperation with the police and courts*. New York: Russell Sage.

U.S. Commission on Civil Rights. (2000). *Police practices and civil rights in New York City*. Washington, DC: USCCR.

U.S. Department of Health and Human Services. (2007). *Results from the 2007 National Survey on Drug Use and Health: National findings*. Washington, DC: Department of Health and Human Services.

U.S. Department of Health and Human Services, Substance Abuse and Mental Health Services Administration, Office of Applied Studies. (2008). *Results from the 2007 National Survey on Drug Use and Health: National findings*. Rockville, MD: U.S. Department of Health and Human Services.

U.S. Sentencing Commission. (1995). *Special report to the Congress: Cocaine and federal sentencing policy*. United States Sentencing Commission.

Unkelbach, C., Forgas, J. P., & Denson, T. F. (2008). The turban effect: The influence of Muslim headgear and induced affect on aggressive responses in the shooter bias paradigm. *Journal of Experimental Social Psychology, 44,* 1409–1413.

Vargas, P. T., von Hippel, W., & Petty, R. E. (2004). Using partially structured attitude measures to enhance the attitude-behavior relationship. *Personality and Social Psychology Bulletin, 30,* 197–211.

Verhovek, S. H. (2001, September 23). A nation challenged: Civil liberties; Americans give in to race profiling. *The New York Times*.

Vescio, T. K., Gervais, S. J., Heiphetz, L., & Bloodhart, B. (2009). The stereotypic behaviors of the powerful and their effect on the relatively powerless. In T. D. Nelson (Ed.), *Handbook of prejudice, stereotyping, and discrimination* (pp. 247–265). New York: Taylor and Francis.

Victoroff, J., & Kruglanski, A. W. (2009). *Psychology of terrorism: Classic and contemporary insights*. New York: Psychology Press.

Viscusi, W. K., & Zeckhauser, R. J. (2003). Sacrificing civil liberties to reduce terrorism risks. *Journal of Risk and Uncertainty, 26,* 99–120.

von Hippel, W., Sekaquaptewa, D., & Vargas, P. (1995). On the role of encoding processes in stereotype maintenance. In M. P. Zanna (Ed.), *Advances in experimental social psychology* (Vol. 27, pp. 177–253). San Diego, CA: Academic Press.

Walsh, W., Banaji, M. R., & Greenwald, A. G. (1995, May). *A failure to eliminate race bias in judgments of criminals.* Paper presented at the 7th Annual Convention of the American Psychological Society, New York.

Walton, G. M., & Cohen, G. L. (2003). Stereotype lift. *Journal of Experimental Social Psychology, 39,* 456–467.

Weber, R., & Crocker, J. (1983). Cognitive processes in the revision of stereotypic beliefs. *Journal of Personality and Social Psychology, 45,* 961–977.

Wegner, D. M. (1994). *White bears and other unwanted thoughts: Suppression, obsession, and the psychology of mental control.* New York: Guilford.

Weiss, A., & Rosenbaum, D. P. (2008). Illinois Traffic Stops Statistics Study: 2008 annual report. Chicago: University of Illinois at Chicago, Center for Research in Law and Justice.

Weitz, S. (1972). Attitude, voice, and behavior: A repressed affect model of interracial interaction. *Journal of Personality and Social Psychology. 24,* 14–21.

Weitzer, R., & Tuch, S. A. (2002). Perceptions of racial profiling: Race, class, and personal experience. *Criminology, 40,* 435–456.

Western, B. (2006). *Punishment and inequality in America.* New York: Russell Sage Foundation.

White, J. (2007, July 16). 16 Saudi detainees return home from Guantanamo. *The Washington Post.*

White, M. D. (2011, August 10–11). *Controlling police officer behavior in the field: Using what we know to regulate police-initiated stops and prevent racially biased policing.* Paper presented at the Roundtable on Current Debates, Research Agendas and Strategies to Address Racial Disparities in Police-Initiated Stops in the UK and USA. John Jay College of Criminal Justice. New York.

Williams, C., & Barrett, D. (2010, March 29). Militia members planned to kill cop and bomb funeral, prosecutors say. Associated Press.

Wilson, J. Q., & Higgins, H. R. (2002, January 10). Profiles in courage. *The Wall Street Journal,* Commentary.

Winerman, L. (2004). Criminal profiling: The reality behind the myth. *Monitor on Psychology, 35,* 66.

Withrow, B. L. (2006). *Racial profiling: From rhetoric to reason.* Upper Saddle River, NJ: Pearson/Prentice Hall.

Withrow, B. L. (2010, June 17). Statement at Hearing on Racial Profiling and the Use of Suspect Classifications in Law Enforcement Policy for the Subcommittee on the Constitution, Civil Rights, and Civil Liberties United States House of Representatives. Washington, DC.

Witt, H. (2009, March 13). Race may be factor in police shooting of unarmed elderly man. *Chicago Tribune.*

Wittenbrink, B., Judd, C. M., & Park, B. (1997). Evidence for racial prejudice at the implicit level and its relationship with questionnaire measures. *Journal of Personality and Social Psychology, 72,* 262–274.

Wittenbrink, B., Judd, C. M., & Park, B. (2001). Spontaneous prejudice in context: Variability in automatically activated attitudes. *Journal of Personality and Social Psychology, 81,* 815–827.

Word, C. O., Zanna, M. P., & Cooper, J. (1974). The nonverbal mediation of self-fulfilling prophecies in interracial interaction. *Journal of Experimental Social Psychology. 10,* 109–120.

Yardley, J. (2000, October 7). The heat is on a Texas town after the arrests of 40 Blacks. *New York Times.*

Youth Risk Behavior Survey. (2007). *Health risk behaviors by race/ethnicity.* Atlanta, GA: Centers for Disease Control.

Zajonc, R. B. (1980). Feeling and thinking: Preferences need no inferences. *American Psychologist, 35,* 151–175.

Zakaria, F. (2002, July 8). Freedom vs. security. *Newsweek.*

Zamora, J. H., (2001, April 20). CHP stops more minorities. *The San Francisco Chronicle,* p. A1.

Zimbardo, P. G., & Leippe, M. R. (1991). *The psychology of attitude change and social influence.* New York: McGraw-Hill.

NAME INDEX

This index contains only proper names. Please consult the separately presented subject index for concepts and keywords.

Rowatt, W. C., 133
Rozell, R. M., 62
Rudman, L., 83–84
Rudolph, Eric, 48, 132, 144
Rusinko, W. T., 210
Russel, Kathryn, 123
Russell, K. K., 26
Russin, A., 208
Ryan, A. M., 83

Sachdev, I., 53
Sadler, M. S., 85, 89, 90, 94, 192, 193
Sagar, H. A., 43, 62
Sanbonmatsu, D. M., 80
Sanga, S., 39, 40, 166
Saunders, Debra, 140
Saxe, L., 8, 54
Schaal, B., 92
Schaller, M., 62
Schauer, Richard, 20, 25, 44, 131
Schell, T. L., 32
Schevaneveldt, R. W., 77
Schmitt, M., 82
Schneider, W., 77
Schofield, J. W., 43, 62
Schuck, Peter, 18
Schuman, H., 54, 71, 74
Schwartz, J. L. K., 81
Sears, D. O., 54, 73, 74, 202
Sekaquaptewa, D., 59
Sen, Amartya, 135
Shah, J. Y., 92
Shelton, J. N., 83
Sherman, S. J., 58
Shiffrin, R. M., 77
Sigall, H., 72
Siljander, R. P., 20
Silke, Andrew, 18, 44, 131, 156–157,
    159–160, 164
Simmons, R., 28
Simon, S., 72
Sinclair, S., 209
Sjomeling, M., 83
Smith, C. T., 93
Smith, E. L., 27
Smith, J., 84
Smith, Scott M., 54, 74–75
Smyth, F. L., 191, 209
Snowden, R. J., 84
Snyder, C. R. R., 77
Sommers, S. R., 8, 22, 31, 213

Specaro, P., 156
Spelman, W., 115
Spencer, S. J., 83
Sriram, N., 93
Srull, T. K., 91
Stack, Andrew, 48, 146
Stacy, A. W., 84
Stapley, G., 149
Steeh, C., 54
Steele, Claude, 56, 83
Steffen, V., 56, 63, 208
Steward, D., 37
Stewart, B. D., 93
Stewart, Jon, 149
Stone, J., 83
Sullivan, E., 62
Susskind, J., 58
Sussman, S., 84
Swarns, R. L., 136, 147
Sweeney, L. T., 22

Tajfel, Henri, 53–54, 211
Tapias, M. P., 54
Taylor, S. E., 56, 187
Teachman, B. A., 191
Tetlock, P. E., 212
Thompson, Larry, 138
Thush, C., 84
Todd, P., 39, 107
Toman, J. E. P., 74
Tompson, T., 93
Tonry, M., 9
Torbit, William Jr., 87
Trone, J., 34
Tropp, L. R., 193, 209
Tschann, J. M., 123
Tuch, S. A., 27
Turley, Jonathan, 13, 129, 140, 156, 163,
    166, 184, 206
Turner, S., 32, 56
Tversky, A., 47, 49
Tyler, R. B., 79
Tyler, Tom, 53, 124

Van Hiel, A., 210
Vance, S. L., 91
Vargas, P. T., 59, 119–120
Vasquez, K., 54
Verhovek, S. H., 133, 135, 152
Vescio, T. K., 67
Victoroff, J., 157

Viscusi, W. K., 133
von Hippel, W., 59, 119

Walsh, W., 55, 61
Walters, G., 60
Walton, G. M., 83
Wasel, W., 92
Weber, R., 59, 60
Webster, William H., 57, 165
Wegner, Daniel, 68
Weiss, A., 36
Weitz, S., 72
Weitzer, R., 27
Western, B., 4, 103, 124
Wickens, T., 54
Wiers, R. W., 84
Wilkes, A. L., 211
Williams, B., 37
Williams, C., 145
Williams, C. J., 74
Williams, D. R., 123
Wilson, James Q., 12, 97, 123, 140

Winerman, L., 18
Winter-Ember, R., 125
Withrow, Brian, 10, 15, 17, 19–20, 23, 24, 25, 186
Wittenbrink, B., 55, 79, 85, 86, 89, 90, 94, 192, 193, 209, 210
Wood, G. C., 58
Word, C. O., 72
Wyer, R. S., 91

Yardley, J., 21
Yzerbyt, V. Y., 67

Zacks, R. T., 77
Zajonc, R. B., 54
Zakaria, Fareed, 135, 159
Zamora, J. H., 35, 36
Zanna, M. P., 72
Zeckhauser, R. J., 14, 133
Zimbardo, P. G., 208
Zogmaister, C., 84
Zuniga, M., 37

SUBJECT INDEX

This index contains concepts and keywords. Please see the separately presented name index for all proper names.

efficiency argument, 97–99
El Al passenger jet hijacking, 134
electrical shock experiment, 72
electroencephalograms (EEG), 70
End Racial Profiling Act (ERPA). *See* ERPA
enforcement mechanisms, 170–171
episodic memory, 75n
equilibrium models, 39
ERPA (End Racial Profiling Act)
  2004 Senate version, 161
  attempts at adoption of, 173–174, 176–177
  clear prohibitions stated in, 175
  data collection requirements in, 176
  definition of racial profiling in, 13, 174–175
  potential benefits of, 174, 202
  procedural requirements in, 175–176
  scope of responses to, 174
ethnicity
  acceptability of profiling by, 2
  definition of, 16
  as invalid indicator of suspicion, 160
evidence of racial profiling
  in airport screenings, 154
  benchmark issue and, 22–24
  in consent searches, 28, 35–36
  from criminal trials/lawsuits, 28–30
  in customs searches, 36
  historical/anecdotal, 25–26
  internal agency analyses of, 36–38
  outcome tests and, 38–40
  real-world examples of, 2, 21, 26
  from scientific studies, 30–33
  in "Stop and Frisk" program, 33–35
  from surveys, 27–28
  varied scenarios of, 21–22
explicit attitude, vs. implicit bias, 92–94
"explicit" stereotypes, 94
"extraordinary rendition," 162

FAA (Federal Aviation Administration), 45, 134, 183–184
Fair and Impartial Policing program, 180
FBI (Federal Bureau of Investigation)
  criminal profiling by, 25
  drug-related arrests, 4
  early drug courier profiles developed by, 9
  institutionalization of racial profiling by, 138–139, 168–170

promotion of terrorist profiles by, 131
Federal Aviation Administration (FAA), 45, 134, 183–184
Federal Bureau of Investigation (FBI). *See* FBI
feedback loop, 10, 48
fMRI (functional magnetic resonance imaging), 70
formal profiling, 9–10, 14, 25–26, 44–46, 206
functional magnetic resonance imaging (fMRI), 70
fundamental attribution error, 58

Gallup poll, 27
GAO (Government Accountability Office), 23, 36, 102, 205
gender, acceptability of profiling by, 2
General Accounting Office. *See* Government Accountability Office
Government Accountability Office (GAO), 23, 36, 102, 205
Guantanamo Bay, Cuba, 144

"hasty generalization" fallacy, 146
Hawthorne effect, 32–33
heuristics, 56–57
HHS (U.S. Department of Health and Human Services), 6
Hirabayashi v. United States (1943), 215
historical/anecdotal evidence (of racial profiling), 25–26
hit rates, 98, 121
HIV/AIDS, increased risk due to incarceration, 125
human thought
  automatic activation, 75–76
  automatization of, 77
  implicit memories, 75
  nonconscious mental processes, 75
  priming of, 77–78
  pros and cons of nonconscious processing, 78
  subvocalization theory of, 74–75

IAT (Implicit Association Test), 81, 84, 92, 94, 149, 190–191, 193
Illinois Department of Transportation, 36
illusory correlation, 58
IMCP (Implicit Motivation to Control Prejudice), 92

mental constructs, 56
mental schemas, 66
mere categorization effect, 54
mere exposure effect, 54
meta-analysis, 24
Millennium Bomber, 146
minimal groups effect, 54
minority communities
  destabilizing effects of incarceration on, 124–125
  effects of profiling on, 121–123, 159–160
  harm to physical health in, 125–126
  increased sanctions borne by, 3
  loss of civil liberties due to profiling in, 12, 123–124
  political disenfranchisement of, 12–13, 188
Missouri attorney general report, 37, 40
Modern Racism Scale (MRS), 73–74, 91
Motivation to Control Prejudiced Reactions (MCPR), 91
MPAC (Muslim Public Affairs Council), 142, 145
MRS (Modern Racism Scale), 73–74, 91
multiple regression techniques, 31, 200–201
Murrah Federal Building, 127–128
Muslim Public Affairs Council (MPAC), 142, 145

National Commission on Terrorist Attacks Upon the United States (9/11 Commission), 137, 164
National Crime Victimization Survey (NCVS), lack of drug crime reporting in, 6, 10, 46
National Institute on Drug Abuse, 6
National Security Unit of the Immigration and Naturalization Service, 138
National Survey on Drug Use and Health
  Black vs. White drug use, 6
  powder vs. crack cocaine use, 7
NCVS (National Crime Victimization Survey), lack of drug crime reporting in, 6, 10, 46
Nebraska State Patrol, 37
"negligence" approach, 203–204
Nevada traffic stop statistics, 38
New Jersey State Police, 21, 28–29, 36
New Jersey v. Pedro Soto et al. (1996), 17, 165

"no-fly" lists, 183–184
non-Hispanic Whites, 4n
NYPD's Street Crime Unit, 33–34

OAGSNY (Office of the Attorney General of the State of New York), 33–34
Oakland Police Department, 29–30
offender profiling. See criminal profiling
offending rate, 105n
Office of National Risk Assessment (ONRA), 134
Office of the Attorney General of the State of New York (OAGSNY), 33–34
Oklahoma City bombing, 127–128, 158
ONRA (Office of National Risk Assessment), 134
Operation Pipeline drug interdiction program, 4, 35–36, 171–172
outcome tests
  in agency-level policies, 181–82
  in ERPA, 176
  evidence of racial profiling using, 38–40
  fundamental insight of, 194
  as solution to benchmark problem, 48
  of traffic stops, 29
out-groups, 53–54, 58

Palestine Liberation Organization (PLO), 132
passenger screening
  evidence of racial profiling in, 135–136
  potential for arbitrariness in, 184
PERF (Police Executive Research Forum), 15
Perspectives on Profiling program, 179
phrenology, 75
PLO (Palestine Liberation Organization), 132
Police Executive Research Forum (PERF), 15
police officers
  core principles for training, 189–190
  power causing stereotyping, 67
  spontaneous discriminatory behaviors in, 94
  stereotypes of African Americans held by, 62
police-civilian contact, 209–211
policy, interventions based on cause, 44
policy recommendations
  accountability, 212

KISHWAUKEE COLLEGE LIBRARY

7943 10126 5153

Suspect race : causes and
consequences of racial profiling / Jack
Glaser.

HV7936.R3 G53 2015
Gen Stx

DATE DUE

PRINTED IN U.S.A.

Kishwaukee College Library
21193 Malta Rd.
Malta, IL 60150-9699